FOLLOWING THE

Alaskan Dream

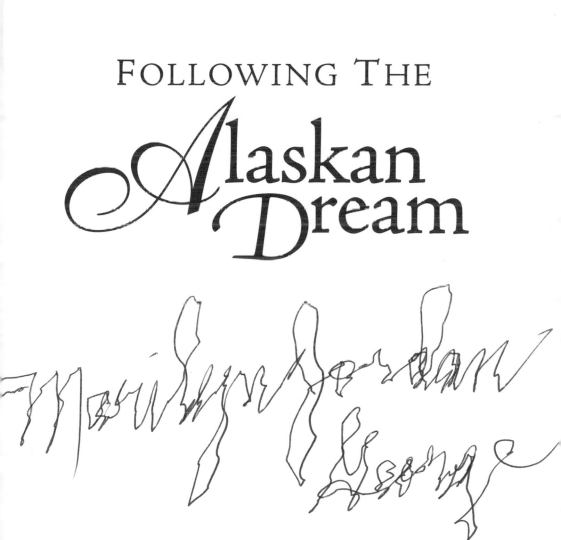

MARILYN JORDAN GEORGE

Fifth printing
ISBN 0-9671639-1-9
Library of Congress Catalog Card Number 99-72997

Printed by Gorham Printing
Rochester, WA

THIS BOOK IS DEDICATED:

To Wilhelm "Skip" Jordan
    who persuaded me to follow his dream to Alaska,

To our children: Eric, Karen, Barbara and Lynda
    who enjoyed life afloat,

To Bill George
    who provided the second chance to make the
    Alaskan dream come true.

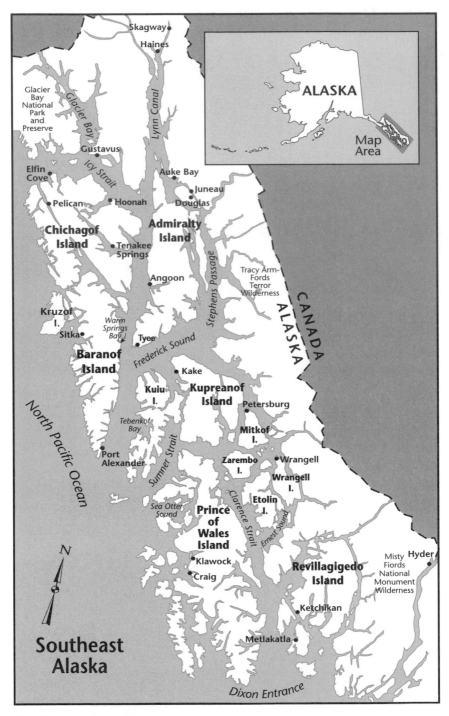

Map By Laura Lucas Design

PREFACE

I HAVE WRITTEN THIS BOOK TO SHARE MY LOVE of Alaska and salmon trolling and the story of the adventure of transforming an Iowa home economics coed into a salmon troller. I inherited my dreams of faraway places from my father. In his youth he worked on his uncles' ranch in Alberta. Before he went into WWI, he managed a ranch in Montana.

I wish I could match my father's knack for story-telling. His stories of ranching and traveling provided the highlights of any party he attended. I led a protected life in Lisbon, Iowa. When growing up, I admit that being an Iowa farm wife did not appeal to me.

In March of 1933, my folks were forced to sell all of their farm animals and machinery during the bank closings. Seeing the pain the depression caused my family gave me a different perspective about my prospects for happiness and security. I recall a well-to-do girlfriend dying. Her mother gave my sister and me each a dress. I cherished that beautiful, expensive dress, and I wore it for many years.

In high school I had the opportunity to play competitive girls basketball. Proudly I made the first team my senior year. My father went into the cattle business and I occasionally traveled to Amarillo and Denver with him to buy feeder cattle. I enjoyed the adventure of these trips.

This book tells the story of my decision to leave Iowa for the adventure of the wife of a Norwegian fisherman in Alaska. Our boat became our home, business, mode of transportation, and window to the beauty of the Alaskan wilderness. Skip Jordan and I raised four children during this time and met many challenges. Sharing the experience of this land and this life has been a goal of mine for 50 years.

I currently live in Petersburg, Alaska, and plan to continue my adventures with family and learning. A highlight is the family reunions I have shared. For my 70th birthday my children and their families, all my brothers and sisters with some of their children, and my out-of-town friends, Betty Bramlett, my college roommate from Ohio, and Irene Ingle from Wrangell, came to Petersburg to celebrate. Barbara and Lynda planned a second 75th birthday reunion at Wallowa Lake in eastern Oregon. Seventy of us came which included my three daughters, my brothers and sisters, many nephews and nieces and their families, and cousins for a great week-end.

Having fished with Eric's sons, Kris and Karl, I longed for activities with my other grandchildren. I spotted Intergenerational Elderhostels in their catalog. Karen's son Richard and I snorkeled and camped in Hawaii. Barbara's son Jake and I traveled to Victoria and onto Campbell River for a rappelling and kayaking week. We ended by visiting the aquarium and zoo at Vancouver, B.C. Barbara's daughter Diana and I did hot air ballooning and studied mining at Park City, Utah and then hiked in the Olympic Rain Forest in Washington state. For Easter vacation, Richard and I traveled to Dillard in northeast Georgia where we square danced and hiked a short ways on the Appalachian Trail. Karen's son Danny and I flew to upstate New York for an Intergenerational at Sagamore, which had been the Whitney's summer home, for canoeing and hiking. When they're old enough, I'll take Karen's daughter Kari and Lynda's son Scott on adventures to distant places. I feel these trips set up rapport with my grandchildren that isn't possible when their parents are present. I also have the opportunity to expose them to the love of nature and philosophy of life that their grandfather shared with me when he brought me to Alaska on our honeymoon.

I thank my editor, Amber Dahlin, and my daughters, Barbara Leachman, Lynda Troka, and Karen Glass, who helped edit this book. My daughter-in-law, Sarah Jordan helped with the final proof-reading. Editors who bought my articles since 1947 encouraged me to keep writing. My instructors in my master's program at the University of Oregon, such as Professor Roy Paul Nelson, helped me start writing this book. Since I started freelancing in 1947, I never imagined that it would take over 50 years to complete this book.

I want to thank Chris Weiss and Joyce Jenkins, who with the help of the State Library, found the sources of many of the quotations. I used *Southeast Alaska Names on the Chart and How They Got There* by R.N. DeArmond.

Editors I wish to mention are: Emery Tobin of Alaska Sportsman and his assistant, Ethel Dassow, who bought my first articles; Robert Crossley of Household magazine; Lew Williams, Jr., of Petersburg Press and Ketchikan Daily News; Bob Pickrell, of New Alaskan; Walt Kisner of Fishermen's News; John van Amerongen, of Alaska Fishermen's Journal; Alaska Magazine; Senior Voice; Dave Fremming, of Alaskan Southeaster; MaryLee Hayes of Alaska Women Speak. The members of the Petersburg Writer's Guild, who include Judy Sarber, Leslie Croxton, Bill Moulton, Betty Winship, Mike Stainbrook, and Marjorie Colpitts, critiqued each chapter as I completed it. I've attended many writing workshops and these instructors were especially helpful: Elaine Colvin, C. Terry Cline, Lee Ribich, Drake Hokanson, Jane Evanson, John Thorndike, Angus Cameron, and Ken Waldman. Jocelyn Bartkevicius at the University of Iowa Elderhostel workshop gave me many ideas on improving my story.

I also want to thank my many friends who provided me material for my stories through the years. Without them, I would have little to write about. Jackie O'Donnell helped me with names and spellings.

My hope is that this book will help you see as Ralph Waldo Emerson wrote "the miraculous in the common."

The longer I live, the more I realize the impact of attitude on life. Charles Swindoll put it so well in his essay "Attitude":

> *Attitude is more important than facts. It is more important than the past, than education, than money, than circumstances, than failures, than successes, than what other people think or say or do. It is more important than appearance, giftedness or skill. It will make or break a company...a church...a home. The remarkable thing is we have a choice every day regarding the attitude we will embrace for that day. We cannot change the past... we cannot change the fact that people will act a certain way. We cannot change the inevitable. The only thing we can do is play on the one string we have, and this is our attitude. I am convinced that life is 10% what happens to me and 90% how I react to it. And so it is with you...we are in charge of our Attitudes.*[1]

---

[1] *Essay titled Attitude by Charles Swindoll. Often quoted.*

All of Marilyn's children and grandchildren help her celebrate her 70th birthday. The five Glasses are Frank (holding Kari), Richard, Karen and Daniel. Next are the Leachmans— Jack, Barbara, Jake and Diana. Bill George and Marilyn are in front, then Lynda and Ben Troka, and the Eric Jordan family of Sarah, Karl, Eric & Kris.

CONTENTS

ILLUSTRATIONS

Cover by Dr. Otto Kruse in Explorer Basin in Tebenkof Bay.
Back cover picture of Marilyn George by Glenna & Charles Paukstis.
Taken at Arapahoe Elderhostel in Denver 1998.

CHAPTER ONE

Is You Is or Is You Ain't

Lyman Bailey visits me soon after getting his navigator wings.

"IMPERATIVE! CALL THIS NUMBER IMMEDIATELY," says the note tacked to my fraternity house door. I recognize my local student minister's name. In 1943 the World War II soldiers took over the Iowa State College's dormitories while they trained. The college administration then housed us women coeds in the empty fraternity houses. My senior class was the smallest since World War I.

My heart jumps. My hands shaking, I dial the number. Is the minister calling to tell me that Lyman Bailey has been killed? I dated Lyman for two years before he went into the service. I care deeply about him and now many of our young men are being killed in the war.

"Marilyn, will you come to our game night at 6:30?" the student minister asks. "I expect quite a few servicemen."

What a relief! I look at my watch, five minutes to six. "Even if you're late, please come," the minister pleads.

I look at myself, I'm not dressed for a game night. This old gray jumper and white blouse won't do. I need something with color to bring out my dark hair and eyes. Pawing through my closet, I pull out a red dress with a fitted bodice and a full skirt. This will do nicely. I run down the street to where dinner is served at another fraternity house.

After dinner I check my watch: 6:20. I almost run the ten blocks to the church. The game night will be over at 7:30. Why do I get myself into these things? I seldom attend these activities because I'm busy with school and am looking forward to Lyman's return from officer's training. The minister sounded so desperate that I couldn't say no.

When I arrive, the group is taking part in a mixer by filling out lists on paper with the name of someone who fits each category. The room is crowded with over 30 people but I notice a Navy man leave a pretty blonde Norwegian girl. He heads my way and with a coy smile and a wink, he asks, "Does your name fit any of these?"

I look them over and laugh, "You aren't supposed to do it that way. Let's see... your eyes are blue and mine are brown. You already have your birthday filled in. I like the out of doors, do you?"

"Oh, yes," he beams, "I've been to Alaska. As ya can hear, I have an accent. I came from Norway when I was 12. Here, sign your name."

I write, *Marilyn Frink.* "Here, you better sign mine, too. There's a prize for the one who gets their card filled in first."

In a flowing script, he writes, *Wilhelm Jordan.* "Everyone calls me Skip. A high school buddy called me Skipper because I was always in charge. The nickname stuck."

We stay together during the other activities. This man is not like anyone

Marilyn as a co-ed at Iowa State College

I know. He's very tall with light brown hair. His twinkling blue eyes make me feel comfortable. His smile lights up his whole face causing me to smile back at him. His accent is quite heavy and at times I have trouble understanding what he is saying. In a way this adds to the intrigue and mystery of this new man. Much too soon, the hour passes and the minister bids us good bye.

"All of you come next week," he says.

"May I walk ya home?" Skip asks with a smile that makes my knees feel weak.

"Okay," I say, a hot blush moving up my cheeks.

We hurry because he must be in his dormitory by 8 p.m. Nearing the fraternity house, he asks, "How about us going out Friday night?"

"That should be fun," I say. Skip obviously is not shy or unsure of himself. "We can dance to a juke box at the Union then." I love to dance. Smiling, I say, "I'll show you the campus on Friday."

He says goodnight and walks off. My heart slows down for the first time since I met him. Wow, what a night! First I am chiding myself for getting dragged into

Skip in his seaman's uniform

going to this mixer and then I meet one of the most intriguing men of my life.

Bursting into my room, I breathlessly tell my roommate, Bonnie Gunsaulus, "I just met a new man. He has an accent and comes from Norway. He's been to Alaska. Doesn't that sound romantic?" I read Anne Morrow Lindbergh's *North to the Orient* and was intrigued by the great territory of Alaska.

Bonnie took the previous term off to get married before her fiance was shipped overseas. She spends long hours writing him. She laughs, "Well I guess the evening wasn't a total waste of your time."

We laugh together and I tell her everything Skip and I talked about. I can hardly wait for Friday night.

Skip comes early, so we walk around Lake La Verne and watch the swans, Lancelot and Elaine. I really like the swans. They are so graceful and beautiful.

"Do ya mean they call this duck pond a lake?" Skip asks.

The central campus has a broad green area with no buildings and the tall campanile at the side toward the Memorial Union. "Someone planned it when they started the college," I say.

"The center is beautiful with the lawns," he tells me. He talks about growing up in Norway and his concern for his grandmother and relatives living under the German occupation. As their letters are censored, all they can write about is the weather and their health.

Too soon the dance starts. I was enjoying having Skip to myself. I'm surprised to find the thin tall Norwegian is a good dancer. He twirls me around the floor effortlessly. When we dance I feel like I'm floating on air. Looking at the other dancers, I think what a fun man Skip is.

When he takes me to my fraternity house, he asks, "What would you like to do tomorrow?"

My mind reels; he isn't going to let me get away. Do I really want to? Is he sweeping me off my feet? Am I falling in love? I had thought to marry a college man. Realistically, I expect to marry Lyman, who will likely stay in Iowa and work with farmers when he graduates. I visualize a routine life like my mother's in a small Iowa town. Skip is nothing like Lyman. This adventurous Norwegian makes my heart pound. But he's a sailor, only an enlisted man.

I try not to seem too eager as I reply, "I changed my major the first of this school year. In order to graduate in June, I'm carrying 20 hours. I must study in the morning, but we can do something in the afternoon and evening. They have a live band in the Union on Saturday night."

After going inside, I confide to Bonnie, "I'm having a great time with Skip. He's fun to be with. He's interested in travel, wildlife, and science. He even asked if he could take me to church on Sunday."

Skip's older than most of the other servicemen, and this worries me. With the war training people far from home, many men fail to mention their spouses. I knew a girl who fell in love with a man only to discover he had a wife and children. I believe in the sanctity of marriage and would never consider dating a married man. I don't know any divorced people so that scenario never crosses my mind. That weekend, I casually ask Skip, "Are you married?"

"No," he answers and moves on to a new subject of conversation.

Luckily, Skip must be in at 8 p.m. from Monday through Thursday; otherwise my grades would suffer. Often we meet after dinner. Spring is so beautiful in Iowa with flowering fruit trees and the grass turning green.

I see why they called him Skip. He always plans activities for us. For the next month, we go on picnics, to dances, and on horseback rides. He takes up all my spare time and I love it. Never have I met a man so confident and interesting. We enjoy discussing world events and the war. Soon the United

States will be invading France. Most of all, he loves telling me about Alaska. His way of telling a story makes me feel I'm there. I actually see what Alaska is like. Skip loves to hold hands and sometimes we just touch each other. I look forward to being with him and having his hand in mine. His eyes always light up when he sees me and his smile seems to say," I love being with you." He makes me feel like no other man has.

Bonnie listens to Skip stories in our dorm room.

One day in April, Bonnie asks, "Marilyn, are you falling in love with that sailor?"

Blushing, I say, "Maybe. Everything's so wonderful. He's fun to be with and exciting. He's more than I ever dreamed of in a man."

When the coeds plan a formal dance the last weekend in April, I invite Skip as my escort. I think this will be the culmination to his time at Iowa State. He will complete his diesel engine training course and ship out May 8th. I know he will have to leave but I hate thinking about it. I'm sad that he won't be here in June for my graduation with a degree in Home Economics.

The last few weeks of school don't go as I expect. I receive a letter from Lyman that he's coming home on leave. He's graduating as an Air Force navigator. He wants to see me the weekend of May sixth and seventh. That's the weekend before Skip leaves. What will I do? I know Lyman will be unhappy if Skip's around. Lyman feels that I'm his, although we both are free to date others.

Skip swept me off my feet. These last months have been fun and exciting, but now my old friend wants to see me before he goes overseas to fly into battle. I hate to make decisions. Neither of these men has proposed marriage so I don't need to decide between them now. I write Lyman that I'll look forward to seeing him on Saturday and Sunday, but I will be busy on Sunday night. I hope he won't ask what I'm doing then, but if he does I'll tell him the truth.

Next, I need to tell Skip that I won't spend the whole weekend with him.

With great effort, I say, "Skip, this old friend wrote that he's coming to see me May 6 and 7." I add, "But I'll save Sunday night for you."

"That's a fine thing. And I'm shipping out the next day," he says, looking at me questioningly.

"I'm sorry."

His eyes tell me that he isn't happy. He must know that I hadn't lived in a vacuum before I met him. I'm trying to walk a middle line by keeping everyone happy, but by not deciding between them, I might lose them both. Oh, I hope not.

When Skip calls for me the night of the formal dance, he looks so handsome in his dress whites. They make him look even taller than his 6'2" height.

He gives me a big smile and squeezes my hand, "You look beautiful tonight, Marilyn, in your red skirt and white top. Red's really your color. Remember, you were wearing red the night I met you."

He sent me a corsage of red roses and white carnations. They're so beautiful. This is our evening and I revel in it while we twirl around the dance floor. He makes me feel like his queen.

At intermission we wander outside and find an empty bench under a tree. The campanile chimes overhead. Skip takes my hand, his voice serious, as he says, "I've something to tell you."

My heart starts beating wildly. Maybe he's going to propose.

"Ya know the night when ya asked if I was married, and I told ya I wasn't? That's the truth, I'm not married, but I've been married. I'm divorced." He says it slowly, all the while looking at the ground. He continues to hold my hand even though I try to pull it away.

With great effort, I make myself ask, "Are there any children?"

He looks into my eyes and continues to softly hold my hand. "Yes, a little girl named Dawn. She's six now and lives with her mother. I see her whenever I'm home in Tacoma. I have her with me often. I know it hurts ya, darling, but I couldn't go on any longer without telling ya. I care so much for ya that I was afraid you'd stop seeing me if I told ya when ya first asked if I was married."

He puts his arms around me and tries to kiss me. I shove him away. I don't want him to touch me. I feel he lied to me. Well, sort of. How could he! How dare he! I don't want to look at him. I just want to go...get far away from him and think. Divorce just isn't acceptable to my family. Good people don't get divorced, no matter how bad the marriage. I try to sort out these conflicting emotions. I feel like crying and screaming at him all in the same breath.

"It won't make any difference, Marilyn. That marriage is a closed book in my life. I never was happy with her." He takes my hand again and smiles.

I want him to leave me, but he doesn't and somehow I stay at the dance with him. The rest of the evening is a blur. Upon returning to the fraternity house, I cry on Bonnie's shoulder, "I didn't want him to be married. What am I going to do, Bonnie? My life is falling in shambles around my feet."

I sleep little that night. I don't consider telling Skip to get out of my life. I really do like him. I enjoy our conversations. We laugh and like doing many things together. His confidence and vibrance make me imagine an exciting life with him.

In the morning I decide that my family needs to meet Skip. What they think is important to me. They won't understand my loving a divorced man unless they meet him. With his shipping out for the Pacific next week, today's the last chance for them to meet. I call and tell my mother that I'm coming home that morning. She doesn't ask why. My family's very close. I don't consider not telling them that he's divorced.

When I call Skip and ask him to go home with me, he says that's fine. Skip and I take the bus to Tama. Dad and Mother meet us at the station. I'm always surprised at how small Mother, who is only 5' 2", appears beside Dad, who's over 6' tall and weighs 275 pounds.

When we arrive home my two brothers and two sisters greet us. I'm the oldest in the family, then comes my sister, Peggy. Unlike Dad and Mother, who have dark hair and brown eyes, she's blonde and blue-eyed. She graduated two weeks ago from the University of Iowa. My brother Lynn, a senior in high school, is the small one in the family being only 5' 10". Next is Dick, a sophomore, who's going to be tall like Dad. My youngest sister, Helen Lucille, is only ten years old. She has blonde curly hair like Shirley Temple.

Skip has a relaxed, natural way of talking to my folks. Helen Lucille enjoys the attention he gives her. No one asks why I brought Skip home that weekend. They probably guess that I want to see how he acts around them. They give me no clues to what they think of him. I guess what I think is all that matters. Skip knows how upset I am about his divorce and holds my hand on the way back to Ames.

When Bonnie asks how it went, I tell her, "Skip did very well, but I have to go slow. There must be a reason for the divorce. We won't have a chance to get better acquainted with his leaving for overseas. Did you have any problems like this?"

"No. We just fell in love and married before he went overseas. Marilyn, at least he told you about being divorced."

I'm not very comforted. All week I think about Lyman. He'll come and everything will be okay. We'll continue where we left off before he went into the service. I'll fall in love with him. I don't need this handsome Norwegian.

"I think I'll wear my red dress when I see Lyman," I tell Bonnie. "I always get compliments with how I look in it. There's an informal ball tonight that we can go to."

She agrees with me.

"I'm going over to Great Uncle Homer and Aunt Cora's boy's boarding house and see if I can stay with them on Saturday night. That way I won't have to be in at midnight." Aunt Cora says I can sleep on the living room couch, and gives me a key.

When I come down the stairs of the fraternity house, I see how smart Lyman looks in his Air Force officer's uniform. I can't help comparing him to Skip. He's shorter and has a round face and brown eyes. I had planned to throw my arms around his neck and tell him how wonderful he looks. But instead I just say, "It's great to see you."

"It's been too long," Lyman says.

We go to a movie in the late afternoon and then out for dinner. I enjoy showing off Lyman at the ball on Saturday night. Lyman can still make my heart throb. When we get into his car, he puts his arms around me and kisses me. How wonderful. I enjoy having the privacy of a car which Skip wasn't able to offer. Lyman drives with one arm around my waist.

Later, when he takes me to Uncle Homer's door he says," I'll pick you up for breakfast. I want to go by the La Verne House where I used to live. Would you like to go to the Methodist Church with me?"

"Yes." He kisses me goodnight.

Lyman and I enjoy each other for the weekend. He has no way of knowing that Skip broke my heart.

I keep hoping Lyman will say, "You and I are the ones, Marilyn. No one else matters." But he seems cool. I wonder if he has another girl. Finally it is time for him to leave and we tell each other to write. I feel Lyman doesn't know how to express his feelings or perhaps he doesn't want to commit himself. I'm disappointed.

Skip arrives at 6:00 Sunday night. He takes me in his arms and tells me how much he loves me and will miss me. He makes my heart throb again. I'll miss him, too. He gives me his home address in Tacoma. He'll be there for a two-week leave before he reports for Navy duty at Treasure Island in San Francisco Bay.

Both men have now left and I'm back to my studies for finals. I can't find the address Skip gave me because I put it in the small top pocket of my suit. I'll just forget him. Then Skip calls to find out why I haven't written. Another man might think I didn't care. Skip never takes anything for granted.

I know that I like Skip, but if he disappears into the sunset, then so be it. I would cry and mourn the one that got away, but my life would be easier. The differences between Skip and Lyman are extreme. The thought of going to Alaska with Skip is too scary. I was born and raised for a comfortable life in Iowa with an engineer or doctor.

In June of 1944, I graduate from Iowa State with a degree in Home Economics and a minor in Journalism. This is the weekend of the Normandy invasion. The war is on everyone's mind. I'm glad neither Skip nor Lyman are fighting yet. One of my old boyfriends, Al Donahoo, was in Europe. He married a girl he met while in the service in Chicago last year. France seems very far away from Ames.

That summer, I obtain a position in A.E. Staley's test kitchen in Decatur, Illinois. Soon after I arrive in Illinois, I meet Chuck Strahl at the Methodist Church. He's a chemical engineer employed on a secret project for the government in Decatur. Chuck and I enjoy dancing and playing bridge with his friends. Agnes works at the Staley micro-biology lab and Leon Elsworth works with Chuck. We also play bridge with others who are also working on the mystery project.

Skip is now stationed at Pearl Harbor in Hawaii. He spends his spare time filling my mail box with his wonderful letters. Each afternoon when I return to my rooming house, I look forward to reading them. As the Navy censor limits letters to two sheets, Skip buys notebook paper and writes as small as possible on both sides. Skip is contemptuous of how other Navy men spend their time. He uses his time to read books by the great thinkers. These include: *Philosophy and Truth of Life*, by Fredrick Nietzsche; *Wonders and Miracles of Science*; *Return to the River*, by Roderick Haig-Brown; *Alaska Challenge*, by Bill Ruth Albee; *Lord of Alaska*, by Hector Chevigny; *Road of a Naturalist*, by Donald Peattie; and *Under a Lucky Star*, by Roy Chapman Andrews. Slowly he develops and shares his philosophy with me regarding what he wants to do with his life.

He sends me some quotes from Emerson, Thoreau, and Nietzsche:

The invariable mark of wisdom is to see the miraculous in the common.[1]

The worst that could happen to me would be: when I came to die, to discover that I had not lived![2]

We have learned to control nature by our understanding, but not how to engender the spirit of love, and we the victims of our own inventions. We can fly round the world, grow food in bottles, build or destroy an incredible city, but how to find happiness on a hundred acres, or how to make men's lives as excellent as their intellects, fatally eludes us.[3]

I send him Henry David Thoreau's *Walden*, and Louise Dickinson Rich's books on Maine. He enjoys them as much as I do, and we discuss their philosophy. I realize his thirst for knowledge makes up for the lack of a college degree. I've not read 17 books this year as he has. He also collects coral, bleaches it and sends it to an aquarium in Oregon.

The second week in April, 1945, President Franklin Roosevelt dies. That week I celebrate my 23rd birthday. I happily receive a dozen red roses from both Skip and Lyman. Skip writes that he saw some beautiful engagement rings at a good price at the PX. "How would you like to become engaged?"

This is not quite the type of proposal I'm looking for. I write, "I'm not sure enough of my feelings for you. I won't accept a ring and hide it in my drawer."

He remarks, "That idea went over like a lead balloon."

Tucked at the end of a letter he notes, "I hurt my back a couple of weeks ago when they accidentally dumped a pile of sea bags on me. I'm just sore and it will soon go away. Don't worry, darling."

Later, I learn that he's in so much pain that he can't sleep at night and must stand to write. He notes in his diary on June 26:

I left old A.B.R.D., Army Base Reshipment Deport, today after over a year here. Arrived at Aeia Hospital in the afternoon. It's sure nice here: clean, cool and quiet and many nice fellows to talk with. After the barracks, where there was nothing but beer parties and radios playing all night, I really appreciate this.

On V.J., Victory over Japan, Day, Chuck tells me that he was working on one part of the atomic bomb. Chuck and I have dated for over a year. He tells me that his job will be shutting down and he'll soon be hunting for new work. I'm not sure about my feelings for him.

On September 7, Skip writes in his diary:

> My name is on that draft. Oh, Boy! Am I happy! My last day in Hawaii! Leaving on the old battleship Maryland tomorrow. Wrote Marilyn and folks last letter from beautiful Hawaii. Aloha Hawaii.

Skip calls me the day his ship docks in California. "Hello, darling!" I wonder who's calling me.

"This is Skip. I'm back in the States. I'm going to have a month's convalescent leave starting October 20. How would ya like me to come to Decatur and visit ya? I can hitchhike from California to Illinois. I just talked to a fellow who did that. He said there's no problem as long as ya wear your uniform. I'll leave here on Monday, the 20th."

How could I forget about his Norwegian accent? "That sounds wonderful. We can get acquainted again." I look forward to seeing Skip.

Before I knew Skip was coming, Chuck had bought tickets for a stage play on October 22.

On October 15, Lyman calls and tells me that he will be discharged from Chanute Field at Champaign, Illinois. He can then be near me. Lyman will be in Decatur on October 20.

I'm happy to see each of them but why do they always have to come at the same time? Maybe they're conspiring against me.

Lyman visited Decatur on leave the previous February. He told me about his narrow escape over Corsica. A few days before, he transferred to another bomber with a different crew. In horror, he watched his original crew get shot down and only three of the five parachutes open. He lost his best friend, who was the pilot.

Lyman and I still didn't discuss how we felt about each other. We had a great time and I thought he might say that he loved me and ask me to marry him when the war was over. But he didn't. Then he headed for the South Pacific and more danger. Lyman's letters were usually one page that said little. He claimed his abruptness was due to the censorship.

Now, after I meet Lyman's bus, we get into a taxi and he takes me in his arms, saying, "It's so wonderful to see you, Marilyn. I could hardly wait. The day seemed endless. I'm going to stay all week."

What a moment for me to blurt out, "Skip's coming Friday." Lyman sits back and looks at me for a long time. Nothing is the same after that.

I hope Lyman will say, "To hell with him. You're mine. I've known you the longest and the best." But that's Skip's style, not Lyman's. I'm forced to tell Lyman about going to a stage play on Wednesday. I don't want to break my date with Chuck for he will leave soon.

I lamely tell Lyman that we can go out tomorrow and Thursday. Lyman makes no comment. The next day he calls me at work to say, "I'm taking the noon train home to Iowa."

I'm hurt at his leaving, but I don't know how to tell him the way I feel because I'm not at all sure myself.

Friday night when I open my rooming house door, I find a tall sailor standing there. My first thought is, do I know this man? Skip is bronze from all of his hours in the sun.

He takes me in his arms and kisses me. "Marilyn, my darling, it's been so long. Ya look wonderful."

"Yes, it's wonderful to be together again. We've been apart a long time."

Never at a loss for words, Skip breaks down my reticence by his enthusiasm. He's arrived sooner than expected because he obtained one ride after another. He seldom waited long with his thumb out. He left California on Monday and arrived in Decatur, Illinois on Friday. I find him a room to rent in a home similar to mine. In the war years, many home owners rented out a room to ease the housing shortage. My meals are at Mrs. Crow's boarding house where we eat family style around a big table. She has room for Skip only for dinner.

While I'm at work, he plans what we'll do in the evening. We go for a walk in the park with a setting sun silhouetting the trees. At the art gallery, we both like the nature paintings. Skip loves music, and we obtain tickets to a concert. We laugh at plays. We enjoy being together. He made up a series of aquarium slides from the days he was the aquarist at Point Defiance Aquarium in Tacoma. He sells sets to the schools.

As the month goes quickly, I can hardly believe that Skip's leave is soon over. Two nights before he leaves, while we sit in the living room of my boarding house, he gets down on his knees.

"Marilyn, I love you very much. Will you marry me when I get out of the

Navy?"

I'd thought about this moment, but I'm still unprepared. A long silence follows. I must say something. All the old doubts come back. Why did he get a divorce? What's his family like? Do they have the Old World values where the man makes all the decisions? How will I fit in? Where will we live? Will we have enough money?

I can only stammer, "I'm complimented that you ask. I...I'll have to think about it."

The next day I help a girl friend cook Thanksgiving dinner. My brother Lynn, stationed in the Air Force at St. Louis, joins us for the holiday. I see Skip fits in well. I trust him to take care of me because he makes me feel safe. Life with Skip will be an adventure. He loves me with a passion.

When Skip and I return to my rooming house, I tell him that I'm willing to gamble we'll have a good life together.

He kisses me. "You'll never regret it, Marilyn."

He's so happy when I put him on the train the next day. At last, I have made the decision, the most important one in a girl's life.

For the next ten days, I ask myself, "Do you love him, Marilyn?" I wish Bonnie were here to talk over the situation, but she's far away. I think, I'm not sure. I like him, I enjoy him. Ours is a comfortable relationship but do I really know him? I'd gone out with Lyman for two years and Chuck for one year. Chuck took me home to Ohio to meet his parents. I only dated Skip for six weeks before he went overseas. The doubts take over. I can't do this.

Finally I write him, "Skip, since you left, I've been trying to sort out my feelings. I'm very sorry, I just don't love you. I think what we need is more time together. When you were here, it seemed right, but now that you're gone, I have many questions."

When he gets the letter, he goes into a trance. He can't eat or sleep for two days. Finally, he says to himself, "She'd feel this way with anyone. She's afraid to gamble on love."

He keeps writing as though I'd never written that letter. I'm surprised when his only reference to it is, "We'll talk about our feelings when we get together."

After his discharge on December 15, 1945, he spends the holidays with his family and daughter in Tacoma. He needs time with his family after all those months in the Navy. I reassure myself that I'm not disappointed.

I'm home with my family when Skip calls to wish me a Merry Christmas.

He closes, "Next year will be our year, darling. Mark my word."

When Skip arrives in Decatur the second week in January, I'm so excited to see him that I take off work to meet his train. He wears an old brown suit that he's slept in for four days. My first thoughts are, "This is what I'm waiting for?" The railroads give the servicemen greatly reduced fares, but the service is terrible.

Skip hugs me and gives me a big kiss. "I wanted ya to see me in a good looking suit, not this old thing. I didn't think you'd meet me." He's handsome and makes the old suit look good.

We begin again where we left off in November. I want him to find a job in Decatur, and we'll think of getting married next summer. When he hears my plan he gets mad, which is unlike him.

"Now, Marilyn, this is ridiculous. Ya just want me here. Ya don't want to decide one way or the other. Ya want to eat your cake and have it too. I won't have any part of it. I must tell the park commissioners whether I'll take the assistant aquarist position at Point Defiance Aquarium. If ya want security, then we can do that. Or we can go to Alaska. If we're ever going up there, it will be right now before I have a job or we buy a home or furniture. Today, we only have our personal possessions, and not too many of them."

Skip enjoys his leave with his daughter Dawn.

I agree with Skip's reasoning but I keep asking myself if I'm up to leaving the Midwest and my family to be with Skip. Do I love him or the prospect of an adventure? While I debate, some friends invite Skip to show his Alaskan slides, which depict the snow covered mountains, blue water and the many boats. As I watch them, I ask myself if we can turn our backs on Alaska for security in the States. So often what appears to be security turns out to be no security at all.

Upon returning to my rooming house, we talk. I sense Skip's reawakened desire for Alaska.

He explains, "We need to decide if we're going to Alaska, because we must find a fishing boat. The king salmon come into shallow water to spawn in the rivers in May and June. If we're going to make a living, we can't afford to miss a day of the short fishing season." Then he draws a picture of a salmon troller. He shows me a letter from his brother-in-law, Frank Johnson, who lives in Wrangell, Alaska. He says the season looks good for salmon.

Skip quotes the question from a popular song, "Is You Is, Or Is You Ain't?" and then gives me an ultimatum, "I'm going to leave here next week if ya aren't going with me, Marilyn."

I lie awake thinking all night. My heart loves him, but my mind has reservations. I think my mind loves the thought of going to far away places, but my heart's afraid. He hasn't told me how he's going to pay for a boat. Skip seems to have little money. Many men wait to get married until they have a job or have savings. Maybe Lyman and Chuck don't ask me to marry because they want to be in better financial states.

I don't want Skip to take the aquarium job as it pays less than my present job, which gives me only a few luxuries. If I marry him, I want to go to Alaska. I dream of traveling around the world as partners like Anne Morrow Lindbergh traveled with Charles in *North to the Orient*. I hate just listening to exciting experiences—I want to be part of them, whether they're good or bad.

I express my dilemma to a young couple living in my boarding house. They say, "What have you to lose? You can always come back."

I don't like that idea. I either go for all or nothing. I may not be sure of my love for him now, but I feel that it will grow. I'm not looking for a rich man, but one that I can work with to build security and raise a family.

The next evening I tell Skip, "I'll go to Alaska with you."

He grabs me and kisses me, "We'll have a wonderful life. Mark my words. You won't regret it, honey."

I take a week's vacation to go home to plan my wedding. The day before I leave for home, Lyman writes: "Here I am back at Iowa State. School isn't the same. The coeds are all so young. I feel like their father."

Too late, Lyman. I'm not turning back again.

CHAPTER TWO
Destination: Wrangell, Alaska

WE STAND ON THE DECK of the *Princess Norah* with the bitter March wind slapping rain against our faces. When I shiver, Skip puts his arm around me. Eagerly, I wait for my first glimpse of Alaska, although in many ways I feel I know Alaska already from Skip's stories and slides.

"Alaska! The Great Land," he points ahead with excitement in his voice.

As I look through the biting rain, I see the tall mountains with snow almost to the water's edge, trees to the waterline and the ocean slapping against the shore. This land differs from rural Iowa. I had never seen the ocean until a few weeks ago.

Marilyn marries Wilhelm "Skip" Jordan in February of 1946.

"I bet it's more wonderful and exciting than we dreamed. Now we're really starting our life together." I squeeze his hand. I'm apprehensive about our life together. Where will we live? Will we make a living at fishing? Will I make new friends?

As we leave Canada, I think back on all that has happened since I told Skip that I'd marry him in January. After returning from Iowa to my job, Skip and I had three weeks in Illinois. Skip helped me pack to leave Illinois, my job in the test kitchen, and my friends.

I picked February 23 for my wedding date, because Peggy, my sister, could come to Iowa from New York City. February 23 was on Saturday and she had Washington's birthday off on the 22nd. I wanted her to sing at the wedding and be my maid of honor. My high school friend, Margaret Siggins, came from Colorado to be my bridesmaid.

While Mother and I made the last minute wedding preparations, Skip went to Tipton to visit my grandparents, the Deardorffs, and Aunt Margery Frink.

Margery wrote to her sister Bee about Skip, "They will go to Washington State and get a boat. Just the two of them will motor to Alaska for several months. Nice boy. Not timid but warm and friendly. Talks easily with enthusiasm and intelligence. A go-getter and likable."

The wedding was beautiful and my "special" day. In all the excitement, Mother and I forgot about pictures. We were leaving town and had to have them done on Sunday. We at last found a retired photographer, whose studio was above a store. Skip ended up sitting on an old nail keg. At least, we had pictures taken.

We left that evening on the Union Pacific's Portland Rose for the West Coast. We called it the Love Train because many servicemen and their wives were aboard. As the porter made up the berths at 8 p.m., the newlyweds spent long nights with each other.

Knowing Skip's first wife became pregnant on their wedding night, I planned that this wouldn't happen to me. When we ran out of protection, Skip decided to go to a drug store at the next stop in the middle of Wyoming. The conductor said they'd be stopped for a half hour and a town was nearby.

In dismay, Skip found it

Eva (Skip's sister), Inga (Skip's mother), and Skip right before they leave Norway for the US in 1926.

was a long way from the train to the main street of the town. He ran into a drug store and requested, "One dozen Trojans. Keep the change."

He was a long way down the tracks when the whistle blew. I kept looking out the window in a panic. What would happen if he didn't make it before the train left? At the last minute, Skip jumped aboard. He puffed, "I never ran so fast in my whole life. I could imagine your heading for the coast without me. I had all the money. How could we explain this to the family?"

We were scheduled to go down the Columbia River Gorge at night. We awoke at 6 a.m. to feel the train stopped. The porter reported they had a derailment on the Oregon side and were switching us to the Washington side. I'd read much about the mighty Columbia and was amazed by the mammoth free-flowing river.

Grandma Deardorff wrote her relatives that we'd be coming through Portland. Mother's first cousin, Mable, and her husband, Joe Fisher, met us. We had a good visit, and corresponded after that.

In Tacoma, Skip's robust father, Kristian Jordan, met our train. Kris was a longshoreman and worked on the waterfront. Kris became a US citizen as soon as he was eligible after immigrating in 1926. Skip and Eva had derivative citizenship because they were underage. Skip's tiny Mother, Inga, immediately won my heart with her warmth. She never took the citizenship exam because she didn't feel her English was good enough. Occasionally I had some trouble with the Jordans' heavy Norwegian accents.

A week later, Skip's sister, Eva Johnson, arrived from Wrangell with her 18 month old son, Chris, and three month old daughter, Ellen. Eva was small like Mother Jordan. As the two youngsters kept her busy, we didn't get well acquainted.

One evening, Skip told Dad Jordan that he taught me to play cribbage on our trip.

Dad Jordan responded sarcastically "Ha! Ya don't know about cribbage, 'Willum.' I'm the cribbage player in this family. Come on, Marilyn, let's play."

I wanted to show him what a good teacher Skip was. I was mad at him for running down my husband. I concentrated and played each card carefully. Skip would wink at me when I made a good play. I ended up beating Dad Jordan five out of six games.

Kris threw down the cards and announced, "That's enough. This isn't my lucky day." I can't remember that we ever played cribbage again.

When we were in Tacoma, our dream of buying a salmon troller and making a living as Alaskan commercial fishermen almost died when we were unable to find a boat. Others, such as shipyard workers, had bought all the good fishing boats in the Puget Sound area.

Skip patiently explained a troller to me. The boat has four long poles onto which are hung four stainless steel lines with a tag line to the end of the pole. The weight of the line hangs from the pole not from the blocks on the side of the boat. Snubbers, which are a piece of rubber with a snap, are attached onto the steel lines at marked intervals. At the end of the snubbers, an Oregon leader dangles a lure with a hook. The boat is called a troller because it moves slowly through the water to attract the salmon to about 20 lures. The number of lures depends on the depth that you're fishing. Once the salmon takes the hook it pulls against the snubbers which give it room to play. If there is no give, the fish would break loose.

I learned that a troller can be either a boat or a fisherman. A troller boat provides a means of earning a livelihood, living area, and a mode of transportation. A troller person makes his living by trolling. Many questions came to my mind, but Skip said that I would learn about them when we started fishing.

We were encouraged when a letter arrived from Frank, Eva's husband. "You're a fool to work for someone else when you can be your own boss up here. In Alaska, you can take out a homesite, build a cabin, have a garden, fish and hunt. No matter how severe a depression, you won't starve or be forced to go on relief. For any sober, hardworking young man, Alaska offers many chances to make good. You've had experience fishing on Puget Sound. There's absolutely no reason that you can't make as much fishing as on any job you could get in the States. There's a boat for sale here in Wrangell. She's a good double-ender."

Dad Jordan graciously took a loan out on his home for the $3500 cost of the boat. We sent a down payment and bought steamer tickets with Destination: Wrangell, Alaska, stamped on them. I was as excited as a small child on her first trip to the city, as we boarded the steamer for Alaska. I enjoyed this fascinating three day honeymoon. The steamer wound in and out among the many islands of the Inside Passage from British Columbia to Southeast Alaska.

At lunch time on the first day out of Vancouver, the steamer rolled easily for two hours in the large ocean swells as she crossed Queen Charlotte Sound, the largest body of open water on the trip. Suddenly I was seasick.

After hurriedly leaving the dining salon, I wanted to lie peacefully on my bunk. Skip may have had misgivings about making this Iowa farm girl into a fisherwomen.

"Come on, get out of that bunk! Ya'll feel better on deck," he said sternly.

I didn't like the idea, but I couldn't say "no" to him when he talked like that. In some ways, he scared me, but then I like a strong man. I found that I was not sick as long as I looked over the bow and watched the ship cutting into the waves.

Now here we are sailing into Dixon Entrance on this 31st day of March. I glance at my husband leaning on the ship's rail and gazing at the snow covered mountains ahead. Perhaps he felt this way when, as a 13 year-old, he came to Halifax, Nova Scotia, from Norway. Skip looked after his tiny mother and his sister, Eva, as his father had come on ahead. Had he learned at that early age not to fear the unknown? He gives me confidence that he'll look after me no matter what the future holds.

I recall one of the quotations he mailed to me when in the service:

> Our main problem is how to do what we want without wasting time and energy making money! This means we plan to live our own lives which diverge from the conventional.[4]

I remember a college instructor who said, "Never dream about what is going to happen. Then you won't be disappointed when reality and your dreams aren't the same. You'll then see that reality is better."

I want nothing to mar this experience and adventure. Skip will prepare me for whatever is ahead.

Two days later, Skip says, "Get up, This is the day."

"What? What time is it?" I see only a faint glimmer of light through the porthole opposite my bunk.

"It's 6:30 a.m. We want to be the first ones off this steamer."

"There's the breakfast chimes. I can smell coffee. Let's go down and eat. The food is free."

"Absolutely not. When ya get dressed, ya carry the two suitcases and typewriter. I'll carry the three seabags. Hurry." He's as excited as a child at his first day at camp.

Walking up the companion way I must go sideways and the luggage is heavy.

"I'll help ya when I get these on deck," Skip says, hurrying on ahead of me. Coming up on the deck, he points with a smile, "That's Wrangell. See the snow covered mountains on the mainland behind the town." I feel a sense of awe as the early morning sun peeks over these mountains.

I wonder what living on a 30-foot boat is going to be like. I envision a small yacht.

"Ya'll love it. You're so much closer to nature on a small boat. Just think of the thrill of landing a big salmon."

"Will I be seasick?"

"Just go out on deck and ya won't be."

"Look at that gangplank! We'll have to climb straight up!"

"It's low tide. Ya'll have to learn about tides if you're a salmon troller."

The custom officer stalks aboard. "Go down to the saloon. You can't get off till I check your baggage." We have to carry all this back? No wonder we didn't see anyone on the deck. They knew the routine.

"I'm sorry, darling. I just wanted to see our boat," Skip says as we carry our bags to the saloon.

"This is April Fools Day. I only hope it doesn't fool us anymore," I remark. He smiles at me and in my heart I know that I can never stay angry at him. When we finally get back to the gangplank, Skip says, "There's Frank. He's that small, wiry man on the dock. His family came from an Indian tribe on the Olympic Peninsula."

Mac McKibben, the boat's owner, is waiting with Frank. As only three can crowd into Mac's pick-up, Frank chooses to walk.

"I wouldn't be selling her, but my wife doesn't like boat life. She's opening a variety store," Mac, a jolly round-faced man, says.

At the boat harbor, we come to a wooden object. In dismay, I see that it resembles a ladder going down to the float from the stationary dock on shore.

Women don't wear pants on the steamer, so I have on a skirt. I see the cleats which are wooden boards pounded crosswise at intervals along one side of this almost vertical incline. Later, I learn they call it a ramp and it changes from vertical to horizontal depending on the tide. Cautiously, I step forward in my high heels.

"Wait a minute," Skip says setting down our luggage. "I don't want my bride breaking her neck the first day." He laughs as he half carries, half drags me down this never ending ramp. At the bottom he gently sets me down and returns for the luggage.

Following Mac, I wonder which will be our boat. I see an old gray boat with a small, homemade cabin perched on its bow. I'm happy when Mac keeps going.

Halfway down the float, Mac stops beside a small white boat. "This is the *Mom*," he says proudly. I see why Mac is proud of her. She has a trim pilothouse. She's an older boat, but very clean. The paint's a crisp white. We're both so anxious to see what's inside that we end up pushing each other to get into the small pilothouse. The interior consists of a wheel, throttle, compass, bench and an exhaust pipe. The fire Mac has going in the stove gives the boat a cozy feeling.

I step down three steps to the kitchen, called a galley on a boat. I realize that 31 feet of boat is far different from 31 feet of house. I'll be living in a cube. The boat's a double-ender, which means it comes to a point in both the bow or front, and the stern or rear.

Knee high lockers line the starboard, or right side. The black iron postage stamp size stove sits on the portside, or left, with lockers opening out along the floor. A table folds down from a dish cupboard on the starboard side. I realize that we will have to eat sitting sideways.

The stove contrasts to the commercial ovens in the test kitchens I used in Illinois. I recall the comic of a stove salesman: "No thermostats, no automatic controls, it just cooks." I have doubts that I can cook on this converted wood stove.

A wooden partition separates the stove from the portside bunk. On the starboard side another bunk folds down over the steps. The remainder of the 31 feet consists of an engine, fuel tanks, fish hold to ice our catch, and the troller pit where we work our gear and land fish. I have maybe ten by five feet of living space. How am I supposed to live here? I'm used to small spaces but this is smaller than I imagined. No wonder Skip didn't describe what our living quarters would be like. I'm feeling great dismay but Skip's busy talking to Mac about the engine. These men obviously care little about where they live. Fishing comes first with them.

Skip checks the engine by starting it. Then he climbs down into the hold. He tells me that he looks for dry rot which must be replaced with new wood. If a boat has too much dry rot, it's unsafe.

While Skip is doing all this I ask Mac, "Where's the sink?"

"You use a dish pan. A water tank's in the bow with a faucet."

I pull Skip's head to my level, "I don't see a bathroom."

"I'll tell ya later," he says. "Yes, Mac, we'll take her."

Driving to the Commissioner's office to sign the papers, Mac points out Chief Shakes Community House surrounded by totems. The town forms an S around Etolin Bay and the streets run in tiers up the hillside. Mac indicates the shrimp and fish canneries and the sawmill.

Wrangell isn't the frontier town I expected. The city has sidewalks and three paved downtown blocks. The modern glass front on the drugstore matches any in Iowa. Looking up, I spot turn of the century cupolas on several buildings.

The Commissioner's office, located in the post office, perches high on a hill overlooking Stikine Straits. Frank waits while we sign the papers and pay our money. Now we must make monthly payments of $50 to Dad Jordan, to pay on the loan. We have made the first step in our adventure as salmon trollers in Alaska.

We walk back to the boat hand in hand. Life is beginning for us! Not only have we bought a business but we now have a home and transportation, too.

Skip stops where we can look out over the harbor, "What do ya think of it all?"

"Alaska is better than I dreamed. The boat is less expensive than anything we saw on Puget Sound. I was afraid the boat would be an old, dirty wreck. I like her." Yet one question has been weighing on my mind all morning. "Where's the sink and toilet?"

"Ya call the toilet a 'head' on a boat. The bucket is the most used object on a boat. Everything goes into the bucket, and ya pour it overboard," he adds.

"What...," I stammer, "No toilet?"

"Ya'll get used to it," Skip continues on down the float to the boat. I stumble after him. First I discover that I'm living in an area no bigger than a horse stall and then I learn that instead of a toilet, I'm supposed to use a bucket! What could happen next?

I'm trying to find places for our clothes when Frank bursts into the cabin. "A big earthquake shook the Aleutians. A Coast Guard Light station just slid into the ocean. A tidal wave may be coming."

"What can we do?" Skip asks worriedly. He stands and looks out of the sky light.

"Tied to a dock is the worst place to be. The tidal wave will hit tonight if it comes this way. Best to head for the fishing grounds together. How fast can you get ready?"

"We'll be ready when we find a place for these clothes. We need groceries."

In the store, I pile more and more items on the counter. With these high prices, little money will be left for fuel and ice. This makes me more cautious. Surely, I'm buying more than enough for three of us for ten days.

"Don't buy your bread at the grocery. The bakery's bread is fresher," Frank says. "If you're done, we better hurry."

After totaling everything, the man asks, "What boat do we deliver this to?"

This surprises Skip, "How did ya know it was for a boat?"

"Most new people are on boats. We'll be delivering in half an hour. Are you at the shrimp cannery float or the oil docks?"

"We're on this side. Boat's name is *Mom*," Skip says proudly, for now we're boat owners.

At the fishing tackle store, Frank says, "You must buy a 22 pistol to shoot the big fish. Otherwise, you'll lose them when they see the boat. Here's a good one for $25. You'll need herring hooks to string up the bait, Oregon Leader and rubber snubbers, and a non-resident fishing license."

As we hurry to the dock, Frank says, "You get ice while I get fuel. If we leave by three, we'll make a good anchorage by dark. Just hurry."

When we step aboard, we find our groceries sitting on deck. Real service, I think. The engine gives a purr when Skip pushes the starter. I sit on a bench that runs perpendicular to the dash board. Skip stands on the second step with his head out the window. The boat tied outside of us is unoccupied. We back out and then push it into the float. I have no idea how to tie it to the float. Luckily, two men take the other boat's lines and tie it to the dock.

"An unwritten law," Skip points out, "says that ya tie any boat outside of you securely to the float. Ya put a tire fender between the float and the boat to keep a passing boat's wake from crashing it into the dock."

Backing *Mom* to the end of the float, Skip puts her in forward gear and turns the wheel to clear the boats on the outside of the float. We're underway. Now Skip's a real skipper. I see how proud he is of his boat handling ability from his many years boating on Puget Sound.

"The cannery with the cold storage in it is ahead on the high pilings,"

Skip says.

"How does the ice get from up there to the boat?"

"Ya'll see. Now ya must help me tie up to the pilings. As the tide's running against us, tying the boat will be difficult. When I slow down the engine, ya climb onto the bow."

Cautiously, I put my feet sideways upon the foot wide ledge between the deck and the trunk cabin. I hang onto the railings fastened there. At last I make it to the bow. I cling to the base of one of our trolling poles.

When Skip slows the engine, we drift sideways away from the piling. Helplessly, I stand there with the end of the rope in my hand and the other end around the bow cleat.

Yelling to be heard over the boat engine, Skip orders, "Get the line around the piling fast. Ya can't be slow. Now! Do it now!"

The transition from bride to deckhand is complete. Well, I think, I wanted to be part of the action. On the next try, he positions the bow long enough for me to put one arm around the creosote piling and grasp the rope with the other hand. Horrors, I see the black creosote sticks to my jacket. I'll never get it off.

He tells the dockman to give us one ton of ice. Skip pulls on his hip boots and crawls into the hold to grasp the end of the ice chute that they lower to him. The ice chute is a rubber tube with metal rings on its end to send the ice in any direction. Skip points the chute into each bin as the crushed, flaked ice crashes down the tube into our hold. Skip tells the dockman to lower two 50-pound blocks of frozen herring for bait. He covers them with ice in the hold.

Climbing out of the hold and up the steep ladder to pay , he sees me standing on the deck. He calls down, "Get some chow, honey. I'm a hardworking fisherman and I can't live on love alone."

When he comes back, he says, "We better catch some fish. Our money's almost gone. I forgot, we must turn off the stove when we put gasoline into the tanks. Ya must wait to cook dinner."

This time as we gently slide alongside the dock, I catch the dockman's line on the first try. I feel better about being a deckhand. We take aboard 150 gallons of gas, 20 gallons of stove oil and 40 gallons of water.

"I don't see a bunch of boats heading out ahead of the tidal wave. Maybe they know something we don't," I say.

"The number of boats doesn't really matter. We came to go fishing and that's what we're doing. This is the moment we've waited for. The start of our first trip in our quest for salmon."

Skip likes to be dramatic. What will this trip bring in salmon, wildlife, and experiences? We pit ourselves against the wind and tide. Rocks and reefs are always just below the surface waiting to wreck a boat. I ask for God's blessing. I sit on this small boat beside my man, who sits on the stool behind the wheel. He feels the magic, too, for he leans over and kisses me.

Looking at his watch, he writes down 3:10 p.m. in the log book. He takes out a chart of Zarembo and Approaches and lays it beside the wheel. He points out the depth soundings and the rocks and inlets. Skip had explained to me that Alaska has a mixture of Russian, Spanish, Indian and American names. Etolin Island, which lies ahead, was named for the Russian naval officer who was Chief Manager of the Russian American Company from 1841 to '45. Zarembo, another naval officer, was Etolin's assistant. Woronkofski Island along which we were traveling was named for a navigator and explorer who worked with Etolin and Zarembo. He was lost when his schooner, *Chilkat*, sank with all hands aboard.

"I'll light the fire so you can finish the meal. There's Frank on the *Roberta B.* heading down...," he peers at the chart, "Zimovia Straits." Zimovia means winter straits in Russian. During the winter most of the small boats travel down this protected passage instead of going out into Clarence Straits, which can get rough.

Where to stow everything is now the question. Skip has already put the meat on ice except two pounds of hamburger for dinner. Standing there with the 25-pound sack of potatoes, I can't find a place for it. Seeing my dilemma, Skip puts it in the coil of rope on the pilothouse's top.

I'm still hunting places to put everything when I hear *Mom's* motor slow down. Now what? Frank and Skip yell back and forth. They tie the two boats together so Frank can show Skip how to make up fishing gear. "Can Marilyn steer the boats?" Frank asks.

"She's pretty good at about everything," Skip replies with the confidence of a newlywed. "Honey, could ya bring us a cup of coffee? That should tide us over till we can eat."

"I can't find the inside of the coffee pot."

"Fishermen never use the insides. They boil their coffee. When the water boils, you throw in a couple of tablespoons of coffee."

I've always had a hard time fixing coffee as I don't like it, but I put the pot on to boil.

I take my place behind the wheel. When are we going to eat? Again, I postpone dinner. Eating must be secondary to fishing. I'd like to ask Frank why more boats aren't leaving.

"See that distant point," Skip points. "Keep the bow heading for it. Watch out for drift. A log can knock a hole in a boat or bend a propeller."

The boats keep purring on their southerly course. I think, this steering is easy. Without warning, the boats sheer to the starboard. I turn the wheel to the port. Nothing happens! In panic, I throw my weight on the port side of the wheel. The wheel spins. The boats take off for the port all right...at a 90 degree angle. Then I try to straighten them out.

Skip yells. "What's happening? Marilyn, look at our wake!"

In dismay, I look over the stern. We're making a figure S.

Skip comes into the pilothouse laughing, "Look, ya landlubber. A boat isn't a car. It responds slower, and with the two boats tied together, they're even slower. Ya must use a light touch on the wheel. Turn the wheel only a fraction each way. Ya have to anticipate what a boat is going to do."

Anticipating and me don't work. I can anticipate what an Iowa mule or cow might do, but a boat...no. Silently, I brush the tears back. Skip smiles at me and goes back out on deck.

Frank changes our course into Chichagof Pass and later into Stikine Straits. We feel so small on our little troller running between these tree-covered islands and distant snow covered peaks. A bald eagle soars and glides overhead. I see no sign that man touched this land. Perhaps the west looked this way to the pioneers.

Luckily, Mac left dishes and two pots, an iron skillet and a griddle aboard because I hadn't thought to buy any of them. I find two cups and two plates and some miscellaneous silverware. I must peel the potatoes with a paring knife instead of a peeler like I'm used to.

"Where's the bread?" I ask.

"Doggone it, we forgot to stop at the bakery."

"I've got enough for tonight," Frank volunteers.

Without yeast, I must make biscuits each day. Skip likes bread with his meals. I resolve never to forget the bread again. I need a hot stove to boil the water in the teakettle. "Skip, you better turn up this stove. It's beyond me."

"See, honey, the stove has a gravity feed from the tank on top of the cabin. Ya turn this valve only a little to increase or decrease the flow. Ya watch how fast it's dripping through the sight glass in the oil line by the stove. I'll turn the oil up for ya."

"I don't have room for both the potato pan and the skillet."

"That's right. Get the potatoes almost done, and push them to the back of the stove. These railings around the stove keep the pans from sliding off if the boat rolls."

I can't believe potatoes take hours to boil. I put the beans on the back of the stove, but they still aren't hot.

At last, I push them to the right side of the stove and put on the skillet for the meat. When the stove doesn't get hot, I turn up the dripper a little.

"Marilyn, what're ya doing?" Skip exclaims rushing down the steps to turn down the dripper. "Big clouds of black smoke are coming out of the chimney. If ya turn it up too much, ya can burn up the boat."

I can't figure out that dripper. "The skillet won't get hot. I hope you like raw hamburgers. Well, everything's done as much as it ever will be. Let's eat while Frank steers."

"Why don't you and Frank eat first? That's the polite way," Skip says.

I'm afraid Skip may have no food for Frank takes seconds. Hurriedly, I eat and climb into the pilothouse to steer.

Upon finishing eating, the men untie the boats near an anchorage.

The sun is setting when we run into a beautiful small bay called Quiet Harbor. Unhooking our 35-pound anchor, Skip slowly lowers it over the small roller on the bow. Fascinated, I watch the heavy chain and rope go overboard. The rope's end, called the bitter end, is tied to the bow cleat.

"Put the boat in reverse to set the anchor." Skip instructs.

Frank yells, "Be sure to let out plenty of scope just in case the tidal wave comes."

"Without enough scope out," Skip explains, "The boat might lift the anchor off the bottom. We could float into shallow water where we'd sit on the beach, or we could float out into the deep water of the Straits."

"I have a lot to learn about boats. I'll trust you to look after everything."

I stand on deck and let the stillness of the place seep into me. Quiet Harbor is a good name. The tide laps at the bottom branches of the nearby trees. Behind us the last touches of color from the setting sun disappear. At nine o'clock the dark isn't completely on us as it would be in Iowa. The shadows from the trees on one shore touch those on the opposite side.

"What a beautiful place this is," Skip says putting his arm around me. I nod.

I follow Skip inside the boat and down the steps into the galley. He pulls the string of the light.

"What a small light!" I exclaim.

"It's only six volts like a car's interior light. We only have three lights: one in the pilothouse, one over the table, and one by the stove."

"I wish one were over my bunk so I could read in bed. Do you realize that 24 hours ago we were on the steamer? So much has happened. Will the tidal wave come?"

"I don't know, but Frank thinks this is the best place if it does."

Skip makes my bed by unrolling my sleeping bag on the mattress on the portside bunk. I pull out my pillow from inside the sleeping bag.

"The skylight's the only place I can raise my arms over my head. You sit on the lockers to take off your shoes," Skip says. "You get undressed first. Here's a wash pan and there's water in the teakettle to wash with. I'll set it on the table."

He gets me a cup of water from the faucet to brush my teeth. At last, I'm ready to get into the bunk.

In dismay, I ask. "How do I get into the bunk? It's too high and the opening is very small."

"I'll boost ya up there. Swing your other leg around."

I get my knee on the edge. I duck my head, and hit the top of the trunk cabin. I finally wiggle into my sleeping bag.

"What a narrow bunk. No room to bend my knees."

"Ya should see my bunk. It folds down over the steps, so it's even narrower and shorter than yours. I give up. I'm going to sleep on the lockers. Good night, my darling," he says kissing me. "This has been a long day and you're a good scout."

"We'll always remember this April Fools Day."

Here I am thousands of miles from home and miles from civilization. I feel no homesickness, only peace as my strong man looks after me. He'll let nothing harm me, not even a tidal wave that might be heading our way.

CHAPTER THREE
Her Name Is *Salty*

THE DAYLIGHT AWAKENS ME. The tidal wave...? What happened?

I lean out of my bunk and turn my head to look at Skip. He's sleeping on the top of the knee-high lockers with his hand under his head and his elbow at a 45 degree angle.

"Skip, did the tidal wave come? Are we all right?"

Sitting up in his sleeping bag, he glances around, "We're still here. The tsunami must have missed us."

He unzips his sleeping bag and stands up to look out the skylight in the middle of the galley. I admire his tall lean body as he begins to dress. He reports, "The tide's way out."

I watch him pull on his one piece long underwear. The boat has no room for both of us to dress at once. As Skip pulls on his wool pants, Frank starts his boat's engine. Half dressed, my husband races to the pilothouse to start our engine.

"Hurry, honey, you've got to steer while I pull the anchor."

I pull my jacket over my nightie and take my place behind the wheel. Carefully, Skip climbs onto the bow. Beads of sweat stand on his forehead as he laboriously pulls up the 35-pound anchor with seven fathoms of 3/8 inch chain and 15 fathoms of rope. At last, the anchor comes up over the roller. Enviously, we watch Frank pull his anchor with a winch on deck that runs from the power take-off on the engine.

Leaving the harbor, we see Steamer Point is only a short distance. We steer down the wide expanse of Clarence Straits following Frank because we don't know the area. When Skip takes over the wheel, I dress and start breakfast. With no bread, I make pancakes from a recipe in my cookbook. I use Mac's iron griddle. After my previous day's experience, I turn up the dripper only a little. Still the griddle isn't hot. I don't like puny colored pancakes. I try to make coffee. While I'm cooking, Skip tells me that Clarence Straits is one of the main North / South passages in Southeast Alaska, running 125 miles from Dixon Entrance below Ketchikan to Sumner Strait. Most of the En-

The smaller trollers laid their bow poles against their mast until 1948 when they learned how to stand them upright with pulleys. Larger boats like the Pauline had a bow mast until then.

glish names were bestowed by Captain Vancouver in the 1790's, who found inspiration from the names of noblemen.

By the time I have breakfast ready, an hour later, we're at Screen Islands. I take the wheel so Skip can eat. He points out the Coast Guard station on Lincoln Rock and Abraham Island named for Abraham Lincoln by the US Coast and Geodetic Survey team in 1886. Without a radiophone we feel isolated.

When we pass Abraham Island, Frank pulls alongside. "Looks like it's kicking up around Point Stanhope ahead. What do you say we go through Three Way Pass? I've never been through it, but I hear there's nothing to it. What's the tide doing? I can't find my tide book."

Skip studies his tide book. He respects the tides from his years of fishing Tacoma Narrows. "It's just beginning to flood."

"Good. That's what we want. If we hit a rock, we'll float."

Skip props up the chart by the wheel. Three Way Pass leads into aptly named Rocky Bay. I pat Skip's hand thinking that the adage, "Fools rush in where angels fear to tread," applies to us. What if we sink our boat on our first trip?

Skip says, "The *Roberta B.* draws more water than we do. If we stay directly on her stern, we should make it. I wouldn't go through here myself, but we'll learn the passage. Marilyn, ya better go up on the bow and warn me if ya see any submerged rocks."

I cling to the cable strung from the bow stem to the mast. I'm shaking as I peer down into the clear water. I can see about five feet down and have no idea what a rock might look like underwater. Time seems to hang in the balance, neither moving forward or back. My shoulders ache from the tension of hanging onto the cable. When will we finally clear Rocky Bay?

On a large exposed rock ten seagulls sit. We pass them and immediately make a 90-degree turn around three rocks and pass them again on the other side. The sea gulls watch us as if to say, "We dare you to disturb us." After the water deepens, Skip calls me to return to the pilothouse.

We run into open water and head for Fawn Island past Mosman Inlet. Looking at the chart, I see that Burnett and Mosman Inlets are two long narrow fjords a fifth of a mile wide. They cut northeasterly into Etolin Island. We follow Frank into Burnett Inlet past Deadman Island.

How beautiful! A mountain looks down on the inlet from steep banks on each side. The sun is behind us now and it shines on the distant snow covered peaks on the far side of the island. The new snow glistens everywhere I look.

Frank yells, "I'm going to put in my fishing gear."

I steer while Skip jumps in the hold for herring. He then climbs into the troller pit and works feverishly in the 30-degree weather to string the herring on the hooks. Fascinated, I watch Skip pull a wire with hooks on its end through the nearly frozen herring, bend the herring and push a stick into its head. This makes the dead herring act alive but injured when we pull it behind the boat. The salmon will strike it and become hooked.

The sun disappears, and suddenly a squall of rain and snow hits us. Looking ahead, I watch Frank let down his trolling poles. The boat is silhouetted against the sky. I laugh, for the bow poles extend like grasshopper antennae. The long wing poles, coming from amidships, look like grasshopper legs.

Skip goes to the bow to let down our poles. Putting the poles into their chalks is one of the most dangerous jobs. He's using both hands for hefting the 15-foot pole weighing more than 25 pounds and cannot hold onto anything to keep him on the boat. If a wave hit, he could easily lose his balance, falling into the icy waters.

Skip returns to the troller pit and puts the 15-pound lead over the side.

He snaps the first leader onto the main line, the one coming amidships. At the end of the 15-foot leader trails the spinning herring. He lets the line out by putting the power gurdy, a mechanized spool, into reverse. Onto the gurdy winds the stainless steel 5/64 wire, marked at three fathom intervals. Skip attaches our lures at every second marker. Thus we have lures at the lead, six fathoms, 12 fathoms and 18 fathoms. He fastens the clothespin on the end of the tag line at the 21-fathom marker. He lets the power gurdy run the line out until it hangs from the pole. Frank impressed upon Skip the importance of the line hanging from the pole and not the block at the side of the boat.

After Skip puts out the starboard wing line, he lets out the port wing line. I watch as he lifts the heavy 40-pound lead sinker on the starboard bow line over the side and snaps on its lures. He does the same with the port bow line. Even though Skip takes much longer than Frank to get his lines fishing, he's soon back in the pilothouse to steer.

We steer along the starboard shore while Frank starts along the port side. Anxiously we wait for the fish to bite. The pole's tips have bells that ring when a fish is hooked. Slowly, we run toward a prominent waterfall that cascades down the sheer rock wall. I spot many smaller waterfalls and some are frozen into giant icicles glittering in the sun. For the first ten minutes, we watch the poles and don't talk. Finally, we relax. Skip feels that the slower we run the engine the more fish we might catch. Each troller must decide his best speed.

Skip says, "We want to go slow enough for our lures to wobble, but not so fast that they spin."

In front of the waterfall, the starboard bow pole jerks. I grab Skip's arm and half push him out the door. "Yippee! Our first fish!"

Skip's pea coat is half on and his rain cap is about to fall off. He shoves the gurdy into gear. When the tag line comes in, he unsnaps the clothespin and

Skip gaffs a large king.

lays it on deck. He pulls in the first leader. Nothing! The rubber snubber on the next leader hangs slack. My heart sinks. Did we lose our first fish? Twenty feet behind the boat, a salmon's silver body leaps out of the water. Salmon don't jump out of the water unless they're hooked or chased.

"This is a big one. Hand me the pistol."

Pulling in the taut leader, Skip aims the pistol at the salmon's head. I gasp when he shoots. "Doggone, I missed him!" Skip exclaims. He grabs the gaff hook and hits the fish on top of the head. Quickly he digs the sharp hook into the salmon and pulls it over the side.

What a beautiful fish! This is my first sight of a salmon and it's at least a 25-pounder. The fish's scales glisten with a purple sheen in the late afternoon sun. Its broad, speckled tail quivers.

"What's the smell?" I ask.

"King salmon have a distinctive smell. Ya can always tell when ya have a king aboard."

We see Frank outside of us. "How many ya got?" Skip asks.

"Two. They bite good just before dark. Don't stop too soon, but we want to get in before it's clear dark because there's a big rock right off the float. You better follow me in."

We troll two more hours and land three more salmon. None are as large as the first one.

"The flesh is white," Skip says sadly. He tells me these bring a third less money because customers prefer the red flesh color. We don't know why some are red and some white for they're the same species. Some think it's the environment, others think it's heredity. I hear many Alaskans prefer the white ones because they're fatter. Unhappily, we find the next one's also white.

I glance at the clock: 8 p.m. "I better pull in our gear," my tired husband mumbles.

Skip puts on rubber gloves and pulls on a navy stocking cap to keep warm. Since he put the bow lines in the water last, he pulls them into the boat first. He carefully coils each leader and throws away the herring. He'll string up fresh herring in the morning.

Coming to the heavy lead weight, he carefully lifts the ball aboard and sets it against the bulwarks. He's slower than Frank who has more experience.

When Skip speeds up the engine, we must follow Frank's running lights in the dark. I wonder if we'll be able to see the rock. The darkness engulfs the area. Skip slows the boat down. It's eerie not to see the shore.

Skip instructs, "Watch for drift, Marilyn. Tree shadows make it more difficult to tell how far we are from shore. There's the rock, over to our port. I see the water rippling over the top of it. After this, I'm going to quit sooner. No more running in the dark for us. This will make me an old man."

We pull alongside a well-kept dock. I see a man pick his way down the float with a flashlight. Frank tells us this is Bill Fox, an old timer. He's the watchman and has a troller tied to the dock. His light finally reaches ours and I see an old wrinkled man. He introduces himself and keeps shaking our hands. I figure he's lonely as he doesn't get many visitors.

I finish cooking dinner while Skip climbs into the hold to throw ice on our four kings. As Frank eats dinner with us, he tells us Etolin Island is known for its wolves. He doesn't know why but some of the biggest ones are trapped here. One year his Grandpap and his pal decided to trap mink down south of here at McHenry Inlet. They just had small, open boats with a little inboard motor, called puddle-jumpers.

For living quarters they had to build a cabin ashore. On the first of November the two brought as much lumber as they could. They beachcombed the rest and built a flimsy one room cabin with moss stuffed in the cracks. Heat came from a roaring fire in the stove made of oil barrels. A blizzard hit right after Thanksgiving. Cozy and warm in their cabin they bedded down for the night. A long howl pierced the silence standing the hair up on the men's necks.

His friend, a newcomer to Alaska, asked, "What'll we do?"

Frank's Grandpap said, "Reminds me of the Three Little Pigs. Pile some of the firewood logs against the door. This damn flimsy house of ours!"

That was the longest night he ever spent. He never did know how many of the wolves there were, but all night they heard them running around the cabin. One howled, then another. Grandpap and his pal sat inside fully dressed with their guns loaded.

"At daylight they slowly opened the door. The wolves were gone but they'd worn a path around the cabin," Frank concludes.

Skip and I sit in silence.

"Are there as many wolves now as in the past?" I ask.

"They're still plenty of them. Haven't seen any numbers of late, but every so often the government poisons the wolves. There's still a $50 bounty on them. Some of the trollers set traps in the wintertime, and sell the pelts."

As the evening progresses the topic moves to plans for the next day.

"What about the fishing tomorrow?" Skip asks.

"There's a few fish here. Sometimes I've come in and got nothing. Changes day to day. You never know." Frank replies.

"What time do we start out?"

"We should have our gear in by daylight. The daylight is getting here by six so we should get up at 5:30."

After Frank leaves, Skip gives me a grin and we head into the cramped quarters in the bow. As newlyweds who are having to sleep in separate bunks, we have to be creative. Skip always makes the evenings fun.

Before I know it, the alarm goes off. We prepare for another day and head out. After we clear the rock, I steer while Skip lets down the poles and strings up the herring. We hope that we'll catch even more today as we're starting at sunrise. The sunrise turns the water red down this narrow fjord. Then we wait and wait. No fish. I make breakfast. Still nothing. I wonder if we should go to another place. The men decide to go back to the cannery at noon and try again in the evening.

Bill helps us tie up. Skip looks up at all the little cabins and other houses and remarks, "Quite a layout here."

"The cannery had a fire in 1940 and they moved all the machinery to Wrangell. During the war, they put the Aleuts from the Aleutians Islands here," Bill answers.

I decide to go exploring and find many cabins with two small rooms and a stove. The larger buildings have a bunk house and a dining room. These cannery buildings were built for summer occupancy, but the government forced the Aleuts to live here for three years. I think the cold winters must have been unbearable.

Old Bill says, "Many Aleuts liked it so well that they came back after the war. You'll find some in Wrangell. Why anyone wants to live on those God-forsaken Aleutians, I'll never know."

After putting out our gear, Skip returns to the pilothouse.

"Look at that bow pole!" He points. Slow tugs pull it down and then pause. The pole slowly returns to its original position. Suddenly the fish starts pulling again, harder this time. We waited all day for this. Skip runs to the troller pit and pushes in the gurdy to pull in the line. After an eternity, he comes to the bottom leader. The salmon stretches the rubber taut.

"Bigger than any we caught yesterday," Skip calls. Slowly, he works the salmon toward the boat. The fish suddenly darts away. Skip lets go of the line to let it run. When the line stops jerking, he works the salmon in closer by pulling in the leader. Leaning over the side, he shoots it in the head. The salmon doesn't move when he gaffs it.

To my inexperienced eyes, this salmon looks gigantic. After putting the line back out on the pole, he cleans it. That night it weighs 34 pounds on Frank's scales. Our hopes soar. Surely we'll catch more. As the hours pass, we become more and more discouraged. Frank only has two 20-pounders.

Skip says, "In Puget Sound these salmon are called kings. In other areas of the Northwest the Indian name chinook is used. Later, we'll catch cohoes, which is the Native name. In the Northwest, they're called silvers because of the silver color of their scales. When they are canned, they are called medium reds for they are not as red as the sockeyes. Why they don't use both Native names in an area, I'll never know. The kings are never canned, for their bones don't soften like those of the other salmon. The kings are only sold fresh, frozen or mild-cured."

Around 6:00, Frank calls, "It's no use. Feed's gone as well as the fish. Let's head for the barn."

I laugh at the expression that I might use in Iowa. I steer toward the cannery float. Skip digs out the ice in a side bin of the hold to make a bed under the four salmon we caught yesterday. He lays the salmon on it back and pokes ice into its belly. He puts each fish side by side with ice around it until he has a layer of salmon. Then he covers the whole layer with ice for starting another layer of fish.

Trollers pride themselves on the quality of their fish. To keep the fish fresh they clean them as soon as possible, then they put them on ice. These kings will be either frozen or mild-cured in preparation for kippering. Seine or gill net fish are dumped into the hold without individual icing. They are cleaned at the cannery. This causes the salmon flesh to be softer.

Over dinner Frank says, "We gave this place a good rub today and nothing. We'll run down Clarence Straits tomorrow."

"Can we listen to the weather report on your radio? Might get rough in that open water," Skip ventures.

Frank looks like we slapped him. He spats contemptuously into his can that he always carries with him for snuff. "I hold no stock in these damn, pardon me missus, weather reports. They make me so mad. Mark my word, you cheechakoes, they're either ahead or behind. If they say it's going to storm tonight and tomorrow morning, I'll bet a 100 to one, it'll be over by then or won't start until tomorrow night. I was always sitting in harbor when they predicted a blow. I could have been out fishing or running. If it hit 12 hours later, I'd end up sitting in that same damn harbor two or three more days. When I'm going to run someplace I'll run out and look at the weather and make up my own damn mind. No weather forecaster is going to tell me what to do. I only use my radio for news and music."

The next morning Frank pounds on our door. "I'm going to the point to see what the weather looks like out in the Straits."

Skip jumps out of his sleeping bag and says, "Ya'd better get right up, honey, and get breakfast. Ya never can tell how rough the water is going to be. Frank'll go in much tougher weather than I would if we were alone."

When Frank returns, I'm breaking the eggs into the skillet. His weight tips the boat so the eggs run to one side; we'll have scrambled eggs.

"It's a little rough, but this ebb tide will push us along. When this tide changes against the northerly, there's going to be hell to pay. We'll leave after breakfast."

We gobble our food. Immediately, I start washing dishes for there's no place to put dirty ones on a boat. Quickly, I set my dishpan on the table and my rinse water pan on the locker below. Frank starts his engine and Skip starts ours. I wash the fifth dish when Skip unties the boat.

"The water's going to get rough. Secure everything. We're going to roll when we're out in the channel."

In dismay, I see that everything is out! Hastily, I put the bars around the stove. What should I do with the bacon grease in the skillet? The skillet can slide under the bars on the stove. I put it on the floor under the faucet in the peak of the bow. Dirty or not I shove the cups and small dishes behind the partition on the back of the table. I fold up the table against its back and put the hooks over the eye bolts. I set the dirty plates, silverware and leftovers on the three shelves built in the port corner by the stove. I look around and think, I've stowed everything away.

When the first wave hits, *Mom* rolls. Over and over she goes. I grab for anything to keep from falling onto the stove. My right foot lands in the middle of the skillet. I'm still trying to grab something when we roll back the other way. The unemptied dish water slops down my leg. The dish of left-overs jumps over the side of the shelf and lands at my feet. The iron pancake griddle flies off the hook behind the stove and narrowly misses me, hitting the coffee pot instead and knocking it over. Hot coffee and grounds trickle down the stove front onto the floor. With my greased foot, I'm skating on coffee grounds. Nothing is worse than coffee grounds. I'm tempted to have nothing to do with coffee.

I finally crawl up the steps into the pilothouse. "I'm going to be sick, Skip."

"Lean out the door and throw up on deck."

He's too busy steering to even look at me. I sit on the pilothouse floor and lean out the door. The saltwater slushes through the scuppers' holes in the side of the boat to let water out. Each time the boat rolls, the seawater washes the decks clean. I throw up and watch the water wash it away. Soon I just gag. I couldn't feel much worse.

"Darling, there's Union Bay. We'll be out of this in a few minutes." Skip calls.

Wearily, I wonder how I'm going to clean up this mess. I crawl up on the bench and Skip pats my hand sympathetically and tries to encourage me. "Look, there's at least 15 trollers fishing here. These are the first boats we've seen since we left Wrangell. This is a good sign."

Skip puts out our lines. He's in the troller pit when the starboard bow pole jerks, then the port bow jerks.

"Two fish at once!" he calls as I race up to watch. This's what we've been hoping for. Then both bells on the wing poles ring.

"Hey, we're on bottom! Speed her up fast, Marilyn."

I pull back the throttle. *Mom* jumps like a bucking bronco. She shoots for open water. Luckily, no boats are outside us.

"Not that much. Not that much. Slow her down."

I get the notched throttle back to its usual position.

"Hope we didn't lose too much. Hand me that chart again. I want to see where we were. Here it is, seven fathoms and we have 20 fathoms out. We'll be lucky if all of our gear is still here."

Skip brings in the starboard bow line first. On the next-to-the-bottom leader is an ugly red fish. Something is hanging out of its mouth, and its eyes look funny.

Skip says, "This is a red snapper. Because of the change in water pressure when we bring it up, its stomach comes out its mouth and its eyes pop."

We land six red snappers. Luckily, we don't lose any gear. Skip spots Frank running full speed up Ernest Sound. We haven't given this place a good try, but we pull in our gear and follow him. Frank tries an hour or two in a place and then moves on. We tag along because we want to run with someone on our first trip. He leads us through narrow, rocky areas.

We wonder if searching for the mother lode is a mistake. You can't catch fish with your gear on deck.

When Skip speeds up the engine, I fall backwards and sit in a pan of water.

"Ya've got to develop your sea legs, Marilyn."

I hear a sharp crack of glass breaking in the pilothouse. Skip laughs, "I forgot I'm standing on the top step. I fell backwards and jammed my elbow through the side window."

"Are you cut?"

"No. I'll tack a piece of cardboard over the window."

"Who should develop their sea legs?" I tease.

Later, I peer into my locker. Not much food left. We have one roast left in the hatch, some macaroni and two cans of meat, which I save for lunches. To stretch what we have, I study my cookbook.

For dinner that night I make scalloped potatoes. I find a recipe called Duchess peas in which I put the peas in a white sauce with chopped up bacon. Of course, more biscuits for bread. I juggle the potatoes on the oven's top shelf with the biscuits.

Frank cleans his plate and asks for seconds. I watch my leftovers for tomorrow's lunch disappear. Taking his last bite, he says, "These potatoes are good, for a change. Nothing beats just plain boiled spuds."

Skip chimes in, "Yes, these peas must be a lot of work. Plain heated peas are plenty good enough."

I stare at both of them. My mouth drops open, but I don't say a word. Later I explain to Skip, "We're running out of food. I really didn't count on Frank eating all of our meals with us. I'm only trying to stretch our food."

"I'm sorry, honey, I just wanted to make ya less work."

The next day Frank again runs into the calm waters of Ernest Sound. From that first trip, I'm fascinated with Ernest Sound, named by Vancouver for Prince Ernest. The snow covers the 3,000 foot peaks of Mount Etolin and Mount Shakes. Shakes was a Tlingit chief.

"I want to work on gear," Skip says. "Will ya steer? See that island on our starboard? We want to go around it and then turn."

Soon I am abreast of the island. When I can no longer see the point, I change our course.

Skip shouts and runs into the pilothouse, "You're cutting the point too sharp." He swings the wheel hard to port.

He sees the tears in my eyes, "Don't feel bad, honey. It's easy to think ya've cleared the point, but ya haven't. Perspective fools ya on water. Ya must have the point off your beam before ya change course. If ya look ahead to the next point, you're liable to run up on the point that you're passing."

We follow Frank through Canoe Pass, aptly named, and between Stone and Etolin Islands. We pass over many rocks. I wonder if Frank is trying to scare us by running to so many places with rocks.

As Frank once caught many fish in Burnett Inlet, he loves to fish there. When we find few fish he heads back there. I hurry to finish our lunch dishes and put them away. I put all the bars around the stove and only leave the tea kettle on it. I throw away some leftovers and give the remainder to Skip to put in the hatch on the shelf above the ice. I check all the wing bolts to keep the lockers shut. Figuring I secured everything, I climb on my bench beside Skip.

We're going inside Stone Island, Skip points out. The island will protect us from swells and this is a shorter way to Burnett. The passage looks like lots of rocks. After Three Way Pass, I figure we know how to dodge them. Skip cuts our engine to half speed. I breathe easier when we pass the rocks. We enjoy watching the sun go down.

We again head into treacherous Clarence Straits. I recognize long low Point Stanhope that juts far out into the straits. After we pass Double and Split Islands, we buck into the swells coming down Clarence Straits. As the boat cuts through the swells, salt spray splashes against the windows.

"How about calling our boat *Salty*. A saltier boat I've never seen," Skip laughs.

I like it, too. From this day, her name is *Salty*.

I congratulate myself on how well I secured everything. Suddenly, we hear a splintering of wood from the bow. I cry, "Have we hit something?"

I peer into the bow. "The stove is falling over. It's leaning at a 90 degree angle," I yell.

"The bolts are loose," Skip exclaims. "You steer."

Water pours out of the teakettle's spout onto the floor. Skip turns off the fire. To hold the stove in place, he sits on the locker and braces his feet against it. Now the steering is up to me. Can I steer our precious boat into Burnett? Since we have slowed down, I see in dismay that Frank is too far ahead for me to steer in his wake. I'm not sure of his course. Fearfully, I look at the chart and see many rocks off of McHenry Inlet. Skip is only four feet away but he's down in the bow where he can't see where we are going. I head for Fawn Island.

In the twilight, I finally spot the lights of the cannery ahead. I see Frank's mast light at the float. I look and look for the wave to break over the rock near the cannery float.

"Where are ya?" Skip calls from the galley.

"Right off the cannery. I can't find the rock, but it must be inside of us. Do you think I can dock *Salty?*"

"Ya better come down and hold down the stove. Ya won't find it too heavy for this short time. I better take her in."

Happily, I relinquish the wheel.

"You're right on course. I couldn't have done it better."

My chest puffs up in pride. He couldn't have paid me a better compliment. Later I try to get the potatoes for dinner from the coil of rope on the cabin's top. In horror, I see the potatoes are gone.

"Skip, did you put the potatoes someplace?"

"No. They must have rolled overboard. That was an expensive coil of rope, too."

"What are we going to eat?" All of the day's tension hits me and I burst into tears. Skip comes in and sits me on his lap,

"Things will be all right, honey. We still have macaroni and rice. There's still a dozen eggs."

Next morning we're discouraged to find no fish in Burnett. Frank and Skip row ashore. Frank is worried because we are running out of groceries. They kill a deer so we can eat venison.

Later, Frank calls over, "Let's try Mosman. No soundings on the chart, but I hear it isn't hard to fish."

"Nothing can be worse than no soundings to tell us the depth," Skip says.

Frank puts his gear in on the portside so we take the starboard. I feel we're driving through a mine field. At the head of the inlet, we see an isthmus sticking out from a small lagoon. Suddenly, the starboard bow pole jerks.

"Is it bottom, Skip?"

"Hell, no. The pole bounces up when we're on bottom. See, it's pulling down. It's a fish, all right."

A salmon is on the top leader. I hand Skip the pistol, from its handy shelf in the pilothouse. The salmon goes wild. It jumps out of water, sounds toward the bottom, tries to lead ahead of the line. The beautiful fish is fighting for its life and doesn't want to come close to the boat. Methodically, like an old pro, Skip works it close enough to shoot.

In the excitement, no one is steering *Salty*. Shall we continue toward Frank or turn around? Skip decides to turn back to where we caught the fish.

As we near the spot, we wait expectantly. Suddenly, the port bow pole jerks again. Then the starboard bow pole bends down. The port main pole's bell jingles.

"Yippee! We've hit the mother lode!" Skip yells like a kid whose wildest dreams just came true.

He lands a 30-pound king salmon from the bow pole, and a 20-pounder comes off the other bow pole. He now doesn't have any herring strung up to put out.

"What shall I do? There's fish on both main poles."

"You better get the fish aboard before they get away."

Then the starboard bow pole bounces. Proudly we look at our five big kings.

Frank comes up and calls, "What's all the shooting? Did you hit something? I see all your gear is on deck."

"It's kings. Great big ones. I was so busy landing them that I didn't have time to string up more herring."

"Haw! Haw! Haw! Only cheechakoes do that. You want to have some lures fishing. It's better to leave the fish on the line anyway. They attract other fish."

Hurriedly, Skip takes a good herring off the main line and snaps it on the bow line to get it out. By the time he has the other bow line out, the first one has a fish on it. He ignores it as he puts out the main lines.

What fun this is! I pull the fish from the bin next to Skip into the bin ahead to make room. With Frank here, we can only take the beach on our starboard side. We fish until the shadows are so long that we can barely make out the shoreline. We end up with ten big kings while Frank has six.

We're ecstatic as we eat dinner. Tomorrow we'll really catch the fish. A large body of kings must be here. With all day to fish, we might catch 20, how about 30?

Frank cautions, "You never can tell about salmon. Might be better tomorrow or might be nothing."

We can't wait until morning. I sleep lightly. Skip pulls anchor while it's still dark. He puts out our lines and then strings up 12 herring to prepare for many fish biting.

On our first pass, a salmon strikes the starboard bow pole.

"They're still here," I cry.

The fish only weighs ten pounds and looks small compared to our big ones from last night. We watch Frank pull in one. Then we wait and wait. Nothing! One hour drags into the next. We fish all day for only three small salmon.

Like a beaten dog, we run to Burnett Inlet that evening. I serve venison heart and liver along with my usual biscuits. After dinner, Frank says we should head for town tomorrow.

The next morning after looking from the point, Frank says we must leave immediately to get around Point Stanhope. We pull out as soon as Skip unties the ropes, and wave good-bye to Bill, the watchman. The water is calm as we start south around Point Stanhope.

"Hang on," Skip yells. "Here come the swells." I can see what Frank means when he says double-end boats like *Salty* roll in a following sea. The swells are eight feet high. We can't see Frank's boat when we're both in the bottom of the swell.

I see the tips of his poles. Now he's high above us on the crest of a wave. There, I almost see his keel. "Skip, it's like a merry-go-round where some animals are up and some are down. On these large waves, our ride is like a rollercoaster."

Skip pays little attention to my talk for he's trying to keep *Salty* on a straight course. I'm glad I'm not steering.

"There, we're out of it," Skip breathes easier. "Screen Islands are a good name for them. Look behind us, the waves now have feathers on them. A half hour later, we would take a real beating."

Salty comes out of Chichagof Pass. I know we're nearing Wrangell when I spot Point Highfield. We follow Frank over to the cold storage dock. Skip is standing straighter for we've had a successful first trip.

Frank unloads his fish into a large wooden box that the man on the dock lowers with a winch. While we wait our turn, I urge Skip to go the two blocks to the post office for our mail. After nine days, I imagine many letters in our rented box. I watch Frank shake the ice out of the bellies of the fish and put them in the box. When he fills it, the man lifts the box with a winch to the dock. On the sorting table, the fishbuyer sorts the fish into mild-cure, white and small red king salmon. Then he weighs them. The red kings over 12 pounds bring a premium price for they are mild-cured in a mild salt solution. Later the smokeries smoke them. They freeze the white and small kings for the fresh market.

While Frank is getting his check at the cold storage, Skip returns with eight letters. He tosses a halibut and a rock fish on Frank's deck. Skip ties the bow line to the piling before Frank backs out. He easily backs the stern in and tightens the bow line to let *Salty's* amidships lie along the dock.

I stop reading my letters to watch Skip fill the box with our bright kings. How proud we are!

When he comes down with our check, he asks, "How much do ya guess we had?"

"$100 worth."

"You're wrong...$150. Pretty good for our first trip. This time of year, we just figure on paying our expenses for the next trip. We'll do better than this after May first."

Running back to the boat harbor, we see Frank carrying the two halibut, two red snappers and a codfish up the float. He's no doubt taking them to some of his friends.

We're feeling good about our success. Skip puts his arm around my waist and kisses me.

CHAPTER FOUR

Tired of Men

Skip proudly holds up a halibut.

ALL THE FISHERMAN around the Stikine River focus on the May first opening. They'll catch upwards of 60-pound "soakers" as they call the big salmon heading into the river to spawn. Some of the fish will travel as far as Canada to lay their eggs in the gravel. The run only lasts through June. These are salmon returning from the ocean to the streams where they hatched four to six years ago. The excitement affects us.

As we wait in Wrangell for the opening Skip has a chance to work on our boat. On the first clear day, Skip scrubs and paints the deck and trunk cabin, the part of the boat built on the hull with the portholes. We are proud of our boat and want it to look its best. My first order of business is to find a laundry. Skip's jeans, coated with fish scales and slime, can almost walk by themselves. Finding no laundromat, I buy a wash tub and scrub board. I think again how much I left behind in Iowa for the frontier of Alaska. After heating the water on the stove, I scrub the fish scales and slime from the jeans. This is no easy feat as scales like to think they are an original part of the fabric and only relinquish that hold after numerous scrubbings. Meanwhile Skip strings a line on deck for me to hang the clothes out to dry.

Later I proudly look out thinking that maybe this life isn't so bad, but when I suddenly see our laundry I cry in dismay, "Skip, our clothes are covered with soot." I burst into tears as I realize the soot must have blown over from the stove. No amount of comforting from Skip can console me. After awhile I take the clothes down and wash them again. This time, I carefully hang them farther back where the soot cannot reach.

Since we have no hot water tank, we have to heat water on the stove and put it in the same wash tub to take a bath. Skip has a tough time fitting in the wash tub as he is over six feet tall. Sometimes I wish someone would invite us to come to their house for a bath or to do laundry. But since we really know no one besides Frank it isn't likely to happen.

Alaska is the land of the midnight sun so each day the days get longer. We are gaining five minutes of light per day. Already it's not dark until after 10 p.m.

When I go into the grocery store, I can't believe my eyes. The shelves are almost empty. I see only two cans of beans, three cans of pork and beans, and no fresh vegetables or meat.

"What's happened?" I ask the clerk.

"Haven't you heard? The longshoremen are on strike in Seattle. The last freighter came in a week ago, and no one knows when the next one will come."

"How long will the strike last?"

"It could be next week or it could go on indefinitely."

Worriedly, I buy the two can of beans, and the three cans of pork and beans.

"What about eggs?"

"None. Your only chance is to get some local ones. The only trouble is they have their regular customers and friends to supply."

I can do without many items because I know how to cook from working in the test kitchens. I understood how to substitute different ingredients and still get good results, but I know of no substitute for eggs. Alaskans, in those days, must ship in as much as 95 percent of all items they buy. If these supplies do not arrive on the ship, you do without. Local chicken farms and dairies constantly have to kill all their animals because feed does not arrive. A strange paradox is that the canned salmon is shipped south to be labeled and then returns to the Alaskan stores to be sold at an exorbitant price.

As May first approaches Skip says, "Let the big ones come. We're ready for them. This lying in town is getting me down. Shall we go out by ourselves? We can go into the area that's open beyond the closed Stikine area. It's not too far away."

"Sounds fine to me. We need to make more money."

Five a.m. and we're heading out. The sun shines brightly with hardly a cloud to be seen and the blue in the sky is so crisp that it almost hurts my eyes. We make our way down Zimovia Straits. The mountain tops are still covered with snow. Everything, the forest, beaches, and ocean sparkles in the morning light.

On our way, we pass the large Native Service boarding school. Skip explains to me that schools have yet to be built in most of the native communities around the state. The Indian, Eskimo and Aleut children come from all parts of Alaska to attend this school.

For the first time since coming to Alaska, we are on our own. When we ran with Frank, we had gone where he thought the salmon were. Now we must figure out where they might be ourselves.

We arrive at Anita Bay on Etolin Island in four hours at *Salty's* speed of six knots. Anita Bay is only six miles overland from Burnett Inlet, but by water it's over 15 miles. The snow-covered Virginia and Helen Peaks, at over 3,000 feet, look down on us from the north side of the bay. Anita Bay is wider and deeper than Burnett Inlet. We're hopeful the salmon will come here.

We put out our gear and see another boat, the *Anna*. I think we can't be too far off if other boats are trying their luck here, too. Nothing happens for over an hour. My heart starts to sink. Maybe we haven't found the salmon yet or maybe we're doing something wrong. This is different from sport fishing—with higher stakes. If we don't catch fish, we'll run out of money.

As I'm preparing lunch, Skip shouts, "Marilyn, hurry. We've got a soaker on."

Never have I seen the pole jerk so vigorously. Anxiously, Skip puts the gurdy in gear. He pulls in the second leader slowly. I catch a glimpse of a large dorsal fin as it cuts through the water. Suddenly, the salmon darts away from the boat. The leader tangles in the wing line, the line with the light sinker which comes from the amidship pole that looks like a wing. We feel a mighty tug and then the line goes limp. Sadly, Skip pulls in the leader. I feel like crying. I slowly turn away and fix our lunch.

Later, we're both in the pilothouse when the bell on the port bow pole gives the tiniest tinkle. "I'll bet it's a fiddler," Skip predicts as he goes out. We call a salmon a fiddler if it isn't big enough to jerk the pole and only fiddles with it. Usually the fish weighs under six pounds and is illegal to keep. Instead of finding a fiddler on the line we find a halibut. This is a large fish with both eyes on one side of its wide flat body. Besides the strangeness of the eyes the fish is brown on the side that faces up and white on the side that lies against the ocean floor.

I am curious about this strange fish and Skip explains, "As a baby fish, a halibut swims upright. Then when it grows, it settles to the bottom. The one eye migrates to the brown side, but its mouth always opens vertically. It's a freak of evolution."

"Are they only along the bottom?"

"Yes. They swim along the bottom. The season isn't open on them until May first. I must shake it off the line." Shaking a fish off a line means to get it off without hurting it. We catch only six salmon that day. They are all white. We learn that Anita Bay has a large percentage of whites.

We take many precautions in anchoring for the night. The last thing we want is to put our boat on a rock or shore our first time out by ourselves. Skip asks me to read aloud from the Coast Pilot about the different anchorages. The trouble with the Coast Pilot is that it's written for larger boats. Often a small boat can find a better anchorage.

When the *Anna* runs by, Skip calls, "Do ya anchor in the small bight on the north side?" A bight is a small bay, one that isn't big enough to get a name.

A good looking man calls back, "That's about as good as any. Sometimes it willies off the mountains." A willy is when the wind makes circles as it blows down the mountain side.

Skip takes his advice seriously. "I'm going to put out that new shoreline I bought. I've heard lots about Alaskan williwaws." Standing on the bow, Skip throws over our anchor. He motions for me to put the boat in reverse. He puts his foot on the rope to test if it digs into the bottom of the bay. Then he ties the shoreline onto the cleat on the bow and rows ashore and ties the end around a tree. Now our anchor won't drag.

Skip invites the man on the *Anna* over for a visit. We learn that he attended college in Oregon. He gives me a jar of blueberries for a pie. With my larder so low, I'm happy to have them. What a tasty pie they will make! After he leaves, we can hear his radio playing music.

"Skip, do you realize this is the first time we've heard music since we came to Alaska? Doesn't it sound wonderful?"

The silence of Alaska seems unique to me. The hoot of a loon or the squawk of a seagull is all that breaks the quiet in the harbor.

After crawling into our bunks, I hear a different noise. The wind whistles down Virginia Peak. "Skip, I hear chimes."

He listens for a minute. "Ya hear the wind in the rigging. The steel lines are taut. The wind makes definite sounds."

Melodious I would say. Every time a gust of wind hits us, we hear the chimes. Skip climbs out of his warm sleeping bag and up into the pilothouse to see if the boat has moved. Reassured, he goes back to bed. Skip takes his responsibility as Skipper very seriously. He hopes someday to find a boat where he can sit up in his bunk in the pilothouse to see out the window. He knows the fate of our boat and both of our lives lies in his hands.

The next morning we troll without a strike. We decide to find another place to fish. After lunch, we run to Sumner Straits to fish right outside the closed line at Woodpecker Cove .

We find three boats fishing there so maybe this place will be better. I'm getting supper when Skip puts out the gear. Immediately the port bow pole jerks. I wait anxiously for Skip to put the gurdies in gear and pull in the first leaders. When he comes to the first rubber snubber, the salmon stretches the leader to the thinness of a pencil. The king runs to free itself. The line whistles through the water. When it stops, the line is taut.

"It's still there," Skip calls. Again he tries to work the fish close to the boat, but it pulls like a lassoed bull calf.

Skip's arms work back and forth when he tries to ease the sudden jerks on the line. Before the fish can sound again, he pulls it alongside. I hear the resounding whack as he hits its head. He gaffs it and pulls it aboard. I can't believe my eyes. This fish is almost black, not like the beautiful silver kings we'd been landing. The upper jaw is a hook with fangs. Skip explains that the salmon use the fangs for fighting off other fish on their trip up the river to spawn. The fishermen refer to these fish as black spawners. The king price usually remains low until these black fish go up the rivers to spawn. As the buyers want the bright feeding kings, they are willing to pay a higher price for them.

After dropping our anchor that evening, Skip calls, "Look at the white troller coming in. Doesn't she have beautiful lines? Maybe they'll like to tie up alongside for a while."

I'm busy with dinner dishes and pay no more attention until Skip says, "Marilyn, come here a minute."

I step out of the pilothouse when the man on the other boat says something to someone behind him. A red haired girl comes out on deck. The men claim that we both exclaim, "A girl!" and throw our arms around each other. I'm so happy that tears come to my eyes. For the past month, I have only visited with men. I miss talking with another woman.

"Come aboard. I'm just finishing my dishes," the girl says.

She braids her long red hair and wears it on top of her head. She's 5'5" and probably weighs 120 pounds. Her friendly smile makes me feel welcome. I think she sparkles. I guess that she's around 30 years old.

I follow her down seven very steep steps. "Not much room here, but you can sit here by the table," she says. "At least we have a big bunk in the bow. It's easy to get in and out of."

Her laughter fills her spotless galley. I find out she always makes light of any problem and makes the best of any situation.

For a 40-foot boat, I admit the *Pauline* doesn't have as much room down below as *Salty* does. The stove and lockers are on the port side while the table and room for two to sit are on the starboard. The boat does have a sink, something I wish I had.

"My name is Dorie Wellesley."

"Mine's Marilyn."

"How do you like fishing? Is this your first year?"

"Yes. So far I like it, but I'm lonesome for a girlfriend."

"This is my second year aboard. We were married last year. I'd as soon live ashore, but Ed needs me." She finishes her dishes, sweeps the floor, and wipes up some spilled water.

"Do you do any of the fishing?" I ask.

"Ed says he did it all for years before he met me. All I do is cook and keep the boat clean. Before I moved aboard, I thought that would be easy. I can't understand how a boat can get so dirty. Sometimes I think herring scales are everywhere from bow to stern including the bunk."

"How did you end up on a fishing boat in Alaska, Dorie?"

"Ed swept me off my feet. He made up his mind that I was what he wanted. He kept after me until I finally said 'yes.' I was working as a secretary in my brothers' dairy in Hoquiam, Washington."

"That's like me. When Skip got out of the Navy, he came to Illinois where I was working. He said, 'Is you is, or is you ain't going to Alaska with me. I finally decided I is.' We both laugh.

"Do you get seasick, Dorie?"

"No. I never have."

"It worries me a little for I have been sick several times." I pause, sharing a thought, "I worry because Skip was married before."

Dorie laughs, "So was Ed. The first time I met him, I wasn't interested in him. He always says we wasted a couple of years while I made up my mind to go out with him. I want to see how it works out before I consider starting a family. Lately, I've thought about it."

"That's just the way I feel. I want to wait awhile."

We have so much fun visiting that Skip has to call for me to come home at around 10 p.m. He reminds me that we must get up at the first light, which in April is around 4 a.m. We fish near the *Pauline* for the next two days.

I'm so excited about seeing a girl that I don't really notice Ed. My first impression is that here is a tough man. He's 5' 10" tall and muscular. I learn that he was a prize fighter in his youth. Like Skip, he appears to be in his early thirties. When he takes off his cap, I see his brown hair. I like his sense of humor and how his brown eyes light up when he kids us women.

The men enjoy comparing catches. Ed always catches four or five more and they're usually bigger.

"We've heard much about the Stikine opening. What's it like, Ed?" Skip asks.

"They'll be some good catches. Lots of boats though."

We wait anxiously for the first of May.

CHAPTER FIVE

The Mother Lode

WE HEAD BACK TO WRANGELL for the May first opening on the Stikine River area. The delta of the Stikine River extends only two miles from Point Highfield on the north end of Wrangell. Each year the delta grows as it fills with more silt. The river is named for the Stikine tribe of Indians. In the 1860's, miners found gold up the Stikine for a miniature gold rush. Some miners from the 1849 California gold rush came to the Stikine hoping to make a strike.

Trollers from many areas of Southeast Alaska as well as Washington come to fish this opening. We have difficulty finding a place to tie at the floats with so many boats. We end up tying on the outside of four boats. We must crawl over all of them to get to the float.

The season also opens for gillnetters, who string out their nets to catch the salmon by their gills. This adds to the confusion.

The day finally arrives. We are up early at 3 a.m. and wait impatiently for enough light to put in our gear. At 4 a.m., we pull away from the dock.

"First boat out," Skip says proudly. "We're getting the jump on the rest of them."

We put out our gear in front of town. The next year we discover that the season opens at 6 a.m. and not at midnight. We don't know we are illegally fishing and, luckily, no one reports us. The regulations weren't out yet when Skip purchased his license. Then he neglected to pick them up when they did come out.

Skip has his first leader down and is ready to snap on the second one when the line jerks. He puts out the remainder of the lines before he works the gear. He lands a 15-pound salmon. He soon has three more.

We troll toward the river only to encounter large chunks of floating ice from the Stikine glaciers. Skip isn't too worried about hitting one, though he does keep a sharp eye out for them. When one of our lines tangles in some of the ice, Skip jerks it loose.

Large flocks of seagulls feed on eulachon, a kind of smelt. We find only spawning kings that are feeding on these "hooligans" as the Natives call the herring sized fish. We catch 12 kings although no 30-pounders. We hope for one of those legendary "soakers."

Skip says, "It's after 9 p.m. and still far from dark. Let's keep fishing." The air is clear, except for a little sawmill haze close to town. Without smog, the stars and moon shine brighter. Distances look closer.

The next day, Skip asks, "How would ya like to get back here in the troller pit with me?" I hoped he would ask me ever since the warm weather came. The troller pit is where the action takes place. I love to be in the middle of the action, not just a spectator. Where April had been a little sun mixed with much rain and some snow, these first two days of May are clear and warm. In our small troller pit, Skip's left hip rests against my right hip. From this angle, the poles appear longer and stick up in the air higher.

"Steer the boat closer to the starboard shore, Marilyn."

Sticking out between us is the tiller, a wooden stick, attached to the rudder. I push it to the starboard. Surprisingly, I watch *Salty* head to the port. It responds in the right direction when I steer in the pilothouse. Helplessly, I watch Skip laugh.

"A tiller works in the opposite way. To go starboard, ya push the tiller to the port. Ya steer a boat by the stern, not the bow as with a car."

Perhaps life was simpler before I climbed into the troller pit. I must remember the difference.

"Look, Marilyn, a big salmon." I watch the starboard main pole jump up and down. When the fish is this shallow, he lets it play on the pole to wear itself out. Slowly, he pulls it toward the boat. The taut line suddenly becomes limp.

"The big one's gone, Marilyn." Disappointment sounds clearly in his voice. He pulls in the leader. "Look, the leader's broken. I use No. 10 wire leader to keep the salmon from seeing it. In sport fishing, I use as light gear as possible. No. 10 wire isn't strong enough. I'll buy No. 12 in town tonight. They won't break it."

Around Wrangell, we receive too much advice, not too little. Some only chock their herring as Skip did in April while others never chock their herring. Skip decides to buy a box of fishing spoons from the advice of still others. He happily greets Silent George, whom he knew from Tacoma. True to his name, he seldom says much. He always smokes a cigarette in a long holder. As Silent George's boat is tied outside of *Salty*, Skip asks him what spoon he recommends. We know of Silent George's reputation as a highline fisherman. Highline comes from the top fishermen running their lines high from their poles.

"These are my favorites, Superior 50-50 copper and brass."

Skip returns with a box of bright spoons which he shows to Silent George.

"I told you 50-50 not half and half. These won't work."

Deflated, Skip returns to *Salty.* "How was I to know that 50-50 are copper on one half of one side and brass on the other half. Half and half are copper on one whole side and brass on the other side. I thought they were the same."

Marilyn and Dorie Wellesley hike on the beach at Point Babler near Wrangell.

"Maybe they'll work sometime," I say.

We find between 20 and 30 boats fishing Point Babbler, named for Jacob

The Jordans go on a picnic with Dorie and Ed Wellesley.

Marilyn's first salmon

Babbler, superintendent of Alaska Packers Cannery at Point Highfield. Others fish at the Nose, which resembles an elephant's nose on Woronkofski Island. The gillnet boats are more of a problem than the trollers. I know the trollers' lines hang behind the boat. The gillnetters stretch their 100-or-more-foot nets in either direction from their boats. Where one net stops, another often begins.

I steer toward Point Babbler and read my mail. Suddenly, a line of corks from a gillnet rises in front of us.

"Skip!" I scream, "I'm going to hit a gillnet."

Shaking, I swing *Salty's* wheel hard to the port. She turns in time to miss it. "If I cut up that gillnet, must we replace it?"

"We sure would. They cost plenty."

"You steer. I'm too weak."

We often see Frank around and wave to him, but we don't get a chance to talk to him. I keep watching for the *Pauline* with our new friends. Sometimes we see them at Pt. Babbler, but then they'll disappear for two or three days.

When we troll back to Pt. Babbler after our gillnet experience, the Wellesleys are there. Dorie and I wave.

"How's fishing, Ed?" Skip calls. Half the fun of fishing is comparing catches.

"Slow today. Only have two for the afternoon. We're thinking of anchoring up for awhile along the beach. We'll fish this evening."

"Sounds good to us. Mind if we join ya?"

"Let's anchor together." We don't like the hard work of pulling our anchor by hand.

We pull on our boots and tramp along the beach. I like walking on land for a change. A long tide-flat extends far from shore. We watch two otters playing. Many clams squirt at us through the little holes which tells us where they are buried.

"See that eagle sitting at the top of that tree," Ed points. "Our national bird, the Bald Eagles are common here. They prey on otter, small birds and other small animals. They dive on fish feeding on the surface. The Territory of Alaska pays a bounty on them of $1 for a pair of claws." I learn that the bounty was put on eagles in 1917, repealed in 1945, reestablished in 1949 and finally repealed in 1953. Approximately 93,000 eagles were bountied in those years.

The next morning we watch two deer cavorting on the beach. We laugh when the fawn throws its head in the air and prances away. Finally, the mother nudges it, and they both disappear in the woods.

We know the danger of fishing too close to the mud flats. Skip calls me out of my bunk, "Look at that boat. He's taking out a homestead on the mud flats."

Sure enough, a boat sits high and dry on the mud where the tide left him. He waits nearly six hours before the tide floats him again.

The next day Skip leans over to pick up a bucket of water from the troller pit. He suddenly buckles over in pain. His old Navy back injury has returned. I help him into the pilothouse. The muscles on one side of his back collapse and one shoulder and hip are higher than the other. He is in so much pain he can't even straighten up.

"We'll have to head to town and get my brace out of storage. Do ya think ya can steer her in?" I am thankful he has taught me how to handle the boat. When we arrive in town, he steers into the cold storage. When the dockman lowers the fish box, I climb in the fish hold and put the salmon in it.

"I'll get the fish check and then get your brace. You just take it easy." I climb onto the bow to reach the ladder to the dock. The tide moves the boat away from the ladder. I attempt to pull the boat to the ladder. Splash! My purse falls into the water. Horrified I watch it sink.

"Help!" I scream.

Thinking I've fallen overboard, Skip pulls himself up into the pilothouse.

"My purse! I dropped my purse!"

That purse has everything in it. Most important are two checks for fish, a check from the Illinois company for which I worked, my wrist watch, both our rings, all our keys and my jewelry and cosmetics. What a calamity! I cry. Skip calmly surveys the situation. Even with the pain from his back, he is going to take action. He rigs up a jigger and lets it over the side. At this minus tide, the water is still 20 feet deep.

"I've hooked something," he calls.

By this time, 15 people have gathered at the top of the dock to watch our efforts. I hold my breath, but it turns out to be only an old raincoat. For 45 minutes he pulls up old coats, boots, halibut heads and other objects from the harbor.

"If we don't find it in five more minutes, we'll give up. I'm just too tired, and the tide is getting too high."

The purse is of cloth material which might make it easier to snag than a leather one, but still I give up all hope that he'll hook it. Then for the twentieth time, he says, "I've got something."

It is small and black. "My purse!" I gasp. Leaning down, I grab it when it comes to the surface. I throw my arms around Skip and kiss him. The people on the dock cheer.

The only casualty is my wrist watch. The bank accepts all the checks.

We pull around to the loading dock on the other side of the cold storage for me to walk up the ramp. First, I find the storage place locked. I wait for the owner to return from his oil deliveries before he can open the storage area. They have moved our belongings. After I find them, I can't see the brace. Finally, I remember Skip pushed it into a seabag. Then I can't untie the seabag. I keep thinking of poor Skip down there lying on the boat suffering. Frantically, I work to undo the knot. At last I untie it and pull out the brace. I tie the seabag together again and put everything back in place. Walking back, I keep thinking how Skip must be worrying about me.

Climbing onto *Salty*, I look in. No Skip! Maybe he's gone to the hospital. I walk up on the dock where a group watches the boats unload. Happily, I spot Skip talking to a stranger.

When he sees me, he beckons for me to come over, "I've been visiting with this lady. She and her husband hope to have a boat like ours someday. I want ya to meet

Marilyn enjoys kitty on Salty in 1946.

Sue Barrow. She and her husband teach at the Indian School."

I smile at her. Maybe this is a silver lining to an otherwise hectic day. Skip puts on his metal back brace which makes him stand very straight. He is determined not to let this injury interfere with our fishing.

The next morning we fish the river flats again. As soon as Skip has the lines out, he returns to his bunk and I take charge of the fishing. The bell on the main pole jingles. Grabbing my jacket, I dash to the troller pit. Shaking with anticipation, I put the gurdy in gear and begin bringing in the line.

"How large is it?"

"The salmon is small, just my size." Carefully, I pull in the leader.

"Play it awhile. Then hit it a good one on top of the head and gaff it," Skip says.

The first time I hit at it, I miss. I never could hit a moving target. The next time I hit it squarely which makes a dull thud. I dig the gaff hook into the head and pull my fish over the side. My first salmon! Even though it only weighs seven pounds, I'm so proud.

After breakfast, Skip insists that I help him into the troller pit. I assist him in landing any fish over 20 pounds. He shoots it, then both of us pull it aboard.

"I hurt my back, so it takes two of us to land the big ones," he calls to a nearby fisherman. He's embarrassed for them to see me helping him..

Pulling into the float, I watch a fisherman throw a gray and white kitten onto the float. "I don't want this on my boat."

"Poor little kitten with no home," I remark to Skip. "I'll give her our fish hearts." When Skip doesn't object, I bring her aboard. She revels in the attention and likes the food. Sadly, I discover she's gone the next morning.

A couple of days later another fisherman pulls into the fish dock where we are unloading our fish. He asks, "Does anyone want a cat? I found this one curled up in my cabin when I pulled out this morning."

"She's the same kitten we had before. May I have her?" I ask Skip. "She'll keep me company."

He consents and the fisherman tosses her aboard. She busily laps the milk I give her. When Skip starts the engine, she darts for the deck. She puts her front paws on the railing and looks at the disappearing shore. She doesn't like the engine's noise. She wanders about the deck meowing and tries to find a place to lie down. At last she spies the skiff tied upside down over the boom. She jumps on the trunk cabin and then onto the top of the cabin and over the top of the skiff. She crawls in under it from the back side. The skiff protects her from the weather, and the engine's noise isn't so bad. When we cut the engine to trolling speed, she returns to the cabin.

She provides many hours of enjoyment for me and the Wellesleys. Whenever we start our engine before Ed does, she dashes for the *Pauline* and spends the day with them. She is a friend to all.

Walking up the float, we hear that the Shrimper is in port. "Come on, Marilyn, that means fresh shrimp. I'll buy a bucket."

As we near the cannery, I again hear the squawking sea gulls and watch them dive for the shrimp pickings. These are the first shrimp since the season opened on May first. We smell the pungent odor of cooking shrimp. Stepping through the open door, we find ourselves in a steam box. I make out a shadow of a man who is removing shrimp from a cooker.

For 50 cents, we buy our bucket of cooked whole shrimp. Skip shows me how to pick the shells from the shrimp. Slowly I pick a small mound of shrimp. With no lettuce, I make shrimp cocktails. Skip buys a six-pack of beer and we and the Wellesleys laugh as we pick the shrimp. Ever since that day I love to eat shrimp.

That night everyone says that the salmon run is at the Nose on Woronkofski Island. We hear tales about the $100 days there. With high hopes we start for the Nose the next morning. We think we left the harbor early, but 50 boats are ahead of us.

I refuse to steer among this many boats. We take the beach on our starboard, then turn around while another troller takes the beach. Skip maneuvers *Salty* well. We find no fish. We only catch one 25-pounder. The boats scatter in all directions.

"They'll be here on the next big tides," one fisherman calls.

I learn fishermen are always waiting for the next big tides. When nothing comes, they shake their head and say the fish will be here on the next tides. If the weather is bad, the next tides will change it. No conversation on fishing is complete without discussing the tides.

This proves not to be one of my better days. Returning from the Nose, we see a squall heading our way. Without warning, the wind lays *Salty* on her side. A pound can of coffee upsets on the floor. In horror, I watch an empty pie pan slide along the top of the bench. The pie filling is a little pile at the base of the shelf on which the pan rested. At least, I console myself, my white rice is safely cooking on the stove. I take off the lid and see I have brown rice.

Marilyn lands a salmon while kitty looks on.

Skip had dyed some leaders with brown net dip to make them not be seen by the salmon. Then he had hung them over the stove

I helplessly say, "There goes my pie and rice and our last can of coffee. I'm sorry, Skip. I know how much you like your coffee."

I back down the steps and put my foot squarely into the garbage bucket and spill its contents. Upon our arrival at the dock, I clean and scrub everything

Ed suggests Skip go to the Finnish chiropractor.

Returning, Skip says, "I'm not sure that he helped me but it isn't worse. When he found out that I was a newlywed, he told me that I couldn't do 'it' every day."

Everyone laughs. Ed and Skip talk in the pilothouse, and we girls only catch an occasional sentence:

"This fishing certainly is slow! Can't be much worse other places and still be any fish at all. We should find some halibut soon. I'm anxious to try somewhere else," Ed says. The men make no decision to leave the Stikine area.

The next morning we try Shoemaker Bay, 45 minutes south of Wrangell. "They're really here," Skip calls. "Three poles working!"

We start landing them when 20 boats bear down upon us. As the spawning kings swim in schools, the many boats scatter them. We only land four kings.

"We've had enough of this fishing," Skip states firmly as he pulls in our lines. "I'm going to find Ed. If he wants to leave, we'll go today."

"Skip, we can't leave until we find our kitty. She jumped off the boat onto the dock this morning."

"If she's around the float, we'll take her. I'm not going to spend all summer looking for a cat."

Whether the chiropractor helped or nature takes its course, slowly, Skip's back gets better. Soon he doesn't need the brace. We find the *Pauline* tied in the harbor. The men decide to leave an hour and a half before high water. We'll go through Dry Straits at the delta of the Stikine River.

"Have you seen our kitty, Dorie?"

"We'll keep our eyes open for her when we go to town."

We tie *Salty* outside a large cannery tender at the loading dock and climb the ladder. We race uptown to stock up on groceries now that the longshore-man strike is settled. A freighter arrived yesterday with supplies from Seattle. We buy all we can afford. This time I remember the bread.

"Looks like we bought out the store," Skip remarks when he carries the third box of groceries down to the dock. "Here, give me those eggs. I'll carry them down the ladder. Then drop this box to me."

"Are you sure you can carry all these things? Those eggs are precious. They're my first ones in a long time."

He disappears behind the cabin of the boat. Suddenly, I hear a large crash. He falls between the boats, but tosses the groceries on our deck. He catches himself waist deep in water. He cuts his leg and it bleeds through his pants.

"Oh, my eggs!" I wail.

"To hell with the eggs. I almost broke my leg."

"If we're going to make this tide, we've got to leave right away," Ed calls. "Can you make it, Skip?"

"I think so."

"Look what I found for you," Dorie calls.

For a minute I can't remember what I'm looking for. Then she hands me the kitten. Our crew is complete. I find dry clothes for Skip and bathe and bandage his leg. He only has a limp to show for his injury.

On a beautiful afternoon we leave Wrangell. Now to search for the elusive salmon in new areas.

CHAPTER SIX

*H*alibut, Here We Come

"I LIKE HEADING FOR NEW PLACES and adventures," I say, taking my place on the bench beside Skip. He sits on his stool steering the boat.

"We couldn't ask for a better day," he replies.

"Ed really knows the area. I prefer running with him more than Frank."

"I know how much ya like having a girlfriend. Alaska has been lonely for ya since we came here."

I smile because Skip seems to know what I'm thinking and always tries to understand. We are heading for Dry Straits. On our right is the mouth of the Stikine River. The headwaters of the Stikine are to the east in Canada.

As we pass Dry and Farm Islands, it's hard to believe that in three or four hours, this will be mud flats. If you're in the channel, which is the deepest part of a body of water, you have lots of water. If you're out of it, you'll sit high and dry whatever the tide.

The white of the mainland mountains stands out against the azure blue sky. The temperature is in the low 80's when we leave Wrangell. As we pass Ideal Cove, a gust of cold wind hits us and the temperature falls 15 degrees.

"What's that white along the far shore, Skip?"

"Icebergs! All these icebergs are dangerous when ya run at night," Skip says. "Le Conte Glacier empties into salt water between those mountains. It's the farthest south salt-water glacier in North America. I read John Muir's book. He named the river of ice after Joseph Le Conte, a glaciologist at the University of California. The Indians said it was the home of the Thunder Bird because of its noise."

A few minutes later he asks, "How about steering for Horn Mountain? I want to polish some fishing spoons."

I easily spot Horn Mountain for it truly resembles a saddle horn. Captain Vancouver named it because "it presented an uncommonly woeful appearance rising to a vast height from the water's edge." A sheer cliff rises directly from the water's edge. Like a river of ice suspended in the sky, a blue glacier glistens in the afternoon sun. I'm so busy looking at this spectacular scenery that I have difficulty keeping *Salty* on a straight course. A low point of land blocks my view of the glacier coming to the water's edge. These mainland mountains are steeper and higher than the island ones. They're always covered with snow, even in the summer.

We pass many large and small icebergs. Seagulls rest on one that resembles a horse. We head toward a long, low point called Point Vandeput, named by Vancouver for Admiral George Vandeput of the Royal Navy. The point juts north of the opening to Thomas Bay. The Bay was named by the U.S. Coast & Geodetic Survey for Lieutenant Commander Charles Thomas, who commanded the survey vessel *Patterson*, in the 1880's.

In the distance we spot Devil's Thumb, a pointed rock peak stuck up like a thumb. It's the highest peak in the area. Native Alaskan myths tell how a family tied their canoe to the top of the Devil's Thumb. This saved them at the time of the Great Flood. When the flood receded, the rope was petrified around the top of the Thumb which left a crack circling the top. The crack can be seen from airplanes. How did the Natives know of the crack as it is

Devil's Thumb, one of the boarder peaks with Canada, east of Petersburg.

over 10,000 feet up a sheer rock wall?

Kate's Needle is the highest of the sharp pointed peaks clustered together. These are the border peaks between the United States and Canada. In 1825 the Anglo-Russian Treaty specified that the boundary should run along the crest of the coastal mountain range but also that it should not lie more than ten marine leagues from the coast. It wasn't until the gold rush of 1898 that it became a problem. Canada claimed that the heads of all major inlets lay in Canadian territory. If this had been true, it would have provided all Canadian access to the interior. In 1903, President Theodore Roosevelt appointed Secretary of War Root, Senator Henry Cabot Lodge of Massachusetts and ex-Senator George Turner of Washington to represent the USA. His Britannic Majesty appointed two prominent Canadians and Lord Alverston, Lord Chief Justice of England. They met in England. Roosevelt refused arbitration and wrote to the three American representatives that there could be no compromise. In the end Lord Alverstone sided with the Americans in a four to two vote. This set the border between Canada and Alaska on the mountain tops and gave the Canadians no seaports.

I know I'll always remember the perfect reflections of clouds and mountains in the water that day. The ocean doesn't even have a ripple. We proceed up Frederick Sound, named by Vancouver for Frederick, Duke of York who was the son of King George III.

"If ya look behind us, Marilyn, ya can see the town of Petersburg, which lies at the north end of Wrangell Narrows. Wrangell Narrows was named before Petersburg was founded. The narrow stretch of water flows along the west side of Mitkof and east side of Kupreanof Islands. Even though the narrows has many beacons and lights, boats still run aground. Every five years, the US Coast and Geodetic Survey ship and crew must dredge it to 24 feet. The narrows keeps filling in with mud and rocks."

I spot a few houses from this distance. The *Pauline* continues north heading for Farragut Bay, named by Lt. Commander Thomas in 1887 for Admiral David Farragut, who was the civil war hero of the battles off New Orleans and Mobile Bay. Between Cape Strait and Pt. Vandeput, I see snow-covered mountains on Admiralty Island, which was named by Vancouver for the British Admiralty under which he sailed.

The *Pauline* is faster than *Salty*, and Ed is fishing when we arrive. Skip puts out our lines. We troll along the west side of the bay and Bay Point. After two hours, we haven't caught anything.

"I'm going to pull up our gear and try inside the bay. The depth is 23 fathoms in there. Plenty deep enough to fish," Skip remarks.

When we are safely past a shallow spot where high tide covers a large rock, we put out our gear. Seeing one pole jerk, I ask, "Is it the bottom?"

"Tut, tut, Mrs. Jordan," Skip laughs. "After two months, ya can't tell bottom from a fish? He's a big one. With my new soaker line, he can take all the line he wants when he runs."

Skip pushes the gurdy into gear and the steel line winds on the spool. I see a large splash about 50 feet behind the boat.

"He's on the next leader, Skip."

"Hurry, get the pistol!" Skip shouts as he loses his usual composure. Slowly, he pulls the leader toward the boat. The salmon sounds and Skip's soaker line spins off the ball. More and more of the line goes through Skip's hands. The fish easily takes 50 feet before he stops.

"Am I ever glad I rigged up the soaker line! When he ran, he would have broken something if I hadn't."

Again Skip slowly pulls the fish toward the surface. This time the salmon swims toward the bow. Skip keeps pulling in the line to make him come closer. Only then will the fish be within shooting range. Finally I hear the shot and then he gaffs it.

"What a fish!" I exclaim.

"It should go 45 pounds. Our biggest of the season." He watches the *Pauline* pass us. "Ed's putting down his anchor. I hoped to fish until dark but maybe we better stop. Tomorrow might be better."

The harbor is so peaceful that evening. The squawking of circling gulls is the only sound. What a difference from fighting the boats in the Wrangell area! I get to visit long into the night with Dorie. Finally Skip calls me home.

The next morning we fish inside the bay again. Skip points out the promising sign of birds everywhere. He lets the last line out on the pole when a shiny mass of herring flips on the surface under our starboard bow.

"Yippee! Look at those salmon rushing the herring. The diving birds chase the herring into a tight school," Skip says. "See the herring jump out of the water in a line in the middle of the school. That's salmon chasing them. The salmon swims through the school and hits the herring with his powerful tail. Knocks 'em dizzy and then the salmon turns to grab them. We ought to get a fish soon." His eyes glint expectedly.

The starboard bow pole bounces up and down like a yo-yo. The 35-

pound lead doesn't slow the fish down. Then the starboard wing pole jerks.

"He's not satisfied with playing with my lead! He races over and winds around my wing line too. Ya, he's really fighting."

Slowly, he pulls in the two lines and pulls the leader with the salmon on around the wing line. I marvel at how much more adeptly he handles the lines since we started a month ago. The fish makes only one run. Then Skip shoots it. It takes all his strength to pull it over the side of the boat. This is our largest fish yet. The purple sheen of its scales shines. Its head is wide and heavy and it's as round as it is long. It reminds me of a fat little man with a large belly. After cleaning the salmon, Skip grunts as he lifts its tail off the deck and sticks the scale's hook in its mouth.

I look at our scales. "It's over 50 pounds!" I exclaim. Our scale just goes to 50.

"Look for the herring again. Maybe we'll catch another."

I climb on the bow. I shade the sun from my eyes. I recall the pioneers standing on the hilltop peering at the land ahead. In some ways I feel like they must have 100 years ago.

"There's the school, Skip. Along the far shore."

What fun chasing those herring around the bay! Every time we come near the herring we land at least one fish, and sometimes we catch a double-header (two on a line). Two salmon break our leaders, three come unhooked and swim away, and some strikes are gone by the time we pull in the line. We catch 12 of our biggest kings yet.

Three hours later we're circling the bay without a strike. Did we catch them all or are they not biting? We pull in our gear and run outside of the inner bay where Ed tells us that he has only five fish.

Skip says, "Let's polish those half and half spoons we bought in town." Polished spoons always attract more salmon then those that are dull.

Busily, I rub on the special spoon polish. When I hand three to Skip, the copper and brass glows in the sunlight. I watch him snap each on a leader. We're only fishing a short time when the bell rings on the port wing line. Skip sees the salmon on the third leader.

"It's on the half and half you gave me. Polish up more."

Those spoons are hot that day. We're catching twice as many fish as Ed.

Skip, never one to keep success to himself, calls, "I'll loan ya three of these spoons, Ed."

Getting the spoons to him with our gear out will not be easy. We run directly behind his stern while Skip puts the spoons in a sack. He stands on Salty's bow and throws the sack into the *Pauline's* troller pit. Then Ed pulls ahead. Ed catches more salmon with the spoons we've given him. Our biggest day ever has us excited.

"I don't think Ed likes our catching more than he does," Skip says that evening. "People like to teach ya, but not beat them."

The next morning we run to Bay Point at the mouth of the bay because we spot the seagulls diving on herring there. We catch five kings while Ed catches only three. We'd been smart not to tell him how many we catch. Two other trollers arrive, and we watch them land fish, too.

As we troll by Ed, he calls over, "I think the halibut should be at Tyee now. We can do better than this there. I'm picking up my gear."

"This looks pretty good to us, Ed." Skip says, "But if you're leaving, we'll follow."

Reluctantly, we pull our gear and follow the *Pauline* west. Later we hear that the two boats caught over 2,000 pounds of kings there in seven days. You're forever faced with the decision of staying where you are or hoping for greener pastures.

Skip is sleepy, and instructs me to follow the *Pauline*. After sitting on the bench for sometime and reaching to turn the wheel this or that way, I discover that I can lean back and steer with one foot. Now I enjoy the scenery more, but I don't steer too straight a course. Oh well, let them wonder what's happening back here.

Little wisps of fog hang over the mountain tops. I enjoy watching them cover up a section of trees then move to reveal a mountain topped with snow. On one ridge the trees look like a sentinel of soldiers.

I spot one solid line of jagged peaks along the horizon. My chart says it's Baranof Island, named in 1805 by Captain Lisianski for the first chief manager of the Russian American Company. It bounds Chatham Straits, named by Vancouver for John Pitt, Second Earl of Chatham. Along with Lynn Canal, it is one of the world's great fjords. Vancouver named it for his birthplace, King's Lynn in Norfolk, England.

From this 35 mile distance, it looks like the snow comes to the water's edge. Baranof was the most rugged of early Russians, so the island that bears his name is the most rugged in Southeastern Alaska.

We head toward the southern point of Admiralty Island where Frederick Sound branches off from Chatham Straits. What a broad expanse of water!

Skip puts Salty on the grid at Tyee. The two room cabins for the Native families can be seen in the background.

We run for three hours before we can distinguish tiny Carroll Island named for Captain James Carroll, who ran U.S. steamboats in the 1880s. Yasha is the small island to the south. It looks lonely out there so far from Carroll Island. The only boat we see is the *Pauline*.

"Do ya realize, Marilyn, ya can count the present settlements here in Southeast Alaska on the fingers of one hand? Ya know, back in Norway, people live in every fertile valley. Sometimes they transplant dirt from one place to another for a little place to grow fruits and vegetables." Stretching out his arm, he says, "Here's all this fertile land untouched. True, it takes a lot of work to clear it, but it can be done. I just can't see why so many people are satisfied to live in crowded, smoky cities. They could live in a beautiful land like this!"

We enter Murder Cove, named by Commander R. W. Meade, because two white men had been killed there in 1869 by the Kake Indians to avenge the shooting of one of their people by a sentry in Sitka. Tyee is located there and has many rocks. Entering at low tide, we spot the ledges that protrude from the west shore. A light and a marker show us the rocks along the east shore. Skip has a book written by the Works Progress Administration, (WPA) during the depression. It tells me that Tyee was first a whaling station in the 1900s. The post office was established there in 1907.

Many large cannery buildings, docks, and a gas dock with its large tanks loom ahead. I spot green lawns as we head for the harbor. We tie to a small boat float that lies inside a large dock and cannery buildings. Nearby they've built a large grid to copper paint boats and scows.

After we dock *Salty*, Ed calls, "Come to the store with us."

I run a comb through my hair, and we hurry after them. I like the feel of solid ground again. We dodge a jitney, a mechanized cart, carrying lumber. We pass the cannery superintendent's house and enter a newly painted combination store and post office. The store has groceries and fishing gear.

"They sell only whole hams, but they're good." Ed says.

"Let's get one," I say. "It'll taste good for breakfast."

All their meat is one price—50 cents a pound. We also buy some steaks and a roast. As we didn't think we could afford hams or steaks in Wrangell, we feel these are reasonable prices.

We don't sell our salmon as Ed wants to search for halibut immediately.

"This halibut fishing is tricky. If you are in the right spot, you'll get fish. If you're even a few feet away, you'll get nothing and you might hook up and lose gear," Ed explains. "You only use your bow lines and let them right off the blocks on the side of the boat through which our trolling lines go overboard. You'll probably do better to use one line at a time until you get used to it."

We follow the *Pauline* out to the fishing grounds. We watch Ed lower his lead on the bottom of the line. Skip hooks on three large silver spoons baited with a piece of herring on the hook. He fastens them a fathom apart and lets our starboard bow line reel off the gurdy until it suddenly stops. Bottom! He puts the gurdy in gear and winds up ten feet of line. With his hand on the line, he can tell when he hits bottom or has a fish. Whenever the line goes slack showing the lead on bottom, he winds up more line. He often tests to see if the water is deeper by letting out more line.

Ed runs north, and then turns around and makes the run again keeping his bow into the tide. He runs as slow as the engine will go. Skip follows, and we wait hopefully.

Skip calls, "I hooked something!"

I dash out on deck and wait while the gurdy winds in the line. As we fish at over 40 fathoms, it takes a long time for the first leader to come to the surface. The first two leaders are empty, but the third leader stretches straight down, not horizontal as with salmon. Skip pulls in the leader, gaffs and pulls aboard a 25-pound halibut. Excitedly, we let our line down again. Alas, we drag and drag, but nothing. I learn that trollers don't drag even though they always use this expression. Trollers tack back and forth but only draggers drag along the bottom. The monotony is broken only when a king salmon takes a halibut spoon.

"Halibut never bite after high tide," Ed calls. "Let's go in." Later Ed says, "We'll wait for the next big tides."

The next morning we sell our salmon at the cold storage. We tie *Salty* below the fish house and Louie, the fish buyer, lowers the big fish box to our deck. When he fills it, Skip proudly yells, "Lower it again. There's more."

"Ed's and our checks are within $10 of each other," Skip says. "That's the way it should be with running partners. It makes hard feelings if one has a lot more than the other."

We search for kings and wait for halibut to come into this area. We run to Security Bay where we fish on the outside of a large pile-driven fish trap that catches salmon later in the season. Skip explains that the pile-driven traps stay in one place year around and the wires on the leads are cut at the season's end. The floating traps are then moved to a safe storage during the winter. The canneries and individuals put out fish traps in Alaska after they proved to be such a successful way to catch salmon in Washington and Oregon in the 1890s. The Territorial Government and the US Fish & Wildlife Service limited the number of trap sites. The Kingamill Trap at Security Bay was labeled a Million Dollar trap because it caught that many salmon in a season. Traps made some individuals and canneries very rich.

We find nothing at Security Bay and continue down Chatham Straits to Washington Bay. In the morning and evening, we catch one or two kings inside the bay and four or five outside during the day. Washington Bay has very steep sides.

One morning Skip calls, "Come see the sunrise on Mount Ada."

The sides of Washington Bay are still dark as I gladly crawl out of the warm bunk. Through the opening the rising sun makes the twin peaks on Mount Ada look like pink ice cream covers them. The glacier makes its crown

We climb aboard the Pauline and run to Warm Springs Bay for their delightful hot mineral baths.

jump out. As the sun rises higher in the sky, it highlights the trees on the opposite side of Chatham Straits. We spot the many indentations to the shoreline from numerous bays and coves. Later in the day, the flat lighting obscures these breaks in the shoreline. This country is more rugged than I had imagined.

We fish for five days, catching only a few fish each day. After the success at Farragut Bay, we are disillusioned.

"We better head back for Tyee. The tides are beginning to increase now," Ed says that night.

The next day we can't ask for more beautiful weather. Little did I realize that many claim the roughest spot in SE Alaska is Point Gardner at Tyee. This beautiful weather lulls us into complacency.

The next day we only fish about an hour. When we catch nothing we run back to the cannery. The cannery superintendent says that Dorie and I can use their wash house with the electric washing machine. What a joy! I like living on a boat until I have to wash. Then I'm willing to trade it for almost any kind of life. Dorie and I visit while we wash clothes and hang them on the lines behind the cannery worker's homes.

Few places are more segregated than Alaskan canneries. Tyee has homes for the families of the superintendent, the cannery foreman and the head engineer. The single white workers have their own bunkhouse and dining room. The Filipino bunkhouse with its kitchen is in another part of the cannery. Then a third bunkhouse for cannery workers who married Natives is built in still another area. The Native women and their children live along the beach in little red two-room cabins. In them are a small wood cook stove like mine on the boat, a table and bench, and a second room of four bunk beds. These last two groups only have outhouses. Their cabins have even less space than the company-provided homes for African Americans in the southern United States.

Returning to the float, I can't see *Salty*. Where's Skip?"

"Marilyn, over here. I put the boat on the grid," Skip calls. "Come help scrub off these barnacles and moss."

I start only to find myself scrubbing alone. Skip goes to the store to buy more copper paint. I'm already tired from washing clothes. Why did he have to take on such a big job now?

Skip returns with one gallon of red copper paint as this is the only color the store has. We already have a gallon of dark brown and Skip doesn't want

A new friend, Joe Cash, who loves to fish halibut and ironically is killed by one many years later.

to mix the two paints. We paint *Salty's* port brown and her starboard red.

I find painting above my head difficult. My arms tire easily.

"Ya've more paint on ya than on the boat," Skip laughs.

We rush to scrub and paint *Salty* before the tide comes in. Water laps around Skip's boot tops when we finally finish. While we wait for *Salty* to float off the grid, we visit with Dorie and Ed.

Dorie says, "Look at yourself in the mirror, Marilyn."

I'm speckled brown. We all laugh. We always find something to talk and laugh about which makes the loneliness of boat life more tolerable. When we row back in the skiff, the tide is still not high enough to float *Salty*.

Looking up at *Salty* from the skiff, I realize getting on board is going to be difficult.

"How are we going to get in without touching the wet paint?" I ask.

"Lift your knee up on the stern."

Standing in the skiff's bow, I see nothing to grasp.

Skip says, "I'll climb up. Ya sit in the middle of the skiff." Easily, he pulls himself over the stern. He is taller and can reach the cleat.

"You row over to this side which is lower."

After much effort I position the skiff and hand him the painter. I still look up to the deck. The top of my head is six inches below the guard rail.

"I can't scale it without touching the paint, Skip."

"Come over here then and hang onto the guard rail."

I stand on the skiff's seat to grab the guard rail. I have a good hold but my feet are dangling in mid air.

"What'll I do, Skip?" I yell frantically.

Without a word he reaches down and grabs me by the seat of the pants and pulls me over the side.

"What a way to come aboard," I laugh.

The next day the halibut still aren't biting. Ed decides to go to Warm Springs Bay for baths. We tie *Salty* to the dock and climb aboard the *Pauline*.

Dorie and I are in the galley when Ed excitedly calls, "There's a strange creature up here, girls. Come look. I've never seen anything like it before. It has long whiskers and is bigger than a seal or sea lion."

Right before we get there, it dives. The men tell tales of sea monsters. Have we sighted a rare elephant seal?

An hour and a half later we enter Warm Springs Bay where they've located the village of Baranof. The steep mountains loom all around the bay with the snow line only 50 feet above the tops of the wooden houses. The snow is lower on the hillside than other places we've been. Our gaze focuses on a large waterfall where water cascades down with a deafening roar. The melting snow makes the falls really big at this time of year. None of the previous waterfalls were as wide or had as much water. The white water churns below the green trees while a snow-covered peak sticks its sharp spire into the evening sky.

We tie the *Pauline* to the float and climb the ramp. The high boardwalks between the store and homes remind me of the Alaskan school child who tries to classify objects as animal, plant or mineral. When she comes to sidewalk, she asks the teacher, "Is it wood or cement?"

Baranof's hot mineral spring baths make it a resort. Many fishermen as well as residents from SE Alaska towns come here. We walk by large unpainted weather-beaten houses. I wonder if resort people rent them. In the past, Baranof had brothels.

Before we take our baths, we climb the trail above the houses to the hanging bridge across the falls. I hold tightly to Skip's hand as we walk out on the bridge. The water swirls in large eddies before going over the falls. The deafening roar and the velocity of the water frighten me.

Ed leads the way. "We better hurry and take our baths," he says. "It'll be midnight before we get back to Tyee now."

We pay for our baths at the store and receive towels and soap. We all head for the bathhouse where we find little rooms with wooden bath tubs in them. The Wellesleys select a room on one side and we on the other. The water runs constantly into the tubs. Skip puts the wooden plug in the tub and it is full by the time we undress.

I put one foot in it. "It's hot. This should be called Hot Springs, not Warm Springs.

Dorie calls from their room, "Turn it off and let it cool. There's a bucket in the waiting room in the front. You can get cold water from the faucet outside the door."

Dressing again, I carry in the cold water. Skip and I take our bath together in the long tub. The bath is worth the effort. Our aches and pains, cut and bruises disappear in the hot mineral water. We soak a half-hour.

It is still daylight when we leave Warm Springs and head for Tyee even though it's 10:30 at night. The sky has streaks of red that turn to orange and then a golden yellow behind the jagged peaks of Baranof Island. The peaks resemble castle fortresses. Soon we spot the light at the mouth of Murder Cove.

The next morning Ed pounds on the door. We are both still in our bunks but Skip calls for him to come in. "Remember those two trollers that came in yesterday—*Old Cliff* and *Little Joe Cash*. Well, they each caught ten halibut on high water slack yesterday. They wander all over the country and don't know the spots. If they can catch that many, we should be able to triple it. The fish are here, man. Climb out of that bunk. We're going out in a few minutes."

"What time is it? Can't be very late."

"It's a little after six. It was low water at six. The halibut bite on the tides and tides wait for no man."

After Ed leaves, we pile out of our bunks so fast that we almost knock each other down trying to get dressed.

"This is what we waited for, honey," Skip says giving me a big hug. "Get that breakfast going."

We can't order a more beautiful morning. The long row of white peaks of Baranof Island looks over the top of the low isthmus that separates Murder Cove from Surprise Harbor, named by Meade either for the white men who were murdered or for his plan to surprise the Kake Indians there.

The blue water, the evergreen trees, white mountains and the blue sky are all the colors of Alaska. I stack the dishes and climb into the pilothouse to see if I can help. If Ed hadn't been so efficient in doing everything himself, I think Skip would use me more. He reasons that if Ed does it alone so can he.

Ed runs the *Pauline* into position and lets his gear down. When it comes to trolling halibut, Ed is one of the best. He knows the grounds, understands how to keep his boat into the tide, has the best landmarks to keep him right on the spot, and cleans halibut fast. Being a prize-fighter, he developed strong arms. All in one motion he grabs the spoon, throws the halibut over his head into a fish bin, and with a snap of his wrist removes the hook. He lands five halibut while the rest of us are thinking about pulling one over the side of the boat. The best fishing occurs during the last three hours of the flood or incoming tide. How fast we land the fish determines the size of our catch.

"I can feel fish on our line, Marilyn. See how my arm jerks back and forth," Skip says as he pushes the gurdy into gear. He tightens the big wheel on *Salty's* power take-off on the engine to produce as much power as possible. We tell how big a load we have by how fast the gurdy pulls in the line. If we have 100 pounds of fish, it groans and comes in slowly. If we have only 20 or 30 pounds, it winds up fast. When Skip pushes the gurdy into gear, we watch how far the block on the stanchion is pulled to estimate how many fish we have. When Skip lands three halibut on the first line, he asks me to bring two more leaders and two more spoons. Like Ed, he fishes five lures.

"Hey, Skip, look! That line is hanging funny. It's slack, not hanging back like it usually does."

"Oh, my God! I forgot all about it when I was landing fish from the other line." He pushes the gurdy into gear but it only growls. "We're hooked up on the bottom," he says. He tries to jerk it loose. Suddenly, we rise with a swell. Snap! The line hangs loose.

"There goes our 40 pound lead. It's just like throwing a $20 bill over the side and watching it sink."

Ed warns us that the tide sets you into shallow water, and you can lose all your gear in minutes. Later a line snaps at the side of the boat, which is more tragic than losing a lead. Not only is the lead gone, but the 50 fathoms of stainless steel line, our lures, rubber snubbers, leaders and hooks. The trolling spools hold 100 fathoms of line. The length of our leaders determines what intervals we mark our lines. For halibut, we mark them every nine feet and for king salmon, 18 feet which is three fathoms. When we lose a line, Skip snaps on another lead sinker and makes a breaking strap which is supposed to break and drop the lead before the line itself breaks. He snaps on new leaders and lures and soon we are back catching fish.

The first day we catch 500 pounds of halibut, lose two 40-pound sinkers and one whole line. Ed catches 1200 pounds and loses no gear. We make money on halibut that first year but spend 20 percent of it for more gear. I think halibut fishing makes us better salmon fishermen. We aren't afraid of losing gear if we are making money. Ed says it's the cost of doing business. Many fishermen are so afraid of losing gear that they never fish near the bottom. They catch fewer fish.

Depth sounders are expensive so we don't have one yet. A depth sounder would let us know how deep it is under the keel. Skip turns into deeper water or speeds up when it becomes shallow. Landmarks and charts help some.

The next day, after three hours of fishing, our bins are full of halibut. Then, a 60-pound halibut goes wild when Skip brings it to the surface. It thrashes the water with its broad tail, throws spray all over Skip and then sounds by heading for the bottom.

"Hand me the pistol!" Skip shouts.

I run out with it. When Skip shoots the halibut, it goes berserk. He can't stop the halibut as it heads for the bottom. It breaks the leader and takes the spoon and hook.

We learn another lesson that helps decrease our gear losses. I turn on a line two or three times before Skip frees the lead from the bottom. Many times I hear his joyous exclamation, "It's free." We may get it all back or only lose one or two leaders.

We've lost a lot of gear so Skip decides to have only one line on the bottom at a time. He will let down the other line the minute he puts the gurdy in gear to pull in the first line. That way the second line begins fishing while he lands the fish on the first line. The only time we fish halibut with two lines is when we each fish a side.

When a halibut weighs over 80 pounds, a fishermen will describe it as having two barn doors.

In the 1940s, a market existed for halibut livers and viscera (intestines) for vitamin products. On the fishing grounds where the price is less, they pay $1.65 a pound for livers and 40 cents a pound for the viscera. This easily pays for our fuel and groceries.

Halibut never seem to stop flopping. They still beat the deck with their broad tails hours after we land them. Halibut have a distinct smell and slime. Halibut gives your bilge an odor that takes many hours of scrubbing to remove. Everything about salmon is easier than halibut. We catch more total pounds of halibut in a day than we catch king salmon. Many trollers refuse to fish halibut, but Skip says we'll fish anything that makes us money. Ours is a fishing boat not just a salmon troller.

The next night we invite Ed and Dorie and the Petersons, who work at the cannery, over for peach pie and coffee. A steamer whistle interrupts our visiting.

"It's the *North Sea*," someone calls. Everyone is eager to greet the passengers arriving on the big boat.

People come from all directions—off floats in the harbor, out of the cannery buildings and the bunkhouses. We push our way through the crowded dock. I hadn't realized so many people live in Tyee. We watch the steamer come in and turn around so its bow heads out the channel. The steamer looks so large in the small channel.

"Make way for the jitney," the driver calls. Someone else commands, "Get back everyone. The men must catch the heavy heaving lines and tie up the ship."

For a few minutes, pandemonium reigns. Everyone mills around while the crews tie her broadside to the face of the dock. The passengers line her decks.

"They want to see what we native Alaskans look like," Dorie laughs.

In a matter of minutes they secure the steamer. The ship's crew lowers the gangplank. As the steamer only comes at high water, the gangplank is horizontal.

First come the superintendents and their families and the white workers. Then come the Filipino, Japanese and Chinese. I estimate 100 people disembark from the *North Sea*.

The *North Sea* will never see another season. She'll run up on a reef in British Columbia in a snowstorm the following winter and slowly break up through the years. Alaska and British Columbia are called the graveyard of ships for so many have been lost in the narrow rocky channels.

I see that the canneries are a large operation. After the people are off, the crews unload the supplies for the canning season as well as food for the crews. Later in the season the steamer returns for the canned salmon. In the fall, it returns again for the crews and the remainder of the salmon pack. Then the cannery closes for the winter except for a watchman and a couple of families who live here year around.

We little realize that we are witnessing the last of an era. The canneries will consolidate and move their operations into larger towns. They will no longer move the crews into the outlying canneries during the fishing seasons. Eventually only Excursion Inlet Cannery and Cold Storage will remain.

The next day we are back at our halibut fishing. Every day more boats arrive. We find that the fleet follows the salmon. If you find the salmon, you can't keep it a secret. We hope we are lucky and are the first ones on a school of fish. We might get three or four days of fishing before the fleet arrives. We contend with the boats and tides.

Later Skip calls, "Look at that boat! They didn't watch and they drifted over that skiff's anchor line."

After much tugging and losing a good deal of fishing time, the skiff's owner frees its line, but, alas, he loses his anchor. The troller finally agrees to buy him another anchor.

Later we troll alongside the *Pauline* and another boat is fishing ahead of us.

"Keep clear, Skip. I'm hooked up!" Ed calls.

Just then the other boat swings around and heads directly toward us. We have no place to turn, with the *Pauline* on one side and the bank on the other.

"Take her out of gear, Marilyn," Skip shouts.

The other boat hits us but luckily only a glancing blow. The skipper runs out on deck, "Sorry. My carburetor isn't working right, and I went down to look at it."

"You better take your boat out of gear or run into harbor if you leave your wheel. It might have damaged our boat."

Later two boats run together. A plank is split in the bow of one of them.

Having caught 600 pounds of halibut on a hectic day, Skip suggests prospecting by ourselves. We drag in various places for an hour with no results. We talk with each and don't think too much about the fishing. Suddenly, Skip feels a tug on his line. Happily, he lands three 20- to 30-pound halibut. We welcome them after catching the chicken halibut. Buyers call halibut under ten pounds chickens. The ten pounders make medium. They pay eight cents per pound for chicken and ten cents per pound for the mediums.

"If ya let down the line on your side, we can fish two lines."

Obediently, I follow his directions. I feel the line jerk. "Fish! Fish!" I shout. After putting my gurdy in gear to pull in my line, I see three good-sized mediums on my five hooks. Skip lands them and puts his line in gear.

We find the halibut in a 100-yard circle. We make accurate land-marks to stay on it. We land halibut as fast as our gear hits bottom. With our two regular fish bins full, we close the pilothouse door and put them in the two forward bins next to the mast.

Soren Anderson on the *Nan*, a good Norwegian friend, pulls alongside and calls, "You folks about ready to go in?"

"Hell no! There's fish here. Get your lines in the water."

I decide to go below for a drink of water. As I open the sliding pilothouse door, a halibut slides across the pilothouse floor and slithers down the steps into my freshly scrubbed galley. Hastily, I pick up the flopping fish in my arms like I would a baby. I scramble up the steps and drop it on deck amid Skip's and Soren's laughter.

An hour later a stiff southwesterly blows up against the ebb tide and forces us to quit. With so much fish on deck, the halibut might slide to one side and we could capsize. Sadly, we pull our gear aboard and head for harbor.

Now Skip must clean each halibut. Tyee's small no-see-ums come out in the evening. We figure out that if we clean the fish outside the harbor, the no-see-ums don't fly that far.

To no avail Skip tries to hire one of the cannery workers to help clean fish, after they are off for the day. Skip finally finishes cleaning our 2000 pounds at midnight. We have a good-sized check when we sell the next day.

As everyone saw us fishing on the other side of Yasha Island, we can't hide where we caught the fish. The next day I'm forced to steer because everyone wants to catch those big halibut. We only catch 1000 pounds that day. By the fourth day the fish scatter and everyone returns to the first fishing ground.

On June 6 the announcement from the International Halibut Commission is posted in the fish house. Area two closes on June 11 as the quota will be filled. Our halibut fishing ends. We made money even though we lost a lot of gear. Halibut fishing is hard work.

"I'm glad to go back to salmon fishing," I say.

"Yes, I don't think I could keep on with this much longer. I'm worn out."

CHAPTER SEVEN
Glacier Dangers

"HOW'D YOU LIKE TO GO TO THE GLACIERS and hunt seal?" Paul Binkley on the *Anna May* asks. "Three boats of us are going: Fred Manley on the *Chester L*, Sandy and the children with me on the *Anna May*, and the Wellesleys on the *Pauline*."

Skip immediately says, "We'd love to go. I don't care much for seal hunting, but a trip to the glaciers sounds exciting."

We talk the superintendent of the cannery, Cliff Erickson, into opening the store for us, as we need supplies for the trip. Why do men always decide on a trip late at night and then want to leave at daylight? The women are the ones who have to work out the particulars.

The thermometer registers 79 degrees when we leave Tyee at 4 a.m. I put on my shorts and halter top and lie on top of the cabin to suntan. As we near Holkham Bay, a cold breeze from the mainland blows from the glaciers down Stephens Passage, named by Vancouver for Sir Phillip Stephens, Secretary of the British Navy. Brrr...my sun worshipping ends abruptly.

That night we anchor by Harbor Island at the mouth of Holkham Bay, named by Vancouver for a town in Norfolk, England. We row ashore to visit Mr. and Mrs. Ernie Kohlhase, a German couple. Ernie tells us that if he had contributed to the German Bund, a political group of the 1930s, the government would have interned him during World War II. He was glad he didn't contribute.

A deep blue iceberg drifts by on the tide, silhouetted by the golden sunset. I sit on the hatch and enjoy the tranquil beauty. The icebergs that have just broken off or recently turned over are always the bluest.

Early the next morning Paul on the *Anna May* leads the way into glacier country. *Salty* takes up the rear. I'm fascinated by the icebergs as we wind our way to Tracy Arm, named by Lieutenant H. B. Mansfield for Benjamin Tracy, Secretary of the Navy from 1889 to 1893. Some are as large as warehouses while others are mere bits of floating ice.

"Marilyn, only one-eleventh of an iceberg shows above water."

"It's fun imagining the various shapes. Look at the horse with flying mane and tail."

"That's from the action of the waves. The water and waves melt the bottom part before the top part melts. When the iceberg becomes top-heavy, it can turn over, creating a dangerous hazard for any boats close to it."

We hear that one curious family was so interested in the icebergs that the wife and three children climbed out on one while the husband took pictures. Old timers shake their heads at the foolishness. The iceberg could have easily turned over and dumped them all into the water. You only survive in the waters this far north for about 15 minutes before hypothermia sets in. We hear another story of how an iceberg turned over near a boat and lifted the boat on top of it. The skipper pushed the boat off and he didn't sink. As in the North Atlantic, icebergs are dangerous to navigation. They don't show up on radar. A Petersburg boat hit one and sank in less than ten minutes.

Through millenniums, the ice wears away the rock to make sheer rock mountains with walls that rise thousands of feet. Many streams of water cascade down these walls. We watch nature at work. It's awe-inspiring. The channels are hundreds of fathoms deep.

In contrast, at a bend in the channel, we spot a grassy, gradually slopping area. A glacier stopped there and then receded millenniums ago. Picturesque valleys and bays are left where glaciers cut channels and eventually melted. Most of Southeast Alaska was formed by glaciers millions of years ago. I feel so small and inconsequential in this country.

The Coast Pilot states no anchorage is available in Tracy Arm, but we follow Paul to the base of a large waterfall. He lets his anchor down fifteen fathoms to keep from drifting to shore. He rows ashore and fastens two shorelines to make a V at the base of the falls. This keeps the boat from floating out into the channel. The current from the falls keeps the ice away from the boats, and the boats away from shore.

The *Chester L* ties on one side of the *Anna May*, the *Pauline* to the other. *Salty* ties to the outside of the *Pauline*.

That night something hits *Salty's* side with a thud. As he bounds out of bed Skip exclaims, "Did we hit the beach?"

He calls, "Bring me the pike pole."

Peering out, I spot a large iceberg nearby. Skip doesn't need the pike pole for the current from the falls catches the ice and it drifts away. In the semi-darkness the icebergs form eerie ghosts floating around us. All night the ice-

Skip lies in the bow of Ed Wellesley's skiff to make a path through the glacier ice as they attempt to hunt the elusive hair seals.

bergs grind against the walls of the bay and crash into each other as they float by on the ebb tide.

Early the next morning the men put on their warmest clothing and set out in skiffs to hunt hair seals. The territory of Alaska pays a $3 bounty on them because they eat large quantities of salmon every year. They placed the bounty on them in 1927 in all parts of Alaska. In 1946 a demand for the hides exists in Europe. Each June, the seal pups are born on the ice beneath the glaciers. With the cows and pups traveling together, a hunter can usually shoot both.

Ed and Paul lie on different points waiting for the seals to swim by. Skip and Alvin, Paul's boat-puller (helper), huddle in the skiffs waiting for the riffle shots. When he hits a seal, the hunter calls, "Go!"

Then either Skip or Alvin rows rapidly to the seal before it sinks. He'll pull the bloody carcass into the skiff. Fred on the *Chester L* picks up the dead seals from the skiffs. He and his 18-year-old brother skin them. Skip marvels at the men's expert shooting. He's cold and stiff from sitting in the skiff.

"I don't have enough dog blood," Skip later confides. "This retrieving business doesn't appeal to me. Yesterday a seal starts flopping as I reach for it.

Zing! Ed shoots it. I tell him not to try that again or he can find another re-
triever."

Sawyer Glaciers at the head of Tracy Arm slough off many icebergs; con-
sequently the men can't get near it. Their seal take is small.

The second day Fred asks if we women want to come along. We eagerly
climb aboard with Sandy and the two Binkley children. Fred's brother stands
on the bow pushing the ice away with a long pike pole as we creep toward the
glaciers. In an hour we only move a quarter of a mile and are still far from our
destination. When we find no opening among the icebergs, we wait for the
tide and current to shift the icebergs in hopes an opening will appear. While
we wait, we watch the many waterfalls cascade down the perpendicular walls.
One looks like a wrist with five fingers.

Slowly, we round the point and the panorama of Sawyer Glaciers unfolds
before us. Two carpets of iridescent blue roll over the mountains into the sea.
The smaller one is on the left, the larger one on the right. A deafening roar
fills the air as the glacier calves large chunks of ice into the water. We're silent
because we know no one can hear what we say.

Ed and Skip have difficulty rowing over to the *Chester L* for lunch and
hot coffee. Skip lies in the bow of the skiff to push away the ice with a
gaffhook and to pull the skiff forward. They find no place to put the oars into
the water. Often the ice jams together so tightly that they must just wait for
it to move.

"We'll have to turn around. This ice is so thick we can't find a path
through it," Fred says after we pick up Paul's seals.

The next day the men try the southern arm of Holkham Bay, Endicott
Arm named by Mansfield for William Endicott, Secretary of War from 1885
to 1889. On our way we pass Sumdum Glacier, which has receded and lies
high in the mountains. Old Natives still remember living at and visiting the
large Indian settlement there. John Muir even wrote of stopping at Sundum
in the 1870s. A mining camp operated here for ten years starting in 1895.
They had a post office from then until 1942.

Endicott Arm is less rugged than Tracy Arm and is much less publicized.
I like Endicott better because trees grow beside the deep gorges.

"Look, honey!" Skip exclaims. Against the dazzling ice, we spot the face
of Dawes Glacier. It looks like a frozen river in the valley between two mountain ranges. This is more awe-inspiring than Tracy Arm. We weren't able to
see the faces of Sawyer Glaciers as clearly because the icebergs blocked our

view.

A real anchorage lies behind a grassy point covered with wildflowers. At the north end of Endicott Arm, I spot a receding glacier made grotesque by a stream flowing over the mud at the glacier's face.

"Come on, let's go seal hunting!" Paul calls. "The ice isn't as thick here. We should find many seals."

The men jump into the skiffs and disappear among the icebergs. This time Paul and Alvin run nearer the glacier to scare the seals toward the point where Ed and Skip wait. Again we women board the *Chester L* with Fred and his brother to pick up the dead seals.

Nearer and nearer we inch toward the face of the glacier. I see cracks and crevasses on its face. Dirt and debris cover its surface.

"There goes a slide," says Dorie pointing to the snow and ice cascading down the face.

Though we're more than a mile away, the face of the glacier towers high above us. Skip tells me the glacier stretches more than 100 feet above the surface of the water, and even more of it is underwater.

When we come to the point of land where Paul is waiting, he and Alvin row out to the *Chester L*.

Fred says, "How about my going with you, Paul? Alvin can run the boat."

Paul agrees and our crew changes. Fred climbs into the skiff, and they row away. The boys tell us that this is their first trip to the glaciers. We women are so busy exclaiming over the slides and watching the scenery that we pay little attention to the change in our crew. The boys decide to run the *Chester L* closer to the glacier for better pictures.

Skip and Ed think Fred is aboard. Seeing the *Chester L* head nearer to the glacier's face, they shake their heads.

"Glaciers are no plaything," Ed remarks. "They better turn around. You never can predict what a glacier is going to do."

Skip nods, "I wish we had a horn or something to blow at them. But with the noise of the glacier, they wouldn't hear it anyway and the noise might cause the glacier to calve. What do ya think we can do to get their attention?"

"Would take us 45 minutes to row over there. We better just sit tight and hope Fred has enough sense to turn around. He knows the score with glaciers. We should stop worrying."

We sit spellbound on the hatch of the *Chester L.* as the boat zigzags among the many icebergs. The glacier comes closer and closer.

Suddenly, a piece of ice the size of a house cascades down the front of the glacier. The agitation breaks off a piece larger than a skyscraper at the base of the glacier. It shoots straight up in the air like a rocket taking off. It doesn't become airborne but collapses in a spray of ice chunks larger than the boat. They fly hundreds of feet skyward. This chain of violent action jars the whole ice face. On the far side, half of the glacier's face sloughs off. With a roar, the icebergs slide over the top of each other. In awe, we watch a surge of water come toward us. It never even crosses my mind that we're in danger.

Alvin yells, "We better turn around, this looks bad. Everyone sit down! You better bring the two little girls inside, Sandy."

On the point, Ed calls to Skip, "Row out 50 feet. When this surge hits, you don't want to set down on this point. It might break up our skiff. Can you see the *Chester L?*"

"Thank God they're turning around. Will they make it ahead of the ice?"

"I can't tell yet. Just so they keep their heads. If all that ice catches them, the boat hasn't a chance. The ice could cut it in two."

Alvin climbs up on the bow and methodically makes a path by pushing the ice away with the pike pole. We're still well ahead of the cascading ice when the surge catches us. We rise up, up, up. Then we go down, down, down into the trough. Behind us, the new icebergs are slowly gaining on us. I hang onto the mast. I know that we're in grave danger. I realize that life-preservers will be of little use in this icy water except to float a dead body. Our only hope will be for the boat to be pushed on top of an iceberg.

If the boys worry about our situation, they never show it. Alvin keeps pushing a path through the ice with the pike pole.

Sandy, who has seal hunted many times with Paul, worriedly says, "This is the largest slough-off I've ever seen."

"It's a good thing it wasn't on this side of the glacier," I say. "We couldn't have gotten away from it. Look, there's our anchorage ahead."

We all cheer and clap. We're safe. We congratulate the boys, "You did well." The boys have just anchored when both skiffs come alongside. When Ed sees the situation, his eyes blaze, "What do you mean leaving these women and children on the boat with only these boys, Fred?"

"I didn't think there was any danger."

"Glaciers are always dangerous."

"You must have agreed to it, Paul."

Dorie runs to Ed's side, "It came out all right, Ed. Nothing to worry about now."

The tension hangs in the air for a moment and then Ed smiles. The tension evaporates.

Later, aboard *Salty*, Skip holds me and whispers, "We really worried about ya. Ya'd never have made it if the glacier had calved on this side. Ed was so sure Fred was aboard."

The next morning the bay is a solid mass of ice. The wily seals move to the thickest part. No more seal hunting at Dawes Glacier.

"Maybe we can find some seals in Ford's Terror," Paul suggests. "It's worth a try before we leave."

Mansfield named it for his crewman on the *Patterson*, Henry L. Ford. He added Terror for the 16-knot tides that pour through its narrow opening. We can only go through the opening when it's slack water because we must make a 90-degree turn. The tide is slack for only a few minutes on each tide. On this low water, we spot a rock which is covered at high water. A running tide will set a boat on this rock. Paul rows to the point and climbs it to watch for slack water. He motions when it's safe for us to go through.

When Paul throws over his anchor, the largest flock of Canadian Geese I've ever seen takes off from the lowland ahead. They circle overhead and keep honking in their harsh voices. Going ashore, we discover their nests. We wager that we're their first human visitors in years.

As the men find no seals, we leave Ford's Terror at the next slack water. We again anchor around the point. One steep bank is amass with flowers. Skip and I row ashore. We find chocolate rice lilies, Indian paint brush, columbine, buttercups, a new variety of violet and some other wildflowers I can't identify. I'm surprised to find them growing so abundantly in this cold terrain.

As we leave the glacier country the next day, we laugh at an iceberg stranded high and dry on a rock. Then we follow the *Pauline* back to Tyee. I will always remember our escape from the cascading ice.

CHAPTER EIGHT

Sink The Scow

"I'M GOING TO JUNEAU ON BUSINESS. Would you like to come along, Marilyn?" Dorie asks.

I jump at the chance. "Can I go, Skip?"

"Of course, ya can. You girls deserve a vacation." As an after thought, he comments, "This will be the first time that we've been apart." I smile and wink at him. We've been together 24 hours a day, seven days a week since we married four months ago.

Early the next morning Dorie and I leave Tyee with Wally and Wilma Peterson on their cruiser, *Kayak*. *Salty* and *Pauline*, being fishing boats, are less roomy than Peterson's boat.

In calm water, we run by Pybus and Gambier Bays, named by Vancouver for James Gambier, a fellow officer in the royal Navy. In Stephens Passage, we spot icebergs from Holkham Bay's Tracy and Endicott Arms. Nearing Juneau, we turn into Gastineau Channel where Wilma points out the abandoned gold mines. She tells us that Gastineau Channel was a fishing grounds for Tlingit Indians, but in early 1880, a local engineer offered a reward to anyone who brought him gold samples. A local Tlingit named Kowee of the Auk Tlingit Tribe provided gold ore to George Pilz who prospected with two partners in the Gold Creek area of Juneau. They struck it rich when they discovered the mother lode of Quartz Gulch on October 18, 1880. One month later the first boat load of prospectors arrived. The first Alaskan town, Juneau, was created by the Gold Rush. When the loose gold in the stream beds ran out the town became the center for large-scale hard-rock mining. One of the largest gold mines in the world is built up the mountainside in tiers at the edge of Juneau. Gold production peaked around 1915. Soon after, a cave-in flooded three of the four mines and production fell off for the Treadwell mines. In the 1920's the high cost of mining effectively halted most of the gold mining.

"The Alaska-Juneau closed completely during the War when the price of gold fell," Wally says, "but they hope to reopen soon."

On the way to Juneau's boat harbor, in the late afternoon, we run under a long bridge across the channel that connects Juneau with the town of Douglas, named by Vancouver for John Douglas, bishop of Salisburg. Wilma tells us that before the bridge there was a ferry that ran back and forth but somehow the territory came up with the money to build the bridge.

Dorie and I wait anxiously as Wally ties up the *Kayak*. We hurriedly thank them and climb onto solid ground. Juneau is spread out before us. Considered by many to be the most beautiful capital city in the United States, this picture book community is nestled along the base of the mountains with winding streets, totem poles and colorful store fronts. Dorie and I exclaim at the colors and beauty. I feel like a kid taking her first trip to the big city. In a taxi, on the way to the hotel, we pass the unique triangle building and Triangle Bar.

Dorie says, "There's the Baranof Hotel. Let's clean up before we do any sight seeing."

After two and a half months on a cramped boat bunk I dream of how good a bed with an innerspring mattress will feel. What a luxury!

"I can't wait for a good bath and shower," Dorie cries. "I'm going to take both."

"I can stretch up my arms without hitting the top of the trunk cabin," I exclaim from the bed. "No engine noise. What wonderful silence." We both laugh and spend the next hour enjoying the luxuries of hot water that never runs out and a bed you can actually stretch out in.

We like putting on our dresses, hose and heels. Dorie unbraids her long red hair and fixes it in a page-boy style where the ends are rolled under. I roll my dark hair into a reverse bang on my forehead. Walking into the ultramodern dining room with linen napkins and beautiful Alaskan paintings on the walls, we look far different from the girls in blue jeans just off the *Pauline* and *Salty*. I admit that I'm tired of my own cooking and savor the chef's delicious entrees.

When we left Tyee on Monday, Superintendent Erickson said the power scow might come to Juneau toward the end of the week and that we could return on it. We also could catch the mail boat, but it leaves tomorrow and won't get to Tyee until Friday. We decide to wait for the power scow so that we can have four days in Juneau.

The next morning Dorie takes care of her business and I go shopping. We decide to visit the museum and scenic spots another day.

Upon my return to the room at noon, I find a telegram: "Power scow coming to Juneau today. Come if you like. Ed and Skip."

Dorie laughs when she reads the wire. "I'd like to see what would happen if we didn't like."

Now we have four hours instead of four days. We literally run from store to store doing our errands. They lock the museum doors as we climb the steps. "It's sad to have only two nights in a good bed," I lament.

"Yes, and I wanted to go to a movie, too." Dorie says. "Let's find a different restaurant tonight."

I thoroughly enjoy this welcome respite from fishing. In the morning, the bell hop asks. "Are you ladies catching the morning plane?"

We merely nod. We don't want to tell him that we're hitching a ride on a power scow. The *Robert S.* is a large boat with a high pilot house in the stern. The rest of the boat has high wooden side bins. The crew uses the winch to brail or dump salmon into these bins from the salmon traps.

The *Robert S.* is much faster than the little *Kayak*, and we pull into Tyee around 3 p.m. We expect the men to be waiting for us after the telegram they sent, but neither is there to help tie up the *Robert S.* Skip doesn't know we arrived until he hears us laugh as we walk toward the float from the dock.

"Hey, Ed, look!" Skip shouts.

In their mad dash up the ramp, they nearly push down an old man, bewildered by the commotion. Neither of us knew they could move so fast. "They must have really missed us!" I whisper to Dorie. She winks and then we're both swept off our feet by our men.

The next day Skip paints the cabin while I give Kitty a bath. "She must have crawled in a coal pile," I exclaim to Skip. "Didn't you take care of her?" Skip rolls his eyes at me and continues painting.

Soon Ed climbs aboard and sits down on the bench. He wipes the sweat off his face. "We're heading for Kalinin Bay," he says. "Often we find good king fishing there before the cohoes start. You kids want to come with us? We'll leave in a couple of days. First I must put away the halibut gear, and mark my lines for cohoes."

We like being asked. "Yes, we'll go with ya." Skip says.

Skip carries rocks from the beach to put in our fish hold as ballast since most of the ice has melted. I write both of our folks to write to us in care of Kalinin Bay. I am not sure I will get letters that are sent there as nothing is final with a fisherman. We may start for one place, then talk to someone or hear reports of good fishing in another area. We'll turn around and end up 200 miles in the opposite direction. I learn the hard way to wait until we actually arrive at a place before having our mail sent there. Still, we may be gone when it arrives.

I overhear one fisherman talking about another troller, "He's been galloping up and down the coast like an express train. Last I heard from him, two days ago, he was at Cape Muson. He's probably at Cape Spencer now. Too bad he didn't stop his train to fish."

That afternoon Captain Eddie Williams, a fish buyer, arrives with a deck load of cohoes on his packer, *Progressive*. The news flashes up and down the float, "Cohoes are in Tebenkof already. This will be a big year."

Ed and Skip discuss the situation. If they work hard, they'll be ready to leave by 9 a.m. the next day. Watching these two men, I decide that nothing causes fishermen to move faster than a reported fish run.

As the sun is setting, Ed discovers a problem with his carburetor. Skip contemplates staying to help fix it but Ed tells us to go ahead. As soon as the cold storage and oil station opens at 8 a.m., we take on ice and fuel and head for Tebenkof alone. Skip and I miss our friends but each time we run alone we become more confident in ourselves as fishermen.

I don't expect the Point Ellis tide rips and my chocolate pie slides off the table and falls to the galley floor with a loud crash. Looking at the mess I realize that the pie plate has cracked. Oh well, no pie for dinner, and no more pie until I can buy a new pie plate. Pies are one of my specialties that Skip loves.

Safely through the tide rips, Skip gazes intently at the chart trying to understand the area. Thirty to 50 trollers are fishing over a wide area. We've heard this area called the Tebenkof flats so Skip is worried that a large shallow area might lie far from shore.

"Ya know, a new place never looks good to me until I land the first fish," Skip says.

On one side of us are the low rolling hills of Kuiu Island and on the other side are Baranof Island's towering peaks. The contrast is striking. I read from my guide book that Tebenkof is named for a Russian Naval officer who made the first navigational charts of Alaska. For years his charts were in Tebenkof's Atlas. A Coast & Geodetic Survey Captain tells us that they are now replacing the final Russian charts.

Tebenkof Bay is eight miles long and extends seven miles into Kuiu Island to form three distinct arms. Over the top of Davis Roch, which lies two-thirds of the way between Pt. Ellis and low Troller Islands, we see only a fraction of the water inside the bay. Gedney Harbor is 11 miles south of Pt. Ellis past Tebenkof Bay on Kuiu Island.

We troll for more than an hour without a strike. Skip steers from the pilothouse. We try to see if any boats are catching fish but the distance is too great. Suddenly, the starboard main pole jerks. Skip runs for the troller pit.

"Do you want the pistol?" I yell.

"Sure." I know he isn't listening to what I'm saying. He only wants to land our first king from Tebenkof. The salmon vigorously jerks the pole and stretches out the rubber snubber. He leads away from the boat and heads for the bottom. He puts up a real fight before Skip manages to pull it aboard. After the sluggish, slow moving halibut, we've forgotten the fun of landing a fighting salmon. It weighs 25 pounds. That afternoon we only catch four kings and two cohoes

"This is no big run." Skip mumbles, "Maybe those who know this area will have done better." Looking at the chart, he continues, "Looks like a big rock near the opening to Gedney. I see Paul over there. I think I'll follow him."

We find 40 trollers anchored in the horse-shoe shaped cove. Six trollers are tied to a float attached to a red scow which lies along one shore. In the middle of the cove, we see the *Sea Lad*, a large packer, anchored. Boats are waiting in line to sell to him.

"The *Sea Lad* is paying three cents more a pound than the scow is. I'm going to sell to him," Paul calls.

The float looks inviting, but we think the extra money is worth the trouble of anchoring. The Sea Lad has fresh fruit and vegetables for sale. I buy as much as we can afford. This is our first fresh produce since we left Wrangell. The store in Tyee won't sell their limited supply to the fishermen. I eagerly buy apples, oranges, grapes, lettuce, celery, and carrots.

"How are the others doing?" Skip asks the buyer.

"Not too much. They get 200 pounds of cohoes and five or six kings a day. Everyone thinks it'll improve on these tides."

Is everything connected to the tide, I wonder? We tie up to Paul's boat that night. When I hear Paul's engine start the next morning, light is just beginning to show on the horizon. Looking for my watch, I remember I dropped it overboard. "What time is it, Skip?"

Port Alexander in 1946.

"It's 3 a.m. When ya tie alongside someone, ya have to leave when they do," he mutters as he rolls out of his bunk.

I steer while Skip readies our gear. I do exactly what Paul is doing; when he slows down so do I. After putting the belt on the engine for our take-off to run the gurdies, Skip crawls into the troller pit. Immediately, the wing line jerks, but it's not the long, slow tug of a king salmon. Skip ignores it until he gets all the other lines out. He then puts the gurdy into gear to pull in that line. As it nears the boat, the fish jumps two feet out of water, doing a perfect somersault. Skip reaches down for the leader, but it's limp.

"He's gone. It was a coho, all right. They have soft mouths and pull loose if they fight."

When we lose four more, Skip makes a decision, "We're trolling faster than for kings. We're still not hooking them. Speed her up another notch."

Finally Skip lands a six-pound coho. I can't figure out how these small fish can put up such a fight. Skip tells me that cohoes, unlike kings, bite only on the top leaders. When we hook them, they roll to the surface which makes them a difficult target. Paul tells us that cohoes go in schools, and we need to put as many fishing spoons in the water as possible. That evening we have only 30 cohoes and two kings.

One old-timer says emphatically, "You think you're really in a school when all four poles are ringing. You'll be lucky if you get two fish aboard out of the lot because they have soft mouths. Blasted fish are so small. Takes a year to clean them all."

Remembering all the chicken halibut he cleaned at Tyee, Skip doesn't agree; he thinks the cohoes are easier.

Ed and Dorie arrive that evening and we tie alongside the *Pauline*. Ed climbs aboard and says, "I hear they're having $100 days at Port Alexander. Shall we go across Chatham tomorrow?"

I am reminded of the days we ran with Frank. We were always following the rumor mill of where the big run was. No matter how good the fishing was it was always better somewhere else.

"I had $55 today," Skip says slowly, "But if ya think it's better over there, we'll go."

To us, being with friends seems more important than making the big dollars. Ya never know where the fish will be so maybe the big dollars are at Port Alexander.

We're underway before sunrise. I steer while Skip makes up gear for the hundreds of fish we're dreaming of catching.

At Port Alexander we see a long line of trollers fishing from Breakfast Rock, named because trollers keep hitting it while they're making breakfast, to Wooden Island. Captain Vancouver named the island for George Wooden, his crewman, who fell overboard here. We get into line and wait eagerly for the poles to work. Nothing happens. I am reminded of the second day at Mosman. We watch the other boats. Many fishermen are sitting in their pilothouses or in their troller pits, but no one is landing any fish.

Tired and discouraged, we carefully follow the *Pauline* past the marker and kelp patch into Port Alexander's main harbor. Port Alexander, named by the Russians for Alexander Baranof, also has an inner harbor, but the fishermen can't get through its narrow mouth at low water. I estimate over 100 boats are anchored around the bay. Not since leaving Wrangell have I seen so many trollers in one place.

"Where are all the fish?" Skip asks an old-timer while he is unloading the fish. "I heard ya had a run here."

"Well, we had a good three or four days at the first of the week. Slacked off now. It'll get good when the tides increase."

After tying to the float, we climb the ramp to shore. Here Skip gets his check for only $15.

We walk along the boardwalk past three gambling halls with black jack tables and slot machines. I now understand why they call this the Las Vegas

Trollers tied to Buckshot's float in Gedney Harbor

of Southeast Alaska. We see two brothels and when we walk along the boardwalk into the inner harbor, we find another one. We stop at the post office to mail letters to our folks.

The next morning I wake up to Skip saying, "That damn cat is gone again."

"I'll go look for her," I say as I climb out of the bunk and quickly pull on my pants and put my jacket over my nightie. I slowly climb the ramp calling "Kitty, Kitty."

I follow men going into the saltery where the lunch counter is. I ask the cook if she has seen a stray cat. She says, "Yes, I saw her and fed her some scraps, but now she's gone."

I leave and start calling, "Kitty, kitty, kitty."

A girl in a bathrobe sticks her head out of a doorway and says, "She ran between the buildings."

I run down the boardwalk between the two building and catch a glimpse of her. I finally corner her at a doorway when she comes to the end of the walkway.

"We almost left you, kitty," I say as I cradle her against my chest.

We run *Salty* back to Tebenkof and luckily the cohoes and kings are still there. We've learned our lesson and when Ed and Dorie keep leaving for places where they hope to catch more fish, we stay behind. They'll be gone four or five days and then return. This doesn't bother us because we catch some salmon every day, and don't have to waste time searching.

We've learned that fishing is seldom good every day. When it slacks off, other places tempt you. Skip theorizes that the fish bite simultaneously in all places. One area may be better than another but then it slacks off everywhere. If we're on our way to another fishing area, we miss the first of the bite and only get in on the tail end. Often when a fisherman chases fish, he will be just a few days late at each place. The experienced fisherman guesses when to sit and wait for the fish to come to him. One fisherman remarks that he did better the first years because he didn't know all the different places to fish.

After we fish in a bay for two or three hours with only one small fish, our tendency is to say, "I knew it was a wild-goose chase." Then we'll leave. One of our friends tells us that he makes it a rule never to leave a place until he fishes over two slack waters, one low water and one high water.

We learn the drags, fishing patterns, in Tebenkof. We also find that the "highline" fishermen learn one area thoroughly. We always look for areas where herring and needlefish concentrate because the salmon are never far behind their food supply.

"Buckshot" and Irene Woolery and their two daughters, Marian and Lauran, buy fish on the Gedney Harbor scow. As the nights grow longer, we fish south toward Port Malmesbury and Table Bay or north to Tebenkof. One decision we must make is whether we will sell our fish to a fish buyer or ice them every night and run to Petersburg for three to five cents more a pound. Running to Petersburg means a one-way trip of 12 to 14 hours. We decide it's better to sell for less but have an extra day of fishing.

I cook dinner after we tie up to the float. Skip always asks how long until dinner. Even though I say only ten or 15 minutes, he'll disappear for at least an hour. He then gets to eat his dinner cold. Finally I say, "It won't be long. Don't you dare leave."

After I clean up the dishes, I always visit with the other wives on the boats. I'm lonely for my friends and family in Iowa, but I enjoy making new friends. Sometimes Skip has to hunt for me. "How am I going to get up at 4 a.m.?" he asks. "I can't go to sleep until ya come aboard." Like a little child, I follow him back to *Salty*, wondering why he has to have me there.

Hazel and Herman Hintz are among our new friends that we meet in Tebenkof that first year. They fish on the *Betty K*. Hazel seems to do all the talking. "Last night we anchored in Troller Islands. I told Herman to stay away from the right side. When he anchored, I asked if he was sure he had enough scope out? Everyone knows how the tide runs in there and we don't want the *Betty* to sit on shore. Everything turned out okay."

"I'm certainly glad that ya aren't like Hazel," Skip tells me later. "She worries if he's doing everything right."

"I figure certain jobs are yours," I answer. "I've got faith you will look after us."

Silent George on the *Helena* arrives. He got his name because he never talks much. George is tall and slim. He has a sixth sense about the fish. I know when I spot the *Helena* that the fish are there.

Dave Harrison, an old-timer, has the *Chance*. Dave has a voice like no one else's. He was born in New England but moved to Virginia at an early age. His Southern accent covered his New England brogue like syrup over southern biscuits. Years later, we recognize Dave by his accent when he calls to us from his new boat, *Norma*. The shortest radiophone conversations in the fleet are between Dave and Silent George. Their five-word conversations are a record of brevity.

Another old-timer is Irish Bennett. Irish keeps his boat immaculate. The native girl living on board got sick and threw up all over his galley. So Irish found her a good home on the boat of his pal, Pat Patterson.

One night someone tells Skip to put the marks on his lines closer together for cohoes. He puts one mark with Oregon Leader between each of his three-fathom markers. This makes the leaders only one and a half fathoms, nine feet, apart. Skip works far into the night to tie up that many leaders, polish fish spoons and attach hooks to them. He fastens these to a leader with a snap. When fishing 24 fathoms, 144 feet, he puts 16 lures per line.

The next day instead of catching more fish, we catch less. That many lures cause the lines to pull so far back that the lures tangle and wind around each other. We take a long time to pull in one line. Disgusted, Skip takes off the extra coho lures on the top half of the line making them three fathoms apart. He also keeps the king lures three fathoms apart on the bottom half of the lines. We will learn the secret to running this many lures sometime.

I meet a young couple, Janie and Gene, who fish on an old broken down boat which cost them more than *Salty* cost us. Every hour they have to pump water out of the boat. Janie wears short skirts and I can see the other boats move closer at pumping time when she has to bend over to raise the plunger of the hand pump. Janie and Gene adopted a dog from the Seattle pound. The dog sits on the stern and barks at every fish that Gene catches. Once a day, the dog falls overboard. Gene turns his boat at a sharp angle to get the dog. This maneuver always tangles his lines.

"I would have said, good-bye dog," Skip says.

Our kitty sits on *Salty's* stern behind the troller pit and watches Skip land fish. One day a whale blows behind the boat. The cat jumps up in the air, but, thank God, doesn't fall overboard.

When trollers tied to Buckshot's float keep finding their baits eaten, they look accusingly at Kitty. I know she isn't eating the bait but I can't convince them. One morning, Lyman Lagalle, the skipper of the *Lydia S*, climbs out of his bunk early and solves the mystery. He catches a mink eating halibut hung from his boom. The mink jumps into the troller pit and the skipper leaves him alone, knowing how vicious the little animals can be. When the boat is a mile from shore, the mink crawls out of the troller pit and jumps over the side. Who knows if he made it to shore from that distance?

A week later we buck into a swell as we run from Point Ellis to Troller Islands. We watch Kitty crawl around the top of the trunk cabin and jump to the top of the pilothouse on her way to the skiff. I must hang onto the bench to keep from falling to the floor. When we run into calm water inside Davis Rock, I look under the skiff.

"Kitty's gone," I cry. "She fell overboard."

"Kitty wouldn't make the two miles to shore," Skip puts his arm around my shoulders. "I'm sorry."

I wipe my tears. "She's been good company. I loved Kitty; too bad I didn't leave her in Port Alexander."

A howling northwester blows on the Fourth of July. No boats venture out of the harbor. The packer arrives in early afternoon with supplies, mail and ice. He brings fresh milk and ice cream, which we haven't seen since Wrangell. I wait anxiously for Irene to sort the mail. Happily, we have three letters. My mother is good about writing, and Skip's dad often writes. This is our first mail for three weeks.

On the fishing grounds, they identify people by the name on their boat. Often we don't even know their last names. If a boat is over five tons, it's documented. This makes it difficult to change its name.

I admire the *Linda Jo* from afar. Then the woman invites me aboard.

"This is Linda Jo ," the proud mother says. She is pointing to a blonde, curly-haired girl of two. For the first time, I meet the person for whom a boat is named.

Many boats are a combination of names such as *Stanmarg* and *Vermae*. *Tern*, *Lone Eagle*, and *Robin* are named for birds. Others are places: *Cape Cross* and *Adak*. Indian names include *Illahee* and *Taholah*. Others are descriptive, such as *Greyhound*, *Crack*, *Surplus*, *Sea Jeep*, *Moonlight* and *Grampus*. Some bring a smile: *Don't Worry*, *Who Cares*, *Ma's Mink*, *Green Pea*, and *Crow Bait*. We hear of a Prince Rupert boat named *Guess Who*. After scraping the boat paint to the original name, the police find it was stolen.

After the day's rest, the fleet heads out early on July 5th. A large school of cohoes has come into the area and everyone catches fish. I climb into the troller pit to help Skip when all four lines jerk with fish. We pull in salmon as fast as we work the gear. I easily pull in the six to nine pound cohoes and Skip designates the port side as mine. During a lull, I land fish from all four lines while Skip cleans. I have more fun landing the cohoes than catching the other fish.

That night a woman asks, "Do you clean fish?"

"Skip says if he can't clean the fish he catches, he better give up fishing," I reply.

I remember my mother's comment on milking cows, "Once you begin, you have a lifetime job." Neither she nor I were looking for a lifetime job because we already had one just by being wives. Luckily, we didn't first run with someone whose wife cleaned fish or Skip may have thought it my job.

When the *Sea Lad* leaves for the cold storage, Buckshot is the only buyer. The scow sinks lower and lower in the water from the weight of many fish. Buckshot ices fish until daylight. In three days, we sink the scow...an expression used to describe the scow when it's full of fish and low in the water.

Buckshot announces that he can buy no more fish until the packer arrives. Luckily on the fourth day, we find few cohoes, which we put on ice in the hold. With the arrival of the packer that day, Buckshot again buys fish.

Slowly the number of kings increases. As he learns the area better, Skip observes that the kings bite on a certain stage of the tide. "We're going to sleep in tomorrow. The kings won't bite until 11 a.m.," Skip announces.

The next morning we're the only boat in the harbor. Laughingly, we tell Irene that you can't expect us honeymooners to put in such long hours. Leaving the harbor, we meet three boats.

"Nothing out there," one calls. "Only three fish and we've been out since dawn."

I steer while Skip puts in our gear. He has no more than let out the last line than I notice the bow pole jerk.

"Yippee! The kings are still here," Skip exclaims.

The kings come so fast that I again climb into the troller pit to help. They average 20 pounds with an occasional 35- or 40-pounder. We even have double-headers which is two fish on one line.

We sell 25 kings that night to Buckshot. This surprises many fishermen. "He was the last boat out of the harbor," one says. Getting out early isn't as important to Skip as being fresh and wide awake at the right stage of the tide when the fish are hitting.

A few days later we hook up three times on a reef. Skip announces that it isn't our day and heads into the harbor. Skip talks Dave into showing us the trout stream called Sockeye Creek in Tebenkof Bay. Skip is an avid trout fisherman. We find rainbows, cut throats and Dolly Vardens in the creek. I don't like sport fishing and am more interested in a 100 year old Native summer camp. Dave tells me that in the middle 1800s, everyone died except an old grandmother and her small granddaughter. Theories are they were killed by eating poisonous clams, or they got smallpox from the white explorers.

One morning, I see several large boats cruising around outside the bay. "What are they doing, Skip?"

"They're herring seiners. That's how I first came to Alaska. I crewed on them in Prince William Sound and Washington Bay here in Southeast."

"They're really large, but you told me seiners can only have a 50-foot keel?"

"The herring seiners can be any size. There's no limit on them. They'll scoop up our feed, and then the salmon will leave," Skip worries.

I think, here is another problem with which to contend. Skip watches the boats worriedly while the *Pauline* pulls alongside.

"We're heading north to outside waters. I hear there's good fishing above Cape Spencer," Ed calls.

Skip looks at me and then out to the herring seiners. I have no idea what we should do. Finally, Skip calls, "Thanks for asking us but we'll stay here where we know the drags. See ya in the fall." We both wave. I'll miss Dorie.

The next day a westerly blows and keeps us from fishing off the flats. Skip decides we should go exploring. We invite Mary and Del MacGuire on the *Mary Ann* to go with us and have a picnic. They're older and this is their first year.

We explore Happy Cove together. It is aptly named because it is like a park with its green, grassy shores, a babbling creek and the honking of geese overhead. I was told two homes were here, but we find no evidence of them now. Only low wooded hills encircle the inlet. I spot a bald eagle in a tree and one circles overhead.

"This is a bit of paradise," Skip announces. "Look, Marilyn. There's a black bear with triplets."

They amble along the beach. When the sow starts for the trees, she calls

*Mount Ada with her twin peaks and glacier looks down on the
Jordans as they run into Gut Bay.*

the cubs. One comes slowly. She cuffs its ear.

After Skip anchors, the *Mary Ann* ties alongside *Salty*.

Mary says, "Let's launch a skiff and row along the shore. I'm afraid there
might be other bears and I don't want to go ashore."

Climbing into their skiff, we each take an oar and head along the shore.
Looking into the water I exclaim, "Look at the crabs on the bottom. Do you
think we can pew them with the pike pole?"

We row back to the boats and I take a short pike pole, which has a sharp point at its end. Holding the pole, I lean over the bow while Mary rows. When she has the bow over the crab, I stab at it. The crab slithers away into deep water.

"I missed it, Mary. Row over this way." When the crab changes direction, "No, wrong way." Sometimes when I stab a crab and bring it to the surface, it somersaults and falls back into the water. After much effort, we catch six Dungeness crab and turn them belly-up in the bottom of the skiff.

"Marilyn, look!" Mary points. "One just turned over and grabbed your pant leg."

With difficulty, I pry it loose. I don't realize how strong it is until I try to turn it back on its back—it's almost a struggling match.

"Come over here, Del and I will show ya how to do it." Skip yells.

The men are faster and have better coordination. They land ten crabs in half the time it took us. We have crab for dinner that night.

Ed's prediction is right and the fish slack off. Skip talks Del and Mary and their son-in-law, Mel, into searching for salmon in Washington Bay and along the east shore of Baranof Island.

We notice clouds of smoke coming from the herring reduction plant at Washington Bay. Skip spots the boat he worked on in 1943. He and I row ashore to visit his old skipper and the plant superintendent. This is old home week for Skip as he knows many of the crews from seining in 1943. He doesn't realize that this will be the last time he sees his skipper. The skipper will die when he is overcom from fumes when cleaning the engine with ammonia.

Soon, we are catching five kings a day on the Washington Bay drag. Then one evening Mary asks, "Are you afraid of the water? I keep thinking about the boat sinking and being dumped in that cold water."

"I don't worry. I figure Skip's been around the water enough to save me. If he doesn't, it's the chance I take. You take chances when you ride in a car or an airplane, too."

We make a circle of middle Chatham Straits. At Hoggatt Bay, named by Liet. Commander E. K. Moore of the survey steamer Patterson, for Ensign Wilford Hoggatt of his survey party, we back *Salty* near the glacier at the water's edge. The men row ashore and chop up the ice and put it in wash tubs. These they dump into their holds. We each use it to ice our fish until we unload our kings on a packer.

The twin peaks of Mount Ada look down on Gut Bay, so named because its shape resembles a human gut. I marvel at the blue of the glacier on its crown. On Gut Bay's north shore is a 50 foot sheer rock wall, where Tlingits say you can see Raven's fishnet. Lichens and small shoots of evergreen trees cling tenaciously to the smooth rocks. I see no beaches as the rock walls come to the water's edge. A narrow opening leads to a small inner harbor located on the southwest corner of the bay. We wait until high water to venture into it. It contrasts with the outside bay with its gentle beaches and many trees. Canadian honkers break the silence. We hear reports of hot mineral springs here, but we can't find them. Here is another paradise like Happy Cove.

On the drag between Gut and Hoggatt Bays, we catch a 55-pound king but the next morning we are still skunked at 10 a.m. "The kings are gone. We might as well head back to Gedney," Skip says. "Maybe more cohoes have come."

Upon our return, we find the fishing hasn't improved and perhaps is even worse. On August first, the packer comes in with the unbelievable news that President Truman re-established price controls. The fish buyers announce the coho price will be 12 cents a pound, down from 18 cents. For three days, the fishermen tie to the docks and debate what to do. Our prices for fuel and groceries remain the same.

Someone reports that prices are higher in Cross Sound, named by Captain James Cook in 1778 as May 3 was Holy Cross Day. We discover later that this price was before the roll-back.

Finally, Skip comes back to *Salty*. "We're going to Icy Straits. Irish is going to lead Hazel and Herman on the *Betty K*, Hazel's relative Lonnie Kellar on the *Ytka*, and Mary & Del McGuire on the *Mary Ann*. We'll leave in the morning."

Salty runs by the cliffs on the northside of Gut Bay. The Tlingits call this Raven's fishnet.

CHAPTER NINE

Back From The Frontier

LIKE A LITTLE ARMADA, EIGHT BOATS follow Irish Bennett up Chatham Strait. After baths at Warm Springs Bay, we wait our turn to wash clothes in the hot mineral water. Skip and many of the men help with the chore. The wash house rings with laughter.I hang our wash from lines Skip strings from the bow. *Salty* resembles a Chinese junk with clothes blowing in the wind. Walking to the boat, Skip says, "I like this camaraderie among the fishermen. Everyone is friendly."

Some of the fishermen decide to copper paint their boats. The storekeeper tells of a good trout stream at Hidden Falls Lake in Kasnyku Bay, north of here. Skip decides we'll look into it, since we have already copper painted our boat. He persuades the *Janie* to accompany us. The *Janie* is one of the boats that is named for someone actually in the crew. We'll join the others when they pass the bay the next day.

The couple living at Hidden Falls shows us their one-man saw mill, optimistically describing their dreams of supplying lumber to all who will build cabins. The falls splash 200 feet down the mountainside. While Skip and Gene fish for trout, Janie and I pick blueberries. We have more luck than the men do. When a salmon hatchery is constructed here in later years, the remains of an ancient camp site that dates back nearly 10,000 years is discovered.

The next day when the wind blows up Chatham Straits, Skip predicts the others won't head north. We run back to the Hidden Falls wharf. The weather is worse the next day, but we buck the waves to Whitestone Harbor in Icy Straits. Icy Straits got its name from the many icebergs from Glacier Bay. As we run past, I watch the shore line, admiring the red fireweed flower that contrasts sharply with the white rocks.

The next morning we run into the Tlingit village of Hoonah. I notice three rows of natural-colored two-story wood houses standing empty on the shore. I learn the government built them for the Natives after a disastrous fire two years prior.

Trout fishing.

We learn our group left there early the previous day. We must go through South Inian Pass alone. North and South Inian Passes connect Icy Straits with Cross Sound. All the tide that flows into and out of Lynn Canal and Icy Straits must go through these two narrow passes. It's less than three miles long and only three-eighths of a mile wide. South Inian is the narrower and hence has the stronger current. Many trollers have sunk in the whirlpools of this passage.

We pass by many icebergs from Glacier Bay. On this clear day, I see the spectacular snow-covered jagged peaks of the Fairweather Range. None of the island peaks compare to it. Brady Glacier at the base of the Fairweather Range looks down on us as we run toward Cross Sound. The light green glacier water makes a line where it meets the deep blue ocean water. I learn that in 1741 the Russian explorer, Alexi Chirikof, was the first white man to view the Fairweather Range. He was with Vitus Bering's expedition. The Spanish explorer, Bodega y Quadra, reached this vicinity in 1775 but had to turn back because his crew developed scurvy.

Long before we reach the eastern entrance, Skip figures out when slack water will occur. He announces, "We'll have to wait an hour and a half."

We anchor south of the pass entrance. Suddenly, Skip jumps from his bunk where he is napping. "I hear boats coming! Maybe we can follow them

Skip climbs the mountain behind Elfin Cove to take this picture of Cross Sound,
Brady Glacier and the Fairweather Mountains. Three Hill and George Island are
on the right side.

through the pass. We don't have a large-scale chart of Elfin Cove. It might be tricky to get in there." On deck, Skip shouts, "Marilyn, here comes our gang!"

Luckily we join the eight boats from our original group.

"Irish will lead us," Herman calls. "Where have you been? We looked and looked for you the last two days!"

We are fifth in the line. We feel safe following Irish. At this smooth slack water, it's hard to imagine an eight and a half knot ebb tide running through here. As all the water must flow out of Icy Straits on the ebb tide, it's stronger than the flood tide coming in from the ocean.

We swing around Point Lavinia at the western edge of the pass. Irish points ahead, "Elfin Cove. Stay behind me."

In the distance we see Cape Spencer which separates Cross Sound from the open ocean. We spot many boats inside the cove, but Irish continues on. We come to a very narrow opening with kelp growing from each side. We wonder if it's deep enough to enter but we follow Irish through it.

Elfin Cove is a small year-round village. The name comes from the boat of the fish packer, Ernie Swanson. He not only buys fish but owns a modern store that sells food, clothing and fishing gear. Ruth, his wife, is the postmistress and radio operator. George Williams and his wife buy fish and run another store. They each run an oil dock similar to those in Wrangell. This is more efficient and convenient than our pumping fuel out of drums in

Gedney Harbor.

Once we tie up we learn that the trollers are striking because 12 cents a pound doesn't even pay the bills. During the strike, I become better acquainted with many other women. Inez and Gerald Hilbert and their two children have come north with another group on their little boat. Gerald is a very large man in both height and weight. When he stands in their troller pit it comes only to his knees. I imagine him holding the boat above his head like Paul Bunyan.

One day we all dig clams at low tide. Another day we pick luscious wild strawberries in Dundas Bay where there is an abandoned cannery. In the rain, Skip and I pick five three-gallon buckets of berries in two hours. I make enough jam to last all winter. We also pick blueberries.

Finally, they settle the strike for 15 cents a pound for cohoes. At daylight the following morning the fleet streams out of the harbor. We run outside of Three Hill Island and put out our gear. I see *Salty* edging closer to Three Hill Island.

"Look at Irish in there among those rocks pulling one coho after another. If he can do it, so can we." Up come our lines and we run in beside Irish.

"I'm fishing seven fathoms and you follow me exactly. The tide can set you on the rocks if you aren't careful."

Our course resembles an S. When we come to the top of the S, we turn into deep water and start over. We catch the most fish during the last half of the flood tide. Often, every hook has a fish on it. Hearing the poles jingle makes my blood run, it is so exciting.

As long as everyone keeps in line and runs the entire course, Boomer Rock, as they call it, is not too difficult to fish. When someone only runs half the course or runs up and then back down, chaos ensues. One cocky little red-headed troller who was a navigator in the war keeps trying to take two turns to the rest of our one. This causes the fisherman he is crowding in on to turn out for him and miss the best part of the drag.

We tolerate this for a few days as we know this is his first year fishing. We think he's not doing it intentionally and will soon learn.

Irish finally goes up to him and says, "Young feller, if you crowd me once more, I'll strip you."

The next day Irish steers along Boomer Rock. The red-head comes half way in and makes a jack-knife turn right in front of Irish. By the time he turns, Irish is alongside him. Irish stands in his troller pit and acts like the other boat isn't there. I'll wager Irish had shallowed up his lines so they wouldn't drag the bottom.

"Hey, you're forcing me onto the rock," the red-head calls. Irish never shows that he hears him. Just then both the red-head's lines break on his inside poles. He has no place to go. He doesn't want to break his poles. Finally he slows down behind Irish.

He loses all four lines and all his gear.

The red-head is still mad that evening. He wants to fight Irish, an old man. Irish says he's not afraid for he's done a lot of fighting in his day. The red-head finally calms down. He seems to have learned his lesson and he takes his turn after that. All the fishermen shake Irish's hand.

The days get shorter, fall is coming. We have a good year financially, and we make many friends. Now we start to think about where we will spend the winter.

I have a chance to visit with Dorie when the *Pauline* pulls into Elfin Cove. "We found some fish, but were stormed into Lituya Bay for three days," Dorie says. "I've had enough fishing."

Lituya was originally called Frenchman's Bay because la Perouse first surveyed it in 1797 and called it Port Des Francis. On Tebenkof's charts he called Ltua. They named the glacier there La Perouse.

Ed says, "We're going inside. Want to come with us? Ernest Sound usu-

Skip paints fish spoons.

ally has cohoes that go up Bradfield Canal this time of year."

The next day we take off through Icy Straits and down Chatham Straits. Usually Ed steers a straight course. Today, the *Pauline* tacks one way and then another. He doesn't have an automatic pilot.

"Wonder what's going on over there?" Skip laughs. He reaches over to me. These men have something on their minds other than piloting their boats.

About 15 minutes later, I back into *Salty's* hot exhaust pipe. "Ouch."

We make Tyee that day and enjoy seeing familiar faces. Ed says, "The tides are right tomorrow to go through Rocky Pass. Want to follow us? It's shorter to Wrangell."

"Sure would, Ed."

The cold storage in Wrangell is short on ice, and we don't have enough if we do hit a big school of cohoes. We fish three days when the *Betty K* and the other boats that we went to Icy Straits with finally arrive. After four days of fishing, Herman calls over that they are heading for Ketchikan and then South. Alaskans always refer to the lower 48 states as South.

We bid them good-bye. Sitting there watching a half dozen boats run up and down the beach, I ask Skip, "Why don't we go South with them? We can show the boat to your folks. It'll be easier to do the many fix-up jobs down there."

"That's a good idea."

Frank is fishing in Ernest Sound. Eva, Skip's sister, is sick in Tacoma with their two children. Skip asks if Frank wants to go South with us. He says yes.

We run back to Wrangell for Frank to leave his boat there and for us to get our extra items out of storage. We bid the Wellesleys goodbye.

In Ketchikan, we find that the gang heading south left two days ago. The first night we anchor in Kah Shakes Cove, which was the site of a Native summer camp. We're on the Alaska side of Dixon Entrance. The next day is beautiful. Frank relieves Skip at the wheel. They decide to run all night and all the next day.

At dusk, we pull into the Canadian Indian village of Bella Bella. Joyfully, we see the *Betty K* and the rest of our friends. After that we stay with them to Puget Sound. They leave us for their home in Bremerton, and we head for Tacoma.

Seeing the lights of Tacoma, I say to Skip, "It's been a great year. Alaska's better than I expected. We've made a living, seen lots of beautiful country, and made many friends. Importantly, we've learned to live together on a 30-foot boat."

"I'm so happy that ya like it," he says as he kisses me. "You're a good scout even when everything doesn't go smoothly."

"That's part of the turf. I can't be a partner without taking the bitter with the better."

For Christmas, we take the train back to Iowa to see my family. We even get to visit my friends in Illinois. We tell everyone about Alaska and salmon fishing. We feel Alaska is the Great Land for us.

Skip's sister Eva remains hospitalized. She may have had a nervous breakdown. Living on a remote island with a baby and a toddler had been rough on her. Mother Jordan, Inga, takes care of one-year-old Ellen. Little Chris is placed temporarily with a foster family.

We rent a one-room apartment with cooking facilities, in Tacoma. One evening we invite Gordon Rahn, a former high school classmate of mine, and his wife, Caroline, for dinner. Gordon is taking his medical internship at the University of Washington in Seattle. We proudly show them *Salty* and describe our lives in Southeast Alaska.

CHAPTER TEN

$\mathcal{A}$ New Homesite Cabin

AS SOON AS THE DAYS START to become longer in January, a fisherman's pulse quickens, and Skip is no exception. He spends every moment working on *Salty* and the gear. On the bow he puts a hand capstan, a vertical rotating drum, for pulling up the anchor. The fishermen also pour their own lead sinkers. We have a cabinet made for the galley with drawers for my linen, silverware and pots and pans. Its top provides me with a work place to prepare meals which makes cooking so much easier. This is much nicer than sitting down at the little table.

Hazel on the *Betty K* informs us that eight boats will head north from Bremerton on April first. We decide to go with them.

Two weeks before we're to leave, I get a pain in my side that will not go away. The doctor informs me he must remove my appendix.

When Skip takes me to the hospital, he slowly states, "When ya've been married as long as we have, a man usually takes his wife to the hospital for something besides an appendix."

"Too bad, no baby." I grin.

I have to stay in bed for five days after the operation which makes the day we are supposed to leave for Bremerton the first day the doctor allows me out of bed. There is so much to do to get ready for the voyage north. I give Skip a list of food to buy and clothes to pack, hoping that nothing is forgotten.

The next morning we make quite a sight with eight fishing boats following Herman under the Bremerton bridge. When we arrive at Friday Harbor, two boats have to turn back with engine trouble. This makes our little flotilla even smaller, but we are still quite a sight. Ernie Kimball and his son, Ernie, are the last boat on this blustery day. Later Ernie tells us that when they looked back at Alert Bay they saw a steamer coming straight for them. They turned starboard toward Alert Bay to stay out of its way. It continued for them and appeared to go into Alert Bay. They changed their course to the port and open water. Ernie later tells us, "The steamer kept coming. We were sure it was going to hit us. We started looking for our life preservers. We were ready to abandon ship. I've never been so scared."

Someone said, "Even if you have the right of way, who wants to argue with a steamer?" Though I do remember one guy who did argue with a steamer. An old timer who was always rowing from Pennock Island to Ketchikan had the right of way and never looked right or left. One day the *Prince George*, a sleek Canadian passenger ship, was coming into Ketchikan. It blew its whistle at him, but he paid no attention. The captain had to send two crew members up on the bow to look where the rower was. The captain slowed the engine. It finally passed within 50 feet.

After a week we arrive in Alaska to find all the trollers striking for higher fish prices. We thought we would earn money as soon as we arrived like we did the previous year. We earned our last income in September and spent a great deal of it re-rigging *Salty*. Because of my operation, we're now very short of cash.

After sitting in harbor for two weeks, Skip figures a way to use our trolling lines to put out a skate of halibut gear. He lets it lie on the bottom for five or six hours and then pulls it in with the gurdy. We make $50 from the halibut.

One day we visit the Wellesleys. Dorie happily tells me they are expecting their first child in May.

Ed says, "That's what happens when you're stormed in three days at Lituya."

"I'm staying home this year," Dorie announces. I will miss her on the halibut grounds. In May they have a little boy they name Charlie.

Skip and I, seeing how happy they are, decide to have a baby and quit using birth control.

While we wait in Wrangell for the strike's settlement, Skip learns that the Forest Ranger from Petersburg is in town. He talks the MacGuires and their daughter and son-in-law into looking over available homesites on the Island. We all ride out to the homesites with the ranger. He shows us many places that have no electricity. We talk to Hank Wells, who has a small sawmill out there. He assures us that they'll put electricity out there in about a year.

Three homesites nearer to town have been turned back to the Forest Service. Two of them are next to each other and one already has a house on it. These all have electric and telephone lines.

Skip says to Delbert, "Why don't you two take the two together, and we'll take the third one?" Delbert isn't too sure. He wants to think about it.

Skip tells the Forest Ranger that we'll sign up for ours right now. When Skip makes up his mind, he doesn't waste time thinking about it. MacGuires and their daughter and son-in-law finally sign up for theirs.

Skip looks over our homesite with its fallen trees and brush.

We fish more halibut until they settle the strike. Skip is more confident this year although he still doesn't like to run long distances alone. He feels if one boat has trouble, those on the other boat can help. He finds someone to run to Tyee and then Tebenkof with us. Now we'll catch the kings and cohoes. This year, though, no feed shows up on the Tebenkof flats.

The first of August, we head north again. The fish we catch in Cross Sound save the season for us. Many fishermen gross less than $1000. Fortunately, we make as much as we did the previous year, though we were hoping for more. Delbert kids Skip that if he falls in a sewer, he'll come up with a king salmon in each hand. Already Skip is building a reputation as a good fisherman.

In the fall, we have enough money to build on our land. We find it full of windfalls and a jungle of blueberry brush and trees. Skip spends three weeks clearing the bushes by hand just to have enough room to build the house. Since we can't afford a chain saw, he uses a cross cut saw to cut the trees. He has to strip the bark from each tree and cut it by hand. It's a lot of work. We live on *Salty* while he builds. He buys a bicycle to ride the four miles from the harbor to our homesite. We plan a 12-by-16 foot cabin. Skip hires another man to help him build. They build the cabin totally from scratch. No architect, no building plans. They put the heavy paper on the outside. They put caneite, a particle board made of cane, on the inside walls. Skip comes home each night exhausted but fulfilled. We're like pioneers. I'm very proud of him.

In letters, some of my friends from the Midwest ask me about how rough living in the Alaska wilds is. Frankly I don't think it's too bad. We have power

Marilyn goes hunting with Skip.

and a road, and the school bus even goes by. This is the life I choose.

We move into the cabin on Halloween. We have a shiplap floor. We buy a good bed, a little wood cook stove and a wood space heater. Then we purchase a sink, a used cabinet, a card table and a set of folding chairs. I remember that eggs and oranges come in wooden boxes and ask the grocer to save some for me. I stack one on top of the other horizontally and some vertically. In these, I keep my canned goods, flour, sugar and other staples. I use a friend's sewing machine to make curtains for the egg crates. MacGuires sell us a cardboard closet they sent for and don't use. We buy a dresser from a neighbor who's a cabinet maker.

Since we have a view, Skip wants a big window to look out on Woronkofski Island and the water. In front of the window, we put our table. We enjoy eating breakfast and watching the ducks swim south in the morning and back in the evening. I'll always remember the moonlight on the snow-covered peak of Woronkofski Island across the straits. We have a big attic that we climb into from a ladder on the outside of the house. We store everything in the attic that we don't have room for downstairs. This includes fishing gear and clothes.

We dam a small creek above the house for water. I have to carry our drinking and wash water with a bucket. The following year we will buy a hand pump that will make my work much easier. Another modern luxury we do not have is a toilet. I haven't had to use an out-house since my family left the Iowa farm back in the 1930s. Skip builds it over the creek south of the cabin.

The first week in November, Irish comes to Skip while he's pumping out *Salty*. "What we need is some good venison. Why don't a group of us go out one of these days? I know a place where I'm sure we can all get two or three deer apiece."

We only can afford a crosscut saw to cut the trees into firewood.

"We need some meat for sure. That sounds fine with me. I'll see if Delbert wants to go. John on the *Carol Ann* said something to me the other day about going out. Why don't we take *Salty* and the *Carol Ann*?" They plan to leave early in the afternoon for Roosevelt Harbor on Zarembo Island to the west of Wrangell.

Irish says, "If we get storm bound for a week this time of year, we'll need lots of grub. I'll go up town and buy more." Skip watches Irish leave, wondering if this is more a boy's outing than an actual hunting trip. Since it's a place Skip has never been, he worries that it will be dark before they anchor. Both Delbert and Irish go with Skip while John is alone on the *Carol Ann*. On the way across the sound Irish drinks half a bottle of whiskey and is as happy as a lark.

"I've been here 1000 times," he slurs to Skip. "You think you'd anchor way out here, but you don't. You go way in at the mouth of the creek. There's the tree I've tied my herring net to a hundred times."

Skip wishes Delbert or John knew this anchorage instead of just Irish. Irish can hardly stand up straight let alone know where he is after drinking all that whiskey. Not knowing what else to do, Skip follows Irish's directions. Del crawls onto *Salty's* bow to watch for the bottom. The shadows are long and it's hard for him to see anything, but he's willing to try.

Suddenly Del shouts, "Bottom, bottom! Back up."

Bob Rooney and Skip trap at Jadeski Cove.

Skip throws *Salty* in reverse. Bump, bump. Skip takes her out of gear, realizing that he has run her aground. Behind them, John has time to put the *Carol Ann* in reverse and back out. Skip softly curses under his breath. Del stands up on the bow, shaking his head. Irish droops in the corner. The tide is dropping fast and soon *Salty* is lying on her side. Skip climbs out on the tide flats and yells at Del and Irish to help him prop her up with whatever driftwood they can find. The last thing he wants is for *Salty* to be totally on her side. Back aboard *Salty*, everything is in chaos. Nothing was made to lay at a 90-degree angle and everything has fallen out of the cabinets. Skip pushes things aside and tries to keep some composure.

"I can't understand this. How can it be shallow here?" Irish keeps mumbling.

Del finally manages to talk Skip into leaving *Salty* and going down to the *Carol Ann* to warm up and get something to eat. "There is nothing more you can do right now. We must wait for the tide to see if she will float."

It's a long walk down the beach. John has rowed his skiff in to pick them up. Irish is starting to sober up and can't believe what has happened.

When trapping is over, the Jordans winter fish around Brownson Island.

Skip goes back to *Salty* a little after midnight. He's in a quandary: will *Salty* rise with the tide? He doesn't have any insurance. What if he loses the

The Robert Rooney family in December of 1947 with their new baby, Robby
From left to right: Marilyn, Janice, Buck, Kathleen, Bob, Robby, and Betty.

means of earning a living? Sometimes boats will swamp and fill with water instead of righting themselves and floating. This would ruin the engine. Skip pounds down the troller pit hatch and the fish hold hatch, tightens all the ports, and fastens the skylight.

Del and Irish come back about 2 a.m. They figure *Salty* will float about 3 a.m. Even though it's dangerous, Skip chooses to stay aboard *Salty* while the others watch from the beach. If he could, he would physically pick *Salty* up and make her float, but all he can do is feel helpless. Her fate is in God's hands now. He puts a peg in the door to keep it shut in case it floods. If she doesn't rise, he'll have to get out quickly. He puts on a life-preserver. Del and John have the skiff ready to pick him up if he needs to abandon her.

Slowly the tide comes in. He anxiously watches through the pilothouse window even though it's still dark. Maybe by sheer determination of will he can make her float. He feels her shift. He cannot breathe, for this is the moment when *Salty* will either float or lay over. Suddenly, *Salty* rights herself. He slowly draws in his breath and says a silent thank you to God. He hears the guys cheering as he starts the engine and backs *Salty* off the flats. He ties her to the *Carol Ann* and waits for the men to row out to her. They all try to get a little sleep.

The next morning they decide to hunt in two groups with Del going with Skip and Irish with John. Del and Skip head south. They don't see anything and start back at noon. They come out on a bluff and look down on a wannegan, a float house.

"Where do you think we are?" Skip asks Del.

"You got me."

Skip starts calling. At last a woman comes out of the wannigan. "Where are we?"

"Roosevelt Harbor."

"Are there two trollers anchored in the mouth of the bay?"

"I don't see anything," the woman shouts back.

"What do you make of it, Del?"

"They can't have drifted away, can they?"

"The way this trip is going, anything can happen."

"Maybe the boats are in Deep Cove," the woman shouts back. "I think a couple of boats went in there last evening. It is right on the other side of the spit you're on."

"That's it! Irish got his bays mixed up. No wonder we went high and dry."

When they get back to the boats, they ask Irish if that is the tree up ahead where he hung his herring net a hundred times. He knows something is up, but he says it is.

"We think this is Deep Cove, not Roosevelt Harbor."

They laugh at Irish's mistake. He never admits he was wrong. They only get one deer and return the next day. Del and Mary end up eating those groceries all winter.

We enjoy our little cabin even if we don't have much money. A mile down the road is Wrangell Institute. The superintendent asks me if I want to work there.

I ask Skip and his reply is typical: "I make the living in this family. You just be my little wife."

This angers me because I want to help earn the money. I don't argue with him even though my working would enable us to buy more items for the house. If that is the way he wants it, I will do what he tells me. I blame his attitude on his Norwegian heritage where the man makes the living and the woman works at home. I guess being a part of the fishing business is a good compromise.

Skip and I meet Bob and Betty Rooney who with their three children arrived in Alaska the previous spring. The sawmill has closed and these new-comers are having a difficult time finding work. Skip and Bob decide to go trapping. Irish tells them that Jadski Cove south of Burnett Inlet is a good place. In Southeast Alaska you sit in an area and claim it for your trap line. The season doesn't open until mid December, but the men head out the week before Thanksgiving to scout it out.

Betty is due to have a baby in December. I stay in town with her and their three children. On Dec. 11, Betty announces, "I better go to the hospital."

I and her friend Tana (short for Montana) Piatt walk with her to Bishop Rowe Hospital, perched high on the hill overlooking the harbor. We are allowed to sit in the delivery room with her. This is a new experience for me. She is very courageous and takes the labor pains in stride. Helping Betty makes me unafraid of childbirth. Finally they roll her into the operating room, where no one but the doctor is allowed.

We're all happy when they have a boy. This is the second one. While Betty is in the hospital, I take care of the three older Rooney children. Bob and Skip arrive the next day. They name the baby Robert. The men only stay one day in town as the trapping season opens on December 15.

While in town, I join the Presbyterian Church Choir. We practice often for the Christmas program. The Presbyterian minister's wife, Roma Crowell, takes me to Mrs. Person's home. She makes sealskin moccasins. When I buy some for my family, I set a tradition which I repeat each year we live in Wrangell. Mrs. Persons is such a dear person, I enjoy just visiting with her. Her children are Soboleffs, which are leaders in the Southeast Native communities.

The Presbyterian Christmas program combines the children's program with the choir's special music. Both the white women's Aid Society and the native women's Missionary Society help with the program. I'm suddenly in the Christmas mood. I buy small gifts for the Rooney children. After our building expenses, we don't have much money left. With the local sawmill shut down, Wrangell's economy is tight. We hope the men are having good luck trapping.

On the afternoon before Christmas, Betty and I look out her big front window, which faces the harbor.

"Wouldn't it be great if *Salty* came around the breakwater," I say. Later, we're preparing dinner when I hear a knock on the door. It will no doubt be the neighbor children coming to play.

I open the door. "Skip! Bob!" Betty runs over and we throw our arms around our husbands and kiss them.

"We wanted to come in for Christmas," Skip explains. "We can't let both of you spend your first Christmas in Alaska alone."

Bob's children, Kathy, Buck and Janice, joyously run to him. Having them home for Christmas is the best present either of us could have.

We're so busy on our cabin that I don't see the Wellesleys as much as I want. They invite us to Christmas dinner. Dorie has made a 24-hour fruit salad. I obtain the recipe and plan to start a tradition for our family.

At Christmas time the men think they've done well trapping with 29 mink. When the men return, they only trapped five more mink. Later they hear that two fellows have illegally pit-lighted the mink. With bright lights, they can see the mink's eyes and shoot them. This happened when the men came to town for Christmas. Skip and Bob work hard in cold, miserable weather for only 34 mink. Skip has found a way for me to go along. He talks our friends, Hank and Sue Barrow who have left Wrangell Institute, into taking their cruiser, *Harlequin,* with me aboard down to Jadski Cove.

We celebrate the 1948 New Year on the *Harlequin.* Suddenly, a loud shot rings through the clear air.

"What is it?" we exclaim. It sounds so loud, for a minute we can't identify it. No one is within 50 miles of us. Skip bounds into the cabin shouting, "Happy New Year!" We all kiss each other and then we discover it was Skip shooting his rifle. We pray 1948 will be a good year.

After the trapping season is over in February, we winter fish in Ernest Sound and Union Bay, where we fished the first year. We make a little more than our expenses. That time of year, we fish at least 50 fathoms, for the salmon are in deep water. I must remember not to turn sharply because the bow and main lines will tangle at that depth. We average five kings a day.

We often go into Niblack Island where old Albert Carlson lives. He and his partner, now dead, came to Alaska in the early 1900s to start a mink ranch.

That time of year, we have short fishing days and long evenings. After Skip ices our fish, we climb the ramp to Albert's little house. Albert makes home brew beer, which he insists we drink. Usually six to eight of us are there. Albert plays the concertina, Ed Loftus the guitar, and we all sing. We look forward to these get-togethers.

In March, we return to Wrangell to ready *Salty* for the new fishing season.

Eva, Skip's sister, and their two children, Chris and Ellen, return to Petersburg to live with Frank. Skip's parents come to visit and bring Skip's daughter, Dawn, with them. She's a beautiful blonde ten-year-old. She's in third grade and starts school in Wrangell. She and I get along well. I enjoy helping her with her school work.

Halibut fishing opens and Skip, his dad and I go out to try our luck. The Tyee Cold Storage pays us 17 cents a pound for medium halibut. We always need money at the beginning of the salmon season and the $1000 we make clears our bills from rigging the boat and other miscellaneous items.

We take Skip's dad back to Petersburg. We stand on the dock and wave good-bye to Skip's folks and Dawn when they leave for Tacoma on the steamer.

Ed tells us many times that our biggest mistake was going to Tebenkof last year. According to him, it's a starvation hole. We know Tebenkof, though, and head back there after the Fourth of July, but trollers aren't catching anything. We head north early to what we hope is better fishing. We trade our little skiff to Paul Binkley for his 12 foot skiff for the summer. We tow it for safety.

Arriving at Elfin Cove, we find the fleet has gone to Dixon Harbor around Cape Spencer. Bravely, we set *Salty's* course around the Cape and out into the Gulf of Alaska. We are no longer in Southeast Alaska.

In Tebenkof, we were one of the highliners. Up here we're only average and Skip's morale suffers a real blow. Perhaps life is like this, I think. If you're riding the wave as one of the top ones, you work harder to maintain that reputation. If you're one of the also rans, you don't put out your best effort.

After a good day, we arise with great expectations. From Graves Harbor we head northwest for Icy Point. Skip looks over the situation. "Let's put in our gear outside of Graves' Rocks. I don't like the looks of that thick fog to the south of us. I hate to get caught out here in that. I hear that it often doesn't lift even at night."

The cohoes are biting fast and furiously, but an hour later he calls, "Marilyn, you steer. That fog is closing in like I said."

We no more than anchor when the fog sets down so thick that we can't see the side of the bay. Only three boats anchor in Graves Harbor that morning. True to Skip's prediction, the fog never lifts. As evening approaches, a boat slowly emerges from the fog. A few boats have depth sounders, but the price is too high for most. Even with them, the fog is dangerous. In the fog a seagull looks twice its normal size. A rock you've fished around for months appears different when you can't see the hills behind it. In the fog, you can be on top of that rock before you see it. Enviously, we watch the boats unload. One calls over that he has $300 worth of fish that day. I admit that I am sad that we haven't fished.

When we turn on our radiophone the next morning we hear tragedy struck on the fishing grounds at Dixon Harbor. The *Emla* had such good fishing that it stayed out until dark hoping the fog would lift. A woman on the *Emla* stood on the bow looking for the harbor's entrance. Suddenly, with a big bump, the *Emla* hit a rock. The woman catapulted over the bow into the water. Her husband, without thinking, dove into the icy water after her. The boat following them pulled the wife out of the water. The man apparently suffered a heart attack and died before they could pull him aboard. They tried artificial respiration, but they couldn't revive him. The true irony of the tragedy is that the boat was not damaged.

Fog scares me more than rough water because we seldom fish far from a good harbor. I want to steer far from shore into deep water, but Skip always looks for a safe harbor. The night the man was lost, friends lay off shore in their boat all night. They wouldn't take any chances of not finding the harbor.

We call Del and Mary on the *Mary Ann* with our radiophone. With our code Skip tries to persuade them to come up here. They won't come. They neglect to tell us that many fish have come into Tebenkof and they are doing well there. When we find this out, we feel bad. We've helped Del many times. Hard feelings are generated when one fisherman calls in another on the fish and the action isn't reciprocated.

We fish Three Hill Island and Boomer Rock in August. We have a good season. Before we know it, September is here. Eagerly, we head back to Wrangell and our cabin in the wilderness. We figure we now have enough money to build two more rooms.

CHAPTER ELEVEN
Forty-Two Months For A Baby

SOON AFTER WE MOVE FROM SALTY into our cabin, Eva becomes very depressed. She flies South with her daughter, Ellen. They hospitalize her for an extended period. Frank asks us if their four-year-old son, Chris, can live with us. We happily agree. Chris is a cheerful, well-behaved little boy. Skip and I love him. We call him Little Chris because his grandfather is Big Kris.

We still think about having a family. We have been married for almost three years. By chance we meet Dr. John Bangeman, Wrangell's only doctor, and his wife the day they arrive. He forever endears himself to us by asking if we are the Jordans he read about. The previous year I'd written six articles for the *Alaskan Sportsman* on our experiences. Skip suggests that we both go to Dr. Bangeman and see why I can't get pregnant. After thorough examinations, Dr. Bangeman recommends a procedure to pump air into my fallopian tubes.

During this time, Skip undertakes to burn out a stump in our yard. He keeps a fire burning in it constantly. Occasionally, I help him. Little Chris loves pilling sticks on the fire. Usually the guys only come into the house for meals.

One afternoon, as I'm making dessert for dinner, I hear Skip's steps outside. Surprised, I look up. Skip is all bent over and holds little Chris's hand.

"What is it, Skip?" I cry, running to him. I help him

Little Chris Johnson rides Dolly, whom Marilyn rode as a child, during a rare visit to Uncle Russell Willer's farm in Iowa.

Little Chris Johnson helps Uncle Skip clear the brush at the Zimovia Straits cabin.

climb the steps.

"I lifted a log wrong. The disk went out in my back. Help me into bed."

This is one of the worse times he has with his back. He wears his brace and is in a lot of pain whenever he moves. At the end of the first week, he has improved little.

Our supply of wood is getting lower and lower. He tells me to see if Ed and Bob will cut us wood with their chain saw. We'll pay them for it. In a half day, they cut enough wood for three weeks. Then they won't let me pay for it.

One day I say to Skip, "Why don't we go South for the holidays and visit both our folks? You can't clear any more land this winter. We'll get back the middle of February in time to get ready for another season."

Skip seldom says no to me. He agrees. Little Chris goes with us on the *Princess Norah* on December 17. Little Chris is fun to travel with as he enjoys the scenery and people. He's reunited with his two-year old sister, Ellen, who now lives with Skip's parents. He visits his mother at the hospital. We have Dawn with us on weekends.

We take Chris with us on the train to Iowa to visit my family. We visit my Grandma and Grandpa Deardorff in Tipton. They enjoy Chris as he is the closest they have to a great grandchild. On their farm we visit Uncle Russ and Aunt Dort. When Chris rides their pony, Dolly, I remember riding her in my childhood. We also visit Aunt Margery, who is taking care of Great

Aunt Lily. I think Aunt Margery enjoys Skip as she did before we were married. By the middle of January, I know I'm pregnant. Everyone is excited—including my parents, as this will be their first grandchild.

Skip tells friends, "I'm flat on my back. Can't even move. Defenseless, I tell ya."

Upon our return to Alaska, Skip finds dry rot on *Salty's bow*. He puts her in the shipyard in April. A boat in a shipyard reminds me of time clocks ringing up the dollars. Three days costs $500. We have the most bills we've ever had as we start the season. We pray for a good year.

I have an easy pregnancy and gain little weight. At halibut time, we have a dilemma. Should I go with Skip? If I do, what will we do with Little Chris?

"I always feel better when I can keep my eye on ya," Skip remarks. "Why don't ya go halibut fishing and then I'll bring ya home the middle of June. That'll be the first of the seventh month. But I don't think it's fair to keep an active boy on a small boat."

I quickly agree. I hate missing any of the fishing, but at least having the excitement of halibut fishing makes it easier. I also think Skip's right about Little Chris. I ask a girl friend to take care of him for a few weeks. While we are gone, Frank finds some one else to care for Little Chris. I'm so sad and really miss him. He'd been a part of our family although we knew it was only a temporary arrangement. Frank had only paid us for one month of the child support that he promised us and we wonder if this is why he took Chris.

We do well on halibut. After the halibut season closes, we find kings in Saginaw Bay, named for Meade's ship that shelled the Kake Native villages. We bring the kings into Wrangell on the 10th of June.

Skip hires a teenager, Shirley Ronning, to live with me. As Skip thinks he can fish longer hours, he hires a young man to fish with him. He pays him 20% of the gross.

A group of trollers, including Del on the *Mary Ann* and Emil Niemeyer on the *Sidney*, all head for Kalinin Bay. They have good fishing there but low prices. We're paid only 12 cents a pound for cohoes and 1946 king prices. With increased expenses, we are squeezed to make a profit.

Skip works hard, and he does better than most of our group. One day he finds the kings off of Gilmer Bay, named for William Gilmer who served on the *Patterson* under Lieut. Commander E. Moore. Skip's plugs are "hot" that day and he out fishes our friends. Soon after the Fourth of July, one of our friends calls him on the radio and says in code that Dixon Harbor fishing is good. He heads there.

Skip writes me long letters and tries to include me in all the happenings. It isn't like being together, though, and I miss the action.

"The fellow is doing all right, but he isn't you, honey."

Skip sees they aren't catching enough fish to keep

The cabin that Skip built on the homesite on Zimovia Straits near Wrangell.

them both busy. They part on good terms in time for the man to go seining.

At the end of July, Skip needs to make more money for me and the baby we'll soon have. He pulls his gear at Cross Sound and runs to Tebenkof where he arrives on July 30. He has 20 days of average fishing but it adds up.

Our baby is due August 12, but I'm still at home on the 14th. I hear Skip talking on his radiophone when he runs through Rocky Pass.

I'm so happy when he says, "Marilyn writes that she and Dr. Bangeman can take care of everything. But I think I better go home. Women need men around at times like this. None of her family will be there." We hadn't planned this pregnancy around the fishing season.

A big fish run develops in August with Wrangell in the middle of it. Writing a column for the *Pacific Fisherman's News*, I describe this unexpected run. One seiner's set at Anan Creek in Ernest Sound nets him $20,000. As his boat isn't big enough to hold that many fish, he shares them with two other boats. The Tlingit legends tell of the great salmon runs at Anan Creek.

Wrangell's a very busy place. Everyone talks about fish. The full tenders bring fish from the traps. Seine boat skippers put on larger crews to fish longer hours, and the canneries need more workers. The crews work 16 to 20 hours a day to put the fish into the cans before they spoil. The stores sell more supplies to the crews. In the days before oil wells and pulp mills, Alaska has only a fish based economy.

I had only heard tales of Alaskan life when a phenomenal run of salmon hits. This particular run won't be exceeded for 35 years.

Before the coming of the white man, the Alaskan Native's calendar only had ten months. When the salmon are running, August to October is one month. I decide their idea has merit.

Everyone works. If I wasn't very, very pregnant, I, too, would be working. When Skip arrives in town, they want him to work immediately. He insists on spending the first night at home.

The next day he reports for work as a mechanic on what was called the "iron chink", a machine that replaced the Chinese who originally cleaned the fish. Skip works around the clock. Some nights he sleeps four hours in the cannery loft and other times he sleeps on *Salty*. He might as well be fishing, as much as I see of him. But at least I know I can get him whenever I need him.

The tenders, power scows and barges come deck loaded into the canneries. As they land salmon in every port, each town competes to ship their fish. The steamers take the canned salmon South as fast as they can, but there aren't enough freighters. The cannery stores cases of canned salmon everywhere. They fill the Fire Hall, and park the fire engine in the street. The only storage place left in Wrangell is the basement of the hospital, which is half full. Where next to store cans?

Dr. Bangeman wants to go see his dying father down South but he is waiting for me to have my baby. On September second, the baby shows no sign of coming.

He examines me closely and says thoughtfully, "It's very small. I hope it weighs six pounds. With your first baby, I can't leave you here with no doctor."

I go to the cannery and tell Skip. He informs the foreman that he must go home that night. To start labor pains, I take castor oil. The pains start soon after midnight. At 3 a.m., Skip calls the taxi and takes me to the hospital.

At 9 a.m., Dr. Bangeman asks Skip, "Do you mind if I X-ray her? It might be a breach baby."

Skip says, "That's okay with me. I was a breach baby myself."

The doctor finds the head is in the correct position, but the baby is larger than expected.

Skip stays with me until they roll me into the delivery room. At noon, I have a seven pound 15 ounce boy. As I'm interested, Dr. Bangeman explains how the baby lay before being born and the miracle of birth.

Suddenly, he instructs the nurse, "Run out and tell the father. We forgot him."

Later, Skip enjoys telling how he hears the baby cry, and then it is 15 minutes before anyone tells him anything. He glues his ear to the door trying to hear through the physiology lesson whether he has a daughter or a son. How proud he is to have a son! After debating about names like Trygve, Sigrud, Olaf, and Lloyd, we finally decide on Eric.

The Episcopalian minister's wife, Margaret Hall, comes in the next day and gives birth to a little girl, Susan. Our babies are the only babies in the hospital. Even though we have private rooms, we become well acquainted. Father Hall is longshoring (loading freighters). He explains that even though the church expects him to give them his outside wages, he gladly helps.

Skip brings me home from the hospital five days later. He says, "Work is over at the cannery now that they closed the seining. We need more money. There's a good price on dogfish livers and I hear Nore's Fur Farm will buy the carcasses. Someone says you can catch them with a net so I bought a net from a fellow for $150."

"Gosh, Skip, $150 is all you made at the cannery these two weeks. Are you sure you can catch them?"

"Yes, I'm sure. I'm a hard worker."

He brings the net home. He finds that he should have investigated the business more thoroughly. He must send the livers on consignment South. You don't know what you'll get after you pay the freight. Nore's fur farm has more scraps from the cannery than they need. They say the dogfish are too rich for the mink.

Luckily, Eric is my first baby for he takes much of my time in the cabin. He awakens and nurses for ten minutes. Then he promptly falls back to sleep for two hours. Then he wants to eat again. Nothing I try keeps him awake for 20 minutes. Every time I start a job, he wants to eat again. I finally give him water or orange juice every two hours.

I buy a combination bath and changing table, which makes life easier. I lay him on it to change his diapers. Washing becomes a greater problem with a baby. From Sears, I order an apartment size washer that is a round tub about the size of a pressure canner. It has an agitator and a hand wringer. I heat water on either the kerosene or wood stove. I keep forgetting to put wood in the wood stove. I'll find only a few coals which will take hours to get hot again. I learned at college to boil all the diapers and rinse them in three waters. Conscientiously, I do this even if it kills me.

When Skip installs a pump, I happily pump water into the sink or tea-kettle. What a difference it makes not carrying water from our spring.

Two weeks after Eric's birth, friends stop by on their way South. They fished Dixon and had a good season.

"It was too bad that Skip left there so soon," they say, "The fish came in August." Their visit upsets me.

I know we only have $500 left after we pay the bills. I cry to myself. Why, Skip, can't you make more? How will we get through the winter? Where will the money come from for our addition? We need lumber, roofing, and materials for the walls. Prices for food and clothing keep climbing. We have no money for Christmas. What will happen to us?

When Skip walks in from riding his bicycle home from town, our friends are gone and I'm in bed. "Marilyn, what is wrong?"

"I don't feel good."

He takes my temperature. It is 102. Skip calls the doctor who is filling in for Dr. Bangeman. He and the health nurse immediately drive out. They worry about infection. They bundle me up and take me and Eric to the hospital. Because of my fever, the doctor wants to dry up my milk fearing it may make Eric sick. I want to keep nursing my baby. The health nurse and Skip argue in my behalf. The doctor agrees if I will stop nursing until my temperature drops. We don't know what caused my temperature, but after 24 hours, it's back to normal.

Lying in the hospital, I have time to think. By getting upset, I only made matters worse, for now we have hospital and doctor bills. No amount of worry will put money in our pockets. If Skip had stayed at Dixon, he might not have caught more fish than he did in Tebenkof. These friends know Dixon better than he does. They might not have made more than Skip did. They have less expenses as their family is grown, and they have their home and boat paid for. We still make boat payments and pay child support for Dawn every month.

I ask myself, "Where, Marilyn, is your faith? The good Lord will take care of you as he does the lilies in the field. You wish to be a good mother, and you've a wonderful husband. Now quit this nonsense." I determine to keep a firm hold on my emotions and "not fall to pieces" as my father would say.

I discover some truths about fishermen. At the end of the season when they're ashore, few admit that they have a poor season. This reflects on their ability as a fisherman. Of course, they always like to make more, but when talking to others, they say they have an all right year. Second, they never say exactly how much they make. What might be an average year for us, might be a good year for them. What might be a poor season for us, might be an average year for them. Unless I know what each fisherman terms a good or poor season, I have no basis for judgment.

Skip says, "Fishing is the biggest gamble there is."

I find this uncertainty is the price we pay to be independent business people on the frontier.

CHAPTER TWELVE
The Baby Salt

FROM BIRTH, ERIC KNOWS WHAT HE WANTS as soon as he awakens. He responds at three months to my talking to him with sounds of his own. His big brown eyes follow me around the tiny cabin.

The new addition to the cabin must be done by the time the snow flies. Skip and I draw many house plans until we settle on one we like. We'll add two rooms now that eventually will be the utility room-workshop and bath. The third addition will be the living room, kitchen and bedrooms but we won't do that until next fall. With friend Delbert's help, we plan how the roof will fit on the third section. We end up wasting a lot of space because the roof has to be slanted to accommodate our amount of snow.

With the delivery of a load of lumber, we start building. Skip works from sun up till late at night.

The first week in October, Dan Bates, the Fish and Wildlife agent, offers Skip a ten-day job checking the seiners at Port Camden. Skip jumps at the chance, because we need the money and he loves to do anything involved with fishing.

He cuts lots of wood and then hides the ax. "I won't sleep nights if I think ya might be chopping wood," he explains. "I see ya chopping off a foot. Ya can handle cooking related tools, but when it comes to anything else...."

I never complain about his hiding the ax. I know a woman

Skip adds an addition to the cabin.

The Jordans

whose husband showed her the wood pile and ax and expects her to use it.

A new friend, Gene Fisher, accompanies Skip. Now that we will have a little money, I happily order our Christmas presents from a catalog. One night I hear the wind blowing harder than usual through the nearby trees. The weather sounds bad but Eric and I feel cozy and safe in our little cabin.

When Skip returns, he says, "I never spent such a night as I did during that storm. I imagined that big spruce tree that is growing on top of that windfall behind the house toppling on ya. I'm going to chop that tree down right now. Gene's gonna help me build a scaffold. I won't spend another night worrying like that."

After working three days, they topple the 100-foot tree away from the house The wood provides us heat all winter.

Skip busily builds our addition. Eric soon learns that when the hammering stops his daddy will soon come into the room. We spend much time talking to him. For Christmas we cut a little two foot tree from our yard. The lights on it fascinate Eric. We set the tree on a little table in the corner.

Eric always watches our kitty, Frisky, walk around the cabin. Frisky is black with four white boots and a white circle of fur under her chin. When Eric is in his jumper that hangs from the doorway, he tries to reach her. His first word is not mama or dada, but "kee" for his beloved kitty.

On January 19, Skip saws the door from the new addition into the cabin and kisses me through the hole. I worry that with the temperature in the 20s, the nails will freeze to his fingers, but he works on.

The new rooms gives added ventilation. With more space the air can circulate and the icicles are gone from under the bed. In the morning my feet don't freeze on the floor because Skip put in a sub-floor with an air space between the sub-floor and floor. Skip has difficulty doing the finishing work. He measures and saws the board to fit, but it's either too long or too short.

Nothing is ever quite right.

Skip proudly tells friends, "Marilyn said she'd live in a house if I'd build it. I know more about engines than carpentry, but I did it."

In February, we discover that I'm pregnant again. Skip takes it philosophi-

Eric in the bird cage

cally, "We wanted a family, didn't we? Why should we prolong it?"

Dr. Bangeman laughs, "First she complains that she can't get pregnant, so I pumped air into her tubes. Now she's complaining because she is."

I resolve not to worry. I'll drift with the tide and let Skip make the decisions. Before we had any children, we decided that I would stay ashore after the children came.

In March, Dan Bates offers Skip another job for six weeks counting the salmon fry as they swim downstream to the sea. Happily, Skip takes off in *Salty* for Olive Cove.

Eric enjoys his playpen in the fish bin.

Eric and I do fine alone, but we do miss Skip. Ten days later he returns for supplies. He excitedly says, "Marilyn, that's a beautiful place in Zimovia Straits. Praders live there in a house, and have a well-built float where I tie *Salty*. Dan says the Fish and Wildlife doesn't care who's on the boat. Would ya and Eric like to move on *Salty* and live there with me? I don't worry about ya if you're with me."

I love Skip dearly and miss being with him. He's great company and in the cramped quarters on the boat and in the cabin, we have become very close in many ways.

"I'll love to go if we can make *Salty* safe for Eric."

He looks at me with that smile I love

Salty is called the Didee Boat during our six weeks in Olive Cove.

so much. "Would ya really like to go?" Fearing I might change my mind, he continues, "Come on then. Let's look at her and see what we can do." Pushing his steel measuring tape into his pocket, he helps me bundle Eric into his snowsuit. We take a taxi to the boat.

"Everyday when I walk up the stream, I see something I want to share with you. Of course, I miss your good cooking. I'd love to return to the boat and find hot coffee waiting for me, even if it's your coffee." Reaching over and patting Eric on the head, he continues, "Most of all, I missed my boy these ten days."

The engine is the most dangerous. Skip places a board in front of it. He has to continually get to the engine to put the belt on the flywheel. This provides power to our trolling gurdies. The belt comes off when we run or anchor. I vividly recall a kitten who fell against the flywheel. The spinning wheel picked it up and threw it onto the galley with a smack. Fearing it had internal injuries, I made Skip check on it. Luckily, it only had a nosebleed.

I give up my bunk on the portside and take the starboard one which must be folded up before anyone can climb into the pilothouse. Eric's bunk is three feet off the floor. I picture Eric falling over the edge onto the galley floor. Boards won't do because then we won't be able to see in and Eric can't see out.

After some thought we decide on fastening fishnet to a frame. It lets him see us and we see him, plus it gives him room to crawl. We call this the bird cage because that is what it reminds us of—with Eric being the bird.

"If you hinge a piece of plywood the length of this locker in the bow, it will make a playpen for him when you fasten the eye bolt at the end," I say. This playpen stops him from falling out. I buy a broad based highchair that folds down into a play table. It proves to be very steady in rough water. We can sit the play table on the hatch or a float when we are outside. I decide a dishpan has more uses than an inflated bath tub.

We get all of this done and move onto the boat in one day, for Skip must return to his job. Solving these safety problems leaves us hopeful that taking Eric aboard will be a success. We're happy to be together as we head for Olive Cove. Eric sits on my lap and watches the wake of the boat out of the pilothouse door. The purr of the engine soon puts him to sleep. I lay him in the bird cage.

Olive Cove is as beautiful as Skip said. We put out our crab pot and some days we'll get as many as four crab. I never tire of eating crab, but I do tire of the clams that we dig at low tides.

My biggest problem is washing Eric's diapers. On a clear, bright day, I heat water until it boils in a large kettle. I fill two wash tubs for rinsing with cold water and attach my hand wringer. Skip strings lines to the ends of *Salty's* poles for hanging the clothes. *Salty* becomes the Didee Boat. I should have washed a few each day, but it was such work that I always put it off and ended up with a pile. I can't hand wash the sheets we use inside the sleeping bags. When we go to town, Mrs. Bates offers the use of her automatic washer. I appreciate this more than anything else she could have done for me.

Eric thrives the six weeks in Olive Cove. Like most children, he likes both parents to be around him.

The ramp from the float leads to Prader's house. We become acquainted with Zelma and Walt and their son, Steve, who flies in from boarding school for Easter. We enjoy their friendship. Zelma, from Latvia, is an outdoors person. She loves to take off on her snowshoes to trap and see the country. I wish I could be as capable and self-sufficient as she is. They started with Zelma's boat called the *Ark*. Now Walt has a combination troller-gillnetter called the *Irish*. They travel together, but often fish different areas. They usually meet at night.

When Skip comes down from his counting, he often says to Eric, "How is my boy today?"

This happy, curious baby coos and laughs. He lies on his big stomach and kicks. One of these days he'll get his knees under him and creep. On bright days, I sit him in his high chair on the float. He laughs when he slings a toy. I see he will be a fisherman as he develops a good arm for tossing fish aboard. We hang a trolling bell and a fish spoon from the ceiling in the middle of the bird cage. When he awakens, he hits the spoon as if calling his maid. I always race down the steps or step over from the stove to take care of him.

When visiting another trolling couple, we hear how much she hates life aboard. "I spent the entire summer sitting on the floor of our new boat holding our two-year old. I was scared something would happen to him. I couldn't even see where we were."

It must have been a terrible summer for that little boy who only wanted to play and the mother who was so full of worry. We hear of another couple who panicked when they couldn't find their baby. They were sure he fell overboard. After searching frantically and steering the boat at a high rate of speed to where they'd been on the fishing grounds, they found him curled up asleep in a locker. I don't know what I would do if Eric fell overboard, but the child proofing of *Salty* has worked for now.

Too soon, May first comes and we must make the decision if I and Eric will go fishing with Skip or stay at home. Hundreds of thoughts go through my brain: Can I keep Eric well and happy on *Salty* while we fish? Will I be able to keep those diapers washed or will we be constantly lying in harbor while I do laundry? We only have four and a half months to make our winter stake. After much discussion, we both decide that if it doesn't work, Eric and I can fly home or run in on a fish packer.

Working on his halibut gear, Skip says, "Well, do ya think we can make Eric into a baby salt?"

I smile, "Yes, a baby salty. I'm willing to try if you are."

We pack everything aboard. Frisky, the cat, makes the fourth crew member. Les Watkins on his pumpkin seed shaped boat, the *Helen*, will run with us to Tyee. We worry Eric will not like rough water. I anxiously watch for his reaction as we buck into the waves. He's oblivious to the motion of the boat. Eric laughs and wants me to hold him in the pilothouse. He protests loudly if I move so he can't see out the door.

Later, he continues to play with his toys in the bird cage. We hope that we are raising a future salmon troller. Maybe he will surpass his father and me in his ability to catch fish.

Skip prefers running through Rocky Pass to going the long way through

Wrangell Narrows. I hear Skip slow down the engine as we run out of Keku Straits. "There she is!"

I race to the pilothouse to see the line of towering, jagged peaks on Baranof Island. "There's Mount Ada. Ya can see her twin peaks today. Don't ya think the snow's lower this year? It comes to the water's edge."

Standing on the top step, I kiss Skip. "Thanks for bringing me. I love seeing these places."

Skip figures we'll reach Tyee by dark. When a westerly blows off the Baranof mountains, we duck into Halleck Harbor in Saginaw Bay. A westerly means the wind is blowing from the west off the mountains or in some places off the ocean which makes the water rough. At Point Gardner, Chatham Straits, Stevens Passage and Frederick Sound all come together. The combination of wind and tide makes this one of the roughest spots in Southeast Alaska. David Stuteen, and elderly Native from Kake, tells us about a look-out on top of a big rock.

When we head across Frederick Sound the next morning, the water is glassy calm. Skip predicts that the halibut won't bite until bigger tides, but he decides to try. He methodically fastens his leaders to the line and lets the steel line down with the power gurdies.

"Marilyn, look at that line jerk! Yippee, we're in fish already! Come up here and steer. I didn't figure on this. I must bait the rest of the hooks."

What a day this is! The only time I leave the wheel is to change Eric, give him his bottle, and fix sandwiches for lunch. I use landmarks to keep on the spot. I like to take some of the credit for *Salty* becoming one of the highliners for halibut.

I set the play table on the hatch. I put Eric's baby food and cereal in front of him. He likes feeding himself even if he often misses his mouth. When Skip throws a 30-pound halibut into the fish bin, it beats the deck with its powerful tail splattering water and blood all over Eric. He yells in fright.

"It's time for your nap, little fellow," I say as I wash the blood off and give him a bottle. I carry him to the bird cage. He lies there gurgling and discovers the porthole alongside his bunk. He peers out of it. The motion of the boats, waves, and birds intrigues him.

When we pass another boat, a woman leans out of the pilothouse door. She points, "Look, there's a baby at that porthole." Soon everyone looks for Eric's face at the porthole when they pass.

Usually the halibut only bite the six hours of the flood tide, but this day they keep biting. We always have three or four on each line. After three hours, the ebb tide passes, and the halibut finally stop biting. When I speed up to head for the Tyee harbor, *Salty's* bow is high in the air. We have over 2000 pounds of halibut on deck.

Skip asks Les, who is running with us, "Do ya know how to clean halibut?"

He says, "Sure."

Skip thinks no more about Les as he's busy cleaning. At midnight, we pull under the cold storage to sell. Les pulls up behind us.

The fish buyer takes one look at Les's fish and says, "You haven't scraped out the sweetmeats, which are two little pieces of meat attached to the backbone. You must redo them all."

Poor Les. After cleaning until 3 a.m., he finally hits the sack. Skip feels that he should have checked Les's cleaning, but Les sounded so confident.

Skip isn't used to the hard work of cleaning that many little halibut. I rub his back and arms with Ben Gay because every muscle in his body aches.

The next day is much like the first, but we quit fishing a little earlier this time. Skip calls, "Marilyn, come look who is coming into the harbor."

It's the *Pauline*. Dorie and Charlie must be aboard, for children's overalls are hanging in the rigging.

How I miss Dorie since they moved to Pelican! She hasn't been fishing in four years. When they come over, I throw my arms around her. I discover Dorie is also pregnant.

Ed surveys the situation and remarks, "If these women ever figure out what makes it, we'll be sleeping on the couch, Skip." We all laugh.

"Have you any morning sickness, Dorie? I worry that I will on the boat, but I haven't so far. Of course, we just left town two days ago."

"I'm like you. We just left Pelican yesterday." Pelican is named after the boat of the town's founder, Carles Raatikainen.

Our combined families include Charlie, age three, and Eric at eight months. Eric hasn't been around older children and is fascinated by Charlie. We all laugh when Eric wants to feel Charlie's face. Perhaps he wonders if he is real or a doll. Eric is creeping now, but I only let him creep on top of the lockers and in the bunk.

We awake the next morning to find a thick fog blanketing the area. Without radar and depth sounders, we could easily run onto a submerged rock or ram another boat, but we cannot afford to take a day off. We lessen

our chances by running with our poles upright which takes less room. We also run at half-speed, and twice we stop to listen for other boats. At last Skip says, "We should be there. See anything?"

Suddenly, I hear a loud splash on our portside. "Skip, there's our whale. We must be there."

Each year this whale swims around us. One year when the whale didn't come, we caught very few halibut. We put in our gear, and the halibut are there. Later in the day when the fog lifts, we see we are exactly where we are suppose to be. We catch our 1000-pound goal.

On very rough days, Dorie and I and our babies stay ashore. Eric likes to crawl in the grass while Charlie loves to run and

Marilyn takes Eric on the beach in Gedney Harbor when Skip puts Salty on the grid to copper paint her.

play. Dorie and I wash our clothes in the cannery's wash house. I fill a bucket of cold water from the outside faucet.

Suddenly, I hear water running. In surprise, I see Eric has toppled the bucket of water onto his lap. Even though the water drenches him, he doesn't cry. I wipe him off, glad I brought a clean shirt and overalls.

Then we hang our wash on their lines. How much easier than hanging it in the boat's rigging. When we come in the next evening, I take down my wash.

Whenever we sell at the same time, I visit with Dorie. We enjoy telling each other about what our babies did that day. On a clear day, we often sit on the hatch of one of the boats and let the boys play in the fish bins. Charlie enjoys playing with Eric.

Good fishing continues for the next week until the small tides. At night

I rub ointment on Skip's aching muscles.

We run with the *Pauline* into Warm Springs Bay. While there, Frisky disappears. The next day, I walk by the houses calling, "Kitty, kitty, kitty." They tell me that the community has only one tom cat. He must be lonely. His owners haven't seen our little female, but they report that the tom acted strangely that morning. In the end, we leave without Frisky. She is over a year old and has never had kittens.

We dream of five more good fishing days before the season closes the last of May, but we end up finding few halibut. We make only $50 in the last five days for only a mediocre season. We bid farewell to Mrs. Short and the cooks at the mess hall, who took care of us when we stayed ashore. Sadly, we wave good-bye to the Wellesleys as they head for Pelican. We don't realize that Ed will not be able to pursuade Dorie to fish with him again. The boat may be too small for their growing family. We put our halibut gear away for another season.

"Let's go to Warm Springs. Another bath will feel good and I can wash."

"All ya want is that cat back. Well, we might as well go."

Upon our arrival, Skip goes up to the tom cat's owners. They tell him how the tom looks after Frisky. He hides her until they put out food. Then he comes down and stands beside the dish and calls her. He always lets her eat first.

Skip calls and calls. At last, Frisky sticks her head out of the loft, but the tom manages to stay between her and Skip. She is his prize, and he isn't going to let her go. At last, Frisky runs past him into easy reach of Skip.

I am feeding Eric in his high chair when Skip sets Frisky inside the cabin door. She jumps down beside me purring. Eric sees her and cries, "Kee!" Trying to reach her, Eric nearly tips over the highchair. Happily, Frisky is home.

That night we put *Salty* on the grid to copper paint below the waterline. We are up so high that we think that Frisky can't get off the boat.

Skip comes back to bed from checking how *Salty* is rising with the tide. He says, "That cat's gone. If she's not back by morning, she's gone for good this time. I'm not chasing her."

At 3 a.m., Les calls from his boat on the grid, "Marilyn, your cat is crying."

Frisky is sitting on top of the piling ahead of us. When she tries to return after bidding her lover farewell, the tide is too high for her to climb aboard. She climbs as far as she can. Now she might drown for the tide is lapping around her perch. Skip puts the skiff in the water and rows over and rescues

*On the fish packer, Rande A, Eric and I pass Skip and Frisky on Salty
as they head out to fish.*

her. I have tears when he hands her to me.

Eric and I are planning to go back to Wrangell when Skip says, "I have a
half notion to see if I can find any salmon around here. Would ya two like to
go with me? If we don't find any, I'll send ya home. Then I'll fish outside of
Baranof and Chichagof Islands like I did last year. You two can't go out in
those big ocean swells."

"Oh, Skip, I hoped you'd say that," I say kissing him. "It's more fun than
going home." I look down at Eric, sitting in the bird cage playing with the fish
spoon. He says, "Goo."

"Eric says 'fine'. He's happy to be with his Daddy on *Salty*. What a baby
salt he has turned out to be!"

As Skip feels safer when two boats are running together, he's happy when
Les decides to runs with us. To keep any king salmon we'll catch, we fill *Salty's*
and *Helen's* holds with glacial snow from Hoggatt Bay. The snow still comes
to the water's edge.

We search from bay to bay. When we fish from dawn to dark for seven
days without a salmon, our spirits sink. Les has no better luck.

Skip remarks, "It's certainly dead around here. I'll try this one last place.
If nothing, you're going home."

"I'm sure you'll find some there."

"You're always an optimist, Marilyn."

Letting the last line out, Skip sees the starboard bow pole jerk violently. "It's a big one!" he shouts.

He lets the large ones tire themselves by fighting the pole. Finally, he puts the gurdy into low gear. The king doesn't fight anymore. Skip lands it. Before he lets that line out on the pole, another king strikes on the port main pole. We are in a school of feeding kings! Eric hears the commotion on deck and cries. He wants to see, too. I take him out of the bird cage and hold him on my lap in the pilothouse. On the top step, Frisky waits expectedly for the fish hearts that I cook for her. She hasn't had any for a long time. When Skip has the bow line fishing again, he finds that the salmon on the main line has broken the leader. Now *Salty* is in deep water. He turns her around and heads back along the reef. Suddenly, both bow poles pull down.

"Bottom!" I yell.

Skip turns *Salty* away from the reef, but still the poles jerk. He shoves the gurdy into high gear.

"The lines can't be on the bottom now. Maybe it's fish."

He shifts the gurdies into low gear. The first and second leaders hang slack, but the third rubber snubber stretches taut behind the boat. Carefully, he pulls in the leader until he grabs the swivel fastened to the lure. Sinking his gaff into the king, he lands it. A 40-pounder!

"Look, Skip, the line is still jerking."

"Say, maybe there's another on the bottom leader." He slams the gurdy into gear. "You're right. A double-header of kings! Is that other pole still working?" He asks as he lets down the line.

"Just look at it pull! Hurry, Skip, maybe it's a 50-pounder." Eric and I are jumping up and down we're so excited.

He lands two kings from that line. Cohoes do this double header bit all the time but we've never had kings do it. I estimate we already have 150 pounds aboard.

One king jumps high out of water and throws the hook at us. Skip and I are speechless but Eric sadly says, "Oooh."

We can only keep our fish six days before we sell them. We leave for Gedney on the sixth day around 9 a.m. after fishing the morning tide. Les follows us.

We work fast to lose as little fishing time as possible. Skip unloads his fish, scrubs out the fish hold and takes more ice. I heat water and use the scow's gasoline washing machine. I also buy groceries. Having only a six-day

Pregnant again, Marilyn works at her new cabinet on Salty.

supply of diapers, I dry them as fast as possible by hanging them in the rigging. We leave Gedney Harbor at 6 p.m. We have diapers hanging from stem to stern.

In the beautiful June weather, Eric wants to be out on deck. In one fish bin, we make his second playpen by putting the boards three feet high. Now he can stand up and move around by hanging onto the sides. The salmon don't scare him as the halibut did. He also enjoys standing in the galley playpen and throwing silverware onto the floor.

As soon as the motor stops, Eric wakes from his nap. I fold down the table that covers the small cupboard and set the dishpan on it. I hang a towel over the front of the cupboard and put Eric in for his bath. With a gleeful look, he peeks under the towel and grabs the salt and pepper. After a fast wash down, I lift him out of the tub. He protests with loud cries.

Skip calls in, "What are ya doing to my boy?"

"If he won't stay out of the cupboard, he's getting out."

We make a couple more trips from our "hole" before the fish are gone. We decide to fish closer to Gedney and sell our fish daily. We stay in the harbor when a good southeaster blows, but I have little time for visiting with the other women. These are the only times I have to wash clothes and clean the boat.

One morning toward the last of June we hear the start of the Korean War on our short-wave radio.

The wind blows on the Fourth of July, making it another harbor day. All of the women make ice cream in a hand freezer, and then in the evening we have a dance. Buckshot Woolery, the fish buyer, clears the floor in the scow

Skip holds Frisky on Salty when we leave in August of 1950.

and furnishes beverages. Lee and Ann Holderman from the *Lady Alyce* play the saxophone and guitar. We take Eric for awhile and carry him around the dance floor as we dance. The musical instruments fascinate him.

We don't go out on July 5 and find lots of fish as we had done in 1946. The fishing is slow, but it slowly adds up when you fish every day.

Having Eric on the boat does have its drawbacks. "I can't sleep with Eric wanting to play when we shut off the motor. Here it is 10 p.m. and he's wide awake. How do ya expect me to get up at 4 a.m.?" Skip complains.

"I'm tired, too." I try lots of things like giving him his nap in the morning and keeping him awake after 3 p.m. Hanging a towel over the fish net door to darken the boat is not successful. Both Skip and I are suffering from sleep deprivation.

One day Skip asks Hazel and Herman, "How many did you get today?"

Hazel says, "I'm just sick. We lost 12 straight."

Skip nods, "Everyone loses some. How many did ya get?"

"Lonnie hardly loses any," Herman mumbles.

"Maybe he doesn't count his strikes. I know we don't. How many did ya say ya got?"

"Thirteen! Think what we would have if we got our strikes."

Skip shakes his head, "That's more than we got. We only got eight."

Then one of our friends brings in 1000 pounds of cohoes from Port Malmesbury for two days of fishing. Skip and I work late that night polishing small spoons that cohoes like. Skip re-marks our lines to put out more lures.

With high expectations, we leave the harbor the next morning. In dismay, we see fog rolling in from Coronation Island. We like to follow other boats when the thick fog sets in. Finally, Skip slows down and puts in our gear. When the fog lifts a little, we discover all the other boats are behind us.

Even though the boat is riding up and down in the ocean swells, I start breakfast. If I stay below, these lazy swells bother me. When Eric awakens, I give him his bottle. Then he sits up in the bird cage and throws up his milk.

"My poor baby ," I say as I lift him out of the bunk. I sit down on the lockers and take off his nightie and put on a clean undershirt, shirt and overalls. Then I hear Frisky get seasick at my feet. After cleaning it up, I manage to eat my breakfast. Then I throw up.

"I'll steer while you eat, Skip."

"I'm sorry. I've lost my appetite seeing the rest of the crew throw up."

"Where are all those cohoes we were going to have on deck by breakfast?" I complain.

We only catch seven. We can put up with some unpleasantness if we're making $50 to $100 a day, but for only seven cohoes!

"Well, I've had enough," Skip says with disgust. "I'm heading back for protected waters. We did better than this."

We meet Les, who stayed in our usual place. Ironically, he has $130 worth and we have $15.

I am starting Eric's bath when Skip calls me to steer. I leave Eric on the locker playpen in his pajamas. Suddenly I realize I haven't heard any noise from Eric in awhile. When babies are too quiet you know they've gotten into something. Fearfully, I look down into the galley. Eric is busily rubbing bacon grease from the jar on himself, on the blanket, on the bench, and on the walls.

"Skip, you steer. Our boy is at it again. He's really made a mess this time." I climb down into the bow.

"Naughty boy."

He whimpers a little, but

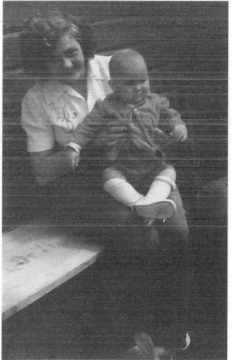

Hazel Hintz holds Eric on Buckshot's scow.

smiles when he sees me get the dishpan for his bath. I must get the grease off of him. I have to wash all the woodwork before Skip can make his bunk on top of the lockers.

Every night we put Frisky in a box under the high chair with the idea that tomorrow we may have baby kittens. Frisky had been born on *Salty*. Now, she will have her first kittens here.

Skip remarks, "What a pregnant boat this is."

One night Eric and I awaken to the sound of kittens mewing, "See, Eric, tiny kittens. Don't touch."

Frisky is so proud of her kittens she lets Eric look at them. She seems to know that he won't hurt them. She purrs and lets Eric drag her around as he usually does.

With the birth of the kittens, I start to worry about my own pregnancy, "My seventh month begins the first of August. I better go home."

I figure this is an ideal time to leave because Eric is trying to walk. Last week he pushed himself over the top of the galley play pen. He isn't satisfied to stand in the fish bin on deck. He wants to crawl all over the deck. He learns how to crawl from the bird cage onto the bench in the pilothouse. I decide that the best time to have a child aboard a small boat is before he walks. I am starting to feel like the mom who sat on the galley floor holding her two-year-old all summer long.

"Marilyn, how are ya going to Wrangell?" Skip asks.

"I'm going on the packer *Rande A* with Beaver."

"On that broken-down old sub chaser. That engine's liable to conk out."

"It's been running all summer. It has two engines."

"Ya do it against my better judgment."

"A plane will cost $100. I'd rather spend that $100 on the house."

We only keep one of Frisky's kittens. We run around Point Harris on the way to Malmesbury. *Salty* rolls and hot water pours out of the spout of the teakettle into the cat's box on the galley's floor. Frisky isn't in the box, but it scalds the kitten. Frisky works and works licking it.

Looking at Frisky, Skip says, "I need some company on the boat. Why don't ya leave Frisky with me?"

"You'll take good care of her?"

"Of course, Frisky and I are pals."

Two hours before leaving, I remember the house key. We look everywhere, but no key. "It's terrible. I'll have to break in." Skip finds it two weeks later hanging under the calendar in the pilothouse.

Eric and I board the *Rande A* at 10:30 a.m. and Skip kisses us good-bye. He and Frisky take off for the fishing grounds. When we run by him, I take pictures of *Salty*. I've wanted to do it for a long time, but since I'm always aboard, I can't.

Everything is going fine, and I think how silly of Skip to worry about us. Captain Lowell Beaver remarks casually at dinner that their usual engine has gone out. They are running on their second engine. I'm glad Skip doesn't know that or he wouldn't have allowed us on it.

I put Eric to sleep in one of the bunks at 8 p.m. We pass Point Baker and will be in Wrangell by 10 p.m.

Suddenly, clink, clank, clunk, the engine dies. The engineer runs to the engine room. The deckhand runs up on the bow and throws over the anchor. Silence reigns.

Beaver calls the cannery in Wrangell on his radiophone. They will send a power scow to tow us into Wrangell. Luckily, the engine hadn't stopped at Cape Decision where we could have drifted onto rocks.

I wonder if Skip is listening and saying, I knew it, I knew it. I crawl into the bunk with Eric, who is sleeping peacefully. At 1 a.m., I hear the power scow come alongside. At last, we're underway.

When I awaken, I find the *Rande A* tied alongside the cannery. Out on deck, I see in dismay one of the lowest tides of the year. The ladder from the dock doesn't reach the deck of the *Rande A*. How are Eric and his pregnant mother going to get off the boat?

We eat breakfast. At 9:00 the tide starts in, but we still can't climb to the dock. Finally, I flag down a passing skiff.

"Will you take Eric and me to the City Float?"

"Sure."

The crew helps us into the skiff. Looking at my watch, I see it is 10:30 a.m. I visit a girl friend until high water at 3 p.m. At the cannery, the crew helps unload all of my gear including the highchair. The taxi is so full that Eric and I crowd into the front seat. When the taxi driver offers to put the items inside the house, I tell him to set them outside by the house steps. I'm not going to admit that I have no key.

I sit Eric down on the ground while I try to figure out how to get into the house. He creeps around eating sticks and berries, laughing and cooing. I see there is no chance of getting in the locked front door. Eric finds a mud puddle and splashes mud on himself. I set him on the wooden walk and give him a toy, which he throws into the grass. He wants to explore this place he doesn't remember.

With visions of hammering the door down, I walk around back. Happily, I discover the utility door open, but we've locked the door from it to the bedroom. I know that it only has a hook and eye lock. Shaking it vigorously it suddenly opens. Home again! What a good feeling!

Skip gave me money to have an oil heater installed and an oil tank set up. I am glad because there is only enough wood to last until the man installs the oil stove.

Eric is a problem the first week we're home. He likes nothing around the house, and only wants to watch for any boats going by our cabin. Land life must be too tame for him I think. We look forward to Skip returning from fishing.

When he comes home the first of September, Frisky is not with him. "But you promised." I cry.

"Well, the kitten died and Frisky decided to go frolicking again. When I woke up, she was gone. I called and called and then saw her on shore. I even fell in trying to crawl to shore on that stick that connects the float. I called to her, but she kept just out of reach. Finally, I just went fishing. I figured I'd get back there to get her. Then the fishing was all up in Tebenkof, and I never got back. Old Adam Wilson on the *Spanko* lives there. I talked to a couple of boats and they say he adopted Frisky. He has a tom cat, too. Ya remember Adam, he's the one that hand trolled out of a dory starting in 1902 at Port Alexander."

"I'm not interested in Adam's history."

"Maybe we can get her next year."

"But, Skip, you promised Eric and me." I cry again.

"I'm sorry. I just figured I'd get back there."

Eric will miss playing with his Frisky. I watch him toddling around the cabin. Yes, we had a good summer. Whenever someone asks about taking a baby on a small fishing boat, I always reply, "Don't worry about the baby, he'll love it. It's whether Mama and Daddy can survive."

Skip did well trolling in August. It's a much better year, financially, than the previous one. We also are pleased that Eric enjoys life on the *Salty*. No doubt, when we hear the geese flying north, Eric and I will be longing for the life of a fisherman again.

CHAPTER THIRTEEN

*M*issing The Excitement

WAITING WITH ERIC FOR the baby to be born, I meet Carmen and Jerry Loomis. Jerry works at Alaska Communications Systems station in Wrangell. Eric's age is between their little girl, Bonnie, and baby boy, Robert. Carmen is due the first of March. We agree that we will look after each other's children when we are in the hospital giving birth.

Dr. Bangeman predicts another six pound baby due about September 20. I am expecting a

The only four generation picture that was ever taken with Marilyn, Karen, Grandma Deardorff and Mother Frink.

boy but Skip wishes for a girl. Skip arrives home the tenth of September, and I go into labor on the evening of the sixth of October. God blesses us with a seven pound 15 ounce girl. We name her Karen, which the Norwegians pronounce Kar-en, like car. I pronounce Kare-n like care. She's named after Skip's Norwegian nanny.

After holding Karen, Skip laughs, "They certainly didn't throw away the mold."

I join in, "The Jordan mold you mean."

Karen is round-faced and bald but I can't see any other family resemblance. Eric is at the Loomis house and when I leave the hospital, Carmen insists we all stay with them for five days. I agree, being too tired to think about staying in our cabin. Karen is a good baby, and unlike Eric, she isn't lazy about nursing.

Finally, we move home. I like having my own space but miss the comforts of living in a nice house and Carmen's care. Soon after we get home Skip announces, "I can work on one of the cannery tenders as a deckhand while they haul canned salmon to Seattle or Bellingham. It'll just be for a couple of trips."

I'm as excited as he is. We need the money. Dad Jordan writes of job opportunities in Tacoma and Seattle due to the Korean War. We will be ahead financially if Skip obtains a good job in a shipyard for the winter. Skip can work on the tender until he finds work, then I'll fly south with Eric and Karen. We pack our most needed items, including the highchair, for Skip to take when he leaves three days later, just in case he does find work.

Life isn't easy taking care of two babies in diapers by myself. Heating the water to wash all those diapers takes up most of my time. I don't have to worry about wood with the oil heater, but I still catch a bad cold and have to go to the doctor.

When Skip returns ten days later, I throw my arms around him, "You're a sight for sore eyes."

"How has it been? I know it isn't easy for ya."

"The water is still running. I did have a little cold." I want him to see how well I'm doing, and to keep this job.

He sizes up the situation, "It's too hard on ya out here alone. I'll quit this job."

No, I think, please don't, but I realize I could argue with him until I'm blue in the face and he still would quit. I sigh, "Okay."

We fly south October 31 and stay with his folks. Skip has visions of jobs like he found during World War II in the shipyards. Alas, our rush is for nothing. He has to belong to a union, and Skip hadn't renewed his union card when he went into the service. No one will hire him without that card.

Suddenly, Skip gets sick with a high fever. The doctor comes to the house and diagnoses mononucleosis. The doctor tells me that Eric, Karen and I cannot be in the same room with Skip. It's hard trying to keep Eric away from his dad, but I manage and Skip gradually recovers.

Eva and I bake pies and make Dorie's special 24-hour salad for Thanksgiving. Since this is the first Thanksgiving I have spent with Skip's family, we're trying to make it extra special. Eric, Karen and Ellen are under foot as we set the good china on the table. No one knows where Grandpa Jordan is. I heard him leave early in the morning. Noon arrives and we're all just getting ready to say the Thanksgiving prayer when Grandpa comes in and sits down at the head of the table. Skip is sitting to his right and Grandpa immediately attacks him, "Why don't you get a good job!"

Skip looks startled. "I'm doing the best I can, Dad. I should have kept that union card so I could return to the shipyard."

Grandpa seems so angry, I think he might hit Skip.

At this moment I notice Grandma Jordan rising out of her chair at the foot of the table. She walks around to Grandpa's side facing Skip and calmly puts her hand on his shoulder. "Calm down, Kris." Turning around she walks back to her chair and sits down. I could have heard a pin drop.

Grandpa picks up the knife and starts to carve the turkey as if nothing has happened.

Dawn holds baby Karen.

Later that day when Skip and I are alone, Skip says, "We're going home on the next steamer." I nod. Within an hour my folks call to wish us a happy Thanksgiving. When they hear we're leaving they insist we come to Iowa for a visit. They want to see their first grandchildren and they'll pay our way. Knowing how much I want to see my family, Skip reluctantly agrees. He hates to accept the free ticket.

One night on the train, I suggest Skip take Eric to the diner while I nurse Karen. When they arrive at the diner, Eric announces he wants milk. The waiter says they are out of milk until Cheyenne. This means nothing to a 16-month old boy. Skip offers him juice, but he keeps protesting. Then Eric stands up in his chair and turns around to grab the hat of the woman sitting behind them. This is too much for Skip.

"Just hold my dinner while I take him to his mother."

Skip opens the door, "You take him. He embarrassed me in the diner. I would have spanked him if I hadn't been in front of people."

After Skip returns from eating, Eric and I go to the dining car and eat with no incidents. Skip is from the old school with children. He believes they should be seen and not heard. Skip expects his children to have impeccable manners. He doesn't understand that Eric is still a little young to know what manners are.

Getting off the train, I throw my arms around my folks. "It's so good to see you."

The folks love the children. My youngest sister, Helen at 16, is the only one still living at home. Over Christmas my brother Lynn and sister Peggy introduce their spouses, Etta and Harold. We visit my 80-year-old grandparents. We take a four-generation picture of my grandmother, mother, Karen and me. It feels great to be home with my parents again and to show off my two perfect babies. Skip, though, is restless during the holidays as he doesn't like living off my folks. When he sees an advertisement for a writing course, he sends in the coupon. I do a lot of the writing in the family for I have a minor in Journalism, but he figures if two of us are writing we might produce more. He writes the Veterans Administration to see if the course will qualify for free tuition under the GI Bill.

After the holidays, Skip announces, "I'm heading back for Alaska. Frank is suing Eva for divorce now that she's out of the hospital. We want to get Chris back and to make sure Frank doesn't get him." We are not sure how Frank is treating Chris. We hope that Eva will get back her son. She has suffered severe depression. We would also love to have him. If they won't let us have him, we would rather he be in the foster home than with Frank. "Dad and I will go to Juneau for the divorce hearing. I also need to get *Salty* ready for next season."

It hurts Skip's pride to ask the folks, "Mother, can Marilyn and the children stay here until spring? With two babies, it's too hard for her alone in the cabin."

The folks are delighted for us to stay longer. It warms my heart to have such wonderful parents to be willing to put three generations under one roof.

Two days later Skip leaves. He spends ten days with his folks before he and his dad take the steamer to Juneau for the divorce hearings. The judge grants the divorce but takes Chris's custody under advisement. He seems to forget about the case until two years later. Instead of awarding Chris to his mother or us, he gives him to the foster family with whom he first stayed. With great sadness we lose all contact with little Chris.

Skip writes long, newsy letters just like he did in the Navy. One letter states that The Veterans Administration wants to test Skip's aptitude. He takes the tests while he's in Juneau for the divorce proceedings.

Excitedly, he writes, "They feel I would make a good teacher. They want me to go back to college. I filled out all the forms for the University of Washington. How would ya like that, honey?"

I think this an excellent idea. We have talked about his taking advantage of the GI Bill. Marine biology and fisheries interest him. He can start college in March. He finds someone who will pay $2500 for *Salty*—$1500 down and the rest at the season's end.

We paid $3500 for *Salty*. I know boat deals are risky if you don't get all of your money. People will charge bills against the boat which you must pay if you repossess it. We spent a lot of money on *Salty*, and boat prices have increased. Anyway I feel she is worth at least what we paid for her. We will be short of cash if he goes to school now. Why not fish another season and start school in the fall? That way we'll have enough money. I wire: "Don't sell *Salty* for that price. Fish this season and start in September. Love, Marilyn."

Skip doesn't show the enthusiasm for going to school after this. He busily fixes *Salty*. He writes that Carmen is due to have her baby any day and I better return as not to renege on my agreement to look after her children while she's in the hospital.

The end of February, I bid my folks good-bye and thank them for looking after us. With the children, I take the train to Tacoma and then fly to Wrangell. I'm exhausted from traveling and getting up at 4 a.m. to catch the Wrangell plane.

"It's great to see you, Skip," I say after kissing him.

"I've missed ya. I've a surprise for you." Skip picks up Eric.

After pilling all of our bags into the taxi, Skip instructs the driver to go to Lemieux apartments. "I rented an apartment for us. It's too hard for ya out in the cabin."

I'm thankful, but worried too. How can we afford this? But it will be nice to live in town, where I can visit, walk to the store and not be isolated. Eric will also be able to play with other children his own age. The comfortable, but not fancy, apartment consists of a kitchen, dining area and one bedroom. It's furnished. We share the bathroom with other residents but at least it isn't outside. This will also make it easier to potty train Eric.

Around 8 a.m. Carmen brings Robert to stay with me as she heads for the hospital. We all laugh that she waited for my arrival. She has a beautiful baby boy, Craig.

I enjoy living in Wrangell. Carmen and Jerry Loomis and Clell and Ruth Bacon help celebrate my 30th birthday in April by playing canasta.

Skip asks Jerry to go halibut fishing with him instead of taking me and the children. We haven't decided if we can handle Eric, who never stays in one place for long, and Karen on the boat. The week before they're due to leave, Dan Bates from the U.S. Fish & Wildlife Service asks Skip if he wants a tagging charter. It's a dilemma. Skip loves working for Dan and he has helped us financially a few times by throwing work our way. But the charter would only pay us $500, whereas halibut fishing might make us more. We have come to rely on the halibut fishing as we usually make $800 to $1000. Besides, Jerry had already been approved for his time off. We couldn't very well leave him hanging after we'd told him how great it is. Skip turns down the charter and on May first Carmen, I and the children wave goodbye to the men as they pull out of the harbor.

We wait anxiously to hear from them. Sadly, we learn that the men find no halibut at Tyee. They only make $200.

While the men are gone I hear that the Wrangell Institute is trying a new system that year. The 13- to 15-year-old girls who do not go home for the summer will work for their board and room, and some spending money. They expect their host families to buy them school clothes. I sign up, and Susie Johnson comes to live with us. Her mother was a Native and her father Norwegian, whereabouts unknown. Sadly her mother recently died of tuberculosis.

Susie is a godsend to me. She reminds me of the hired girls my mother had during my childhood. She especially loves Karen, a real doll. Karen still has no hair. All her baby fat is still there, which is probably from the way she loves to nurse. Susie loves to hold her and take her for rides in the buggy. Eric, at 18 months, is not the lovable type, and I decide Susie is afraid of him. He knows what he wants, and no one argues with him, except Skip or me.

Paul Binkley, with whom we went seal hunting, makes a special effort to find Skip in June. "The kings are really hitting at Quiet Harbor, where we anchored our first night on *Salty*. You better run with me."

Skip has a good trip with Paul, which help makes up for the halibut. We are thankful for Paul's helpful fishing tips.

On June 20, Skip leaves for Chatham Straits to catch kings. He calls me on the radiophone, "Marilyn, it looks good out here. Why don't ya see if ya can buy a tent? You can live on the beach and be very comfortable. I'll come in for ya around the Fourth of July."

I ask the Institute if we can take Susie to the fishing grounds with us. They say yes. I buy a ten- by 12-foot wall tent. Skip buys shiplap for the walls and floor. We move items to the cabin that we aren't taking. Then Skip loads aboard the lumber, and all the items we'll need with the children. With all the weight *Salty* sits low in the water.

We leave after the Fourth of July parade. It's a beautiful, warm day. We stop in the middle of Rocky Pass to wait for the tide. I go swimming which is unusual in these frigid waters, but today this shallow water is warmer than usual. When Eric sees me dive off the bow, he wants to do it, too. I let him wade nearer the beach. Susie takes Karen ashore while Skip naps.

I'm happy to be back out on the fishing grounds. That evening as we weave in and out among the islands in Keku Straits, I let the beauty of the country seep into me. We run into Little Halleck Harbor as the sun sets. Skip throws over our anchor. The clink of the chain is the only noise. Such peace!

"Thank you, Skip, for bringing us."

I put Eric in one end of the bird cage and Karen in the other. In the bow, we open out the board for the playpen and set it on a corner on a bucket. This widens the sleeping area on top of the lockers for Skip and me. Susie sleeps in the bunk that folds down over the steps.

At daylight, we pull anchor and head down Chatham Straits. Susie likes to sit on the hatch and hold Karen. We are in Troller Islands by 10:00. Talking to other fishermen on our radiophone, Skip learns the fishing is very slow. He still decides to put the tent in Troller Islands.

Gene Fisher and two other fishermen help construct the walls and floor of the tent. By evening we move ashore and sleep in it. We bring one baby bed for the two children. Eric sleeps at one end and Karen at the other. Susie and I sleep on folding cots. We bring a wood heater, a kerosene cook stove, card table and chairs to sit on and wooden boxes for storage. Skip makes a shelf from a piece of shiplap across the width of the tent. We're warm and snug in our tent.

The only problem is we have no water. Skip packs water from Gedney in washtubs. He strings up a clothesline. The next three days Skip fishes inside Troller Islands and outside on the Flats. Nothing. Never have we seen it so poor. It's like the halibut at Tyee. Is this going to be a jinx year?

A friend of ours runs down the west shore of Baranof and calls Skip from Patterson Bay. "What is it like over there, Skip? Worth coming over on that side?"

"I've never seen it so poor. Can't figure it out. Some feed around, too. No herring. The herring seiners must have got 'em all."

Two hours later a fellow and his uncle, who never fished before and have a very small boat, call Skip with their weak radiophone. "I'd come down here

At two, Eric wants to row the skiff when we camp in Troller Islands.

if I were you, Skip."

"Did ya hear that?" Skip asks. "Maybe something is going on down there since I left Gedney yesterday."

He pulls anchor and takes off. Knowing how conscientious Skip is, I'm concerned when he doesn't return for three days. I know that he won't let us run out of water. Later that night I hear *Salty's* engine. Eric crawls over the side of the crib to see his daddy. Karen cries for me to pick her up. We all run to the beach. As Skip left us the skiff, Susie and I carry it down to the water. It's still light as I row out to *Salty*.

"Marilyn, you've never seen anything like it. There's solid cohoes from Gedney to Malmesbury. Ya just go out and fish until ya don't want to land anymore. Everyone is making $200 a day. I made $250 yesterday. Buckshot is sending for Irene even though her baby is Karen's age. That scow is like '46 when it almost sank with fish. Boats wait in line until 3 a.m. to sell. There's nothing up this way yet."

He looks so tired that I feel sorry for him. For ten days he runs back and forth and each time he looks more tired.

The fish buyer pays us cash. Fishermen demand this after fish buyers' checks bounced in years past. I count $1000 in $20 bills. When we pay for fuel or groceries, I find it harder to part with cash than a check. We always send the money to the bank when we have more than $1000. I worry the boat might sink and we would lose all our money.

On the tenth day, Skip says, "Marilyn, do you think you can move on *Salty* for two or three days? I need your help. You're missing the fun of this fish run and seeing our friends."

We plan to sleep as we did when we left town. Like in a Pullman sleeper, we give Susie some privacy with a curtain around her bunk. Skip and I sleep spoon fashion on top of the lockers in the bow. It's cramped but everyone makes the best of it.

We hear some news about our kitty. Adam tells how Frisky and her offspring learned to catch the flying squirrels. One or two cats climb the trees and chase the squirrel to the ground where another cat catches it. If we get over to Malmesbury, we will stop and look for her.

It's good to see our friends when we arrive at the scow. Hazel and Herman are there, and Hazel is beaming from ear to ear. I spot Silent George and Dave Harrison.

Irish Bennett says, "In my 24 years in Alaska, I've never seen fishing like this."

Skip is walking up Buckshot's float when a man yells, "Skip Jordan!" It's Orville Berg, a high school classmate from Tacoma.

I am so happy that everything is working out. Skip can go to college, and we will have enough money. We apply for married student housing. If the fish keep coming for six weeks, we'll have our best season. To help our finances, we can fish *Salty* every summer. We won't need to sell her.

That afternoon the packer brings the first mail we receive since leaving Wrangell. Skip hands me a pile of mail, most of which are magazines. I watch him keep some. They're probably from his folks, I think.

I sit on a bench on the side of the scow reading my mail from my folks, Skip strolls over to me. "Marilyn, guess what?" he says, waving a telegram. "They need a skipper on their Fish and Wildlife research vessel. I can have the job if I come into Wrangell right away."

"You aren't going to take it, are you? You're

Skip with Eric and Karen in 1951

going to college."

"This is bet-
ter."

"What does it
pay?"

"$4000 a year."

"That isn't
enough. How can
we live on that?"

"We can buy a
house with the
money from the
boat...or rather
make a down-pay-

Eric and Karen play on the beach near our cabin.

ment on one. We'll make out fine."

I go to *Salty* and cry. He can't do this. I'm still crying when he comes in.

"I make the decisions in this family. I talked to lots of our friends and
they all think it's a fine deal. It'll give us security. This never knowing how
much we're going to make worries me. Besides, I was a skipper on a motor
launch in the Navy and it's what I love to do. How do you think I got the
nickname Skip?"

"But college, Skip? You'll make lots more when you're through."

"I'll probably start making $800 more a year than I would with this.
What if I flunk out? I haven't studied for 20 years. This is better than the
fishery management jobs as they are political."

"Please, Skip."

"No more talking. I've made up my mind. I'll send them a wire that we'll
be in there the first of August. That will give us seven days of fishing and two
days to tear down the tent and run to town."

Why hadn't I let him go in March? I never thought that he might change
his mind on college or that this temptation would come along. Well, I decide
that we'd better make as much as we can this last week. Good old *Salty*, we'll
have to sell her.

At daylight we head for Point Cosmos with 50 other boats. We troll
along the beach. We only catch ten cohoes on the first two drags.

After breakfast, Skip says, "This isn't as good as it has been. Maybe the
fish moved into Tebenkof. Old Emil Niemeyer said they set up that way ten

days after they hit Malmesbury. It's that time."

We try off the Gap where we had good fishing in '46. Gap Point is named becaus of the gap it forms into Explorers Basin. When we find few fish, we troll toward Point Ellis.

Finally, Skip pulls in our gear. "I'm going to run in there by the fish trap. I see a boat in there."

We come alongside Al, whom we only know slightly. He has a large white troller. "How are they biting?" Skip asks.

Looking at his bins, Al replies, "Looks like 150."

"You're kidding!"

"Come look for yourself."

"Marilyn! Get out here."

"I'm washing clothes. Can you wait until I'm done?"

"Hell, ya can wash clothes all winter. Get out here."

"Susie, you'll have to take charge of the babies and the cooking. We'll pay you well for it," I say. Thank God for Susie, I think.

We only fish seven fathoms as the fish lie along the reef. We fish four spreads on each line with one above the tag on the heavy lines. Every hook has a fish. In this shallow water, they really fight. I have difficulty gaffing the rolling, twisting cohoes.

Now, I must get the fish on deck and the hook back into the water as fast as possible. I devise a method. On the port side, with my left hand, I hold the leader against *Salty's* double-end. This makes a stationery target at which to aim the gaffhook.

Old friend Dave Harrison talks with Skip.

Often I dig a little deep and get a little of *Salty*. I'll never know why we don't sling them aboard.

When Skip pulls in his starboard bow, I pull in the port wing line, and then vice-versa. We work from one pole to the other. As soon as one line goes out, the next one comes in. We never stop. Skip knows that he can't let the cleaning get ahead of him. When he starts his line in, he cleans a fish. I gaff his fish and land it while he cleans. When I empty his line, he puts it back out and I bring in mine.

"This is the life," Skip says as he leans over and kisses me.

Every muscle in my body aches. Eric and Karen feel the excitement. Eric, who is not quite two, tries to help Daddy by pulling the cohoes into different bins with the gaffhook. On the hatch, Karen sits on Susie's lap. I couldn't have stayed in the troller pit without Susie's help. My arms are numb. I nurse Karen once, but the rest of the time, she takes a bottle.

Later, Irish joins us and shares in the good fishing. An elderly couple on the *Silver Fin* arrive. The man calls, "We're only fishing two lines. We can't handle more."

By dark, six of us are fishing there. Skip calls to each, "Let's all stay here tonight. If we run to the scow, the whole fleet will be here tomorrow. In this small area, they'll spoil the fishing for all of us." They all agree.

We have over 1500 pounds which Skip immediately ices in the hold. On this beautiful, calm night, we see not a ripple on the water. The seagulls are diving on the feed. Their squawking is deafening.

"July 24th is Mother's birthday. She'll be happy that it is our lucky day," I say.

"This will buy ya a sewing machine and an automatic washer. Ya need them," Skip says as we crawl onto the locker. He knows I'm still upset about his college decision.

At 3:30 a.m. we pull anchor. The fish are still there. What fun! When an empty hook comes up, we ask where the fish went. Steering isn't easy. Pillar Bay's floating fish trap provides an excellent landmark. We certainly don't want to hook up and take time to rig up new gear. The trap is catching many cohoes, too.

At 4 p.m., Al leaves and the rest of us run for the scow. We never know how much Al had for he sells in town. Skip speeds up the engine to cruising speed. The stern goes down into the water and we can barely see over the bow, which rises high in the air.

All the fishermen crowd around to see our catch. We have 2900 pounds of cohoes and 100 pounds of kings in a day and a half. It comes to $729. Tired and happy, we crawl into bed. The next day the fleet heads for Point Ellis. We stay at Gedney. Susie and I wash diapers while Skip scrubs out the hold and cleans up *Salty*. Everyone reports few fish at Point Ellis.

We fish until July 29 and then take down the tent and load lumber and supplies aboard. We experience the largest troll catch on record. It won't be exceeded for another 40 years. With tears in my eyes, I bid our friends good-bye. We head for town on July 30. Our friends report the cohoes come through all of August.

We move into the cabin and Susie stays with us until school starts. She helped me a great deal, and I know I didn't thank her enough.

On the Fish and Wildlife's research vessel, *Sablefish*, Skip enjoys the men that he works with on their escapment project. In October, the Fish & Wildlife Service announces that they plan to winter the *Sablefish* in Ketchikan.

When Skip prepares to move us to Ketchikan, he needs to do something with *Salty*. He hasn't put a for sale sign on her.

Two days before we are due to leave for Ketchikan, I suggest, "I can steer *Salty* and follow you on the *Sablefish*. Lucia Jewett does that when they go to

The Jordans have a portrait taken for Christmas presents in 1952.

Hole in the Wall."

"Absolutely not. Are ya going to leave the children on my boat?"

"There's more market down there. Maybe you can pay someone to run her down for us."

The next day he comes into the cabin and announces, "Two fellows want to take *Salty* crab fishing. I told them they could."

"Do you know them or anything about them?"

"I told them to charge no bills against her. I gave them the keys."

The next day I stand on the dock and cry as I watch *Salty* leave the harbor. Later that day, we climb aboard *Sablefish* and head for Ketchikan. We find housing very scarce and I wish we at least had *Salty* to live on. At last, we rent an old house that they will tear down when they build a tunnel next year. We make many friends but I miss my old friends in Wrangell. Life in the wintertime is much like Wrangell's though Ketchikan is bigger and has many more things to do.

Skip works hard trying to find a buyer for *Salty*. Finally Skip and a man fly to Petersburg where the crab fishermen left her. Tragically they can't get the engine started and the man decides not to buy her. Skip believes the engine is ruined. We drop the price and sell her to Clell Bacon for only $2500. Clell gets a good bargain because he finds he doesn't need to replace the engine.

In March the new crew arrives from Seattle. Skip soon learns that the man in charge of this project has no water savvy. He thinks the 38-foot *Sablefish* is a steamer and can run all over Alaska in any weather. Skip is in charge but this man insists he run in bad weather. Skip worries that if they wreck he'll be blamed, not the other guy. He's very unhappy. The first supervisor gave him a superior evaluation but this supervisor wants him fired.

Skip leaves in March and returns to town for a day here or a couple of hours there. He doesn't get to see how Eric and Karen are growing, or how much they are changing. No one is happy that summer, including me. I miss the excitement of fishing, but most of all I miss my husband.

CHAPTER FOURTEEN

Nohusit

A COLD NIP IN THE AIR MEANS WINTER is right around the corner. I anxiously await Skip's return. On Sunday, September 20, the *Sablefish* comes into port. I kiss Skip while Karen, who is almost two, and Eric, who just turned three, each hang onto a leg of their dad's. We celebrate his homecoming that night.

Early the next morning, Skip checks on the *Sablefish*. When he returns, he says, "I went over to the Thomas Basin dock in Ketchikan Harbor. The Hoffmans and their son, Donny, are in. I asked them to come for Sunday dinner. Is that all right?"

"Of course. I miss seeing our friends."

On Sunday with the meal almost ready, Skip leaves for the *Doneda* to bring the Hoffmans to our house. When he hurries up the steps alone, I can't figure out what happened.

"Push the dinner back. I just found our boat."

"I didn't know we were looking for a boat."

"We can live on this boat year around. Wait till ya see her."

Confused, I put coats on Eric and Karen and we head for the harbor.

"I saw this for sale sign, but I figured it would be too expensive. I walked on by but the owner asked me if I'm interested in a boat. I told him that I wasn't really. He invited me to come aboard and he'd show it to me. So I took a look. It has great living quarters, a head and even an ice box. Just wait 'till ya see it. It doesn't cost too much either. The fellow's wife left him and he wants to leave town."

Skip tells me that the boat's name is *Nohusit*, pronounced No-who-zit...an unromantic name for such a beautiful ship. It's a 45-foot cruiser that this owner made into a troller. The three areas are a sitting room pilot house; a galley down three steps in the stern, and a bow section with four bunks, full-length closet, a head with a lavatory, and even a full length mirror. Each bunk has an innerspring mattresses and its own reading lamp. The sleeping area resembles the Pullmans on trains.

A large, gas engine powers *Nohusit*. Skip likes the iron bark all around her hull. In fact, we like everything about her, but we tell the owner that we'll think about it.

At the *Doneda*, we greet the Hoffmans and walk to the house. All we talk about during dinner is the *Nohusit*. Hoffmans had a good season, but nothing like '51. After dinner, Don and Skip go back down to the dock and thoroughly look over *Nohusit*. They find some dry rot in a corner of the pilothouse. The Hoffmans like the boat, but I'm not so sure we want to get back into fishing.

After the children are in bed, Skip fixes us each a rare drink and asks, "Well, what do ya think, Marilyn?"

I hesitate, "Like you say, it will make a good home. They're going to tear down this house, and we'll have to find another place. Rents are so high. You can continue with the Fish & Wildlife. Maybe we can take our boat out and anchor it where you're working." I know now that Skip will never let me steer the boat to follow him on the *Sablefish*. He doesn't trust me. Why are we doing this? I didn't know we wanted another boat. We've been apart so much the last year. He seems so excited about *Nohusit*.

"We've gambled before. It's fine with me," I say.

"We can't lose anything by buying it. We certainly can't buy a house for that kind of money. Until the children are in school, we shouldn't tie ourselves down."

After Skip leaves the next day on the *Sablefish*, I fill out a bank financial statement. They will consider our loan application at their Board of Director's meeting the next evening. To own a documented boat, I must take Skip's citizenship papers to the lawyer who will make out the papers on the sale.

Nohusit's price is $6500 but the bank tells me they will only loan us $3000. I count every penny. I take the money from *Salty* and the inheritance from my grandparents. We only have enough money to insure the bank's part of the loan. On September 23, I sign the papers and pay the owner. *Nohusit* is ours. When Skip comes back he hires a man to make the breakfast nook in the galley into a double bed for us. We give our landlady notice that we'll move on November first. We sell our furniture and put our excess clothes and other items in storage yet again.

No one knows what effect President Eisenhower's election will have on the US Fish & Wildlife Service. The middle of November, we learn that they will station the *Sablefish* in Seattle for the winter and will only hire a skipper from March 15 to October 15. We have difficulty living on their year-around salary let alone a half-year salary.

"Well, there goes our security," Skip laments. "Aren't we fortunate to have the *Nohusit*? I'll wager the bank wouldn't have given us a loan if they knew this. We would be in a panic if we had to pay rent on a house." He pauses and takes my hand. "Don't worry. We'll fish *Nohusit*. We can pull in our belts easier on the boat."

Skip on Nohusit

We take it in stride. I talk Skip into letting me get a job during the Christmas season. I haven't worked in eight years but find it enjoyable. Skip takes care of the children the month I'm working. Since they're both out of diapers he can handle it. Eric and Karen love living on the boat. He gets them to help him. To them it's an adventure. Skip plans a party two days after Christmas to show off the boat. It's a big success and everyone loves *Nohusit*. We leave the day before New Years' for Skip hears that one of the supermarkets wants filleted red snapper to sell. He says, "I know just where to get them at Bell Island. Let's start 1953 with our gear in the water." Bell Island was named by Vancouver for his Midshipman, Edward Bell, who kept a journal of the voyage. Bell Island has a resort with a hot springs.

Our friends Hank and Sue Barrow will run with us. We wouldn't have gone out if they hadn't agreed because Skip doesn't like to run alone in a new boat. You just never know what could happen, he says. The *Nohusit* doesn't have a radiophone so if we got into trouble we wouldn't even be able to call for help.

On a crisp clear day with a cold wind blowing down Behm Canal and the temperature in the 20's, we take *Nohusit* on her maiden voyage. After running this course often with the *Sablefish*, Skip knows how to stay in the lee of the wind. The snow-covered mainland peaks stand out against the deep blue winter sky. A silver frost covers the trees. The beauty of this area always takes my breath away and I can't imagine living anywhere else.

I forget how much I enjoyed running our own boat. It's been 18 months since I was on *Salty*. Sitting on the stool beside Skip, I drink in all the beauty that unfolds before me. On the boat, I also have less housework and more time to enjoy Eric and Karen. They like to sit on the ledge in front of the wheel. Even though only two and three, they enjoy watching the scenery.

"This is the life!" Skip says taking a deep breath as if he can inhale it. "We're all together again, which is best of all. I keep thinking of ya when I'm away."

For Christmas, we had bought the children a record player. With our inverter, we change our 32 volt system into 110. I can also use my mixer and sewing machine and Skip uses his electric razor.

Upon arising, the children play their records. To my dying day, I'll hear "Little Red Caboose" and "Little White Duck" playing over and over in my mind.

On New Year's Eve, our old friend, Dave Harrison, comes into Bell Island's float where we're tied. All evening he entertains us, and Hank and Sue, with his many experiences. This is so unlike him that we love every minute of it.

"Did Ah ever tell y'all about the spring Ah went ashore to cut trolling poles?"

We shake our heads. Dave has a heavy Virginia accent. "All Ah took was a hatchet and a saw. Ah was busy chopping when Ah heard a wolf bark to my left. Ah didn't think nothing about it. A few minutes later Ah heard one howl on the other side. Ah stopped when one howled right behind me. A pack of wolves surrounded me! Ah was a good quarter of a mile from that beach. They scared me, Ah'll tell ya. Ah left that saw right in the tree and grabbed my hatchet and ran for the skiff. Ah'd hear one yelp on one side, another answer on the other side. They were gettin' closer, but Ah couldn't see them. Ah jumped into the skiff and pushed out from shore. Three of the biggest wolves Ah'd ever seen ran out of the brush. They sniffed where Ah'd been. One sat on his haunches and put his nose in the air and howled. Have ya ever heard them howl? The hair'll rise on your neck. The next day Ah took ma rifle along. Ah got the pole and saw. Never heard a noise that day. Ah should have known to carry a gun, but Ah knew it would be all Ah could do to drag the pole. Ah didn't want to fool with no gun."

Dave enjoys telling stories, a trait of many old-timers. He shoots only for meat to eat, never just to kill. He views contemptuously the newcomers who are always shooting at something.

"They wound more animals. The animals have a right to live the same as the next fellow," he emphatically explains.

Dave finds trapping difficult this year because the large snow drifts cover his traps. This makes it hard for him to find them. Dave would never leave his traps out because any caught mink would slowly freeze to death. He doesn't want any animal to suffer needlessly. He pulls most of his traps that day and waits for warmer weather.

We all gather at Old Albert's for an evening of visiting and music.

Skip puts out our gear on New Year's Day. We catch eight red snappers. We fish red snapper like we fish for halibut. Suddenly, the temperature drops to ten degrees above zero. *Nohusit* is warm every place but in the bow section. We can't figure out how to get warm air into the lower sections. The only time the bow is warm is when the engine is running. When the engine stops it gets cold. We can't run the engine all the time so I bundle Eric and Karen up in wool clothes and pray no one gets sick.

Someone has given us a little gray and white kitten. This turns out to be a life saver for me because it keeps Eric and Karen entertained for hours. Sometimes the best toys are the ones that cost the least. When the cold spell breaks, we run back to Ketchikan with our red snappers and six salmon. The money only pays for our expenses.

"Let's go to Ernest Sound," Skip says after we take ice and fuel and put groceries aboard. "We've caught fish there at this time of year. We can fish every day up there. Always some place that you can get in the lee of the wind."

When we arrive in Ernest Sound I feel comfortable. We fished here our first years and know it well. "We need you, Ernest Sound, to bring us luck," I pray. We need a good trip to make our bank payments. We don't want to start the season with too many bills.

We spend many nights tied to Old Albert's float in Niblack Island. Often Johnny and Dorothy Melon are there with Sandra, who is Karen's age. The children crawl around the floor playing. Friends from Wrangell often stop in to say hello and see how we're doing. Each morning we head for the fishing grounds from Sunny Bay to the north end of Deer Island, to Brownson Island to the mouth of Zimovia Straits. We average five kings a day. At night we compare notes with the other fishermen at Old

Eric and Karen with their dog and parakeet in Ketchikan

Albert's. We fish for ten days then run into Wrangell to sell and stock up on ice and groceries. I also get to do laundry when we are in town. We have two $200 trips which makes the boat payments. I enjoy seeing our Wrangell friends such as Marjorie and Carl Guggenbickler on the floats in the harbor.

When the fishing slacks off in February, we pull our gear at Point Eaton and work our way back to Ketchikan. I have a nagging feeling, "Drink in all this beauty, Marilyn, you might not see it again for a long time."

On the morning of our anniversary, in Meyers Chuck, Skip starts marking our lines. He unreels the lines off the gurdy by walking up the dock with the end. A full gurdy holds 100 fathoms of wire. He marks each of the four lines every two fathoms with Oregon Leader. I cook a special dinner. Our friends, Irish Bennett and Pat Patterson, come aboard for a cup of coffee and to look over our new boat. Skip's too busy marking. When darkness comes at six, he continues working under the float lights until 8 p.m. He finally comes in and eats my special dinner I've tried to keep warm. Skip yawns, "I'm too tired to even visit."

"You pick the right thing to do at the wrong time."

"It has to be done. I can't fish well with the markers gone. I accomplished a lot today. I won't have to do it later."

I'm hurt for this isn't any ordinary day. It's our seventh anniversary. I tuck the children into bed and silently cry myself to sleep. Men just don't understand how important these things are to women.

The next day we head for Ketchikan where we put *Nohusit* on the grid to copper paint the hull. *Nohusit's* a much bigger job than *Salty*. How many years now have we worked to get the paint on fast enough to beat the tide? Could it be seven years?

"We must have a depth sounder," Skip declares. "I saw a Bendix that looks great in the shop today. I'm thinking of ordering it. I can have it for $100 down and the rest when the fishing gets good."

"Since we paid our income tax, we're practically down to our last $100. It scares me to get so low."

"We'll catch more fish. We'll easily earn its cost back."

The next day he orders it, but it hasn't arrived when we leave on March 16. As we seldom fish in March, we aren't sure where to go. Skip hears they're getting fish at Moser Bay at the north end of Tongass Narrows. We make it to Moser Bay just ahead of a huge snow storm. The bay is named for Lieutenant Commander Jefferson Moser of the USC&GS. He later became general superintendent of the Alaska Packers Association. We end up laying in the harbor for three days before the storm clears. We pass the time visiting with old friends like Charlie Waterson on the *Murellet*.

Finally on the fourth day we're planning to fish. When Skip starts the engine he says, "Something's wrong. There's no water in the fresh water cooler. It's sprung a leak."

"What will we do?"

"We'll run back to town. I'll keep pouring more water in it. It isn't running

Eric and Skip in the troller pit of Nohusit in February of 1953

out too fast. It'll take us an hour and a half to get there."

Another worry. More expenses. Skip puts *Nohusit* on the grid. "I don't think they can solder our keel-cooler. A whole new one is very expensive. I saw an ad for a new system, and the shop by the harbor is handling it. It's called aqua-clear units. You pump the salt water into this bowl, and it takes out the salt. Water with the salt removed cools your engine without hurting it."

"I didn't know they perfected anything like that. Are you sure it will work on this large an engine?" He assures me that it will work, but we have less than $100 left after he gets it installed.

On Saturday night, Skip races into the pilothouse where I'm feeding the children and shouts, "The depth sounder is here! It's at the airlines. Tomorrow I'll call the shop and see if they'll let me have it for the air freight. We'll pay the rest when we get in from our fishing trip."

"How are you going to pay the $100, Skip? We spent that money for the aqua-clear."

"I've got a friend who will loan it to me."

"You haven't!"

"We always pay everyone. Don't get that sick look."

He calls the shop's owner for him to okay his taking the meter out of the airlines office. The owner isn't home, but his wife says it's all right. Skip is like a child with a new toy. He likes the big dial. He puts the transducer in the bilge. He invites Jimmy Sprague to run out in the channel to try it. They report that it works excellently.

"Now, we don't need to worry about losing gear," he predicts.

On the previous day, Grace Durham had flown in from the states. She and Hank on the *Alameda* plan to fish with us. Grace is an attractive woman, whom I guess to be in her 50s, but she looks younger. Hank, who is older, first came to Alaska on charter boats. He knows Southeast Alaska well. Sunday night after I put the children to bed, the four of us discuss where to go.

Hank asks, "Have you fished south of here at Point Alva and Mary Island?"

"Never have. I don't know the harbors down that way at all."

"It's often good this time of year. I'll show you the drags and where to anchor. Your new depth sounder will help."

"I hope so. We're really in the hole." The men continue to make plans. Later, Skip says, "I feel so much better that Grace and Hank will run with us."

CHAPTER FIFTEEN

When Friends Count

EARLY IN THE MORNING ON MARCH 23, Skip listens to the weather report on our radio. "Winds 25 to 40 miles per hour with occasional stronger gusts this afternoon."

Skip leans on the table and holds his head, "I don't like that weather forecast. Let's not untie."

I am insistent. "Let's get ice and fuel, and we'll be ready to go when the weather breaks. I'll get groceries as soon as they open at 8 a.m. so we need to get back."

I ignore his reluctance and continue. "Will you get our 16 mm movies that we took with the folk's camera and slides out of storage? I want to work on them while we're out. I'm going to do the program for my PEO women's group the first week in April. It'll be Easter when we get back, so I'm going to leave some things for the cleaners."

Skip gives me a dirty look and goes up the dock to get the items. I guess he doesn't think we should untie the boat with these weather reports. I just want to help him get ready and I don't want him to be mad.

"Here are all the pictures, Marilyn," Skip says bringing them in. "I'll put them on the top bunk above Eric. How are ya doing?"

"They'll deliver the groceries any minute, then I'm all ready. I'll give this cleaning to Dorothy."

"That overcoat is clean enough. Just send the suit. I'll see if Hank and Grace are ready."

Diane Olson, the six-foot blonde on the *White Light*, knocks on the pilot-house door. She says, "Here are the books I borrowed. You might want them."

Skip backs *Nohusit* out, and I wave good-bye to Dorothy and Diane, who stand on the dock. Dorothy has our cleaning in her arms. Hank and Grace pull out first. They head for the oil dock.

"Let's get ice first," Skip says. "We'll have to wait for them. Now that the Standard Oil dock is being rebuilt after the fire, it has poor facilities." He continues grimly, "I can't understand what we're doing out on a day like this,

Marilyn. Look, the wind is picking up all the time."

"I admit that it doesn't look too good, but how are we going to make the payments tied to a dock?"

We will be glad that *Nohusit* is full of ice. When we arrive at the Standard Oil dock, Grace knocks, "May I come aboard?"

"Certainly. I'm here in the galley stowing away groceries." Eric's playing train in the grocery box in the pilothouse with the kitten. Karen is in the galley with me. "Sit here in the breakfast nook."

I turn off the galley fire, and Skip turns on the exhaust blower that sucks any gas fumes out of the engine room.

Skip announces, "I can barely get 40 gallons of gas in her. We only went to Musher Bay. I'll light your galley stove and then pay the bill. I want to talk to Hank about this weather."

"Skip's mad at me," I tell Grace. "He thinks we shouldn't untie the boat and leave the harbor. Say, do you smell gas?" I sniff and so does Grace. "I suppose it's all right. The blower is going."

Fifteen minutes later, Skip sticks his head in the door and makes a comment. Usually, he comes in to start the engine.

"What did he say, Grace?"

"It sounds like he wants you to start the engine."

I climb the three steps into the pilothouse. Grace sticks her head out the side door to hear him. Skip has untied the stern and stands on the bow untying its line. I push the starter. A deafening roar shakes the boat. Pieces of wood fly around me. I recall Skip saying, "A gas engine in a boat is like sitting on dynamite. It only takes a cup of gas to explode."

I hear Skip's yelling, "Oh, my God, Marilyn, the children."

I don't know how I got the ten feet across the length of the pilothouse. The six-foot engine room doors had blown open. Did I step on a board? Somehow I hurdle them. I hear Karen crying in the galley. My first conscious act is to jump down into the galley. The explosion has blown out the steps.

I pick up the highchair, which lies on top of Karen. Skip comes in the back door and grabs Karen as I lift the highchair.

I think, "Eric! Where's Eric?"

He was in the pilothouse, but he isn't there. Grace has been blown out the door, and Skip pulls her further back onto the dock and runs for the stern. I think, "I must call Eric," but no sound comes out.

Suddenly, I hear, "Mama! Mama!" It's the most wonderful sound I have ever heard! I lean over and look into the engine room where the steps blew out. He is pinned in front of the reduction gear. I see the flames. I reach for his arms and pull with all my strength.

He's free! I pull him into the galley. His clothes aren't on fire. Somehow we get outside. I claim that the windows blew out of the breakfast nook, and I climbed on the seat and stepped out on the side of the boat. Skip thinks this is impossible. I must have climbed out the stern door, but I remember looking back and seeing Skip and Karen to the stern of us.

Luckily, Skip has retied *Nohusit's* bow to the dock. The stern has drifted away from the dock. I get out on deck in time to see the attendant on the dock pull back the line that he threw too short for Skip to grab. On the next try, Skip grabs it and pulls in the boat and secures it to the dock.

We both step to the dock with the children. The attendant takes a big fire extinguisher and points it toward the burning boat and sets it off. He is too far away and the CO2 foam runs out before he gets close enough. In horror, we watch the flames engulf *Nohusit*. This is both our home and our livelihood.

Hank helps Grace up the ramp. "I'm hurt, Marilyn," she whimpers.

"Oh, I'm so sorry, Grace."

Skip carries Eric and he holds Karen's hand. At the top of the ramp, I turn and look at *Nohusit*. Flames are burning the pilothouse curtains. I think, maybe this is the last time I'll see our boat.

"Marilyn!" Skip calls. "Hurry! Ya must get Eric to the hospital."

Two workmen say they'll drive us to the hospital in their pick-up truck. I climb into the front seat next to the driver. I hold Eric while Karen sits on the other man's lap. Skip pats my hand and says he must see what he can do for *Nohusit*. He'll come to the hospital as soon as he can. It's all so surreal that I just nod my head.

I see Eric's hair is all singed. I start to touch it, but the man says, "Don't do that."

Arriving at the hospital, the Sister asks who my doctor is.

"Dr. Stagg."

"Go up to the operating rooms on third floor."

Dr. Stagg's office is only two blocks away. He runs over. He's there by the time I get to the operating room. I look down at little Karen, who is holding my pant leg. She only has one shoe. None of us have coats.

Dr. Stagg methodically bandages Eric. Eric's hands are badly burned. The worst places are his right ear and a round spot like a 50-cent piece in his hairline.

"We may graft skin on his ear and forehead," Dr. Stagg says. "You're so lucky that his clothes didn't catch on fire."

Karen is not hurt badly. Just her hair is a little singed. Before Dr. Stagg finishes with Eric, I turn around to find my friend, Leah Hattrick. She gives me a hug.

"Karen, you come with me," Leah says.

I pat Karen's head. She obediently follows Leah away.

"I heard them blow an all clear siren. Maybe the fire's out," Dr. Stagg says.

I wonder what is happening to Skip and *Nohusit*.

After putting us in the truck, Skip races to the dock to try to save whatever he can of *Nohusit*. In dismay, he sees them cut the boat free, and she drifts out into the channel.

I've got to get a skiff and get out to her, he thinks.

He spies a skiff on the beach left by a construction crew. As he climbs into it, a fireman comes up.

"Get in. We'll pull her onto the beach so you can put hoses aboard," Skip says.

With Skip's precise rowing, they quickly get to the burning boat. The fireman grabs the rope hanging over *Nohusit's* bow. Skip starts to row, pulling *Nohusit* toward the beach. He finds superhuman strength to do it. Another fireman stands with outstretched hands to grab the rope as he nears the beach. Suddenly, he starts going backwards. He stops and lets the skiff drift around until he can see around the burning boat. A Coast Guardsman in a skiff with an outboard is towing *Nohusit* in the opposite direction toward the fireboat. Skip lets go and he and the fireman drift back to the beach.

Unknown to Skip, the regular fireboat captain isn't at the helm. A shoe salesman is running the boat. With the *Nohusit* alongside the fireboat, they pump water into her and the flames die down.

From shore, Skip thinks, "Thank goodness only the pilothouse burned. The bow and galley sections are intact."

Then the fireboat's engine dies when its captain tries to idle it too slowly. In disbelief, Skip watches the flames flare up again and burn the bow and galley. Only the cold ice on the other side of the hold's bulkhead keeps the flames from spreading into it. In the half-hour it takes to start the fireboat's engine, the wind blows the two boats closer and closer to Pennock Island.

I can't row out there, Skip thinks. As if in answer to his prayers, a man runs by in an outboard. "Can ya take me out to that burning boat? It's mine."

The man nods and quickly they run out to the burning boat. "Hey," Skip calls. "Don't let my boat drift on the beach."

"You want the hull?" a fireman asks.

"I sure do. Get some pumps into her. She's going to sink."

"Come aboard and help."

After thanking the man with the skiff, Skip climbs aboard. He takes a bucket of water to douse the flames burning some sacks stowed over the refrigerator. He crawls into the fireboat's hold for heavy lines. With wind whipping in his face, he climbs onto *Nohusit's* bow with the rope. After looping the rope over the cleat, he throws it to a fireman, on the fireboat's bow. He sees that a minute later the *Nohusit* would have drifted onto the nearby beach.

"It's getting shallow, Jordan," the captain shouts. "We must get the fireboat into deeper water."

Skip tests the line as he learned when tug boating. He climbs back on the fireboat, "Now give her full throttle," he says.

Slowly, the partially sunken hull swings to the port into deeper water. They will win the battle unless she starts sinking. They slowly pull her across the channel to the Coast Guard base. They secure *Nohusit* to another Coast Guard ship. The ship's big pumps start pumping out the hull. Skip jumps aboard to search for our important papers, cameras and pictures. Everything is fire-singed and water-soaked. The cameras and pictures are a total loss.

A Coast Guard corpsman discovers blood spurting from a cut on Skip's right hand. They take Skip to the hospital where Dr. Stagg stitches a small artery closed.

I look up from Eric's bedside to see

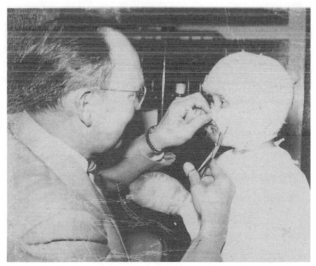

Dr. Stagg cuts Eric's bandages that covered his 3rd degree burns.

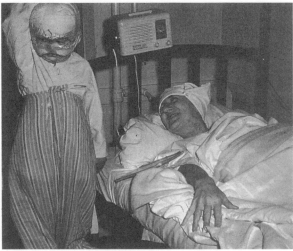
Eric visits Grace Durham in the hospital.

Skip come in with the doctor. I just take his hand. I know I can't start crying as I won't be able to stop. Later, I learn that those watching the boat burn looked and looked for Skip. The rumor started that he drowned. I'm certainly glad no one came to the hospital and told me that. I would have collapsed.

When we're alone beside Eric's bed, Skip and I sit and cling to each other for a long time. We don't say a word. We both know how lucky we are to be alive.

After Skip relates what happened with the boat I tell him, "You did wonderfully. What if we'd lost the hull?"

"We were all clicking. What if we hadn't found Eric? I get sick every time I think of it. The good Lord had his arms around the Jordans today, but he didn't give a damn about the *Nohusit.*"

Grace's condition worries us. The x-ray shows she has a fractured vertebrate. She spends four months in the hospital in a cast. She's a good scout about it all. She never blames us for it and we become even better friends.

I spend long hours sitting beside Eric's bed. Dr. Stagg completely bandaged his head except for his eyes and mouth. One eye swells shut from a big blister below it, and another blister covers his nose. Covered with bandages, his hands look like boxing gloves.

The second morning after the explosion, Eric asks, "Mama, where's kitty?" I hadn't thought of her, but I reply, "I suppose she jumped off the boat and swam for shore."

Sitting there, I wonder what we will do now. Everything is gone. When Skip cleans up *Nohusit*, he finds that our kitten had crawled under a bow bunk and drowned. Our beautiful boat is only a charred hull. Our savings are gone. I wonder what we have left. I feel we're at a crossroads. Next week, it will be seven years since we arrived in Alaska. Shall we leave and start over somewhere else?

A boy brings a newspaper to the hospital. "Eric, look! A picture of *Nohusit.*" With his one eye, he peers at it. "She all burn up, Mama."

For a long time, he looks at the picture and then says, "Daddy go buy new pilothouse. Eric help Daddy on *Nohusit.* Then we go fishing."

Suddenly, I know the answer. We made Eric, a baby salt. We taught our children to love the sea and to love fishing. We make it fun for them. We can't turn to something else. Our children, even if they are only two- and three-year olds, aren't going to let us. Houses burn, but you don't stop living in them. The next time we'll put in a diesel engine, and we'll rebuild *Nohusit* just the way we want to. It'll be our dream boat.

Over the next couple of weeks, we learn how generous and wonderful people can be. The first night when I go to Leah's, I find a box of clothing from the girls in the store where I worked at Christmas. The note says, "We want you to know we're standing by."

Another friend comes to the hospital and pushes $25 into my hand, "I know you'll have use for this."

Jimmy Sprague brings our coats up to the hospital. Letters and packages come from friends all over Southeast Alaska and the West Coast. Diane Olson and Dorothy Sprague organize a trollers' wives committee that launches a drive for money, clothing and household articles.

The committee writes a letter to the editor of the Ketchikan papers, saying, "This is our chance to prove that we really do practice, not just talk about, the Golden Rule."

Friends sit with Eric, which allows me to run errands. A couple we'd never met calls and offers us their home for a month while they

Nohusit is only a charred hull after the explosion and fire.

take their vacation to the lower 48. I never could thank them enough. Some men Skip doesn't even know help him clean up the debris and work on the boat. Harry Kaetz, who has a shipyard on Pennock Island, offers to put *Nohusit* there and Skip can help him rebuild it.

Civic and service organizations, church groups, fishermen and businessmen join to help us. They start a "Jordan Fund" and raise nearly $2000 for us. Everyone's generosity overwhelms us. We can't leave Alaska. It's part of us. When we came, we knew no one, and now we have many friends. They tell us, not by words but by deeds, that this is our home. We resolve to rebuild *Nohusit* and go trolling again. Knowing you don't stand alone is powerful.

Material items can suddenly be destroyed but through the years of fishing Skip and I have gained confidence in ourselves and our abilities. This provides us with true security.

Not much is left after Skip rescues the hull.

CHAPTER SIXTEEN
Our Last Two Dimes

WE MOVE TO THE COUPLE'S HOME for three weeks and slowly get our bearings. Pete Woolery, Buckshot's brother, now owns the buying scows. He offers to set Skip up as the fishbuyer in Tebenkof Bay. It doesn't start for six weeks though.

Every day, I think, "Where will we go?" We don't have enough money to stay in a hotel.

A friend says, "Now, if worse comes to worst, there's our basement. There's a toilet down there, and you can use a hot-plate."

Another friend offers her attic. When the week comes that the house owners are due back, I tell Skip, "You better check out that basement."

He soon returns and says, "We could get along in the basement, but your friend says there's no sink and she doesn't think one can do without a sink. I'll bet her husband said no. She is flabbergasted that we'd even consider it."

The friend with the attic is an even worse situation. You must go through their bedroom to the bathroom. I decide that with two small children this will never work. "What are we going to do?" I cry.

The telephone rings, "Mrs. Jordan, this is Mrs. Kimball." She did house cleaning for me during Skip's Fish & Wildlife days. "We're wondering if you found a place to stay."

"No, we haven't," I say.

"Well, we have an extra bedroom. You can stay with us. It isn't anything fancy. We have a six-year crib for your children. Our grandchildren have outgrown it. They live with us."

"Did you talk it over with your husband?" I ask. I don't want to make that mistake twice.

"Oh, yes, we talked it over first."

"Thank you so much for the invitation. We may take you up on it. I'll call you when I talk it over with Skip."

"It's a place at least," I tell Skip. "You better walk out there and see what it looks like. I don't know where they live. It's probably in the phone book." The Kimball home is on North Tongass Avenue. Skip walks there but finds no one at home.

"It's a two-story house on the water side of the road. It looks all right." he reports.

I call Mrs. Kimball and tell her that we'll be happy to accept their invitation. I hire her to help clean the house we are in the day before the owners arrive. They're arriving on the noon plane, and we leave the house at 11 a.m. We are forever thankful to these people for letting us stay in their house. Skip borrows a truck to take our belongings while Eric, Karen and I go in a taxi. We knock on the door as the Kimballs are finishing lunch.

"Just make yourselves at home," Elmer, her husband, calls.

Mrs. Kimball says, "This is your bedroom here. I think everything is ready. I've a job this afternoon, and Elmer is working now, too."

Mrs. Kimball is a small lady in her 60s. I look around and realize that she must be too tired to clean her own house as there are breakfast dishes in the sink and they just left their lunch dishes on the table. Dust is everywhere. They must not have a lot of money to spend on the house's up-keep. I wish I could paint their walls. The linoleum is well worn.

As they leave, Elmer says, "There's wood for the stove in the box there. If you run out, there's more out front. Lily got a load yesterday. You probably saw the pile."

When they're gone, I push the plates to one side of the table and put my head down to cry. Eric comes over and asks, "Mommy, what you cry for?"

"I can't stay here," I tell Skip. These people have so little and yet they are willing to share with us; I just can't burden them even more. Skip takes me in his arms, and I continue, "I don't know what else we can do."

I crawl onto his lap, and we cling together. "But honey," he says, "They're willing to share what they have with us. I know it isn't much, but it's all they have." He laughs, "Maybe I should pitch our tent in the middle of the avenue. That's all we have to live in."

I laugh, too, and Eric and Karen laugh without knowing why. A sentence comes to mind, "It isn't what happens to you in this world that matters, but the way you react to it." Of course, my pride is hurt. I remember that Christ didn't send away the widow who had only one mite to give. The Kimballs are willing to share their home with us.

I look around again from my vantage point in Skip's lap. "It won't take much to do a little cleaning, because it certainly isn't filthy. You take some of our food and make us some lunch. I'll wash the dishes. We want them to be glad that they shared with us. We'll have it spic and span when they get home."

I get out the children's toys and they play on the floor. I sing as I work just like Cinderalla did. After we eat, I put the children in the crib and read them a story. They immediately fall to sleep.

Skip buys groceries since we want to furnish as much of the food as possible. Then he chops some of the wood, while I wash the dishes and put our clothes away. The Kimball's grandchildren, who are around seven and nine years old, come home from school. They enjoy playing with Eric and Karen. By the time the Kimballs arrive, I have a meat loaf and a pie made.

Mrs. Kimball approves of what I did. She sets the big table in the dining room while Elmer starts the automatic coffee-pot.

"We bought this for $5 at the second-hand store. It makes the best coffee," Elmer says proudly.

Mrs. Kimball says, "Let's stop this Missus and Mister stuff. My name's Lily."

"Please call me Marilyn," I happily say.

Lily explains as we wash dishes, "Elmer was a good shop electrician where he lived down South. Now that he's in his early sixties, he hasn't found steady work. Perhaps, the insurance rates are too high for older men."

I notice Lily puts the grandchildren in the upstairs, a kind of attic. We must have taken their room.

The next morning we awaken to the aroma of breakfast. "Pancakes!" the children cry in glee as they climb out of the crib and race for the kitchen. Lily's grandchildren are already eating.

Elmer turns from placing a cake on Lily's plate. "I made plenty for everyone. Here's the batter. We're all done with the pancakes." He gives a chuckle, "I always end up with two eggs."

"Elmer does all the cooking when he isn't working," Lily explains.

"Hurry, Lily, bus time," Elmer says pushing back his chair from the table. "Time for you children to go to school, too."

"I hope you find everything you want. The washing machine's on the back porch," Lily says as they leave.

We enjoy the three weeks we live with the Kimballs. The only bad time is when I awaken with pains in my side. The doctor diagnoses a cyst on my right ovary so I must immediately have surgery.

We easily find subjects to talk about with Lily and Elmer. I enjoy hearing of Lily's experiences with her Native family. She enjoys the present, especially her grandchildren she is raising.

Eric on the float at the Hole-in-the-Wall.

When Lilly has a hard day, Elmer shakes back his wisp of white hair and says, "When I get steady work, Lily's not going to work anymore. She's worked hard her whole life."

The three weeks go quickly. Suddenly it's time to be fish buyers. Pete claims that he doesn't have the contract ready when we leave town. Then we find that we'll be at Hole-In-The-Wall, located on the west coast of Prince of Wales Island, south of Chatham Straits. This is a good spot to be in early in the season. We also have competition from Bob Smith's buying scow.

We cater to the Native fishermen as most of the white fishermen sell to Bob Smith. One of our Native fishermen always has the largest catch though. As we're to be paid on a commission basis, we work very hard for little money. We use our own money to buy groceries and fishing gear to sell in the store.

When Pete sends out the contract three weeks later, Skip says, "This protects him from us, but it certainly doesn't protect us from him. We're getting out of this business before we lose more than we make."

One of the Natives tells Skip about a boat for sale cheap in Klawock, the Native village about 20 miles away. Skip and Eric go to look at it. As it costs only $700, Skip buys it. I'm excited that we are trollers again and happy to retire from fish-buying, even though we did it for only a month. The *Triking* is only 30 feet long with hardly any pilothouse or living quarters. Luckily, we brought our tent with us as the boat is too small for all of us. Each morning Skip goes fishing and I stay in the tent with Eric and Karen. This time we're near water and the buying scow and Skip comes back each night.

One day, George Anniskett and his son, Alfred, arrive. They rowed their open boat from the Native village of Klawock. We call George our "Old Man of the Sea," because he has fished these waters as long as anyone can remember. They live in a tent nearer the scow than us, and row out to fish. The Native fishermen face the bow of the boat and pull ahead with little effort and in perfect rhythm. We sit outside our tent and watch George and Alfred fish as the Natives have done for years.

I meet Danny and Benny James. Danny tells me, "When Benny goes out with the boys, I used to tag along. I finally decided that was a mistake and now I stay home."

Hazel and Herman on the *Betty K* and Lonnie on the *Ytka* are there. On the Fourth of July everyone takes the day off from fishing and has a potluck picnic on the beach. There is even an impromptu baseball game.

A week later the fishing slacks off. Skip decides to move us and we take down the tent and move aboard *Triking*. Skip builds a triangular bunk in the peak of the bow for all of us. Skip sleeps crosswise at the widest point in the front, I'm next and Eric and Karen have the peak.

We find later that we should have followed Hazel and Herman to Sea Otter Sound for they have good fishing there. We by-pass Tokeen by picking our way up Dry Pass toward Point Baker.

I find it very difficult to live on *Triking*. With only a 15-gallon water tank, I must save my dish rinse water to reheat it for washing Karen's diapers. I realize what a difference it makes between a 10-gallon and a 15-gallon water tank.

We go to Tebenkof through Rocky Pass with the Praders on the *Irish* and the *Ark*. Surely we will find fish there, but alas the fishing is still poor. We hear they're catching fish across Chatham Straits.

"Let's go to Port Alexander," I say. "I like fishing there."

"Absolutely not," Skip replies. "What if this old boat springs a leak on the way over there. We might all drown in the middle of Chatham Straits. Chatham can be really rough."

There's no use arguing with him. I think we will just miss out on the good run of fish there. Skip isn't in the mood to make $10 to $20 a day in Tebenkof. In the end we retrace our route to Port Protection.

Point Baker tides are treacherous. One day, the tide sweeps us over a seven fathom pinnacle. We lose three lines of gear.

"Well, that cleans us. Let's give up this fishing. I'm going to take ya into Wrangell and put ya in the cabin. At least we still have that." Skip exclaims.

We hadn't gone back there when the boat burned because the boat's hull was in Ketchikan. We thought we had more chances of jobs there. I like the idea now though. I beg him to rerig and go out alone for the cohoes are sure to come. He goes after he settles us in the cabin. I'm right, the cohoes do come, and he does well alone.

The children love playing at the homesite. They freely run in the woods. We pick many blue- and huckle-berries, and I make lots of jam and jelly.

When Skip returns the last of August, he announces, "We better head for Point Ward and get in on those fish. Ya going to come with me?"

I don't answer for life is easier in the cabin than on the boat. I point to his hand that has fish poisoning and urge him to go to the doctor.

When he returns with some medicine, he says, "Doc doesn't want me cleaning fish until this heals. I might get blood poisoning."

"That decides it. I better go with you." We pack clothes for the children in a sea bag, and buy groceries, fuel and ice. We head for Ernest Sound on September second. Eric's birthday is the third. One look at Skip's hand tells me that he can't clean fish that day. I never have cleaned fish and to my dismay we catch 47 cohoes. Skip doesn't use a fish trough, which holds the fish upright with its belly upward. He always lays the fish on its side and slits the belly. For me the fish keeps moving around the deck. With much effort, I finally clean the fish.

Skip claims I have blood and guts from bow to stern of *Triking*.

When we get out of the school of fish, I run down into the galley and make and decorate Eric's cake. I remember Eric's fourth birthday as the only day I clean fish.

The next morning, Skip's hand is swollen to the size of a melon. We head back to Wrangell. Dr. Bangeman wants to put Skip in the hospital and give him an anesthetic before he lances it but Skip says no, he must unload the fish.

"It's going to hurt with just a local," Dr. Bangeman says.

"Go ahead and cut, Doc. We need that $200 worth of fish too much for me to go into the hospital."

An hour later he returns to the boat, and tells me that it wasn't too bad. It's raining as we pull alongside the cold storage. I put on all my rain gear and crawl down into *Triking's* hold to unload the fish. Skip is embarrassed that I must do this. To everyone who comes by, he explains his predicament.

As the doctor insists on redressing Skip's hand, we don't leave town for five days. Then we run back to Point Ward. We have good fishing the first day. That night we run to old Albert's place in Niblack Island.

When he sees us, Ed Loftus runs down to the float. He says, "They announced on the radio that you have a wire at the Alaska Communications Service."

"Who could that be from? We've only been out a day and a half. We don't have a radiophone on this boat. We'll just have to head to town," Skip tells me.

All night we worry about who wired us. Could one of the parents be sick? The next morning, we head to Wrangell.

The wire is from Dawn and we are relieved. She wants to live with us. She's almost 15. Four years ago Dawn's new stepfather asked us if he could adopt her, but after much debate we said no. We kept sending child support. Dawn might need us sometime. Skip loved his daughter and didn't want to give her up.

Skip calls her and she tells him she has moved in with some other people and now wants to stay with them. Her mother sent the wire when she and her husband decided to get a divorce. Skip says she can stay with these people for now.

When we run back to Point Ward to continue fishing, the cohoes are gone. Dejectedly, we return to Wrangell.

Skip talks to Alice Conant, whose husband tragically died that summer. She hasn't been able to find a buyer for their 50-foot troller, *Beilby*. Skip talks her into letting us take *Beilby* to Ketchikan to live aboard while we rebuild *Nohusit*. We sell the *Triking* for $1200, which is a $500 profit. Thank God, we need the money.

Once we get to Ketchikan, Diane Olson from the *White Light*, a dispatcher at the Ketchikan police department, tells Skip of an opening at the department. He applies and gets the job of a motorcycle policeman leading traffic through the tunnel construction area.

Skip and I spend hours redesigning *Nohusit*. We want a duplex bed for Skip and me in the pilothouse with large windows. We put the galley in the pilothouse to make it more accessible. Every night he comes home from work, eats and then works until 11 p.m. on the *Nohusit* at Harry Kaetz's shipyard on Pennock Island. He spends six weeks just scraping out the charred embers before they can pull the hull inside the Marine Ways. I help occasionally, but taking two youngsters across Tongass Narrows in a skiff isn't easy.

To help meet the mounting bills Skip agrees to let me look for a job. The first of November, I obtain a position at the Singer shop as clerk and sewing instructor. Our friend, Marjorie Thorson, baby-sits Eric and Karen while I work. We're happy rebuilding the *Nohusit*. Skip says, "We might not have lots of money, but we do have lots of love." The sacrifices of working long hours and not being with Eric and Karen seem worth the price.

At Christmas time, Dawn arrives to live with us. Cramped would be the only way to describe the five of us living on the *Beilby*. Dawn is a beautiful blonde and instantly becomes popular at school. She lifts a load from my shoulders by preparing dinner every night. Without her help, we couldn't accomplish as much on the boat.

The first of March, I start work at the Fishery Products Laboratory. I enjoy the work because it combines my chemical training and my test kitchen work. I experiment with different recipes, finding new and delicious ways to prepare fish. I like the 8 a.m. to 5 p.m. work schedule more than the 5:45 p.m. closing at Singers.

On March 16, we launch the rebuilt *Nohusit* with a new pilothouse and decks. Skip selects a 451 GM diesel engine, and they tow *Nohusit* to Northern Machine Works for its installation. She also needs new wiring and rigging before we can fish.

Everyone works and is happy. Dawn's boy friend, Roger, helps lay the linoleum. Skip offers to take him on our first fishing trip to repay him because we have no money.

My job finishes on June first and we leave on June second.

Skip says, "This is the life!." He puts his arm around my shoulders, "Now we're five Jordans plus Roger for this trip. I hope ya like it, Dawn."

I feel the exultation of heading out for another fishing season. All the hard work has been worthwhile for our *Nohusit* is a beautiful boat. We are scared to add up the bills. We know they are around $15,000 and the bank only loaned us $3000. The rest are current accounts we must pay off as soon as possible. We can't make any false moves. We try not to want it too hard because the pressure could make us fail.

We go to Wrangell to find that the fishing has slacked off there. After trying outside the boundary lines for three days and only catching two fish, we run to Port Protection. Again our timing is terrible because as soon as we leave the fishing picks up.

When we find nothing at Port Protection, we continue to Sea Otter Sound. Hazel and Herman on the *Betty K*, Don & Eddie Hoffman on the *Doneda*, and other friends are fishing there. This is another goldfish bowl. No matter where we are, the fish are biting another place. We arrive a day

Skip works as a Ketchikan motorcycle policeman.

ahead or a day behind the fish. We barely make enough for our expenses of food and fuel. Nothing is left to pay the bills. We send Roger home for we don't have enough food to feed another mouth.

One morning we find a school of big kings and they "walk through our gear," an expression that means the fish break our gear. We finally hook one fish and it breaks the leader. Skip isn't prepared for this as we didn't have enough money to buy extra gear. By the time we make new leaders, the fish are gone.

Another fisherman, Hans Norbisrath, becomes a good friend. He trolls the *Inga*, a 34-foot double-ender like *Salty*. Skip persuades Hans to run 50 miles to Tebenkof with us. Surely, the kings will be there now at the end of June.

We leave Sea Otter Sound for Cape Decision. Upon entering Chatham Straits, the *Nohusit* bucks into a northwester wind. With the rough weather on the new boat, we discover many items that weren't properly secured. Books fly across the pilothouse. Cooking utensils bound off their hooks on the wall, and the sugar and ketchup roll off the table. We bought a pullout clip for the cupboard door under the sink, so when the door flies open, all the glasses and plates fall out. With each roll of *Nohusit*, the broken dishes clatter against the pans. The clatter upsets me more than the rolling boat.

Karen suffers from motion sickness. I hold a pan for her. This makes me sick. All of us except Skip feel terrible. We lay down on the bed in the pilothouse and try not to throw up. All the broken dishes keep rolling under the bed sending a deafening clatter through the pilothouse.

Skip laughs at us, "Some crew this is. All sick."

"I'm not sick," Eric declares.

Later Eric wants something to eat. When I give him a Hershey bar, he promptly gets sick. He accuses me of getting him sick to be like the rest of us. When we come to Port Malmesbury, Skip anchors to make the boat ship shape again.

We look and look for the big run of kings. We run to Washington Bay, which paid off for us in the past, but nothing. Maybe we should be more patient and just relax and take whatever comes. We are trying too hard.

"This has been a wild goose chase," Skip says sadly. "We might as well go through Rocky Pass and back to Tokeen and our friends in Sea Otter Sound."

We arrive in time to celebrate the Fourth of July. Skip does not celebrate with the rest of us because he worries we will lose the boat to our creditors.

We talk Don and Eddie Hoffman on the *Doneda* into going to Petersburg with us to

Eric, Marilyn, Skip and Karen sit beside the newly rebuilt Nohusit.

get ice. Then we'll head north for Tyee or perhaps to Cape Spencer.

I count our money. In Petersburg after Skip pays for ice and fuel, I have five dollars to buy groceries. We always figure on $50 as a minimum for groceries for a trip. I buy a soup bone, ham hock, beans and split peas and potatoes. I have spaghetti and macaroni that I bought in Ketchikan.

Right before we're to leave the Hoffmans receive a wire that Eddie's brother in Montana was struck by lightning and killed.

Eddie and Don climb aboard and say, "We're going to tie up the boat here to go to the funeral. We'll give you our meat, fresh vegetables, and bread."

Hoffmans won't take a rain check for the food. They say that it would only spoil.

We head for Tyee alone. After passing Turnabout Island, we start across Frederick Sound. We're out in the middle when Skip points, "See that black strip ahead. That's the wind coming. This is going to be bad. Secure everything."

This time I know what to secure. The wind hits us quarter on the beam, which is bad on *Nohusit*. We roll and toss. I think we'll never get to Tyee alive. Skip tries to reassure me that with all the ice aboard *Nohusit* won't capsize. Skip tacks north so the wind is more on *Nohusit*'s stern.

Here we are alone with no radiophone. No one knows where we're going. If something happens to us, no one will look for us for weeks. Skip is not worried; he says the boat can take more than we can— and he's right. We three girls are sea sick. We find eating saltine crackers helps. The worst waves hit us on the beam when we turn toward the Tyee light. I'm scared but the boat rights itself. Finally, we run inside the markers and into calm water.

We're surprised to find people still living at Tyee without the cannery. Happily, we tie to the float and all lie down for a nap.

After our nap we hear that the fish trap crew found a baby brown bear and is keeping it in a cage. That afternoon we climb the ramp to see the cub. Dawn puts out her finger through the fence, and he bites it. Luckily, it doesn't break the skin. Later that summer, they sell the cub to a zoo.

Skip learns that the fishermen went to Killisnoo, three hours north of here for kings. We leave early the next morning. Joe Cash on the *Flicka* and Oley and Diane on the *White Light* as well as a half dozen other boats are there.

Skip throws over our anchor and then stands on the bow to talk to Oley. With mud on his hands from the anchor chain, Skip takes out his handkerchief to wipe it off. Out of his pocket come our last two dimes. They roll toward the stern and go plunk, plunk overboard. I am at the wheel and look around sadly at Dawn. Skip sees the dismay on our faces.

He calls, "Our luck has to change. I just dropped our last two dimes overboard."

That afternoon Dawn, the children and I explore with Diane. The buying station had been a whaling station in the 1900s and then a herring saltery in the early 1920s. The main buildings burned at that time. We see only parts of machinery and other buildings which have fallen down or are only half standing. Like Burnett Inlet, Killisnoo had been a "duration camp" for the

Nohusit looks beautiful anchored in a secure harbor.

Aleuts during World War II. Conditions here were worse than at Burnett Inlet. Years ago the Natives moved their village to Angoon, beside Kootznahoo lnlet. Only those with local knowledge visit Kootznahoo Inlet due to its treacherous tides. Diane shows us the three graveyards. The first graveyard consists of 17 wooden crosses with exactly the same small inscription of a foreign language on each. These whitewashed markers are in good shape. I wonder if these were Aleut graves, for ten percent of them died in the camps. The fishbuyer says they're Russian, but it's almost 100 years since the Russians were here. These appear more recent.

Further on through the island we find the Indian graveyard in disrepair. The little picket fences around the grave houses have fallen down. Nothing is intact.

On top of the knoll looking down on Chatham Straits are well-kept Japanese graves. Someone has made little rock gardens with blooming flowers and a running stream. I learn these are two graves of children of the Samato family. Children of many Japanese, who worked in fish processing, are still in the area. Three cultures come together here and at one time as many as 2500 people lived on this island.

The next morning we catch $25 worth of kings and cohoes. No $25 ever looked so good to us.

At noon, Skip says, "Let's go back to Tebenkof and take what comes. I've had all the running around I can take. We can't do any worse than we're doing now."

We sell our fish, and I buy sugar and flour and some other staples for $10. Skip puts in $15 worth of fuel. We run until we arrive at Gedney Harbor late that night.

We find our old friends, Elsie and Pat Kelly, buying salmon on the *ARB 10*. Many of our Wrangell friends are there. Among them are Sharkey Ingle with his three sons, who are Dawn's age. The two older boys, Tommy and Lance, are fishing their own troller while Leonard is with Sharkey. I know Dawn is lonesome for other young people as I was for a girl friend the first year. Skip breaths a sigh of relief for we've come home.

We fish from daylight until 8 or 9 p.m. We are usually the high boat. We average $50 a day, which adds up fast.

Dawn has a good time with the Ingle boys. They take their portable radio and sit around a bonfire on the beach each night. Sharkey finally asks Skip if he will get Dawn to come to the boat a little earlier at night. The boys aren't getting up early enough for the morning bite. Skip laughs. Dawn is able to sleep in on *Nohusit* while Skip and I fish. Skip teaches Dawn to clean fish and we pay her a nickel for each fish cleaned.

On August 1, the Halibut Commission announces a special halibut season. Skip decides Point Ellis is our best bet. We find few halibut and run back to the Gedney float early in the day.

When we pull alongside the float, everyone seems excited. I find Elsie and she explains, "The *Pearl* came from Table Bay with a big catch of cohoes."

Skip hurries over to *Nohusit*. He says, "Table Bay is about an hour south of Malmesbury toward Cape Decision. Even though it's exposed to the open ocean, we'll go wherever the fish are."

We run to Malmesbury that night and start early the next morning. Twenty boats are fishing there. For the first time, we fish around the black whale birds. They come in from the ocean only when a certain kind of feed is present. Another name for whale birds is sheerwaters. True to their name, the whale birds sheer up and down the waves until they find the feed. Then, they settle down on the water and pick at it. A larger bird that often accompanies the whale birds is the white albatross. We find the best fishing when we circle the feeding whale birds.

When the whale birds take off, Skip calls, "Which way now?"

I run to the front of the pilothouse and look in all directions. My eyes follow the whale birds until I see where they come down. Eric and Karen sit on the ledge underneath the pilothouse window and watch for us. They point excitedly, "There they are, Mama."

Skip pulls and lands fish on one side, and I pull the other. We fish 27 fathoms and put out nine lures on each side. Often every hook has a rolling, fighting coho on it. Eric helps pull the fish into the bins.

The first day we catch 1200 pounds, the second and third days 1800 pounds. When we land 2400 pounds the fourth day, Skip says, "Look at these fish for we might never catch this many again."

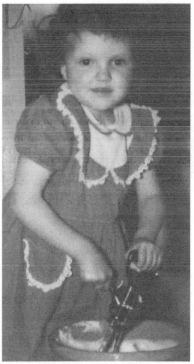

Karen beats the eggs for angel food cake.

Skip thinks the Table Bay anchorage is poor. He insists that we run to Malmesbury each night to unload. When we leave Malmesbury the next morning, we see Earl and Jackie Prather on the *Emla* .

"How are you doing, Skip?

"Ya never saw anything like it. Just follow us."

Earl makes the mistake of putting down their gear before he comes to the main body of birds. We have our gear in the water by 7 a.m. The fish never stop biting. Every muscle aches and the bins are full. Dawn starts cleaning right away. We shut the pilothouse door to make a bin for uncleaned cohoes in front

Dawn cleans over 300 fish on one of the biggest fishing days in 1954.

of the door. To get inside we walk along the boat's side to crawl through the slanted window. Skip puts the cleaned fish in the hold.

After Dawn cleans 300 fish, Skip takes over and lets her pull with me. He's afraid that if she is too tired, she will cut herself. As we are fishing much deeper than in '51, we land many more fish in the same amount of time.

Skip says at 3 p.m., "We can't be so greedy that we kill ourselves off. Steer for Malmesbury."

Proudly, we pitch off our cohoes onto the ARB 10. We have 3100 pounds. The price is less than in '51 and we don't have the kings that we had then. Even though our total check is a little less, it is our biggest day of cohoes in our years of fishing.

Skip climbs aboard exclaiming, "We did it crew. We couldn't do it without ya, Dawn. I'll bet we'll never top this for total poundage."

Bob Rooney, Skip's trapping partner, arrives two days later on his troller, *Chief*. We fish together the rest of August. We catch fish from Table Bay to Point Ellis. When one place slacks off, the other place becomes good. We make $4000 that August.

Later, Skip confides to me, "I worried that we couldn't pay our bills and the bank would foreclose on the boat. With this money, we won't lose the *Nohusit*."

God has answered our prayers.

CHAPTER SEVENTEEN
Coho Machine

WE RUN INTO WRANGELL to enroll Dawn in high school which starts September first. We pay our neighbor, Judy Krepps, for taking care of her until the fishing season ends on September 20th. When we return we receive a message from the Ketchikan police department wanting Skip to come back to work for them this winter. Dawn doesn't want to leave Wrangell as she's been

In 1955 Dad and Mother Frink visit for the first time.

elected Freshman Class President. After much discussion, she convinces us that she will work for her board and room with Judy. We reluctantly leave without her.

We live on *Nohusit* when we are in Ketchikan. I work as a chemist at the Ketchikan Pulp Mill. Skip and I work opposite shifts with my working during the day and Skip at night. Living near us on a 50-foot coast guard patrol boat are Oren and Lucia Jewett and their children, Debbie and Mike. For a modest amount of money, they agree to take care of Eric, who is in kindergarten, and Karen while Skip sleeps.

I cook dinner every night when I come home and then we clean up and all go to bed. Skip sleeps best from then until he awakes at 10 p.m. to go to work. With only our utilities and moorage rent we are able to pay $300 a month on our bills.

One December evening we're surprised by a visit from Clinton Miller. He's a senior on the Wrangell basketball team. Tall and handsome, he tells us that he is Dawn's boy friend and asks us to allow Dawn to move in with his brother, Dale Miller, and sister-in-law, Lillian. We listen and then thank him for coming by. He seems so earnest. We immediately find a telephone and call Dawn to ask her about the situation there in Wrangell. She agrees with what Clinton told us. We tell her to come down to Ketchikan and live with us, but she doesn't want to do that. Finally we hang up and discuss Dawn's situation. My theory is that those taking care of your children are either too lenient or too strict. Few find the middle ground. We know Dale Miller, who is the US Marshall in Wrangell, and like him and his wife, Lillian. I went to the baby shower when their little girl was born. Skip argues that they will let nothing bad happen to Dawn. In the end we realize that we cannot make Dawn come to Ketchikan. If we did, she might run away, and since she is getting B's in school, we should trust her. We call Dawn back and tell her that if her grades fall or we hear of anything bad going on, she will have to come to Ketchikan, but if she abides by these rules she can live with the Millers.

Matt Stuckey, a fellow police officer, buys a troller and Skip and Matt spend hours talking about when to start the season. They finally decide to quit the force in March and be out on the fishing grounds by April first. I quit my job at the pulp mill at the same time. We take the Stuckeys to our first fishing area in Ernest Sound. We spend the nights tied together visiting. Bessie is a small shy women who jumps whenever Matt tells her to do anything. She is far different from the independent Dorie Wellesley. Fishing is slow as we wait for the May first opening on the Stikine River. Fewer trollers come there because more gillnetters fish the area which cuts the trollers' area.

After nine years in Alaska, we have finally persuaded my folks to come for a visit. They come in May for we tell them this is the best month for clear weather. Little do we realize that this May will be one of the wettest since we came to Alaska. The only clear days they have are the first day and the last.

Skip shows Dad how to fish. He quickly learns how to run the gurdies and lands a 15-pound salmon. One night we run to old Albert's place on Niblack Island. Albert, as always, offers his home brew and is hurt when my mother refuses. No one tells him she doesn't drink.

Mother adapts to boat life and enjoys playing with Karen, who is a very lovable little girl. After mother meets the Stuckeys she sums up their relationship. "Stuckey's my picture of an army sergeant. When he gets excited, he yells at poor Bessie." I agree and we all laugh. If Skip yelled at me like Stuckey did, I'd have left the first month. Stuckey, though, is all bark and no bite. I soon discover that under that rough persona is a man who genuinely cares for people and who will go out of his way to help you.

Stuckey has an old rifle with a hair-trigger that someone gave him. One day, he decides to shoot a big salmon. He yells for Bessie to bring him the rifle. When she hands it to him, the rifle fires and grazes his finger. They head for the doctor who stiches it. Poor Bessie feels so bad. We soon see them back fishing.

My dad and Skip are a great pair. One is always seconding whatever the other says. Each night they hope to catch one more salmon before going into the harbor. Sometimes we're out to well after dark.

Since we are near Wrangell, mother and I decide to go to Dawn's boyfriend's high school graduation. As the men don't want to stop fishing, we are late getting into town.

"We'll let you off at the loading dock," Skip says. "It's closer to the school than the boat harbor."

As we pull into the dock I remember Clinton's graduation gift in the bow and run down to get it. Skip pulls alongside and is still at the wheel in the pilothouse. Dad and mother are on the deck waiting to get off. *Nohusit* is still moving when mother steps off the boat. Just then the tide pushes the boat's stern away from the dock. Mother steps into air. In horror, I see her go down between the boat and the dock. Luckily dad has her hand and hangs on. Skip rushes out of the pilothouse and grabs mother by the other arm and they pull her back into the boat. She is only wet to her knees but is shaking from fright and the cold. I take off her wet clothes, wrap her in blan-

Eric waits for a salmon to bite.

Grandma Frink walks with Karen on a beach.

kets and make her lie down. She keeps assuring me that she is all right and not to worry.

Later in bed Skip says, "I should have told them to stay in the pilothouse until we secured the boat. I didn't think she'd step off."

"Me either. I shouldn't have gone below for the gift. You can't blame yourself. You can't second guess accidents."

"What a narrow escape! If Dad Frink hadn't kept hold of her, it might have been tragic. I don't want anything to spoil their trip."

"For some reason, she's always been afraid of the water. She encouraged all of us children to swim, but never learned herself," I tell him.

We work and work but never have a $100 day while they are with us. On May 28 we celebrate Skip's 42nd birthday. He buys a bucket of shrimp from the cannery and Eric shows Grandpa how to pick them. Mother helps me bake a cake and decorate it. Even though *Nohisit's* stove is easier to regulate than *Salty's*, we still must rotate the cake while it's baking to keep one side from getting too brown.

Too soon the time comes for them to leave. Dad now has fishing stories to share with his cattle-buying friends. I don't think mother would have liked spending too much time fishing because of her fear of the water. She might have ended up shooting herself like Mary MacGuire did instead of having to go fishing again. I remember Mary telling me in 1946 how afraid she was of the water. I think that instead of telling Del she wasn't going, she committed suicide. This broke Del's heart and he gave up fishing and moved south.

I start to cry as my parents board the *Princess Louise* for Vancouver, B.C. Seeing my tears, Skip puts his arm around me.

The next day, we take on ice and fuel. As we decide to visit Dawn, we ask the Stuckeys go on ahead. We try to talk Dawn into going fishing with us.

Skip shows Grandpa Frink how to gaff a salmon.

She says no and surprises us with the news that she and Clinton are engaged.

Skip angrily tells her, "We want you to finish high school!"

She reassures us that she will. With lumps in our throats, we leave her in Wrangell.

We speed after the Stuckeys. We're passing Vinchnefski Rock at the west end of Zarembo Island when we finally spot them.

Skip radios them on our new radiophone. "Matt, where are you going?"

"Out Sumner Straits."

Smiling, Skip replies, "You're heading down Snow Pass. That will take you back to Ketchikan."

To me he says, "It's a good thing we weren't five minutes later. He would have been out of sight and ended up somewhere he didn't want to be." Skip shakes his head, "Matt hasn't learned to read charts. He sees an opening and heads for it."

In 1955, we fish between Port Alexander and Gedney Harbor on both sides of Chatham Straits. On a rainy day in August, I'm running out of Gedney Harbor while Skip is putting on his rain gear when he yells. "It's too rough around Point Cosmos. You steer north of it."

As the last line goes out on the tag, he hits the gaff on the deck. This is our sig-

Eric explains cleaning clams to Grandpa Frink.

The fog is a constant danger when fishing. Here it rolls in at Point Harris at the mouth of Port Malmesbury.

nal that he wants me to come back and talk to him. "Look Marilyn, whale birds!"

"Oh Skip, the fish must be here."

We always have good fishing when the whale birds come. They seldom come this far up Chatham Straits, preferring more open water. I put on my rain gear and crawl into the troller pit with high hopes. With our new automatic pilot, Skip can steer a straight course. He sets it and it holds the course until you change it from either the pilothouse or troller pit.

We see a fish on every hook. When Eric and Karen awaken, I climb out of the troller pit to feed them. This is the only time all day I end up out of the pit. After breakfast, the children watch us from the pilothouse door. They also climb on the bench behind the table and look out the back window, but mostly they stay in the doorway. We're pulling in fish so fast that the action is much more exciting then anything else they could do. I work the portside and hold the coho's head against *Nohusit's* stern to gaff. It isn't as easy as with *Salty's* double end because I could hold the fish's head against the stern's point instead of nothing.

The Stuckeys, Bob Rooney, and Oley on the *White Light* spot us going back and forth and join us. The rain continues to pour and the visibility varies from ten to 50 feet.

"This is the life," Skip exclaims as he throws another fish aboard. He doesn't need to gaff the fish like me; he slings the cohoes aboard and the hook jerks out right before they hit the deck. As we did in '51, he cleans while I work both sides. We wish we could have convinced Dawn to come with us.

"Well, *Nohusit* is the coho machine again," he laughs.

My arms get numb

Karen, Skip, and Eric show off the large kings they've caught.

and I can barely feel my hands. At 6:00, the rain is coming down even harder.

"Where shall we sell tonight?" Skip asks.

"Beaver's paying two cents more a pound at Malmesbury. With this many fish, it'll make a lot of difference."

Skip shakes his head and warns me, "We'll take a beating getting in there with this southwesterly."

Just then Stuckey trolls by. "Where are you going to sell, Matt?"

"Maybe we better go where we get the most money."

We head for Malmesbury. It's smoother than we thought going around Point Harris. The boats line up three deep to sell. We have 2500 pounds, Matt 1800 and Bob 2000 pounds. We fall exhausted into bed that night. Later we learn that Oley sells 2400 pounds in Gedney.

The next morning the wind blows hard off the hillsides and the rain continues. I expect Skip to take off early.

"It's storming a gale out there. We went through lots of leaders yesterday. I'm going to make up new ones. There's always another day."

"Everyone except us and Bob has gone out. Even Stuckey," I argue.

Skip knows I'm mad, but he ignores me. I see absolutely no reason for not going. I wish we had gone into Gedney so it wouldn't be such a run.

Beaver buys so many fish that he pulls anchor and heads back to Sitka. On our radio we hear a Sitka fisherman ask him, "What gives, Beaver? You just went out night before last and here you're back already."

Eric and Karen enjoy a rare day of sunshine.

"I filled up this subchaser in one night. The cohoes have hit down there. Some had 2500 pounds in one day."

Skip looks at me in alarm, "Everyone hears that. The Sitka fleet will be here soon."

"We'll get our share if we keep fishing."

Later that day we hear Jimmy on the *Trilby* at Port Protection. Skip turns to me and says, "If Beaver tells his friends, we might as well tell ours. Remember how bad we felt when Del didn't tell us about the good fishing?"

"How are you doing, Jimmy?" Skip radios.

"Not good. No fish here."

"We've got some here. Everyone's calling their friends."

I give Skip an angry look. I'm against telling anyone. If we'd fished that day, he'd be too busy to use our radio. Matt has 1200 pounds, but in the rough water he breaks two of his steel lines. We don't know what Oley catches off Gedney.

The home fleet is not happy about the arrival of the Sitka fleet. Some that heard Skip tell Jimmy about the fishing blame us for calling them in. I blame myself for encouraging him to go to Malmesbury. The fleet is very serious about not letting the word out to everyone as it can ruin the fishing. The word is, "Don't tell Jordan. He calls in the fleet." Many times even our best friends won't tell us where the fish are.

The next day we only catch 600 pounds probably because of all the boats. A storm blows the feed to Security Bay where the boats coming south find the cohoes. We also head there because the fishing slacks off in the Gedney Harbor area. We're fishing among lots of boats for the salmon who are following the feed.

We finally run back to Gedney two weeks later. I think the cohoes may have set along Port Protection shore. Skip corrects me, "They don't set in."

"Well what do you call it? One day they aren't here and the next day they are."

"They come in on the tide or they follow the feed in."

Skip persuades Bob and Stuckey to follow us through Rocky Pass to Port Protection. We catch some cohoes there but no big numbers. Bob says he's going home the last of August and we run with him to Wrangell.

As soon as we come to town we find Dawn. She informs us that she and Clinton are planning to marry as soon as Skip will sign the marriage consent form. Because she is only 17 the law requires a parent consent form to be signed. Skip asks if she is pregnant and she tells us she's not. We can't see that any good will come of this marriage. Clinton doesn't even have a job. We talk and talk to Dawn trying to persuade her that this is a bad thing. But she and Clinton say they are in love and nothing can persuade her otherwise. Finally Skip tells Clinton he will agree to the marriage if he gets a job and Dawn can finish high school. He informs Clinton that the road widening project is looking for surveyors. Clinton gets the job and agrees that Dawn can stay in school. Skip reluctantly signs the form. I call my mother to send my wedding dress. We put new netting on it and Dawn is married the last of August. She is a beautiful bride in a lovely wedding at the Presbyterian Church.

We immediately take off for Ernest Sound in search of cohoes. We are trolling along Deer Island when the Savikkos on the *Jowal* pull alongside.

Walt calls, "Why don't you apply for the home economics position in Wrangell at the school."

Skip and I discuss it. It will be money we need to pay off the boat bills and give us some security through the winter. We pull our gear and run into Wrangell and I apply for the position. I get it and start teaching in September. Since I have never taught school children, I find it exhilarating but hard. The eighth graders are the most challenging. Their hormones are changing daily. It's like a team of horses: if you relax one minute, they'll take off. Eric is in first grade and Karen in kindergarten. Working all day and coming home to our children is hard.

When Skip goes to Ketchikan to get our things out of storage, he buys a Willy's Jeep and ships it to Wrangell. I ride the school bus every morning to and from school. We buy an electric stove, deep freeze and chain saw. I send the clothes to the laundry. We dream of building a new house with our money. Skip says the way to get it is to trade some of our land to get the site cleared and bulldozed. I'm not sure that's a good trade, but I do want a better home. Ken Dorman bulldozes an area for a new house and we sign over a 100 foot section on the south part of our land.

Dawn starts her sophomore year in high school. Her teachers report that she is doing very well. After six weeks she tells us that Clinton insists she quit school. The next month she becomes pregnant. She won't tell us why he wanted her to quit but we speculate Clinton is jealous of her friends.

In February Skip says, "Let's let nature take its course and try for another kid."

I'm surprised but excited. I become pregnant the first month. Skip's sister Eva, who married Walt Osterbauer, writes that she is expecting too. Skip laughs that the Jordans are adding to the population explosion. He's going to be a grandfather, uncle, and a father in the same year.

Being pregnant I struggle to finish the school year. I don't let any of the other teachers or administration know I am pregnant. I prefer working as a chemist because no test tube ever talked back to me. When summer finally arrives, I decide not to keep teaching. I will stay home with this new baby like I did with Karen and Eric.

CHAPTER EIGHTEEN
Desperate For Fish

READING A LETTER FROM DAD JORDAN late that summer, Skip says, "My mother is very ill. What do ya say that we take *Nohusit* South? Maybe we'll decide we like it down there, and I'll just come up from April until September."

"I thought we were building a house where we had excavated at Wrangell."

Skip argues that he wants to see his mother. I know how close they are and how much it will hurt Skip if she dies. I relent and we run into Wrangell to pack. The fishing season has been good, not great. With our bills paid, we don't worry about losing the boat.

While we're packing Ed and Arlene Duncan knock on the door. "Are you interested in selling the house, Jordan?" Ed asks.

This surprises us as we had never thought of selling the cabin. We go in the back room and talk about it.

Skip comes out and says, "We'll just sell the house and 100 feet of the lot. We'll keep the excavated portion and the land behind the house."

We settle on a price. We end up taking only the new stove and deep freeze. We pack everything up in the trunks. I cry as we leave our little cabin for the last time. This cabin has signified more than just a home. Skip built it with his own hands, and my babies have been raised in it.

Before we leave Wrangell, I visit Dr. Bangeman as our next baby is due in six weeks. "Please list the steps Skip should take if the baby comes. It's many miles between settlements along the Canadian coast."

He writes ten steps on a slip of paper which I keep in a safe place. The trip should only take a week but a baby decides when it wants to be born and it doesn't matter if you're in a modern hospital or in the middle of Queen Charlotte Sound.

By the time we do the paper work on the house it's September 25. All of our stateside friends have left. Running alone, we make 100 miles a day. We are at the mouth of Rivers Inlet at the north side of Queen Charlotte Sound in only four days. On the fifth day we awake to gale force winds. Luckily we are in a secure anchorage and decide to wait out the storm.

I try to keep Eric and Karen busy. The boat cabin seems even smaller when everyone is trapped inside because of the weather. Eric decides to play with the parakeet and lets it out of the cage. When Skip walks out on deck, it flies out the door. Having had the bird for two years, we all start to cry. Karen says tearfully, "I bet you were teasing it, Eric. It never flew out before." I reassure them that our bird will want to come back and they hopefully set the cage on top of the cabin. After three days, Eric and Karen sadly take the cage off the top of the cabin and put it in the hold.

We pull anchor and buck across the Old Queen, as Hazel Hintz always refers to Queen Charlotte Sound.

I awake every morning and laugh, "Well, no little Canadian today." This always brings a smile from Skip who doesn't seem to be as worried as I am about the baby suddenly wanting to be born.

We arrive in Tacoma on Karen's birthday, October 7, 1956. We rent a house at Dash Point. I enroll Eric in second grade and Karen in first.

Each day Karen comes home with names for the baby. I laugh at some of them, but since we are not set on any one name we encourage her. One day she says, "What do you think of Barbara?"

"I had a good friend by that name. I'll ask your father."

Skip likes it. "How about my grandmother's name for her middle name, 'Adele'. Norwegians pronounce it with soft e's...A-dayla."

Barbara is born on November 15, 1956. Again I have a short labor and no problems. The Jordans, in less than five months have added to the population by three: Dawn's baby boy, Jeffrey; and Eva's little girl, Marle; and now Barbara.

Barbara is a lovely little baby with big blue eyes, which turn brown, and blonde hair. But this is the only resemblance she has to Eric and Karen. Her facial structure is totally different with a longer face instead of being so round. We joke that Barbara comes from the Jordan side of the family. Like Eric and Karen she's a happy baby and gives me little trouble.

My winter is spent caring for the children. Too soon, April first comes and Skip is ready to head north. Ted Threlfall, an old friend of mine from Decatur, decides to go along as cook. At the last minute, Dad Jordan, who has retired as a longshoreman, also wants to go.

"Skip, three is not going to work," I argue.

"How can I say no to Dad? We've been planning on Ted going for months. I can't tell him no this late. I think it'll work out. Dad's having an apartment built in the barn for him and Hilmar, Mother's brother. He's going to put Mother in a nursing home. We'll live in their house on Waller Road. Dad's had a rough year with Mother being so sick and he wants to get away."

"That's not a good idea. Are we going to keep living out there when you come back? I think putting three generations together will be too hard. We will also have to move the children to a new school and they have friends and are doing great here."

Karen, Skip and Barbara in Nohusit's pilothouse. Barbara plays safely in her play pen behind them.

"You're moving out there. I've made up my mind. When I come back, we'll keep living in the house. Three generations in one house worked just fine in Iowa with your family."

I can't change his mind. Reluctantly, I move. I wish the children and I could go with him, but they need to finish school.

With Barbara in her basket, I drive the three men to the harbor and kiss Skip. "Good-bye, darling, catch lots of fish."

"Take good care of our children. I hate leaving when Barbara is getting so cute." He pats her on the head and grasps her little hand. With tears in my eyes, I wave good-

Nohusit looks like a grasshopper with her bow poles down.

bye to them as *Nohusit* pulls away.

Skip writes his usual long letters and reports a good trip north. He praises Ted's cooking but misses mine. In April, most of the trollers go to Noyes Island and Hole in the Wall where we bought fish. Between the lines, I read that they aren't catching many salmon. I'm hoping they will go to Tyee for halibut. Without a fish packer there, Skip writes, *Nohusit* can't pack enough fish to make it pay for the long run into Petersburg.

When they drag their lines through the water for hours without a fish, they become discouraged. Dad Jordan always felt Skip could do better than making a living by trolling. When they find no fish by the end of May, Dad knows he is right.

He tells Skip, "You're just on a picnic here with your family. Why don't you get a decent job?"

Angrily Skip stamps out of the pilothouse and climbs into the troller pit. When he pulls in a line without a fish, he hits the deck in disgust with the gaffhook. The gaffhook flies up through the glass in the pilothouse door, spreading glass both outside and in. Startled, Skip realizes that his dad will only keep saying those things. No matter how hard Skip tries not to get angry, his dad seems to know exactly what to say to take him from total calm to seeing red faster than he could say "fish."

"Let's pull in the gear. We're running into Wrangell and you're going home, Dad. I'm sorry, Ted, that you're in the middle of this."

No one talks as they run into Wrangell. As Skip is waiting to put Dad Jordan on the plane, he thinks of me and the children living in the Jordan house. Quickly he obtains the last seat on the amphibian plane to Annette Island where the DC-6 takes them to Seattle. Skip calls me from Ketchikan to meet him at the airport in Seattle. He tells me that he and Dad had a falling out, and he does not want us to take the brunt of Dad's anger. Since Dad is not speaking to Skip, we are ignored when we offer him a ride home from the airport.

We quickly pack our belongings, including the stove and deep freeze, and put them in storage. I call the school and ask Karen and Eric's teachers if they can be passed as there is only a week of school left. They agree. The car quickly sells and we buy tickets to fly to Wrangell. We move so fast that we don't get to visit the nursing home where Skip's mother is to say goodbye. Maybe if she hadn't been so sick she could have smoothed things over between Skip and his Dad but as it is, our living down South comes to a disastrous end.

Once we arrive in Wrangell, Ted prepares to leave. There just isn't enough room on the boat for all of us. I never tell Ted how sad I am that his Alaskan trip turns out this way. Tragically, he dies before I see him again.

By this time, the Stikine River area is closed. We try fishing at Quiet Harbor. After dragging for four hours, we pull our gear and run to

A group gathers on Nohusit. Karen is in the left hand corner, Marilyn holds baby Lynda with Barbara in the right foreground. Bob Rooney is next to Marilyn and Bill Boren is next to Bob.

Port Protection. Again we find few fish. We run through Snow Pass to Ratz Harbor. It looks good, but again we catch only two kings after four hours. We spot lots of birds at Onslow Islands, but we've never fished there so we keep running. After trying Brownson Island and Sunny Bay, we return to Wrangell. We visit with Carl and Marjorie Guggenbickler on the *Sarah E.*

"It looked good," Skip says, "but they wouldn't bite for us." Later, we hear that Carl and Marjorie ran to Ratz Harbor the next day and had excellent fishing. We're probably trying too hard, and lack patience. We should relax and try a day and a half at each place.

"Let's run to Frederick Sound," Skip says. "Hans is there. Between the two of us, we should be able to find fish."

We don't do any better there. If we're fishing the Brothers, the fish are an hour away at Cape Fanshaw. If we troll Big Creek, the boats load up at Last Chance, so named because it's the last chance to catch the salmon on their way to the spawning grounds. We find a large school of herring at Pybus Bay. For a day and a half we and Hans troll back and forth. The salmon should be there.

Finally at noon on the second day, Skip calls to Hans, "Nothing can be worse than this, only three small kings in two days. Shall we leave?"

Hans reluctantly agrees, and we head south. An hour later three trollers arrive at Pybus Bay. For three days, they have fabulous fishing, 2400 pounds of big kings per boat. We never knew if the kings arrived after we left or were there all the time but not biting on our lures.

We're desperate by the end of June. We've spent all of the savings from my teaching and selling the cabin. We debate where to go. For the first time, Skip's self confidence ebbs. Skip's dad did more damage to his self-esteem then I had realized. Skip seems to secretly believe what his dad said about his being a bad provider. In a way it's starting to be a self fulfilling prophecy. How can I get his self-esteem back and make him realize that we feel he is a good man? Even though I hadn't been completely sure at the beginning of this adventure, I now know I love Skip more than I can ever tell him. He let me fulfill all the dreams of adventure I had as a young girl. Times have been hard, I know, but without adversity you can't have true happiness. The only thing I wish is that money wasn't so hard to come by. It's hard for me to think about getting through the winter with only $400 in our pockets.

"You decide where to go," Skip says. "I'm a complete flop."

I should say, "I don't have any better ideas." But I say nothing.

We discuss going to Tebenkof, but then hear a rumor of fish in Cross Sound. I say, "I think we should go. We've had good luck there in the past."

Skip tells Hans that we're heading up Chatham Straits. He's at Last Chance and will meet us in Elfin Cove. He's going up Stephens Passage.

We arrive at Elfin Cove only to find the fish are farther down the coast off of Deer Harbor and Khaz Bay. They're also around Cape Spencer. Skip doesn't want to go around Cape Spencer even though we fished there before. He says that we don't know the Deer Harbor drags. It's like he's trying to defeat me now. We end up fishing three weeks for as few fish as we caught in Frederick Sound.

I try to keep our family life normal aboard the boat that summer of 1957. We are not finding any fish so there is no money for anything. I worry that we will not have enough money to live through the winter, especially since we will have to pay rent because we sold our cabin. I try not to let the children know our worries. Barbara is only seven months old. We buy a play pen that makes into a bed. Barbara looks so cute peering out through its bars. She sleeps in it because I'm afraid that she'll roll out of the bunks in the bow.

One day I notice that she can get out of the pilothouse. "Skip, we must buy a gate for the pilothouse door. She can crawl out on deck."

Dutifully, Skip installs the gate. Barbara crawls over to it when she hears excitement on deck. She also crawls around the pilothouse. Life is much easier with a baby on *Nohusit* than on *Salty*. All the machinery is in an enclosed engine room and the sink is big enough to give Barbara a bath in.

Nohusit has higher railings and a larger hold hatch to sit on than *Salty*. On calm days, we put the bin boards in the slots on the side bin on deck. Like Eric did at that age, Barbara peers over the top of the bin at her daddy landing fish. She claps her hands like her older brother and sister did when a big king comes aboard. On a bright day, Karen will sit with Barbara on the hatch. Karen still gets sea sick and I must give her Dramamine every morning. Barbara takes after Skip and never gets sick. Karen treats Barbara like a doll and is a big help.

One day in June, Buz and Donna Goldsberry give us a puppy, whom the children name Tiny. We also have a cat on the boat. The animals supply hours of enjoyment for the children even providing a lesson about birth when Mama Kitty has kittens.

Someone asks, "What do the children do aboard?"

As soon as they arise, they put on their 45 rpm children's records, play games, or read books. Eric and Karen love to read books to Barbara. One day we teach Eric to row his sisters ashore in the skiff. They are always happy when we pull in our lines and head for the buying scow or the anchorage because they can go exploring. Elfin Cove is a favorite place. They have room to play ashore with other children.

On July 31, we return to Chatham Straits and find Hans at Security Bay. "I was heading for Icy Straits when I saw all of these birds working. I put in my gear. Big spawners were biting. I can't keep up with them. I tried to call you, but you were too far away. When they were still there the second day, I heard Ollie on the Tomolee so I called her. They got there in three hours. It lasted for five days."

I have a sinking feeling in my stomach. Nothing has gone right this year. The next morning we put in our

Our friends follow Nohusit through Rocky Pass.

gear at Security Bay. After landing only five humpies and three cohoes, Skip says, "Let's go to Tyee. I've a hunch kings may be there."

When we arrive, we find the *Tomolee* fishing there. We catch five big kings and a dozen cohoes in two hours.

"This looks good," Skip says. "I better call Hans."

By the time Hans arrives two hours later, we have ten kings. Our spirits rise. That evening we tie to the float at Tyee. Hans comes alongside and then Tom and Ollie come aboard.

Hans's eyes blaze as he demands of Tom, "Why didn't you call me when you found these kings? I called you on the other fish."

"You run with Jordan," Tom replies. "He calls in the fleet."

"That's the last time I ever call you in on fish," Hans says.

I'm afraid they are going to fight in our pilothouse.

Later, I tell Skip, "I wanted to tell them we just arrived yesterday, but I didn't want to get in the middle of it."

"You were wise to keep your mouth shut. Tom is just hunting for excuses. I hope Hans sees through it."

"It all goes to the time in '55 when we were blamed for calling in the fleet," I say sadly.

We catch a few cohoes at Security Bay, Port Camden and Port Protection. Ironically, I spent nine months waiting for our summer fishing season to make money, and now it's over and we are worse off than when we started.

Soon, we head for Ketchikan to register Eric and Karen in school. Skip feels it will be too difficult for me to keep a baby on the boat. We borrow money on Skip's life insurance to rent an apartment in the Ferris Court. We pray for a better season next year.

CHAPTER NINETEEN
Steering For A Divorce

LIFE PROVES MUCH EASIER AT FERRIS COURT than our Wrangell cabin. In our one bedroom apartment Eric and Karen share a bed in the bedroom and Skip and I sleep on the hide-a-bed in the living room. Barbara sleeps in her crib beside us. Karen is in second grade and Eric in third. We are a close family and love just being together. Every evening we play board games. Careers is one of the favorites.

After our disastrous year we are discouraged. Skip says, "Two poor years back to back will wipe us out."

With a baby, I haven't looked for work. I do find time to do an article, "We Go Fishing Every Day," for *Household* magazine. I do one for *Singer Light* called "Troller Wives," and a children's story called "Puttin' Finds Her Place," for a Sunday School magazine. I dream of writing a book of our experiences.

The University of Alaska Cooperative Extension Agent visits one day and asks, "We have an opening for a part-time home economist. Would you like to apply for it?"

I think about it but reply, "No. I want to spend my time writing and fishing." I wonder if I will regret this decision.

Skip tells me, "A man down on the float has a machine for bottom fishing with wire gear. He'll sell the whole outfit for $500. *Nohusit* doesn't have enough deck room for conventional halibut gear. He'll take $100 down and the rest at the end of the season. What do you say? I can fish red snapper right now with it."

Remembering previous get rich quick schemes, I ask, "Will it be like the dogfish you were going to fish in Wrangell?"

"I'll talk to the stores and see if there's a market for red snapper."

The next day he excitedly reports, "Two of the grocers said they'll take all I bring in. Ya know what a hard time we've had fishing kings. We can fish halibut with this gear early in the season."

Skip buys the halibut gear. On the float he meets Dick, a young fellow who is looking for a job. He lets him live on the boat and gives him a percent-

*An end of an era. Everything in Port Alexander is deserted and falling apart.
The children love exploring these old buildings.*

age of what they make on red snapper. They sell their red snapper both to the stores as fillets and in the round on the dock. After he pays Dick and buys the gear and food, there is little money left.

Skip is working on the halibut gear when an old Norwegian comes by. Skip explains his set-up. Finally the Norwegian asks, "Jordan, how are you going to steer this rig when you're setting and pulling your gear?"

"My wife is good at steering."

"I give her exactly ten days. She'll be in here suing you for divorce."

Skip tells me about the conversation. "Ya wouldn't leave me over some gear, now would you, Marilyn?"

I laugh and agree that I wouldn't. Not over something as trivial as how to steer a boat.

With high hopes, Skip, Dick, Eric, Barbara and I head for the west coast of Prince of Wales. Eric's teachers say he can leave early because he is doing so well but we leave Karen with the Thorsons to finish school because she gets seasick.

The first day I realize what the Norwegian meant. I can't steer to please Skip.

Skip yells, "Further to the port. No, not that far. Now go to the starboard. Marilyn, you've got to do better. Ya caused us to break the line and lose a lot of gear."

"I'm doing just what you tell me."

After a week, I see I can't satisfy him no matter how hard I try. I'm in tears most of the time. Skip has no way to steer on deck. The Norwegian was right, I'm ready to fly to town and sue for divorce. If he hadn't warned Skip, I might have done it. I find if you know the obstacles, you are better able to handle them. I lay awake at night and realize that of all the years aboard, I have come the closest to giving up this spring.

Slowly, we learn how to fish the gear. The wire doesn't stretch as rope does in halibut skates. We can pick up the wire from the buoy on the other end. We still lose much gear when we can't retrieve the wire from under the rocks.

As soon as school is out, Karen flies out to Tokeen in a small seaplane. She looks very sick as she gets off the plane. The pilot tells us how she got airsick and threw up all over herself and the plane. He had to make a special landing to clean up.

Skip decides that the cohoes should be showing in Tebenkof. We store the long line gear in the hold and engine room and on top of the cabin. We head through Rocky Pass. I enjoy the beauty of Baranof Island's snow covered peaks.

Arriving in Gedney, we find Bob and Mary Shields buying fish on *NEFCO XI*. Their little boy is between Karen and Barbara's age, and they play with him when we tie to their float at night.

Both Eric and Karen help by pulling in or cleaning fish. Whenever Skip doesn't need them on deck, Eric and Karen, who are both avid readers, head for their bunks and curl up with a book they've borrowed from the buying scow.

Happily we find salmon and don't have another disas-

Barbara pumps water into Nohusit's sink.

trous year. By the end of August we stop fishing to enroll the children in school. We decide to go back to Ketchikan as we've had luck finding work there.

Upon arriving in town I immediately check our mail and find a letter from my dad asking Skip to come work for him in the cattle business.

Skip mulls it over and smiles, "I would like that."

Skip writes Dad Jordan that he would like to see his mother on his way to Iowa. Dad Jordan immediately writes back saying that she wouldn't know us and it would be a waste of our time and money.

Dad Frink sends us a train ticket from Prince Rupert, British Columbia to Waterloo, Iowa. The ticket includes a bedroom which he says we need with this many of us.

After we make arrangements for someone to look after *Nohusit*, we fly to Prince Rupert. Our biggest problem is how to take Tiny, our dog. The small airline to Prince Rupert doesn't have a box for her. We put her in a cardboard box but this will not do for the train ride. When the plane lands on the Canadian Thanksgiving, all the stores are closed. Skip asks anyone he can find to direct him to a carpenter and finally he finds one. The man agrees to make a wooden travel box with air holes and a hinged lid. Tiny travels well in the box on the trip across country.

Arriving in Iowa, I happily greet my mom and dad. We haven't seen them since they came to Tacoma in 1956 to see Barbara soon after she was born. I immediately notice that Dad has lost 50 pounds. I discover that my brothers, who are now doctors, have put him on a strict diet. I worry they think something is the matter with him.

Skip enjoys working with Dad at the stockyards. Skip does the heavy work which frees Dad to talk to the customers. Dad is a stocker-feeder who buys cattle in the west and resells them to the farmers to fatten.

"I get along with Dad Frink better than I do my own father," Skip says. "I could learn the cattle business. It would work in well with our fishing. Its busy time is September until Thanksgiving. We could fish in the summer."

Eric and Karen find Iowa a lot different than Alaska. "Mother," Eric says, "It rains different in Iowa than Alaska."

"How is that?"

"When we go to school here and it's raining, the sun is shining by recess. In Alaska, it's still raining when we go home."

I laugh, "Yes the weather is different. We can't see any mountains here like we can at home." The children catch grasshoppers and snakes. With only evergreens in Alaska, they haven't seen the colorful leaves on trees. They jump and play in the huge piles of leaves. The cows and chickens fascinate them. They spend many hours playing in the large park across the road. I miss the beauty of Alaska but enjoy visiting with my folks.

In November, we receive word that Skip's mother, Inga, has died. Unable to go to the funeral, Skip worries about his father.

Our Alaska slides and fishing stories fascinate my old school friends. Several groups invite us to talk to them. After one of them, Skip says, "We aren't catching the excitement of the fishing with stills. We need a movie camera."

I'm surprised at how well we get along with two families in one house. I thought two generations living together would cause a lot of strife but my folks are adaptable and easy going. Both grandparents love playing with Eric and Karen. Mother especially enjoys Barbara who is a lovable two-year old. Just as I did when little, Eric enjoys playing checkers with my father.

In January, the folks leave for a visit with my brother, Dick, who is doing his medical internship in Stockton, California. Unexpectedly a load of cattle arrives. Skip calls Dad to find out how to price them. Skip assures Dad that he and the other man at the stockyards can take care of them. But Dad immediately cuts their visit short and heads back to Iowa. I am saddened that Dad doesn't feel he can trust Skip yet, but maybe this will come with time.

Winter is also a slow time of year in the cattle business and Skip has no work to do. Never one to sit still for long he starts to make plans to head back to Alaska. We worry about wearing out our welcome since we've been here for four months. Sadly, I kiss my folks good bye and thank them for the visit.

CHAPTER TWENTY

Oh, Ye of Little Faith

WHEN WE RETURN TO KETCHIKAN, I am happy to be home. The snow-covered mountains contrast to the flatness of Iowa. Being away always makes me appreciate Alaska more. We move aboard *Nohusit*.

Skip buys an automatic pilot to help with the steering. From Idaho, a man who read my article in *Household* magazine writes that he would like to fish with us. Skip needs help with our wire gear, so he agrees to take the man and his wife. At the last minute their 20-year-old son decides to come. Skip agrees to pay them a 35 percent share of whatever we make after we take out for food and fuel.

Before they arrive, Skip buys a used 16 millimeter movie camera. "I dream of lecturing on our fishing life. We can only capture it with motion pictures. This was a good buy."

"Skip, we're short on cash. How could you! Film and developing cost money that we do not have. I'm not sure this was the time to buy it." I see his face start to take on a stubborn look and I quickly add, "You do the movies and I'll do the stills."

Again, we leave for the May first opening on the Stikine. Eric is allowed to finish school early and go with us while Karen stays behind at the Thorsons again and will fly out at the end of school. We have room for all with Eric and Karen sharing a bunk and a bunk for each of our crew.

Three weeks later, I see Skip has not touched the camera lying on the dashboard. I read the direction book and learn how to run it.

Skip now knows how to direct the steering so I can understand what he wants. We catch many large halibut with our new expertise. After two months we head for Petersburg to buy ice and celebrate the Fourth of July. On this special Fourth of July in 1959, we celebrate Alaska becoming the 49th state. We worked a long time for Statehood.

Petersburg, known as "Little Norway," is a colorful community. It was originally founded by Peter Buschmann, a Norwegian. Many of the residents are of Norwegian descent. I can hear people openly speaking Norwegian on the streets, many with deeper accents than Skip's.

"Ya know Petersburg looks good to me. See how clean this community keeps their homes and yards." I can tell that this place appeals to Skip because of his Norwegian background.

"I hear that the same house costs less here than in Ketchikan," I say.

"I'm getting tired of racing to Ketchikan each fall to find where we'll live to know which school to put the children in. Petersburg is

Grandpa Jordan and Barbara celebrate Alaska becoming a state on the Fourth of July in 1959.

located in a more central location to our fishing grounds," Skip says.

We return to Tebenkof and fish halibut until the middle of July in South Chatham Straits. Then our crew flies out of Gedney for Ketchikan. When we pay them their shares, we find little left for us because of not figuring boat and gear shares.

I sigh. "It's good to be alone again."

"Ya worked hard steering and cooking for all of us. I only wish it had turned out better."

In the harbor, we head for *NEFCO XI* where we stored our trolling gurdies while fishing for halibut. Upon our arrival, Bob Shields informs us that he knocked them in Gedney Harbor with his boom. We do not have the money to buy new gurdies and we cannot troll without them. They are like the spools on a fishing reel and are what lets the lines in and out and keeps them from tangling.

Bob helps Skip drag the bottom of Gedney Harbor in hopes of snagging them. I remember the luck Skip had finding my purse that first season. I cross my fingers and say a silent prayer to God. For hours, Bob and Skip drag the bottom. Finally, when it looks like they will give up they hook something. As it breaks the surface I give a loud whoop— they've found one! New enthusiasm keeps them going for another couple of hours. As the light is slowly fading from the sky, they again hook something that feels the right weight. We anxiously watch the line reeling up and the second gurdy breaks the surface as the sky behind it turns a fiery red. I breathe a sigh of relief and thank God for again answering my prayers.

When Skip returns I hug him. "I'm happy that you got them. Think how much it would cost to replace them, plus we'd have to put on new wire, mark it, and replace the motors."

"Yes, we were lucky," Skip agrees. "Now to catch some salmon." With high hopes, we head for the trolling areas the next day. We troll every day for mediocre catches. The price isn't good, and we find no large amount of cohoes as we have in the past.

The first week in August, Skip announces, "Let's go to Petersburg for a load of ice. Then we can prospect in other areas."

Upon arriving, we receive a letter from Dad Frink. He writes, 'How would you like to go into the cattle business with me? You kids can buy your own house here. There's little cattle business in the spring and summer so you could keep fishing too.'

I am so proud. Dad must have decided Skip was worthy of going into business with him. Skip immediately writes back, 'I like the idea.'

Excitedly, Skip says, "Marilyn, we must get ready to move to Iowa. We'll make one more trip as we already have ice aboard. We'll leave the boat in Ketchikan. We want to get the kids in school when it starts in Iowa. We'll need at least a week so we should leave no later than the last week in August. We must take some items out of storage. With some trunks, we can get everything on the train. The big problem is getting it from Ketchikan to Prince Rupert." He adds, "I hope we can find some fish. We'll need the money to move to Iowa. We can't expect your dad to buy us the ticket this time."

I pack before we leave for Security Bay. I'm as excited as Skip. We will not have to give up salmon fishing and yet we will have some financial security. In addition, I will be around my folks, whom I dearly love. Everything I've always dreamed about can finally come true.

We find few fish at Security Bay and dejectedly return to Petersburg to finish packing. At the post office, I find another letter from Dad. I am excited as I rip open the letter to see what plans he has for us. My happiness is shattered when I read: "I was not well last week. I'm sorry, kids, I just can't do it. I'm not able to make enough to support both of us. I hope this change doesn't affect you too much. Love, Dad."

Skip and I look at each other. In the space of a few moments and a few lines on a letter, everything has changed. Skip sums up the situation; "There's nothing to do. We must hunt for fish before school starts. We've wasted ten days of the best fishing of the year while we made plans for moving."

As we walk back to the boat, we discuss where we should go. "It's too far to run to Icy Straits. Maybe there will be good fishing at Security Bay or Tyee; they are much closer." Skip says.

We make only enough money to cover our expenses. We run back to Petersburg with Ben and Louise Gates on the *Kitty T.* They, too, did not have a good season. Soon after arriving, Ben and Skip get a job building a bridge with Arne Trones.

I am thankful that this job will answer our financial needs. Skip talks to Andrew Wikan, whom he met many years ago. He learns that Andrew has bought the Chris Lang house and will rent it to us. It's a small furnished house.

Skip returns after the first day on the job and sadly tells me, "I didn't realize that this construction job will only last three weeks."

I am devastated. In dismay, I grab our checkbook and see that we have only $600 to last until the next fishing season. My mind quickly calculates our expenses; our rent is $80 a month; $80 times eight months is $640. I tell myself that I cannot go to pieces. Skip will find other work. After the construction job, Skip tries to find work but no one is hiring. He runs *Nohusit* to Ketchikan to bring back our stored items.

I see a notice that they want a Webelo leader for Scouts. They refer me to Carlene Wikan, who lives nearby. Then Mary Reid knocks on my door and says she will help if we'll take her son, Tom. These are my first friends in Petersburg. Over coffee, the three of us plan what we will do each meeting. We wait anxiously for seven fifth-grade boys to arrive. Even with our plans, we turn around to find two of them fighting on the floor.

Skip walks in at that moment and points out, "Ya boys should behave and be thankful that these three mothers are villing to have your Webelos group." I'm not sure it does much good, but it calms them down that day.

My biggest problem is stretching our little amount of money. I reason

Barbara enjoys swinging in the bow of Nohusit.

that my nutritional training should show how to feed my family healthful food inexpensively. We take our small amount of money to buy a 100-pound can of powdered milk, a couple of cases of canned milk, two 50-pound sacks of flour and sugar and a 25-pound sack of brown sugar. Skip puts salmon and halibut he catches in our freezer. We all dig clams at Sandy Beach one Saturday. We hand grind them for chowder and put them in the freezer. Skip and Eric hike out the road each Saturday to hunt deer. I am thankful we bought the freezer when I taught school in Wrangell.

As Petersburg does not have school lunches, the children come home each noon. I know we cannot afford canned soup for five of us so I make a large batch of soup stock from the deer bones and add many vegetables. As the children do not like the vegetables floating in their soup, I strain them out. Our neighbors, Twila and Laurence Molver, give us their milk cartons to store our soup. Each week I take out a carton from the freezer, divide it into six portions and add various dry soup mixes and fine noodles.

Breakfast is another meal where I know we cannot afford five eggs a day. One day I make cooked cereal with raisins. Another day we have hot cakes from an Extension Service recipe mix that only uses one egg. I vary this with a different kind of cereal and scrambled eggs using only three eggs and canned milk and water. Each one gets a half an orange for breakfast each day.

For salads, I vary from tossed, carrot and raisin, coleslaw, and Waldorf. Karen enjoys coming home from school to make inexpensive desserts. When Barbara gets sick, Skip treats her to a quart of fresh milk. I pat myself on the back as I do know how to stretch our food dollars.

Karen, Barbara and Kathy Phillips walk to Nohusit on Petersburg's dock.

I use my sewing machine to make clothes for the children. I make a jacket for Eric with a quilted polyester lining. I buy a light coat for Karen and put in a zipper lining to make it warmer. For Karen's and Barbara's birthdays, my mother sends them each a beautiful dress. I'm so thankful for these as they will be their best dresses.

I know Christmas will be a problem. Not only do I need gifts for the children, but we still exchange gifts with the folks and my brothers and sisters. I make candy and send them our canned salmon.

Skip hurries home with the mail. "I've a letter from Aunt Molle in Norway." We anxiously watch him open the letter. "It's a $100 check."

An angel named Molle has answered my prayers. I think, oh, ye of little faith. We cut our own Christmas tree, make decorations for it and buy gifts for the children. To make the money go even farther I buy much needed clothes and only a few inexpensive toys. I think about the previous Christmas that we spent with my family. I know all of my brothers and sisters will be in Tama with my parents. As we have no money for a telephone or even to call from a pay phone, I settle for letters.

On December 27, Twila Molver knocks on the door. "The Lutheran minister just called and left a number for you to call. He said it was an emergency. I'll stay with the children while you go call from our house." Skip and I rush to their house. I see that it is my folks's telephone number on the paper. I can barely dial the number I am shaking so much.

"Hello." It is my sister Peggy's voice. It sounds strained.

"It's Marilyn."

"I've got bad news for you. I hope you're sitting down."

What has happened, I wonder.

"Dad shot himself this morning."

"Oh my God," I whisper, the tears welling up in my eyes. "Oh no, not Dad. Why?"

"We think he was worried about his health." Peggy says.

We talk for a few more minutes, but I am too stunned to really think. Could this all have been averted if we'd moved down there in September? Skip gently puts his arms around me.

I sob, "There's no money. I can't come for the funeral."

"It's all right, Marilyn." Peggy assures me. "No one expects you to come."

I hang up the telephone and stand there crying. To me suicide says that you do not have faith that God has something good for you around the next corner.

Skip cries with me. He became close to my dad when they worked together last year. Slowly we pull ourselves together. Almost within a year we have lost his mother and my father. We do not make it to either funeral.

"We'll just tell the children that his heart stopped," Skip says. I nod. That evening the Jordan family holds each other as we all cry for Dad Frink. He meant so much to each of us that we can hardly believe we will never see him again.

On the day of his funeral I call the Lutheran minister and ask him to come over. "Can we have our own service?" I ask.

He agrees and arrives a little while later. With Eric, Karen, Barbara, Skip and me present, we read different Bible passages that fit our image of Dad Frink. We all bow our heads in prayer and softly say our good-bye's. My tears never seem to stop. I dearly loved and respected my father and will always remember him as a great man.

I find it difficult to pull myself together after the shock of his death. One day the high school basketball coach decides to take over the Webelo group. My only worry now is how to feed and clothe my family. Everything is a blur.

As the snow is softly falling, I hear Skip come into the house. His face is alight with excitement.

"There's a house for sale down the street. Let's go look at it."

"How can we afford it?" I mumble.

"I already talked to the banker. They'll loan us half of the $8,000 price. The owner, Dagne Wikan, says she'll take $1000 each fall for four years plus interest. The monthly payments will be the same as for this house."

I see he has already made plans. We look at the house. It is bigger, and I like the floor plan better than the rental house. I especially like the kitchen with its table looking out on Wrangell Narrows and Petersburg Mountain, which has a clearing near the top that looks like a map of the USA. Luckily, the house is furnished. I agree and we sign the papers that same day. Packing our belongings helps me get out of my depression. A new house was what I needed to brighten my mood and help me get back my sense of humor. Skip always seems to know what to do to help me get my strength back.

We are comfortable in the new house. I still worry about money and how to feed everyone, but the fishing season is just around the corner. March arrives and I discover I am pregnant. We think of names for a girl. I have already decided if we have a boy he will be named after my father, Gale.

Dad Jordan is having a hard time adjusting with the death of his beloved Inga. He misses her terribly and is restless at the house on Waller Road with only Hilmar, Inga's brother, to visit with. There are just too many memories. He sells the house and property. He writes and we encourage him to visit us. We find a small house for him to rent. He eats some of his meals with us and helps with the groceries. I'm glad that he becomes better acquainted with his grandchildren. Skip and his dad are close even through all the disagreements about Skip's fishing. Skip spends much time visiting Dad and usually brings Karen with him. They speak together in Norwegian which fascinates Karen. They tease and laugh together. Dad stays two months and then goes South again.

We find good fishing that summer, but we don't have the $1000 fall payment plus $80 a month to pay the bank.

Skip decides, "We'll have to sell the Wrangell property. I'll take the boat over there and talk to the real estate agent."

I hate to sell the site. We traded property to get the area excavated for a new house. I have no idea what it's worth. I ask Skip to get as much as he can for it.

He sells it for $1800 to be paid at $80 a month. It will make our house payments. The fishing money will pay the $1000.

On November 23, 1960, I give birth to a seven pound 13 ounce girl. During the summer we saw a herring seiner in Warm Springs with the name Lynda. Skip and I both like the name and spelling as it had a 'y' like my brother Lynn's name. If Lynda had waited one more day she would have been born on Lynn's birthday.

Although Petersburg only has a population of 1500 people, three of us have babies at the hospital on this cold Wednesday before Thanksgiving. Florabelle Rice gives birth to George a couple of hours before me and Sigrid Medalen has Kirsten the next day. We sit up late comparing our babies and laughing.

Soon after Lynda is born, I meet Louie and Christine Lahmeyer at the Presbyterian Church. They are new to the area and do not know anyone. I invite them to share Christmas dinner with us. Louie is a building contractor.

He asks, "Skip, I'm building a house and need more help. Would you like to work for me?"

Skip is happy to work. At last, life is looking up for the Jordans. The money Skip earns working helps us get through the winter without major financial trouble.

The next summer, Dad Jordan comes back to Petersburg. He enjoys spending time with his grandchildren. Barbara, at the age of five, is fond of him and they jig herring together off the dock. He buys a tent, skiff and outboard motor and sportfishes out of Gedney Harbor for a month. He is still not happy and when he receives a letter from his sister Molle inviting him to come to Norway, he leaves on the next plane.

Sadly, we bid him good-bye. When he arrives in Norway, he contacts Randi, a lady he knew as a young man, before he met Inga. Randi is now a widow and they marry the next year. Dad deserves happiness.

Grandpa Jordan fishes in the skiff with his sport pole.

CHAPTER TWENTY-ONE
God Is Watching

THE FOUR CHILDREN AND I move aboard the *Nohusit* the day school is out. We'll spend three months trolling. Lynda is a year and a half old the summer of 1962. We know this is the most dangerous age to have her aboard. She fears nothing. She's no longer content to remain in her playpen as she did the previous year. She is more self-sufficient than her five-year-old sister, Barbara, was at that age. She sticks her hand into the five-

Fishers have a picnic on the beach in Gedney Harbor.

pound honey jar and then she can't get it out until she straightens out her fingers. Another time she pokes her finger in an open clam shell and screams when it shuts.

Skip tries to childproof the boat. He fastens down items that Lynda could pull over on herself. We don't allow the children on deck without a life preserver.

I ask him, "Would you like me to stay ashore with Barbara and Lynda in our house this summer? You can take Eric and Karen."

Skip thinks a little. "No, not really. I need ya to steer, and everything runs smoother when you're along. I know how much ya enjoy the fishing. This year I really worry about Lynda."

"I know, I worry, too. We can't relax."

I take Lynda's small hand in mine and she toddles down the dock to the boat. I say a prayer, "Please, God, keep Lynda safe."

This is our 16th season of salmon trolling. When I arise, I have no idea

Skip looks out of the pilothouse window with his daughter standing on the dresser next to him.

how many salmon we'll catch that day or what sea life we'll see. Sometimes I point out a rainbow or a mirage to the children.

Skip subscribes now to the theory that salmon bite best at daybreak, which happens to be 4 a.m. in July. The sun comes up in a blaze of red and golds as we leave the protected anchorage in Gedney Harbor. We head out into wide Chatham Straits.

"Where are we going today?" I ask Skip.

"We'll go north to Tebenkof. Lots of feed on the flats yesterday. What a beautiful day—not a ripple on the water."

Nohusit's pilothouse measures 15 feet long and eight feet wide. At the front bulkhead three steps lead to the bow section, which has four bunks and the head. On the starboard side of the bulkhead is the wheel for steering and the seat for the helmsman. Between the seat and the starboard window, we place a low dresser. Often one of the children sits on it for a better view over the bow when we travel. Against the dresser, we place a trundle couch that makes into a double bed for Skip and me at night. Another dresser touches the couch at its foot. Along the wall we pound hooks for rain gear. The back door opens out on to the deck and troller pit.

A dresser for fishing gear sits on the portside in front of the stove and sink. Across the back next to the door we have built a long locker for canned goods. It forms a bench for sitting at the table.

Skip steers from his seat behind the wheel. On this unusually warm day, he slides the window open above the small dresser. Later, he pulls the drape across the window to keep the bright sunlight from shining on the depth sounder.

Arriving at the place where seagulls circle over a school of herring, Skip says, "It looks good here. I'll steer from the troller pit with the automatic pilot while I put in the gear."

"I'll enter our bills in the account book." It helps at income tax time to do the summer ones and I spread all the bills into neat piles on the seat of the couch.

I've entered only the first bills when I

Eric pulls in a fish while Barbara watches. The Jordans always tow the skiff behind the boat for safety and convenience.

hear Lynda cry from her bunk. I change her diaper and leave on her little white nightie and rubber pants. I plan to bathe her later.

With the back door shut, I feel she is safe as she can't get out on deck. She climbs up on the bench and sets plates out for breakfast.

"Good girl, Lynie," she says.

"Yes," I reply.

A few minutes later something causes me to look up. Lynda is not in sight. Did she crawl along the backside of the couch and climb up on the dresser? I see the curtain blow in the breeze.

"Lynda!!" I cry, jumping up. No answer. I peer into the space between the dresser and the switchboard. Nothing! Then I look into the bow section. I see only the three sleeping heads of the older children.

Screaming, I race for the back door. Surely, if she fell overboard Skip would have grabbed her. Once he caught a kitten that fell overboard from the cabin. He saw it floating by and pulled it alongside with the gaff hook. In horror, I see he is working the lines on the other side of the boat. In surprise, he looks at me.

"Lynda! Lynda!" I cry, pointing at a little white object floating about 100

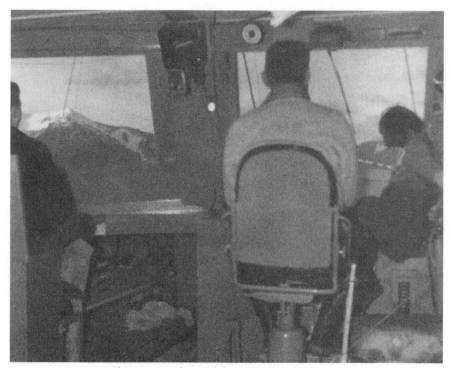

*Skip steers Nohusit while Barbara sits on the low
dresser for a better look.*

feet behind the boat. My baby looks like a sea lion lying on the water's surface.

"My God, no life preserver!" Skip exclaims. "Help me pull in the skiff."

What an old-timer said flashes through my mind: "When you need a skiff, you need it right that minute. There's no time to untie it from a boom or to launch it." I am glad it's already in the water.

By this time, Eric, Karen, and Barbara are standing in the pilothouse doorway. In horror, I watch Skip nearly lose the skiff by unsnapping it from the boom before he climbs into it. Only by super human effort does he keep it close enough to the boat to lower himself into it. We will lose valuable minutes if it floats away. Our eyes are glued on Lynda.

"She floating on her back," I say. "She looks like a little white board floating farther away all the time."

"For God's sake, turn the boat around," Skip shouts as he pulls away.

Nohusit's automatic pilot is keeping her running ahead. We now are at least 100 yards away. Both Eric and I race into the pilothouse to turn the wheel. I speed up the engine.

"She's still there," Karen reports. Lynda keeps floating, never moving at all.

"Hurry, Skip," I call.

Skip, an expert rower, covers the distance in long, smooth pushing strokes. He keeps his eyes on her. Nearing her, he sees her eyes open very wide, but she doesn't cry or move. Breathlessly, we watch him lean over the side of the skiff and grasp her. I hug the children, crying, "She's safe. He has her."

"Touching her warm body and knowing she is safe is the most glorious sensation I've ever had," Skip tells me later. "If she'd started to sink, I was going to kick off my boots and dive in after her. How close we came to losing our Lynda."

We watch him put her over his knee and pat her back to see if she swallowed any water. She doesn't spit out any. I'm shaking as I watch Skip row back. When he comes alongside, I reach over the railing for my precious baby. With tears rolling down my cheeks, I sit down on the couch to take off her wet clothes.

I close my eyes and whisper, "Thank you, God, for saving our baby."

I see no sign of hypothermia. I give her a hot bath and a warm bottle, but she only wants to play around the pilothouse. We are the ones who need to calm down.

"How did it happen?" Eric asks.

"I pulled the curtain across the open window," Skip says. "She must have crawled up there and put her hand on the curtain and tumbled out. We'll never know if she went backwards or forwards."

"She never made a sound," I say. "She must have held her breath because she didn't get any water in her mouth or lungs. Luckily she just floated and didn't thrash around. I'll bet she went out backwards and never got water in her nose."

"If you children ever fall in the water, remember you can float as Lynda did. You only need to keep air in your lungs by breathing naturally until help comes. Even in the 50-degree Alaska water, Lynda didn't panic."

Later that morning I see the starboard bow pole pull down, down, down. All I can think to do is yell at Skip and point. Again he is on deck. Wearily, he looks up as much as to say, "What now?"

Seeing where I point, he jumps into the troller pit to lift the weight off the pole by putting the power gurdy into gear. If the pole breaks, we'll lose at least two days fishing time in cutting, peeling, and rigging another.

"This isn't our day," Skip calls. "Marilyn, get back here and help pull in the gear. We'll have a picnic on the beach before something really tragic happens."

Sitting on the beach, Skip tells me, "I made a mistake by pulling that curtain over the open window. What a relief that she is safe. We just must be more careful. We must not make a big thing of it. We don't want her to have emotional scars from this."

Skip asks me not to tell others about our narrow mishap. Perhaps he is the one with the most emotional scars. I'm sure if we lost her, Skip would have sold the boat and given up fishing. We look forward to a time when we don't need to worry so much about the safety of the children.

Years later, Lynda will read this and remark, "Mom, it's funny. Even though I've taken life-saving, no matter how hard I try, I can never float on my back."

CHAPTER TWENTY-TWO
Alaskan Fishing Family

OUR SENSE OF EXCITEMENT and Skip always seeing the "miraculous in the common" creates an ideal learning atmosphere aboard the *Nohusit*. We make sacrifices in our effort to enjoy fishing as a family. We often stop fishing earlier in the day for the children to row ashore and explore. We also fish inside waters where the water is not as rough. When we anchor at night, the children are like wild horses let out of the corral as they head for shore. No two days are ever the same. Life on the boat with four children is always full of much to see and do.

"Daddy is a most patient teacher," Karen says. "He has a way of making learning fun. Eight is a magical age. That year he teaches us to work the gurdies and coil the leaders and, best of all, how to hold the gaff hook to land cohoes or humpies (pink salmon). Then he teaches us to clean humpies. When we're nine, we can clean cohoes. How proud we are to now be part of the crew. I just wish he would let me gaff something besides cohoes and humpies. I want to gaff salmon," she concludes.

I smile. "There will be time enough to learn how to catch a king salmon. Just be patient."

Skip and I drag the skiff behind the boat for both safety and convenience. Skip also doesn't need to lift it off the boom every day when the children want to go ashore.

Eric or Karen or both of them will sometimes get in the skiff as we tow it about 15 feet behind *Nohusit*. One time they row the skiff around inside Pillar Bay to troll with sport poles. They hook a large halibut. We watch as Eric manages to get it alongside the skiff. They only have a gaff hook to land it.

"It's as big as the skiff," Karen yells. "We need a shark hook or a gun to shoot it. If we pull it into the skiff, it might upset it. Dad, can we have the pistol?"

"I am not giving two excited children a loaded gun," he yells back.

I watch as they try to figure out how to land it. Finally the halibut breaks the leader and disappears into the deep water. Both children have such long faces when they return to the boat.

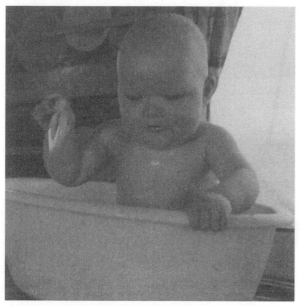

I find it works best if we eat our dinner at noon. At night we have soup and sandwiches, which gives the children the chance to take the sandwiches with them when they row ashore to go exploring.

When the halibut gear soaks on another day, we run into the harbor early. Eric, Karen and Barbara ask us if they can row ashore to explore.

Marilyn finds it easy to give Lynda a bath in Nohusit's sink.

Soon they are off on another adventure.

When they return Karen tells me, "I love playing in the tall grass. I caught a little bullhead and some small hermit crabs in the tide pools. There's so much to see in them. Look, Mom."

I admire her collection and ask Eric what he did. "I got into a pine cone fight with Barbara. Then we ganged up on Karen. It was great."

At the Tokeen Cold Storage the children find Donny on the *Doneda* and those whose parents run the cold storage. In Tebenkof Bay they often play with Robby Rooney on the *Chief*. How well I remember when Robby was born.

On rainy days which Southeast has many of, I teach the children some card games. Crazy Eights is a particular favorite. Karen and Eric try to teach Barbara to play. Lynda also tries to join in. One day when I don't have much else to do, I watch them play. Karen is winning when suddenly I notice Eric cheating. He ends up winning the game. Later when Karen is curled up with a book by her favorite author, Zane Grey, I pull him aside.

"I watched you play Crazy Eights this afternoon. Whenever it looks like the girls are winning, you cheat. That isn't fair."

Eric protests that it isn't true.

"Don't cheat, Eric."

Barbara picks berries when ashore.

The next morning, as happens every morning, the children turn on their record player. Barbara looks at *Grasshopper And The Ant*, a Disney book, as she follows the words from the record player with her fingers. I bet it's teaching her to read. Smiling, I go back to making breakfast.

That afternoon we run into Port Alexander to sell our fish. When Eric is ten and Jackie O'Donnell and his family are buying fish with the *Alaska Maid* here, Eric watches red-haired Nancy unload fish, then returns to the boat and says, "Isn't she beautiful, Mama?"

Coming into the harbor I see that most of the buildings and houses are now abandoned. After tying up the boat, Eric, Karen, Barbara and I head up the dock to see what is left. I discover only 20 people still live here year-around. I tell the children about the bustling community that was here in 1946. The emptiness saddens me and I decide to go back to *Nohusit*. Karen begs me to let them go exploring. I look around. As nothing looks too dangerous, I agree and head back to the boat. As dinnertime approaches the intrepid explorers return to *Nohusit*.

"How did it go?" I ask.

Karen is beaming. "Mom, it looked like people lived here one day and were gone the next. The gambling hall still has the gaming tables, slot machines, and cash registers. Look, I even found

Eric and Karen try to catch a coho from the skiff Skip drags behind.

Lynda watches the fleet in Port Alexander on a stormy day.

a powder puff at the old hotel." She hands me the puff.

"What a find."

Eric cuts in, "The old school still has those old-fashioned desks. It was really neat."

"What a place to find hidden treasures."

One day in July, at Warm Springs Bay, I am out on deck looking at the shore. The ripe salmon berries weigh down the bushes.

"Skip, let's not go out today. The children would love to explore and go berry picking. I could make a shortcake."

"Sounds like a good idea. I love your shortcake," he says, taking me into his arms and kissing me.

Barbara and Lynda are excited to pick berries but Eric and Karen prefer fishing trout at the base of the falls. Barbara fills up the bucket. When she notices me feeding berries to Lynda out of her bucket, she exclaims, "Mom, how could you!" She grabs the bucket.

"Oh, it wasn't very much, Barbara, and Lynda really likes them," I say. Lynda grins at Barbara with berry juice staining her chin, lips and teeth. Barbara gives me a frustrated look and stomps off. A little later I see her on the dock tempting the tame geese within petting range with her berries. Later, we arrange with the Shorts, who live there, to use the big wooden tubs for a bath. Soaking in the hot mineral water is always a treat. We first came here with the Wellesleys in 1946.

The next week while fishing deep inside Tebenkof Bay, Eric pleads with us to go trout fishing in Alecks Creek, commonly called Sockeye Creek.

Knowing how much Skip loves to trout fish, I agree.

Eric, Karen and Skip row ashore late that afternoon and hike up the creek. For bait, Eric carries a jar of salmon eggs he saved from cleaning fish. When they return around dark they have many trout. For breakfast we enjoy fried trout, a true delicacy.

I recall in the early 1950s, the old man who tied his boat here. He was a stream guard for the U.S. Fish and Wildlife Service. The government felt that stationing stream guards kept seiners from making illegal sets. We enjoyed his stories. He claimed his father was a brother to General Custer and was killed in the battle of Little Big Horn. This man, whose name was not Custer, remembers pulling off Uncle George's boots at the age of four. After the massacre, he lived with George's wife, Elizabeth, for awhile and was then adopted by a relative whose name he took. His relation to General Custer got him into West Point. He tells us then he became a body guard to President Teddy Roosevelt. His stories always fascinate us. I don't know if they are true or not but in Alaska you never question a story's veracity.

Later we go into Deep Cove with Lett and Ann on the *Gloria*. We climb

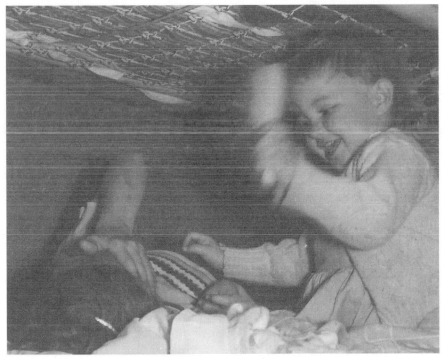

Karen and Barbara play on the bunk in the bow.

Karen rows Lynda and Barbara ashore for an outing.

past the old herring saltery by the waterfall and up the mountainside to a beautiful lake. Skip carries Lynda on his shoulders through the thick brush. We find no trout but the children will remember the day of that long outing. Our favorite trout streams are in the lake above Little Saginaw and in Port Camden.

In our search for salmon, we run into Saginaw Bay. In June and late August, Dignon Fish Co. tows *NEFCO XI* into the bay and ties it to a float by the old cannery. Barbara and Orwan Simpson run the scow and have a small store. Sometimes Skip takes the children into the store to buy a piece of candy and a bottle of pop. Saginaw Bay is another exciting place for the children to explore. They run up the boardwalks. Mac Hammer, the watchman, lives there with his wife, Lois, and daughter, Carol. Even though Carol is ten years older than my children, she often spends time with them. They fish for black cod off the dock or explore the old cannery buildings and abandoned houses.

In Halleck Harbor, we spot a pictograph of a blazing sun high on the rock cliff. Many stories are told of it, but I like to believe it is a peace symbol between the Kake and Tsimpsian Native tribes. Skip and I hear that many fossils and Jasper rocks are found here. While Skip keeps fishing, the children and I row ashore for some archeology exploring. Everyone finds interesting rocks.

When Skip sees our collection he says, "Only pick the best two or three that you find to take back with ya." Everyone looks forlorn and starts emptying their pockets.

Our friend, Hans Norbisrath, a geologist, tells us if he were going to look for oil in Southeast Alaska, he would start at Saginaw.

The boat forces me to get all my housework done. In the house, I feel guilty about not doing all the jobs. On the boat, we must put everything in its place to keep it from falling onto the floor in rough water. When Skip calls, "Wake," Karen runs to the dresser to grab anything that is loose. I run to the table. Luckily, Skip had pounded a piece of wood between the hinges on the table and the wall. This makes three compartments to stow the salt, pepper, sugar, instant coffee, ketchup, and small jars of salad dressing. Dirty dishes go in the sink.

When Eric is 13, he wins a scholarship to attend the Alaska 4-H Club

Barbara studies a book of sea life. She hunted for how many shells she could find on the beach.

Eric lifts a large king salmon aboard.

Congress in Fairbanks. Eric and I plan to fly from Tebenkof to Petersburg for me to get his clothes ready. I awake that morning to find a thick blanket of fog covering the bay. Skip calls Alaska Coastal Air to tell them that we are at Point Ellis. Bill Stedman is their pilot out of Petersburg. He will pick up Eric and me as soon as the fog lifts. Anxiously we wait the day out with the fog getting heavier. The next morning we hear a plane circling above us. At last, we see it come through a hole in the fog and land gracefully next to us. Skip rows Eric and me to the float plane and we take off through the same hole. When we arrive in Petersburg, we find the other Southeast Alaska teenagers have left. I put Eric on a plane to Juneau where the local Extension Agent meets him and puts him on a Fairbanks plane.

The next day I fly back to Tebenkof Bay to rejoin the family. The first night we anchor in Troller Islands and tie up with Lett and Ann Taylor on the *Gloria*. The girls want to explore ashore. Skip agrees and we watch them disappear into the woods. We don't worry because Eric and Karen have explored these woods many times. The children know to come back to the boat before dark. Skip walks out on deck and calls, "Karen."

No answer. From my seat in Ann's galley, I hear him call a few more times. Each time his voice gets a little louder. Finally he returns, a worried look on his face. Lynda is just two and a half, Barbara six, and Karen 12 years old. Skip picks up the radiophone and calls other boats anchored in the area. He asks each one if they've seen his three little girls on shore. Everyone replies that they haven't but they'll watch for them.

Darkness is fast approaching. I stand on the deck shouting their names, while he is calling the boats. Except for the radiophone, and Skip's worried voice, nothing breaks the silence.

As I listen, Skip asks Lett, "Can I take down your skiff and row ashore?"

Lett agrees. Another boat pulls up and the three worried-looking men row ashore. They have flashlights, for darkness has enveloped us. While the men are organizing the search on shore, the three girls walk out of the woods straight for them.

Skip is the first to them, grabbing up little Lynda and Barbara in a hug. I have a lump in my throat as I watch them walk back down to the skiff.

"What happened out there? Ya know ya are supposed to be back an hour before sunset," Skip exclaims once they are back on board.

Karen shakes her head and says, "Barbara wanted to walk around the island on the beach rather than cutting through the woods on the narrow section. The island is larger than we thought and the beach turned into steep rocks. When we were about half way around, I decided to turn around and go back the way we came. We weren't lost at all."

Lynda starts crying and I take her into my arms.

"Don't ever do that again, Karen," Skip says. "You really worried us. At least you didn't panic and run in circles."

Indignantly, Karen says, "I knew the way back."

When Eric returns a week later he has many stories to tell. He describes a workshop that inspired him to become a "Leader for Tomorrow." This means he must get better grades in school. He acts so grown-up that I am happy that he went.

When he hears about Karen being late getting back with the little girls on the island, he exclaims, "See what happens when I'm not looking after my sisters."

I know that Skip worries about having us all aboard. Commercial fishing is a dangerous occupation. If something happens, Skip feels that he might not be able to save us all. The younger children always wear life preservers out on deck and on the docks. I reassure him that as long as we teach the children to stay calm in any situation, everything will be all right.

Where to fish is always a problem.

Eric always reminds us, "You argue about where to fish too much."

"I don't like your father making excuses for not fishing. We have such a short time to make enough money to get through the winter." Eric just gives me a look and walks off. Children never want their parents to argue. They don't realize that sometimes it's the only way we know to express ourselves.

We are running between fishing grounds and spot a school of Dall porpoises coming toward us. They swim back and forth across Nohusit's bow.

The best place to see them is from the two portholes in the bow. The children immediately fight over who can look out.

I say, "Everyone can see out of two portholes if you get really close together. You must take turns. You'll have to hold up Lynda, too."

Often humpback whales breach near the boat. One time, one swims right under the boat. In good weather, the children will put on shorts and sit on the bow to watch the whales jump, dive, and roll on the surface. This is so breathtaking that I often get the movie camera and join the children.

Every morning before breakfast I wash small items like undershirts, panties, and for many years, diapers. I hang them on a line on top of the cabin, where the wind and sun soon dry them.

Whenever we are stormed in on the boat, I heat water in the copper boiler on the stove and wash clothes in our gasoline Maytag washer with the wringer. Then we hang the clothes on a line on shore. Skip claims we have clotheslines strung all over Southeast Alaska.

Now, Skip announces, "We're going to sell the washer and send our clothes to town with the packer to the laundry. Let's have enough clothes for him to leave one bag and bring one back."

I'm happy to do this. If we run to town, Skip puts me and the laundry bags off on the dock as he heads for the cold storage to sell the fish and get ice for the next trip. The children and I take them to the laundry for their fluff dry service. Barbara watches the women run the big power mangles at the laundry.

Upon our return to Saginaw Bay, we hear a rumor about fish in Sumner Straits. As we run through Rocky Pass, I think of Ed Wellesley, who led us through in 1946. The children enjoy sitting on the bow as we pass the Summit and Devil's Elbow. Then we run by Point Barrie, named by Vancouver for Robert Barrie, one of his officers. We head for Buckshot's Trading Post at Port Protection. We've known Buckshot and Irene since 1946 when they first bought fish in Gedney Harbor. We enjoy visiting with then and their daughters, Marian, Lauran, and Claire. I well remember when Irene and I were pregnant at the same time with Claire and Karen in 1950.

A friend asks, "You mean you take four children on that salmon troller?"

I reply, "It's no big thing for they enjoy it." I know that our family is very close because of this experience. Despite safety concerns and financial worries, we all work together to make our trolling a success.

CHAPTER TWENTY-THREE
Too Good To Be True

"I HATE FISHING. The fleet is mad at you if you say anything about the fishing to your friends. They always want you to lie and say how bad it is. They can call in their friends, but you can't call in yours," Skip grumbles.

"Well... you can't be a good fisherman if you don't like fishing. You tried being a skipper on the Fish & Wildlife boat and that didn't work. It's too late now for you to go back to school

The children watch the scenery of Alaska pass by from the bow of the Nohusit.

under the GI Bill. If you don't want to keep fishing, what will you do?"

"I don't know, but I don't like this any more."

In 1964 we decide to take a gamble on our future. We start a charter business of taking fishing and hunting parties around Southeast Alaska.

In one end of the living room, we set up the huge old slant-top office desk which we bought from the closed Pillar Bay cannery. Here Skip sorts, splices and edits our 16mm movie film. Hours and hours he stands there until the film satisfies him for a half hour program. We sell the first rights to a film for the Seattle KOMO's Exploration program. Skip edits out the parts with the

The Jordan family in a rare family portrait taken Feb. 1965.

children and then, ironically, KOMO wants to feature the family. The next film captures our life on the *Nohusit* and he calls it, "Alaskan Fishing Family."

"This makes the first step in our dreams coming true," Skip says as he mails the movies to the Northwest Traveler producer.

In exchange for a big ad about our new charter business, I sell two stories about Petersburg to John Grainger, the publisher of a travel guide. He then asks Skip to sell Petersburg advertisements for him for a commission. Skip sells many ads making me wonder if he should have been a salesman instead of a fisherman.

"You can now become salesman for our charters," I say.

Jim Leekley, the manager of the fur farm in Petersburg, calls, "I've got two friends who want to go bear hunting. Can you take them, Skip?"

"Certainly."

"I'll be the guide," Leekley says.

"Our first charter!" Skip exclaims. "Everything is coming our way, honey.

I just have a feeling."

Skip works from early morning until late at night to make *Nohusit* ship shape. By having a seat built in the front of the pilothouse on the port side, the passengers can look over the bow as they travel.

In April, the producer of the Northwest Traveler program calls for Skip to come to Seattle to narrate the film. I want to accompany him because I took most of the

Karen scrubs the skiff while Lynda and Eric look on.

films and I'm hoping for any inside tips on how to make them better. I also hope that he will let me appear with Skip on the program. We figure and figure, but we can't come up with enough money to pay my travel costs.

As the day approaches for Skip to leave, I set my sights on winning first place in the local Toastmistress' speech contest. When I win, I excitedly tell Skip, "I'll get my way paid to Terrace, British Columbia, to represent our club at the district contest. That's one-third of the cost to Seattle. The contest's on Saturday and you're doing your program in Seattle on Tuesday. The doctor thinks I should have the varicose ulcer on my ankle checked by a Seattle specialist. Can't we make it?"

Skip sees my excitement and wants me to go, too. We add up all the money we have and how much we need. We figure they'll pay us for the use of the film as soon as we narrate it, as the previous producers did.

Suddenly, Skip has the funniest expression and says, "What are we going to do with the children? You'll be gone at least a week." I realize that I cannot go. There is no one to take care of the children and we can't afford to pay anyone.

Like a prayer's answer, the next day a strange woman knocks on my door. She says, "I'm a friend of Don and Eddie Hoffman. They told me to look you up. I'm Mrs. Lemon." During our visit, I discover that she and her husband and little girl are living in inadequate facilities.

On a hunch I ask her, "How would you like to move in here and take care of my three girls for a week? Mr. Jordan and I want to go to Seattle. Eric will be staying with friends."

She is interested but first needs to talk with her husband. That evening she calls to say that they will do it. I can't wait to tell Skip when he comes home from working on *Nohusit*. After adding up the amounts, we decide that I'll meet Skip Monday night in Seattle.

I spend all week making a new suit for the contest. I put aside all my routine housework. Skip and I talk that night. Skip's happy eyes say more than any words, "Everything's going our way, Marilyn."

On Friday, in dismay, I see the house is a mess. Skip sees my look and says, "Don't worry, honey, the children and I will clean it before the Lemons come."

While packing, I notice my billfold is well-worn. I change it for an extra one of Eric's. I carefully put all our money into it.

Skip says, "Don't worry about the speech. Have fun."

I work hard on my speech. The topic is provided just 48 hours before the presentation time. My subject is empathy. Emily Martens and I join members from Juneau and Ketchikan on the trip to British Columbia. I thoroughly enjoy my first Alaska State ferry ride on such a beautiful sunny day. In Terrace, I proudly come in second of five contestants.

Flying to Seattle on Monday, I discover that I hadn't put one piece of identification in my new billfold. I worry immigration won't let me into the United States. As I walk along the tarmac, I see Skip waving to us from the other side of the airline fence.

When the immigration agent comes to me, I explain my predicament. He nods me on and says, "All right."

I run and kiss Skip and explain what happened. "I thought they might send me back to Canada."

Skip laughs, "All your scheming to get down here would have been for naught then."

We are like newlyweds as we can't remember when we've been away from the children. The next morning I go to a hairdresser and have my hair fixed in a bouffant. Skip beams when I meet him for he likes me to look chic.

When we arrive at the TV studio, we preview the film first, because we haven't seen it since Skip sent it in February. The producer gives me some pointers on improving my movie making, but they don't invite me to appear with Skip. Then Skip and the host go before the cameras. I'm proud of how

Skip talks spontaneously and is so natural in front of the cameras. The program is a success but we wont be paid until it plays in May.

The next day we go to the doctor. He wants to operate on my varicose veins immediately.

"As soon as I earn the first money from fishing," Skip tells the doctor, "I'll send her down to you."

"The longer you wait the more chance we'll have to graft skin. She'll be in the hospital four or five times longer then," the doctor warns us.

We fly home on Friday after visiting Eva, Skip's sister, and her family in Mount Vernon.

Skip's first charter is a success. He tells me, "I never laughed so hard. The hunters and Leekley played tricks on each other. No tension, no worry. No better way to make money."

Word is slowly spreading about our charter business. He next takes Larry Gardner and his wife out on a four-day hunt with T. Smith as guide. They usually figure they need a ten-day charter for a successful hunt, but they are lucky. Gardner shoots a nine-foot brown bear and three black bears.

For his last charter of the season, Skip takes two brothers and their wives on a three-day sight-seeing trip. I'm the cook and the Lemons take care of the children again.

With the charter work done, Skip says, "I'll take Eric and Karen and we'll see if we can find some kings. With your going to the hospital with your leg, I can't see your moving on the boat until you return."

Eric is 14 and Karen 13 that year. In June, Barbara, Lynda and I stand on the dock and wave good-bye for the first fishing trip of the season. They find the kings at Point Ellis where we caught the cohoes in 1951.

Upon their return, Eric says, "Mother, it's like pulling cohoes. Two and three big 20-pound kings on every line. One day we had 52 kings."

Before this, Skip had always pulled in the big ones, but now Eric learns how to land them. The three of them laugh and have a good time. When another king hits the deck, Skip says, "This is for your mother's operation. This is our year, kids."

Karen cleans fish as well as cleaning the boat and cooking. Skip lets her pull in the small kings. They also catch halibut. They are proud when they bring in $1200 for a 10 day trip.

"Fine time for Karen to go to 4-H camp," Skip exclaims. "You're going to Seattle. Eric and I must care for Barbara and Lynda on the boat."

Skip's new marine battery for the *Nohusit* arrives that day. When we are lying alongside the cold storage dock, I say, "You better get it off the dock before you leave. The dock company says they need the space."

He gets it. I look up and see him crawling down the ladder. I know immediately that something is wrong.

"I hurt my back when I lifted the battery." He lies down on the couch. I see he is in terrible pain and can't straighten up.

"You better see the doctor and get some pills," I tell him.

As in the past, the muscles on one side of his body have collapsed making one shoulder and one hip higher than the other. He no longer has a back brace as it burned when the boat exploded.

When he returns, he bravely says, "Don't look so worried, Marilyn. It'll get better. Eric and I will fish. Come on, boy, untie the lines. We'll all head out," he says patting Barbara and Lynda on their heads. "The kings may still be there." He kisses me and says, "Now go to Seattle and don't worry."

With sinking heart and a foreboding of disaster, I stand on the dock and watch the *Nohusit* speed up and head past the buoy. Karen leaves for camp on Saturday night, and I fly to Seattle on Sunday.

David Stuteen from Kake tells the children about the old totem in Tebenkof. They are sitting by a clam midden.

In Seattle, I form a close friendship with Marjorie Arnberg, a second cousin who is my age. When I return to the room after the operation, I call Marjorie and tell her the good news. The doctor didn't have to graft skin.

Skip calls the hospital, saying, "We found no fish, but I'm better."

After my discharge from the hospital, I stay with Esther Frink, my cousin. I try to look for home economist positions in the Seattle area. If Skip is going to lecture, we'll need an income while he is getting started. I find nothing.

After ten days, I fly home. Twila Molver, our neighbor, meets me with her car at the amphibian plane turnaround. We still don't own a car. Twila reports, "Skip called that he and the children will be in today."

As the boat docks I'm surprised to see Skip doesn't look well. I tell myself that his back's been bad before, and it

Marilyn and Skip work at the Alaska booth at the Chicago Boat and Travel Show.

gradually went away. When Karen returns from camp, she stays with a friend. We stay in town for the Fourth of July because the doctor must take the stitches out of my ankle the day after the Fourth.

We fish the rest of July. I immediately notice that Skip lets Eric and Karen pull in the fish. He is willing to only supervise us.

In August, we travel across Chatham Straits to Port Alexander. On the first pass along the beach every pole jerks.

"Get Eric and Karen up. The fish are here," Skip says as he sits in the pilothouse at the wheel. Usually he'll pull in the fish while they are dressing.

When Eric and Karen are in the troller pit, he says, "Marilyn, can you steer? I don't feel good."

He lies down on the couch and never gets up all day. The fish are there, all right. Eric and Karen find a coho on every hook. They have a great time. I'm not sure how to stay on the fish. How long a tack should I make? Before, I looked back at Skip in the troller pit. He'd motion me to turn around or keep my course. Now, I must decide. Skip shows no interest and only gets up when we head for harbor. He steers through the kelp at Port Alexander's entrance. We sell 150 cohoes plus a few kings for $250, our biggest day of coho fishing that season. Skip is proud of us.

The next day he is better and he does some of the steering. He never goes outside on deck though. The fishing isn't as good that day. When the fishing slacks off, we return to Tebenkof.

August 25 finds us in Saginaw Bay. That day when Skip awakens, he says, "I'm sick, honey. Take my temperature."

It is 102 degrees. We all try to talk him into flying to town to see the doctor. He won't hear of it. "It's just the flu. I'll get over it."

Skip won't let us fish as we did at Port Alexander. For a week we lie at the float. His temperature goes back to normal. We fish three more days before heading to Petersburg to put the children in school.

Skip feels reassured when he finds others who have been sick. He tells me, "Vince on the Camelot is in the hospital. He has a kind of flu like I did."

He has a chance to work on a surveying crew. George Rice, who has an outboard shop, also offers him a job. Skip says, "I took the outboard shop job. I'm not able to carry the heavy chain around for surveying."

As he seldom admits he isn't able to do anything, I look at him closely. I tell myself, "You're silly to worry. He's in his 50s now and you can't expect him to be as strong as in the past."

The outboard job only lasts three weeks. In September, Skip meets Estelle Krantz, who is looking over the tourist facilities for Gil Boeckmann of the Chicago Motor Club. Skip corresponds with Gil, who encourages him to come to Chicago to audition for the lecture circuit.

He works many hours on our films. He puts together an hour and a half movie which is required for the lecture circuit. By the middle of November, he has it ready for duplication.

We haven't made the $3000 we figure we'll need to finance the trip. "I'm going down to the bank and see if we can borrow it for the trip," Skip says. "This is our investment for the future."

He returns, slamming the front door. He walks over and throws down his paper on the table. "It's all off, honey. The banker will only give us $500, and at the most $1000 on another set-up. Maybe I should go alone and leave you and the children here."

I think for a long time. I finally suggest that we borrow on his life insurance.

His eyes light up. "I didn't think of that. Thank you, honey."

"It's an investment in you, Skip. You're the best in the world," I say giving him a big kiss. I write my mother and ask if the children and I can stay with her in Iowa. We'll put the older children in school at Tama.

We work hard and pack unneeded items in the attics. We need to rent the house to make the mortgage payments. We won't worry about pipes freezing if it is rented.

Skip makes an appointment to see the Sitka orthopedist about his back. We postpone leaving until the night after Skip's appointment. We can make train connections through Canada only on certain days of the week so the appointment slows us down by a couple of days. Then the planes can't fly from Sitka. The orthopedist is coming on the ferry we are leaving on. Skip tells him that he'll make a new apointment upon our return.

We will take Tiny but not Mama kitty. When we find our renter's son is allergic to cats, we don't know what to do with Mama kitty. We worry that we might have to do away with her. On the last afternoon, we find someone to keep her for us.

On the train ride I tell Skip that we must tell the children about Dad. We can't take the chance that someone in Tama will tell them.

Later that afternoon Skip says, "We told you that Grandpa Frink's heart just stopped. That is true, but he shot himself."

"Why?" Eric asks through his tears. He remembers playing checkers with Grandpa Frink.

"We'll never know for sure. We know he worried about his health, and perhaps his business. We all loved him, and you shouldn't think less of him. We felt you should know as we'll be in Tama for six months."

We put our arms around each other and cry.

We arrive in Tama four days before Christmas. Christmas is a sad time for Mother as it reminds her of Dad's death. She hasn't bought a tree. We buy the last one in town. After a delightful Christmas with Mother, we show the children the area. We reason that once school starts in January, we'll have no time for sight-seeing. We visit my college roommate Ruth Elliott, her husband, Elmer, and their family on a farm in Clare, Illinois. Our children are the same ages, and they enjoy riding the farm ponies. We journey to Chicago to visit my first cousin, Phyllis Dolan and her family. We show the children the metropolitan area, aquarium, field museum and zoo.

At the Union Station in Chicago, we put all our luggage in the storage lockers while we tour the station. We go to pick up the bags and Skip is passing them out when he suddenly looks up and says, "Where's Lynda?"

A sense of panic strikes everyone in the family. Lynda is only four years old and the train station is crowded with travelers. We head in different directions looking for her.

Then, over the loud speaker we hear, "We have a little girl at the information desk. We can't understand her name. She is looking for her mama and daddy."

We run to the desk. "I couldn't see you, Mama. I went to the desk."

"You did right, Lynda. You must have missed us when we went behind all those stacks of key lockers." How happy we are that she is safe.

We all board the train to visit my aunt and uncle, Bee & Bill Murray, in Kalamazoo. We enjoy New Years with them. We return to Iowa to register the children in school.

We don't understand why Gil doesn't want Skip coming to Chicago until the third week in January. These are three of the longest weeks for Skip and me. Skip doesn't have anything to do. As Mother is 73 and has a tremor, she is happy for me to take over the cooking, washing and housekeeping.

I have the "what ifs" as the month progresses: What if nothing comes of all this investment? What if we don't have enough money to get back to Alaska? What if we worry Mother with our problems? We might upset her which we don't want. What if we lose the house and boat? We might even end up on welfare.

I don't tell Skip what I'm worrying about, but he senses it. Finally, he says, "Don't ya have faith in me, Marilyn? Ya can't have, if you're worrying so much."

That snaps me out of it. I vow not to let myself get in that train of thought again.

Skip does wonders in Chicago with Gil opening doors for him. Each lead Gil gives him, he runs down. He meets the outdoor editors on the newspapers and television stations. He appears on several of their programs. As he did when we first met, he calls to share each new happening.

"Tonight, darling, I'm on Art Mercier's program. Be sure to listen." As usual, he is great as he tells about Alaska.

Skip returns to Iowa the middle of February for our anniversary. Not to be idle, he gives five programs in three days in the Cedar Rapids and Lisbon areas. For our 19th wedding anniversary, we show our movies for the Lion's Club Women's night at Manchester. On the bus back to Tama we hold hands. We are so happy, for the trip has been a great success.

Skip signs a national lecture contract with Redpath Lecture Bureau for the winter of 1965-66. They title the show, "Alaska Fishing Family." They insist we have a family picture made for their brochure.

"The first year will be a little slow. They figure that by the second winter, they'll book me solid," Skip says.

Skip helps in the Alaska booth at the Chicago Boat and Travel Show. After the show starts he calls, "Marilyn, ya must come in for it. I talk to people all day. You'd like it, and ya can help, too. Ya come the middle of the week, and Eric and Karen can come on Saturday and Sunday."

Peg, my sister from New York, arrives for an Iowa visit on Sunday before I leave. She doesn't want me leaving the children with Mother. I quickly find a woman to come during the day to take care of Lynda while the other three are in school. I know 14-year-old Karen will help with the cooking and look after Barbara and Lynda when she gets home from school. Peg and I take the train Tuesday night when she is satisfied that I'm not expecting Mother to look after the children.

When I get to Chicago at 9:00, I call Skip and joke, "Mr. Jordan, I'm interested in an Alaskan trip. Can I talk to you?"

"Where can I meet you?"

"At the railroad station."

"Marilyn!"

"You knew me."

"I'll take a taxi right down there."

I love seeing him in such good spirits.

"I was on the 7 a.m. TV round-up this morning telling about the Travel Show and the Alaska booth. It went real well. Too bad you couldn't have heard me."

We go to the Travel Show for its 12:30 p.m. opening. We work hard. I sit behind the brochures and say, "If you're interested in Southeast Alaska, Mr. Jordan can help you. Mr. Watlalka knows the mainland. Fred is from the Department of Tourism and he can answer all other questions." Skip and I enjoy doing it so much that we forget how tired we are by closing time at 9:30.

This is a second honeymoon for Skip and me. If the children come to Chicago, we'll need to rent two more rooms at the hotel plus their train tickets. As I feel that we can't afford the expense, I encourage Skip to call them on Thursday and tell them not to come. They are so disappointed.

A group of us goes out for dinner at restaurants after the show closes each evening. Skip loves showing me around the city. In this short time, he already knows Chicago. He makes arrangements to show our movies at Chef Alberto's Restaurant on Wednesday after the Travel Show closes. On Sunday night I need to catch my train at six. We step behind the displays, and Skip kisses me good-bye.

"I love you, Marilyn."

"I love you, Skip. Good luck on Wednesday. Sign up many charters."

Late Wednesday night, he calls, "I've got down payments on three charters. There's a couple more good prospects. Everyone loves your movies, honey."

He always gives me credit, but I only took part of them. They would have been nothing without his editing. He tells Redpath how I am as good a lecturer as he is.

When he arrives in Iowa we celebrate our trip's success. Everything is working out for us.

Skip debates whether to return to Alaska by way of the West Coast and visit Dawn and his grandsons. Dawn and Clinton divorced and she moved to California and married Lowell Myers. They have a son who is Lynda's age.

When the bear hunters change their hunt to April 30 from May 10th, Skip must leave immediately for Alaska. I decide to stay in Iowa until school is out.

"I've always worked on that boat for two to three months to get everything done. I'll be alone with none of you to help, and I barely have four weeks."

We take the children and Grandma to the Des Moines Boat Show on March 27. Skip receives down payments from the Des Moines hunters.

Eric, Karen and I drive Skip to Waterloo at 2 a.m. that night to catch the train. "Please eat right," I tell him. "Eat one meal a day in a restaurant. You can't get sick, Skip."

"I'll try. Don't worry. Everything is coming our way at last." Happily, he kisses us all and boards the train.

CHAPTER TWENTY-FOUR
I Love You ...

FROM THE TIME SKIP REACHES ALASKA, he isn't well. Tucked in the middle of his long, cheery letter is this:

> I wish I could have some appetite. It's absolutely gone, and I never get hungry although I remember to eat at times. I'm losing weight which is O.K. and I feel fine.

Another time he writes:

> I'm not doing very well with my work. I haven't any strength or ambition at all anymore, but it's the same with the rest of the old-timers, too.

Then he writes that *Nohusit* is going into the shipyard for a week. When no letter comes, I worry. This isn't like him.

When he calls, he says simply, "I've been sick most of the week, honey, but I'll be ready for the hunters when they get here tomorrow."

The last letter says:

> The hunters are here, and we'll be leaving tomorrow. By superhuman effort, I'm ready.

I hear nothing until they return 12 days later. I worry all the time. Skip's 15- page letter describes their experiences. On page five he writes:

> I'll have to go to the doctor. I have been quite sick the whole trip. Must have a flu bug that I can't get rid of. I may have pleurisy also. My stomach hasn't been good for

a month, maybe it's an extended case of stomach flu. I just have to feel better soon.

When he arrives in town, he adds to his letter:

Dr. Smith says I have a virus and have to be very careful. It is in my lungs and throat and head. He is afraid it might get into my liver and cause hepatitis . I had a chest X-ray and got some pills. Been running a temperature for a couple of weeks and my gums are tender and sore. Hope I don't land in the hospital.

The next day he writes:

I feel a little better after a couple hours sleep and I enjoy a meal. I think I'll lick this bug in a couple of days. I'm going to get plenty of rest and take my medicines. I'll have time to get ready for the Johnston party who arrive a week from tomorrow.

The next letter says:

I'm sure glad I had fortitude enough to get ready for this last trip even as sick as I was. Now I'll have to get hold of some inner strength again and get everything ready for this next trip even against doctor's orders. I simply can't stop—we will all go to pot if I don't produce now.

On Monday morning I receive his letter written on Friday evening:

I plan on calling you Sunday evening. You'll have this letter after I talk with you. I want to be sure you have enough money and everything is going O.K. before I take off. You'll be on your way by the time I get in. I have managed to get

most of the work done, but I have to lay down often. I bet
you are sick of reading about all of my troubles. Dr. Smith
gave me another shot and a whole lot of new medicines
today. I'm improving slowly and should be O.K. by Tuesday
when the Johnston party arrives.

No phone call comes Sunday. All day Monday I walk around in a trance with a premonition of disaster. Skip always does what he says. Why hasn't he called? By evening I pace the floor, but I don't want to worry the children or Mother. They sense something is wrong.

I run to the phone when it rings. An operator says, "I have a collect call from Mr. Jordan in Petersburg. Will you accept the charges?"

"Certainly."

"Hello, honey."

"I worried when I didn't hear from you."

"I went all to pieces yesterday. I'm in the hospital now."

"Oh, no," I burst into tears.

"I'll be all right. It isn't too bad. They're doing everything for me. I was so sick yesterday. No one came by the boat to see how I was."

All the children talk to him on the extension phones. "Everything is going to be fine. They're going to make me well," he assures all of us.

That is May 17. We are due to leave the first of June. I write Dr. Smith and ask him to keep me posted on Skip's condition. I'll fly home if warranted. I give him my telephone number and address. At school, I ask if the children can leave early and pass their grades. Their teachers agree so we will leave on the train a few days early.

Skip writes two cheery letters about how much better he is. I receive them on Thursday and Friday, and then nothing. On Saturday, friends, who plan an Alaskan trip the following year, invite us to their beautiful home for dinner to show the movies.

Watching the movies, I think, "What if something happens to Skip." I almost cry.

A man from Chicago calls Saturday night about a trip the first week in June. I need to give him an answer. I awake at 2 a.m. Sunday morning. A sixth sense tells me that Skip isn't well. I can't sleep and only doze once before morning.

The next morning I call Skip at the hospital at 9:30. "I can't take anyone out, Marilyn." He can't talk. "I've got phlegm in my mouth. They haven't had time to clean it out yet." His sentences aren't coherent. They are short and jerky.

"Please get all right. I worry about you so much."

"I'll try," is all he says. We don't talk long.

When I hang up, I burst into tears. "He's worse. He's going to die, Mother." I throw my arms around her. "I need him so much." I lay my head on the table and sob, "My Skip! My Skip!"

The next morning the man from Chicago calls back and asks, "What's wrong with him?"

"I don't know. They call it viral pneumonia."

"My wife just got over it. They recover." I feel better after that.

"Others recover," I keep telling myself. Peggy, my sister, flies from New York and helps us pack on Wednesday night.

Skip wires that night, "I'm slowly recovering. I can't meet you in Prince Rupert as we planned. Have a good trip. Love, Skip."

We all feel better. The five of us and Tiny leave Iowa on Thursday and will get into Petersburg early Tuesday morning. It is a long train ride, but we enjoy the trip. Previously, I only made the trip in winter. How beautiful the United States and Canada are with the trees budding and the farmers plowing their fields! I have missed the mountains, trees and salt water, though.

Reverend David Crawford, our minister, meets us at the ferry terminal. For a minute, my heart stops. I close my eyes and pray, "Oh, God, please don't let him have died."

"Skip got out of the hospital today. He's up in my pick-up."

"Thank goodness." I can hardly believe it is my Skip. He's thin and haggard. Later, I learn that Skip almost died as we went through Canada. Dr. Smith had people standing by to give him blood.

As the renters are still in our house, we go to the Crawfords' home. When we are in the bedroom, I lie down beside Skip and cry, "Darling, darling, darling."

"It's gonna be all right now, Marilyn. I thought I was going to die. I'd never see you or the children again."

The next day we move aboard *Nohusit*. Barbara and Lynda want to sit on Daddy's lap. Skip likes to hold them. Eric and Karen plan to attend church camp on Thursday, and I wash and iron their clothes. Skip just lies on the duplex bed in the pilothouse. I put Eric and Karen on the ferry.

Each day Skip tries to do a little around the boat. We have a couple coming on a sport fishing charter on June 13. I feel that with my cooking, Skip appears to regain his strength. He looks better and is getting more color in his face. I'm happy he has ten days before the next charter. The doctor insists he come in for more office calls. I know he is taking many blood samples. When Eric and Karen return, everyone helps to ready the boat for the charter. Skip merely supervises us.

The couple flies into Petersburg on the 13th and we immediately run to Pybus Bay. Skip is the guide, Eric is the deckhand and I am the cook. We pay Susan Fredricksen to board Karen, Barbara and Lynda. Skip's color is much better and he isn't losing weight anymore. For some reason Skip decides not to sport fish off *Nohusit* and has bought a large open skiff.

I am still worried about Skip. When the weather turns cold and rainy, I suggest that Eric be the guide. The couple won't hear of it and demand Skip, saying they paid for him and not a teenager. I don't understand why it matters, as they will be near our anchorage. Skip gives me a warning look and I don't mention it again. The couple fishes every day from sun-up to sun down. Skip runs the skiff, baits their hooks and cleans the fish. In their 12 days, they catch many salmon and halibut. As they hope to land a record fish, he keeps trying.

When we return to town, we find a note from the doctor requesting Skip stop by his office every time he is in town to give a blood sample. Skip and I wonder why. What is going on that the doctor isn't telling us?

Our last charter is due to arrive in a couple of days. Skip, Eric and Karen clean the boat and get everything ready. On the last day Skip stops by the doctor's office but he finds it very crowded. He tells me, "I'm feeling much better. I can't see any reason for so many blood tests. I'll get it when we return."

I know he hasn't regained all of his strength and still weighs the same.

On the first day of this charter, we run out to Pybus Bay with the Buriegies. The weather is bright and sunny. They immediately catch fish. They have a wager on who will catch the biggest fish. Skip loves their sense of humor and enjoys the trip. In the end the wife wins with the biggest fish but the husband catches more.

As the couple flies away Skip turns to me, saying, "We'll get more charters from these groups telling about how much fun they had. Word of mouth

The Jordans and the Kruses go out on Nohusit.

is the best advertising there is."

The girls have missed us. "It's boring to stay in town after being out on the boat," Karen says. "It seems like you've been gone a month."

The next day in the mail we receive a down payment on a trip for a 1966 bear hunt. Skip is excited as he bursts through the door waving the check, "It's all working out like I told you it would. We've already got a great start on next season."

Happily I kiss him and exclaim, "I am so proud of you."

We spend the next four days getting *Nohusit* ready to commercial fish. I've persuaded a classmate of mine from grade school, Dr. Otto Kruse, to bring his Norwegian wife and five boys for a week of fishing. I am excited about seeing old friends and am busy around the pilothouse on July 10, the night they will arrive on the ferry. I see Skip lying down.

"How about your meeting them, Marilyn. I just don't feel like getting up at 2 a.m. to meet the ferry."

I look at Skip closely. Is he getting sick again? "Sure, honey. You just rest."

I stand at the end of the dock and watch the Alaska State Ferry *Matanuska* come in. What a beautiful boat, even in the dark. I see Otto standing on the deck holding their baby, Eric. These are the first friends to visit us in Alaska. I am excited to show them our life and this beautiful land. After hugging everyone, I hail a

Eric celebrates his 16th birthday.

taxi to take them to a hotel. Otto tells his wife he'll come to the room after he sees where the boat is docked.

As we walk through the crisp Alaska night to the dock, I tell Otto, "Skip's been terribly sick. I am worried and don't know what is happening."

Otto nods. I feel better about having another doctor to talk to. When Otto appears the next morning while we are eating breakfast I pour him a cup of coffee.

"I think I'll help Verna make out a grocery list for all of us."

As I step off the boat I hear Skip ask Otto, "Doc, would ya like to see my doctor with me? He insists on a blood test before I leave town even though I am feeling fine now."

I walk up the float. I know Otto will take care of things. At the hotel, Verna and I make out the grocery list. We go over what we will need to feed six boys, three girls and four adults for the next week. We're surprised when Otto enters the room with a stricken look on his face. Verna looks up at her husband and immediately stops talking. My stomach drops. Why is Otto so upset?

"Marilyn, I must talk with you. I went over with Skip to his doctor. Your doctor handed me the lab reports. Skip's blood count is all off. He should have six to eight monocytes in his white count, and it is 68. The lab wrote aleukemic leukemia with a question mark."

My heart stops. "Leukemia," I whisper. My throat contracts and there is a sinking feeling in my stomach. I put my head in my hands. Suddenly I remember Otto said there was a question mark.

I look up, "What does the question mark mean?"

"They can't be sure until they run a bone marrow test. They don't have the equipment to do that in Alaska. He would have to go South. Marilyn, the monocytes count might be way off because of the antibiotics they gave him in May. Maybe he doesn't have leukemia."

I stare at Otto. He must be trying to give me reassurance that everything isn't known yet. I still feel like my world is falling apart. In the back of my mind I realize that I cannot break down. My family depends on me to be strong.

"Doctor Smith is calling Seattle to see what they advise. He'll let us know as soon as he hears anything," Otto says.

Slowly I regain my composure. "I want you folks to have a good time on the boat. You've come a long way from Iowa. Let's not spoil it. When we get back in, the test results should be back from Seattle. We'll tell Skip then."

Unloading the groceries at the boat I see Skip sitting inside. "The doctor says I should go to Seattle for tests, Marilyn. My blood isn't what it should be. I told him it would wreck us financially for me to go now. I want to wait until September. Six weeks shouldn't make too much difference. He said that was okay and to check in when we get back into town."

I am putting cans of food in the cupboards. "Sounds fine to me, Skip," I say, not turning around. I don't want hi m to see my expression.

Later, Eric and I run to the house in the skiff to get another life preserver. As we pull up on the beach I tell him, "Eric, your Dad may have leukemia."

He stares at me, his face blank. Maybe he didn't hear me. "There's nothing we can do, is there?"

"No, I don't think so. The doctor will tell us if there is."

"Then why did you tell me, Mom. I'd rather not have known."

"I had to tell someone, son."

Eric just looks at me; his face has taken on a stricken look that wrenches at my heart. A mother should never have to see that look in her children.

With 13 people on board the *Nohusit*, life at times is a little hectic but never a cross word is said. The Kruses have brought a tent for Otto and the boys to sleep ashore. Verna and I feed the group in two shifts. Otherwise everyone spreads out throughout the boat. Some are below in the bow section, some on Skip's new seat, others on the couch and a few around the table or out on deck.

One morning Otto tells me about sitting in front of the tent at Explorer's Basin watching the sunrise. "It was so beautiful, Marilyn, what with the light hitting the clouds, creating canyons and mountains in them. The sky was a brilliant red with darker textures. It was so peaceful."

They stay for six days and both sport and trout fish. Otto catches a 30-pound king salmon. They fly to town on Saturday after hearing about Eric's plane not being able to pick him up because of fog. When the float plane lands, Eric takes the Kruses to it in the skiff. They don't want to miss their ferry on Tuesday and the small planes don't fly on Sunday unless it's an emergency.

After commercial fishing on Sunday, Monday dawns bright and clear. Skip flies in early Monday to give the doctor another blood sample and find out what they recommend. I do not tell Skip what Otto told me. Around supper time I hear the plane circling and then landing 200 feet away. Eric and

I go out in the skiff to get Skip. The first thing I notice as he climbs in is his eyes. They have a far away look in them. He sits in the bow of the skiff. He doesn't say anything to either Eric or me as we run back to the boat.

Once at *Nohusit* Skip disappears below for a few minutes without a word. I finish putting supper on the table and we all eat in silence. After the dinner dishes are set in the sink, Skip finally says, "Well, family, it's more serious than we thought. They think I have leukemia."

We sit in a tense silence and then Karen softly starts to cry. As I glance around the table I see that Barbara and Lynda don't know how bad leukemia is. They stare at Karen and then back at Skip.

"Doctor Smith wouldn't take my white cell count because he said it would only confuse the issue. He let Otto tell me what they are afraid of."

"Good old Otto. He didn't know what he was getting into when he agreed to come up here for a visit." I shake my head. "What are we going to do, Skip?"

Skip just stares blankly back at me.

"They are getting fish at Table Bay. Eric and I can run with Lett and Ann on the Gloria, while you go South for more tests," I suggest.

"No. You two don't know enough to run a boat alone." There is finally fire in his eyes. "You can drown yourselves, but I will not let you drown my three girls. I'm taking *Nohusit* to town and tying her up. If the renters are out of the house, you can move in there."

Silently we all nod. Skip gets up from the table and goes back to the bunk. He says nothing the rest of the night.

The next morning I am cooking breakfast when I hear him on the radiophone. "Goodbye, Lett. It's been great running and fishing with you. Hope you have a great year."

He calls all his closest fishing buddies and repeats the same thing. I can barely continue cooking as my heart aches so much. Tears silently run down my face. Is this the last time I will see Tebenkof with my beloved husband?

After a silent breakfast Skip runs *Nohusit* the 12 hours into Petersburg. We find the renters are still in the house so Skip runs electricity to the boat. The day is clear but we are all depressed.

As I lay beside him in bed that night I hear him softly crying. "I will never see Eric graduate or give my daughters away in marriage." I gently put my arms around him. At my touch he stops crying. He must think that he needs to be strong. All I can feel is sadness. Why did this have to happen to my

Skip?

On July 17th, Skip flies to Seattle for tests. He kisses us all goodbye before he climbs aboard the plane. His letters come every day and are full of optimism:

> Our prayers are answered. Everything is okay and will be fine with me! They will study the results of the bone marrow tests. Everything is GO with me.
>
> There are three of us Norwegians here in this end of the ward. We have good visits together. It gives me a good feeling that the fellows all like and respect me. Even the doctors treat me with a lot of respect. The sailors ask me why.
>
> Thanks a lot Lynda and Barbara for very good letters. I love you all so very much.
>
> Daddy

The doctors take the bone marrow test on Tuesday and by Friday they still haven't told Skip the results. Skip tells me he is impatient and doesn't want to wait around any longer. He flies home on Saturday, telling the doctors to send any results to his doctor.

On the first of August, Skip arrives back in Petersburg. We are all so excited that he barely gets off the plane before the five of us surround him. He hugs all the children and me.

"I'm so very, very happy you're back and that you're all right," I whisper as I give him a big hug.

Skip says, "We've missed two weeks of fishing. Now we've got to get right to it. Eric, let's fill up with ice and fuel. We'll leave today."

I finish my job at the day-care center and hurriedly buy groceries. At 5:30 p.m. we pull out of the harbor. We anchor at Portage Bay for the night. The next morning I hear Skip on the radiophone telling his friends that it was all a mistake. He doesn't have leukemia.

Our goal is to make $3000 before the children start school. That equals $100 a day. Unfortunately the fish aren't at Tebenkof. We run to Port

Alexander. Nothing.

"Table Bay, here we come," Skip says as we leave Port Alexander. When we approach, we see many highliners.

"Here's for another August like in '54." Skip says. The fishing is great. One day we catch 125 Cohoes.

"After this, I'll never keep your mother away from Table Bay. Ever since 1954, she's wanted to fish here and I haven't let her," Skip laughs.

Skip still doesn't look well because his color is off and he is so thin. I try to keep as much of the workload off of him as possible. Karen and Eric pull the fish and clean them. By the middle of the month the fishing slacks off. When we don't know where to go we decide to head for Icy Straits.

As Skip doesn't like running alone, I am thankful Vince on the *Camelot* agrees to run with us.

"Maybe the fish will come in late up there," Skip speculates.

He radios ahead to see if anyone is fishing Icy Straits. A couple of friends call back and say the fishing is terrible and that we shouldn't waste our time. One third of the way to Icy Straits, at Morris Reef, we slow down and reconsider what to do.

"We can't afford to go someplace the fish aren't," Skip says.

I still want to fish Icy Straits because it's always been good to us.

We ask Vince what he is going to do. He tells us that he will continue on as he didn't hear the conversation about the bad fishing. We head down Chatham Straits and find some cohoes inside Pillar Bay. The children go ashore and dig 17 buckets of clams on one low tide. After cleaning and putting them in freezer bags we send them to Petersburg on the fish packer. This will help our food bill this winter. We end up only making $2500 in August.

As a special treat for Eric on his 16th birthday we run into Port Camden so the men can trout fish. Skip has agreed to let us girls fish *Nohusit* for the day.

As soon as they are gone, Karen turns to me. "How do you think Daddy is, mother?"

"I don't know. He has that little hacking cough all the time. I have a feeling that when he goes out to pull a fish, he is forcing himself to do it. It's like he's saying he'll show his body he can do it. I just don't know." We catch 20 cohoes while they are gone.

As they climb aboard, Skip points back to shore, saying, "It's beautiful in there. We should take movies."

Skip leaves for the hospital in Seattle in 1965.

The next day everyone wants to go trout fishing with Skip. An argument erupts because someone has to stay behind and fish. "Eric, you've already gotten to trout fish. You stay and fish *Nohusit*," I say.

"I am not. I'm going." Eric exclaims.

"If you don't stay then no one can go because the girls can't run the boat. I want to take movies and Skip needs to show us the best fishing spots."

Eric glares at me.

"We'll pull in the gear and all go," Skip says. "It's a long hike up the beach, and I am not sure Lynda can make it. But we will all try."

We have a wonderful day with the whole family. Everyone catches a fish, even Lynda and Tiny. I am busy taking movies of the family fishing. We hope to show them to potential charter customers. As we are walking back Skip whispers to me, "The oldest and youngest are the tiredest."

We head back to Petersburg on Labor Day. The children must register for school on Tuesday. As we walk to the house we see that the renters are still there. As they didn't pay us rent in August, we had thought they would be gone. Tiredly we all walk back to the boat.

On Tuesday, Skip looks for a job. "I asked Lahmeyer if he had a job for me. I can go to work at 1:00 today if I want, but I told him I couldn't work until Thursday. I've got to get the renters out of the house and move us back in."

"Are you sure you can work, Skip?"

"Quit that. I'm fine. They found nothing wrong with me."

"I haven't seen anything in writing saying that."

"We need the money. I've got to work."

I shake my head. We thought that if the doctors found anything they wouldn't have let Skip leave Seattle the end of July. But Skip still looks so tired, I wonder if maybe they are not telling us the whole story.

Skip is unable to get the renters out of the house. On Thursday he goes to work. I am worried about him and talk to my friend, Judy Harle. At lunch time I see Skip slowly walking down the dock toward us. It looks like he can barely put one foot in front of the other. His head droops as he settles into his chair.

"Are you okay, Skip?" I gently put my hand on his shoulder.

"The first day on any job is always the worst, especially in carpentry. I haven't done it in a long time." He sighs. "I can work there until the first of the year which will work well with the lecture circuit. Financially we will be okay."

After eating he slowly trudges up the dock. That night he is so tired we all go to bed at 8:00 so that he can have peace and quiet. I worry all the next day. Is he still sick? Could the doctors have been wrong when they didn't say he had leukemia? Skip can barely lift his head from the pillow, so after he goes to work on Saturday morning, I decide to talk to Doctor Smith.

"Are you keeping new findings from us? Have you heard anything from the hospital?" I ask. He hands me a report dated August 11. I read the words, "Suspicion of leukemia. A complete report will follow once we evaluate the tests."

"What does suspicion mean?" I ask Doctor Smith.

"They have a question. They aren't sure."

I hang my head, tears welling up in my eyes.

"Nothing else has come. Have Skip come in the first of the month, and I'll send them another slide."

"No," I whisper, "That's too long. I want you to have one done now." I slowly walk back to the boat. Skip comes home at noon and I tell him to go up to the doctor's office.

"No, they close at noon. I'll go in on Monday."

Lying in bed that night I ask him, "Don't you think we should stay on the boat until we know more about your condition? We could take *Nohusit* south if you need to be nearer medical treatment."

"Absolutely not. I'll feel better if you are in the house."

I don't argue with him.

Sunday morning we all go to the Presbyterian Church where Skip is an elder. Our family takes up a whole pew. After the church service the worshipers stay around eating sandwiches. Our friends comment on how well Skip is looking. Uncharacteristically, Skip lingers and puts off moving into the house.

The renters said they would be out today. After we change our clothes we head to the house. Sadly I see they didn't leave the house as they agreed. They had moved all of our furniture into the basement and hadn't moved it back. Eric, Karen and I carry the beds and dressers upstairs. It's heavy work but finally we have our bed set up. Skip immediately lies down and falls asleep.

Monday, when he comes home from work at noon, I give Skip his sandwich and gently put my hand on the back of his neck. It is burning up. "Skip, you have a fever," I cry.

"It's okay, Marilyn."

"No, it's not. You go up to the doctor right now."

At the doctor's, Skip has a slide done of his blood for the doctors in Seattle and for my brother Dick, who is a doctor in California.

That night Skip sits in his easy chair holding Dick's slide. "This tells my future. It looks like so little but it can tell so much and dramatically change our life."

The next day he tells Lahmeyer that he cannot work afternoons. For some reason he feels fine in the morning but by noon he has a temperature and is very tired. Lahmeyer says that is okay.

On Thursday afternoon the doorbell rings. I open the door to find Reverend Crawford standing there. He looks very sad. My heart drops. "Doctor Smith wants to see you immediately," he says.

"Who is it, Marilyn?" Skip calls. He is in the back helping the telephone man install our phone. Reverend Crawford comes into the house and starts talking about the weather and fishing to Skip.

"I have a couple of errands to run downtown. Reverend Crawford just said he'd give me a ride."

"That's fine. Ya needn't hurry back," Skip says, turning back to the telephone man.

As I wait to see Doctor Smith I have a terrible feeling in the pit of my stomach.

"They called from Seattle. It has worked into sub-acute leukemia. His white count is 18,000. They recommend immediate hospitalization. The government will pay your way as his attendant if you want to go. I suggest you call the airport right now and see when you can fly out," Doctor Smith tells me.

I leave his office. Unable to get my bearings I don't see Reverend Crawford waiting for me. I can hardly breathe and all I really want to do is sit down and cry.

"Marilyn...Marilyn. Here, get into the car." Gently he takes my arm and leads me over to the door. As we walk into the house I see Skip. His face immediately loses its happiness. He realizes something has happened from how fast we returned and how I look. Reverend Crawford is still with me.

"Skip..." Suddenly I cannot go on, tears stream down my face. "The hospital wired that you have sub-acute leukemia. You must be hospitalized immediately," I whisper.

Skip looks like someone has just kicked him in the stomach. Reverend Crawford puts his arms around Skip's shoulders.

"The government will pay my way as your attendant." I cry.

Skip just stands there, his eyes looking past me. "I'll go alone. The children need you here."

"No, Skip. It's worse than in May. You need me."

"No," Skip says, standing up straight.

As soon as Eric arrives home from school, Skip takes him down to *Nohusit*. He wants to teach Eric everything he can about taking care of the boat before he leaves.

When they return at dinner time I suggest, "We should view all the movies we took this summer before you leave. Four new rolls arrived this afternoon. Maybe we should watch them tonight. Can I ask Harles and Molvers to come over?" I ask.

"Fine," Skip replies. "I'll splice them together when I get back."

When he comes home, he has a bottle of vodka. "We'll have a party when everyone is gone tonight."

He sits in his easy chair with Barbara, Lynda, Tiny and Mama Kitty in his lap. Soft classical music is playing on the radio as he tells the girls that everything will be fine. I busily pack his suitcase.

"I better take all my clothes," Skip comments from the chair. "Then you and the children will have less to bring when you move down to be with me."

We enjoy the films. Later after the children are all asleep, Skip makes us drinks and we make love. Sex may be the best sleeping pill, but it doesn't work for us this time.

Afterwards I am lying in Skip's arms when he says, "Don't ask me to fight anymore. I'm too tired."

At 3 a.m. I sit up and say, "Something tells me I should go with you. Please let me."

"Marilyn, there's little you can do down there. The children need you here. Please, don't mention it again."

The next morning, September 17th, Molvers drive us to school to get the children. While we wait for Skip to get on the plane, a stranger approaches us. I noticed him getting off the plane. "You're Skip Jordan, aren't you?" he asks.

"Ya," Skip answers.

"I'm Jim Walsh, the Pan American representative in Ketchikan. I want you to know how much we think you are doing to promote Alaska."

"Thank you," Skip says proudly.

"Here's the name of our Chicago representative. If you need any material or if he can help you, don't hesitate to call on him."

"That's fine," Skip says, tucking the card in his billfold. "I'm on my way to the hospital now. I'm sure I'll be all right and will go to Chicago the first of the year. I'll give him a call then."

"Thank you, God," I whisper. The good Lord must have put that man on the plane. I know how much it means to Skip to be recognized like this.

Skip lifts Lynda and kisses her. Then he hugs and kisses Eric, Karen, and Barbara. He gives Eric an extra pat on the back. Then he kisses me and walks to his plane. At the top of the stairs Skip turns and waves good-bye.

CHAPTER TWENTY-FIVE
*H*ave Courage

SKIP WRITES EACH DAY. His letters are much like they were in May.

> Doctor Saunders is very sorry he hadn't sent a final
> report of further studies of my bone marrow and blood
> tests. They couldn't really find anything wrong and aren't
> worried about me from the tests and observations they
> made in July. Doctor Saunders is really surprised to see
> me and thinks I look good. He said if I had acute leukemia I
> would be showing definite signs and feeling symptoms by
> now.
>
> Don't worry about me, nobody here is worried or excited.
> Please take It easy, Marilyn, dear!! Don't work too hard
> and don't worry. It would be very ironic if it turned out I'm
> okay (which I am) and you broke down or got sick over all
> this. There is one good aspect of all this. It brings us all a
> lot closer together.
>
> Love, Skip

Early the following Monday morning, September 20th, I dream that a nurse is shaking me and says, "Your husband is dying, Mrs. Jordan." I sit up in bed. The clock reads 5 a.m. I get up and start washing and packing my clothes. I am going to Seattle no matter what Skip says.

After the three older children leave for school, I take Lynda down to Judy Harle's boat. I tell her about my dream. "If you have to go to Seattle, Warren and I and the children can move into the house and stay with your children," Judy says.

"You don't know what that means to me. It lifts a weight from my shoulders." I hug her.

Gay Plumley irons my clothes and shortens Karen's coat. On Tuesday I receive another letter from Skip written Saturday night.

I'm holding up my end very well. There is nothing definite about my condition yet except that things will not be as serious as we imagined regardless of how I am. We will most likely be able to lead a normal life together and even charter and fish. The treatment in most cases is pills and occasional checkups that I can't have done in Petersburg. They will give me cortisone which is easy to take pills. The pills completely check most cases these days, especially when a person is as healthy as I am.

Love, Skip

His letter that I receive Wednesday, written on Sunday the 19th, is very positive.

Dearest Marilyn,

Not much to write tonight. Things will get in gear early tomorrow when several specialists start checking me. They are not at all sure I have leukemia, but there is something wrong that might be easy to fix. I still have the slight cold and temperature from 99-100 degrees. I have lost part of my appetite but eat fairly well. My morale has been sadly shot today but is better now. I sleep most of the time like an old bear in hibernation.

It is beautiful weather here in Seattle. I suppose you have rain up there now. Ask Eric to please check all rifles and the pistol. Take them home and oil them and take all shells out if any are in them.

Did you work hard on the boat? Please don't try to do too much, dear. You are needed to be just you and not only for all the work you do. I have been terribly depressed by the way the children treat each other. They are so smart and good, but are so mean to each other. I'm

worried about Barbara and the treatment she gets
from her older brother and sister. There must be more
true love among them. We don't have much of anything
but lots of love, and we must use it towards each other.

Have courage, dear, this uncertainty is about the worst,
but it won't be long before we know the facts, and then I
can get treatments and soon be with you all again.

I hope you have had time to write a note to some of our
friends here that might come to see me. I wrote Dad a
long letter in Norwegian last night.

One thing you can be sure of—I'll be able to come home
and help you make plans and be with you after I have
started my treatments!

Please love one another children and be good to Mother!
Love, Daddy

On Thursday Mrs. Crawford comes to the house. "You've got a wire at
the Alaska Communications System office. Doctor Smith asked me to come
out and be with you."

"Skip didn't die, did he?" I sob.

"I don't know."

The office is busy. Sitting on the bench waiting for the wire is one of the
longest half hours I ever spent. My eyes quickly take in what is written there:
"Sorry to inform you that your husband is seriously ill here at this hospital."

Mrs. Crawford drives me up to Doctor Smith's office. I show him the
wire. "You should call the hospital and talk to Doctor Saunders."

"I'm thinking of flying to Seattle tomorrow," I say.

"I think that would be a good idea," he replies.

"Does he have leukemia?" I ask.

"Oh yes, of course."

This is the first time they have confirmed that he does have leukemia. I
think of the months we didn't know. I find the Friday morning plane from
Petersburg to Annette Island is full.

Gay comes and helps me pack. I am disorganized and like a robot. She washes my hair, sets it and packs my suitcase. She also cleans my house.

On Friday morning the airport contacts me and says the plane has mechanical difficulties and they can't leave Juneau as scheduled. Mrs. Crawford stops by and suggests I take the ferry to Ketchikan and fly out on the Saturday plane. I can't think, so I decide to stay in Petersburg until the plane can come. Finally, the airline contacts me and says they've added a special flight. They can keep me on the original plane or put me on the special flight. I say no; I want the original plane. Late in the afternoon I say goodbye to the children and board the plane. My mind is a whirl. Skip has only been gone for seven days. In Wrangell Carl Guggenbickler, whom I've known since 1946, boards the plane. He sits next to me and I soon discover he is going to the same hospital Skip is in.

My cousin's wife, Esther Frink, meets the plane and her twin sister takes us to the Public Health Service Hospital. It sits high on a hill overlooking downtown Seattle and Puget Sound. The hospital desk person doesn't know which room is his, but does tell me Skip is on the third floor.

I walk down the long hallway looking into the rooms. One man is propped up in bed with a tray before him. I almost walk past. Can this thin and haggard-looking man be my Skip? Finally recognizing him, I burst into tears as I cross the distance between us. I put my head down on the side of his bed and sob. He takes his big hand and rubs the top of my head.

"I can't take it, Marilyn. You've got to keep control of yourself," Skip whispers. I take a deep breath. I must be strong for him. Rubbing the tears from my eyes I give him a hug.

"Did you know I was coming?" I ask.

"Yes. I told them to send for you."

As I leave the hospital that night I realize that Skip is dying. I can only be with him. I stay at Esther's twin sister's home because Esther is looking after children. The next morning when I arrive at the hospital at 9 a.m. Skip looks worse.

"I can't swallow. Everything comes out my nose." Skip says. His voice is barely above a whisper. I call the doctor who discovers a blockage in his throat. They start an intravenous tube to feed him.

As they are working on him I call Eva, Skip's sister. She arrives a couple of hours later with her daughter Ellen. Skip carries on a coherent conversation with them for an hour, then falls asleep.

Reverend Fine, my relative's minister, arrives at the hospital later that afternoon. "Are you a Lutheran?" Skip asks.

"No, I'm a Methodist."

"That's all right. Marilyn's always been a Methodist."

When Reverend Fine asks if he believes in Jesus Christ, Skip says, "Not 100%, Reverend." Skip is no hypocrite.

I arrive Sunday to find him looking even more tired. Chalky would be too mild a word to use, for now he is white. His skin seems to hang from his bones and he can barely hold his head up.

"Shouldn't we send a wire to your dad?" I ask.

"Good idea. Say I'm getting slowly better and the disease will be controlled." As I stand in the telegram office holding the pen I decide I can't lie. I write, "Skip is critically ill. He hopes he is improving and they will control the disease."

I think of the wire he sent me before I left Iowa in May. He hadn't been out of danger then, but he tried to allay my fears about him.

On Monday Skip can barely talk. I stay by his side through the night. He squeezes my hand, "Ya'll have to leave Petersburg and go back to your profession. Eric is too young for you and him to fish *Nohusit*. If he vere two years older, ya might make it."

A while later he whispers, "Don't take anything but cash for *Nohusit*. Ya might have to hold the paper on the house."

As the morning sun shines through the window I softly cry. Skip is sleeping peacefully. Later Skip and I talk about his decision to give his body for medical research. He doesn't want any money spent on him. We decide that not only will Skip give his body but I will give mine too. Louise Gates, from the *Kitty T*, obtains the forms from her brother, a doctor in Seattle. The University of Washington Medical School is minutes away and they will cover the cremation costs if Skip donates his body.

His condition steadily worsens as the day wears on. He can no longer even pick up his hands or talk to me. Tuesday night the hospital staff refuses to let me stay another night. I hire a nurse to sit with Skip at night so he is not alone. I am exhausted and try to get some sleep. On Wednesday my brother Dick arrives. He talks to Skip's doctors and tells me that the hospital is doing everything they can. This makes me feel better.

On October 4, I arrive at the hospital earlier than usual having made my bus connections without having to wait between buses. As I walk into the room I hear Skip making a strange hiccuping sound. I run down the hall to the nurse's station. She runs back up the hall with me and gets the doctor out of a room two doors down. They race into Skip's room and put an oxygen mask on him. I stand in the doorway and realize that today will be the day my Skip dies. Tears stream down my face.

I call Reverend Fine but they tell me this is his day off, but I might catch him at home. I shakily dial his home number.

"Reverend Fine, this is Marilyn Jordan. Skip is dying. Can you come over," I sob into the phone.

"I'll be right there."

The nurses wheel his bed out in the hall to take him to the operating room to give him a tracheotomy. I wait by Skip's side, holding his hand. Skip doesn't seem to know I am there. Reverend Fine steps out of the elevator. He walks over and takes Skip's hand and says a prayer out loud and then a silent prayer. The good Lord must have planned for him to get out of the elevator at that minute.

I thank Reverend Fine for coming and he sits and talks with me for awhile. I feel better having him there. He leaves before they bring Skip back in the room. I wait by myself until they bring Skip back. He doesn't regain consciousness. He doesn't have very much longer. I can't be in this room alone; I need someone here with me.

I call Marjorie. "Can you come this afternoon? I fear Skip is dying."

Marjorie is in the middle of a construction project at her home but surprisingly the workmen finish up early and she is able to leave sooner than expected. I believe my Higher Power must have helped her come to my side.

At 2:40, Marjorie arrives. "Doesn't he look peaceful?" she asks while hugging me.

"Yes," I sob. "Let's go for a walk." I lean down and gently kiss him on the forehead. We walk down to the lobby to mail a letter I've written to the children. As we look out the window onto beautiful Puget Sound, Marjorie puts her arm around me. Softly I cry.

"Marilyn Jordan, please return to room 311," the loud speaker pages. Marjorie and I run up three flights of stairs instead of waiting for the elevator. I walk in the open door of Skip's room far enough to see that his chest isn't moving. I can't see his face with the doctors and nurses around him. In a split second, I turn around. I don't want to see him in this condition. I want to remember him as Marjorie and I left him, sleeping peacefully on the bed. Marjorie puts her arms around me and we don't say anything.

Dr. Saunders comes out and says, "You can go down to my office, Mrs. Jordan." I do this for I know I'll cry when they wheel Skip out. We wait an hour to find if his body will be accepted by the medical school and then I am free to leave.

I walk down to Carl's room and tell him Skip is gone. He holds my hands for a few minutes. It's good to have an old friend by my side.

CHAPTER TWENTY-SIX
Like A Fish Out of Water

MY BROTHER LYNN flies north with me on Friday. Ann Taylor and Reverend Crawford meet my plane. Lynda looks forlorn standing beside Ann. She cries, "I want Daddy to come back."

"He can't, honey."

I spend Saturday morning looking for Skip's diary he kept in the service. In it, he copied quotations he liked. I provide these to Reverend Crawford to include in the service that afternoon. I want the memorial service to be uniquely Skip's and to try to share the kind of man he was.

Lynda, Karen, and Barbara with Marilyn as the photographer moving to Oregon in 1966.

Some of the quotations that were important to him are:

The invariable mark of Wisdom is to see the miraculous in the common.[5]

The worst that could happen to me would be: when I came to die, to discover that I had not lived![6]

Our main problem is how to do what we want without wasting time and energy in making money. This means we plan to live our own lives which diverge from the conventional.[7]

Before we leave home for the church, I tell Lynda, "We are going to church to say good-by to Daddy. You won't be able to see him. We can only think about him and what he means to all of us."

I know Skip wouldn't like traditional funeral hymns so as we arrive, the organist plays, "Day is Dying in the West."

I am surprised that the church is overflowing. Extra folding chairs are set up and many people are standing. Most of Petersburg is here. As we walk down the aisle, I notice that Karen stumbles and Lynn grabs her arm. Tears are streaming down her face.

Reverend Crawford reads the 121st Psalm; verses 1-4:

> *I lift up my eyes to the hills. From whence does my help come? My help comes from the Lord, who made heaven and earth. He will not let your foot be moved; he who keeps you will not slumber. He who keeps Israel will neither slumber or sleep.*

He concludes with Joseph Fort Newton's Life's Unfinished Symphony. Three sentences I think so apt are:

> *Human life is a symphony, but it is an unfinished symphony and we are waiting, the last movement; the last or undiscovered chord which will give the meaning to the discord at the very moment when it is resolved. The world aches with the stress of a silence that tries to speak, but is tongue-tied as in sleep, because we do not hear. Here and there a hint, a gleam, of the Eternal bursts through, and as much or as little, as we see is our religion.*[8]

The service ends with everyone standing and singing "Blest Be The Tie That Binds." I never realized that this song says so much at a time like this. As the family leaves the church, the organist plays "Let the Lower Lights be Burning."

I say humbly, "Thank you, Skip, my darling, for a wonderful life: for bringing me to Alaska and for making our four wonderful children. You give me courage to face the future."

Many people come to the house to share their condolences. On the dining room table, I set the beautiful arrangement of red roses Dad Jordan sent with a note on how sad he is and how much he regrets not being at the funeral.

Later, I tell my brother that I can't get into my bed because it reminds me how alone I am without Skip. He tells me to make a running jump into it to break the dread. It works.

The next day, I work around the house like someone in a trance and slowly realize taking care of the family now depends on me alone. Lynda is four and Eric a junior in high school. I tell myself to move slowly for I must take care of many business items. Since Skip donated his body for medical research, I have few funeral expenses.

A few weeks later, I ask Eric what is worrying him.

"A friend told me I must now be head of the family. I don't know how to do it, Mother."

"This is my problem, Eric. You just enjoy high school."

I list *Nohusit* for sale as well as the house. In December, Willmer Oines stops by and asks if I receive social security yet. I had applied but heard nothing. He instructs me to call Juneau. I think it speeds up the paperwork for our social security checks start arriving in January. Many friends send gifts for Christmas. I receive the money from the insurance companies, which isn't much as we borrowed against them the previous year. We also borrowed from my insurance. I pay it with money from the other insurance policies. Skip warned me about running out of money. He knew how I always want to pay any outstanding bills.

Adjusting to life without their father is hard for the children. The last time they saw him, he was walking onto the airplane. Accepting that he is really gone and won't come back and walk in the door, is hard. They love and miss him. We are all in a state of shock.

Skip encouraged me to go back into my profession of home economics. How do I do it? I hadn't worked in my field for 20 years. If only I'd taken the Extension Service job ten years ago when they offered it to me, I'd find it easier now. Now, my resume only shows being the week-end cook at the hospital, chemist at the Pulp Mill, and the Fishery Products Laboratory in Ketchikan. Thinking I might work in the Tourism Office, I ask Jean Davis to stay with the children. I take the ferry to Juneau. Sadly I find they have no openings. I try to apply as a writer/editor at the U.S. Forest Service, but I must be on the U.S. Civil Service list.

I send for job listings from Iowa State's Placement Center. Public Relations positions catch my eye, but I have no experience. Then I think about going back to college for my Master's Degree in journalism.

Eric and Karen both say, "Just don't go to Iowa."

Happily, I discover, to attract graduate students, Oregon is waiving out-of-state tuition and charging undergraduate fees. I can go there for $110 per quarter. Eric will start college next year, and I reason that I must receive my MS degree by then. We can't afford for two of us to be in college. I apply to the University of Oregon and am accepted.

Eric graduates from high school in 1967.

Our friends the Gates recommend *Nohusit* to some trollers, who buy our beautiful boat at the end of March. I sell the house the end of May. I come down in price on both of them, but I receive all cash.

One of my most difficult decisions comes when a friend says, "It's a shame to move Eric his senior year. Why don't you leave him with us? He'll be good company for our son who is his age." I ponder the idea. No, I decide, we keep our family together.

Eric works on Wayne Plumley's boat packing fish. He'll fly to Eugene in the fall.

On June 4th, Karen, Barbara, Lynda, Tiny, and I head south on the ferry. I loved fishing in Alaska. I wonder if I will ever return. After 20 years and two months, I'm leaving this beautiful frontier. I wipe away a tear. I must be successful. Four children are depending on me. I am scared.

Joan Maddux and her son travel with us. We take the train from Prince Rupert to Jasper National Park and then to Vancouver, Seattle and Portland. My mother's cousin, Mabel Fisher, meets us and helps me buy a car and then goes to Eugene to help me find housing. We rent for $90 a large house that the Christian College will use for their students in the fall.

I sign up for 12 hours of classes for summer school. Later Dean Hulteng says, "Mrs. Jordan, do you realize that 12 hours in summer school is equivalent to 18 in a regular quarter?"

I reply, "I must take that many hours in order to graduate next June."

Proudly Marilyn receives her Master's Degree in Journalism from the University of Oregon in 1967.

Karen says, "Mother, you go to the library and study. I'll do the dishes and get the girls to bed." To make money for her school clothes, she works in the fields picking strawberries, raspberries and beans. I succeed only with her help.

Eric makes enough to pay for his clothes. Karen takes sewing and makes some of her clothes. In the time between summer school and the fall term, I make pants and a top for Barbara and Lynda.

Money is extremely tight. We try to live on the $225 per month from Social Security and Veterans survivors benefits. I use my savings to pay for tuition and books. The girls help me U-Pick berries, other fruit, and beans to stretch the grocery money. I enroll the younger girls in summer recreation programs. When school starts, I put Lynda in kindergarten and another mother, Jerry Carmichael, looks after her until Karen comes home from high-school.

I enjoy my classes and the students. I see I'd be a perpetual student if I could afford it. I especially like research and reading microfiches of old newspapers. My main courses are in photography and public relations. I take a directed study and work on writing my experiences in Alaska.

At the end of the fall term, I write in my Christmas letter, "Happiness is a 4.0 in graduate school." We plan to spend the holiday with my two brothers in the Sacramento area. Eric has one of the leads in the school play, Marat-Sade, and they practice until 2 p.m. on Christmas Eve. At 4 p.m. we leave for Sacramento and hear on the radio that Santa has been spotted with his reindeer. Five-year-old Lynda asks, "How will Santa ever find us in this car?"

After a fast stop for dinner, we head out in the snow on Interstate 5. With little traffic, I worry that if we break down, no one will find us because we see only an occasional truck. At 11 p.m. we stop at a motel at the foot of Mount Shasta. Lynda and Barbara hang their stockings. I am very tired and worry that I will drop off to sleep. When Lynda's breathing is regular, I crawl out of bed in the dark and fill the Christmas stockings.

The next morning as Lynda opens her gifts, she says, "Mother, you're Santa. I saw you put the presents in my stocking."

As we continue our journey into California, we can't find a restaurant open on Christmas morning. Finally we spot one in the back of a bowling alley that is open 24 hours-a-day, 365 days a year. We are not the only ones happy to find a place to eat for the line for a table is long. From 8 a.m. until 10:30, we join many cars heading toward Sacramento. I'm happy we started the night before.

The trip is worthwhile, for my children have a great time with their ten cousins in Yuba City and Sacramento. We head back to Eugene after two days.

I begin applying for positions in January. I take the Civil Service exam and send out resumes. I'm proud when I'm the only woman graduate student selected that year for Kappa Tau Alpha, journalism honorary. Eric and I both graduate in June. My mother, her first cousinMabel and old friend Inez Whitney all come for the ceremony. It is a happy time for all. I think how proud Skip would be of our accomplishments.

Eric leaves for Alaska to fish on Jeff Pfundt's seiner and I am still job hunting. In June,1967, the US government puts on a hiring freeze making few positions open. I imagine that once I have a degree, I have a choice of positions. I find a newspaper job that pays $90 a week. I can't live on that. I keep looking. With the three girls, I drive to Seattle, Spokane, and Pullman to meet with people but I receive no job offers.

Finally, in October, I am offered a position as home economist with the Idaho Extension Service. They have three openings and I select Mtn. Home because of the largest population, an air base nearby, and its proximity to Caldwell where my youngest sister, Hona, and her family have moved.

The Sunday before we move, I tell the church group at coffee time that I'm moving to Mtn. Home, Idaho.

One woman says, "Oh, out there in the desert."

Upon consulting my encyclopedia, I find the town has an annual rainfall of nine inches. What a change from Petersburg which has 105 inches. Too late for me to change my mind now.

After returning from fishing in Alaska, Eric remains in Eugene and attends the University of Oregon. I move to Idaho with my three girls and our dog, Tiny. As we left Petersburg with no furniture, we have less than a van load. The movers say it might be three weeks before we will receive our belongings. We take our most needed clothes, some cooking utensils, bedding and most important of all, the frozen fruit we picked that summer. We buy dry ice to keep it frozen. We look like Okies from the 1930 in our very full Chevy II. Our first stop on the way is my sister Hona's home in Caldwell, where we arrive at 2 a.m. Hona claims the first thing we say after our greeting is, "Do you have room in your freezer for our fruit? We don't want it to spoil."

On the 65 mile drive to Mtn. Home the next day, we see a desert covered with sagebrush and tumbleweeds. We stay in a motel while I look for a house. I meet the County Extension Agent, Herb Edwards, and the office secretary, Ada McCune. Ada's daughter, Brenda, introduces Karen at school, which helps her get acquainted.

I put my journalism training to use by writing a column for the local paper and doing radio programs for homemakers on the Mtn. Home and Boise radio stations each week. I teach classes in sewing, decorating and cooking in Mtn. Home, Glenns Ferry, at the air base and to a group at Blacks Creek near Boise. One air base wife reports that her husband is so happy she is doing something constructive instead of gossiping at coffee klatches.

I meet Rhea Fenton, who introduces me at the Congregational Church, the American Legion Auxiliary and the Square Dance Club. This helps me fit into life in Mtn. Home.

I help the Worthwhile Club in Glenn's Ferry set up their monthly programs. When Dorothy McFadden hears that I can't find time to save my articles, she volunteers to put them in a scrapbook for me. I have a special place in my heart for Margaret Sims, as well as the other members of the club.

Karen graduates from high school in Mtn. Home and registers at Oregon State University. My biggest adjustment comes when Karen leaves in the fall of 1968. I have no one to talk to about my work or other problems. Eric goes north to Alaska and spends the summers fishing and making money for college.

When I try to talk to Barbara, who is only 12, she says she's sorry but not interested. I so long for Skip. I'm afraid that others will know of my problems and won't keep a confidence. I talk to no one.

Dad Jordan and his new wife, Randi, visit us from their Norwegian home. The children enjoy getting re-acquainted with their grandfather. His longshoremen group is having a reunion in Tacoma.

I promote the 4-H programs. We start a new program at the air base and expand the Mtn. Home and Glenn's Ferry clubs. I'm happy when 250 children sign up for 4-H.

Tiny, our little crossbreed dog that traveled with us for 11 years, dies a few months after Barbara starts training her in the 4-H dog club. Barbara is saddened by the loss and dreams of owning a German Shepherd or a Collie. When we spot an advertisement for a mini-collie or Shetland Sheepdog, we take a look. We buy a lovable little sable female for $55 and name her Gina. She is registered and a smart little pup. Barbara does well with her in obedience competitions. Lynda begs for a dog of her own and I hope it will help her self esteem. We end up with a male named Dandy that Lynda works hard to train. I recruit Mrs. Ken Wicks, an air force wife, to lead the 4-H Dog Club. She knows how to teach the children to train their pets.

Social life as a widow is not what I expected. I know Skip would want me to be, in his words, "damned choosy." I look for someone like him who is caring, intuitive, and someone who loves to just talk, but most of all loves me and my children. The last thing I expect to find is a jungle of married men all looking to have affairs. I still believe in marriage and would never have an affair. Not too many of the single older men want to deal with a family.

A friend introduces me to Glenn Ackerman and we start a long relationship. I feel I need to know a person at least a year before considering marriage. Glenn arrives and cooks breakfast for me while I jog. Then he heads for the Air Base where he is a working foreman in construction. Glenn becomes my partner at the square dance group. After a year, I think Glenn might ask me to marry him, but he doesn't.

Karen will graduate in June of 1972 from Oregon State University. I tell the children that this is the last time we will take a vacation with just the five of us and no in-laws or children. We choose the coast of Oregon. We pick up Karen at the University of Oregon Medical School where she is studying to be a medical technologist. We plan for Eric to meet us at Seaside in the

Marilyn works as a Home Economist for the Cooperative Extension Service in Mtn. Home, Idaho.

middle of the afternoon. When Eric has not arrived by 5:00, I worry. I finally call the Oregon Highway Patrol to find if he had an accident. I am not impressed when he arrives at 6 p.m. and tells us, "I saw the State stocking a lake with trout. I just had to stop and see if I could catch any."

Still, we have a great time. We dig clams, and just lie on the beach. Then we travel to Lincoln City and onto Corvallis for Karen's college graduation. Again, I wish Skip were here to see her.

In the fall, Elmore County has four national 4-H winners with Barbara among them. She won for her work in the dog program. All the winners receive trips to National 4-H Club Congress in Chicago. Four winners is a record number for a small county.

Lynda is only 12 when she enters her dog in the American Kennel Club (AKC) Boise show. We hope that she will get a qualifying score in the obedience class. She is competing against handlers of all ages. After everyone completes their exercises, the group of handlers return to the ring with their dogs and wait for the awards. The judge starts with fourth and works his way up. When the judge calls out, "Highest Dog in Trial—No. 116," no one steps forward. Then Lynda looks at her number: 116. Her legs are so wobbly that I'm afraid she won't make it to the front to receive her trophy and ribbon.

Lynda competes with professional handlers at Caldwell, and the next year at the Salt Lake City Salt Palace and again at Boise. She wins again and again and then can no longer enter at that level. Dandy changes the way Lynda views herself. She and her dog are a winning combination.

In March, 1973, we travel to Eugene for Eric's graduation from the University of Oregon. As he changed his major to health education, he graduates after Karen. To keep out of the draft for the Vietnam War, he must complete 45 quarter hours a year. I consider that a good incentive.

Eric and Sarah Prince walk down the aisle together for the graduation

Lynda at 12 wins Highest Scoring Dog in Trial with her dog, Dandy, at the Salt Lake Salt Palace.

ceremonies. They then come to Mtn. Home for a visit. He takes his physical for the draft, but doesn't pass because of his hearing. He feels it's from the many years around the "screaming Jimmy" engine on *Nohusit*. He is happy not to be heading into war. Eric's best friend had been killed getting off the helicopter his first week in Vietnam. Soon both Eric and Sarah obtain positions teaching in Juneau and then get married in 1973. Skip would be very pleased that his oldest son chose to return to Southeast Alaska.

My relationship with Glenn Ackerman has lasted four years but I'm upset when he asks the girls what they think of his becoming their step-father. I dreamed of his asking me to marry him, and he spoils it by asking the girls first. He helps me out in many ways by fixing up the house such as paneling the basement and laying flooring. I am thankful for this. Whenever Glenn and I have a disagreement, he slams the door and goes to his house. I worry that he keeps everything bottled up inside and will suddenly blow up. Our communication is poor and I don't tell him how hurt I am.

I enjoy socializing with my single friends, Jean Annest and Dorothy Grieve, who are extension agents in nearby counties. We all plan a Fourth of July weekend in the mountains with our children and Dorothy's friend, Harle Hammond. Glenn gets disgusted with too many people in the small weekend rental. He leaves and we soon go our separate ways.

At the Fireman's Ball, my friends Rhea and Tom Fenton introduce me to Bill Bradbury. He takes me in his arms and we dance. As he strongly leads, I easily follow him. I still love dancing and think of Skip's excellent dancing when we first met in Iowa. The twinkle in Brad's eyes soon makes me forget everything else. Before I know it, we are dancing cheek to cheek. He isn't much taller than my 5'7 nor is he an especially handsome man. His skin is dark, and I later learn that his grandmother was Cherokee. We stand in the middle of the floor and talk between dance numbers. Before I leave with my friends, Brad says he'll call me after church the next day.

When Brad picks me up in his red Volkswagen the next day, he says, "How about my showing you some of the back roads around here? I'll bet you've never seen the falls?"

The Bruneau Canyon Falls on the Snake River are speculator. I think this man has charisma. I find that he was recently divorced and lives on proceeds from some investments. Many evenings we dance while other times we play bridge with Rhea and Tom. Brad's eyes twinkle when we play cards. The highlight of my work day becomes his call although I worry that it sounds like he is calling from a bar. He always has a joke for me.

One night, Brad says, "When I'm single, I spend more time in a bar. With a home and family, I'm busy around the place, and we plan activities together."

I decide I've had enough the night of his lodge's Sweetheart Ball, which he invites me to attend. When he hasn't arrived by 10 p.m., I find him asleep on the bed in his apartment. I can't believe how drunk he is. He insists that we go to the dance and then he embarrasses me by showing off on the dance floor. He keeps on drinking.

The next day I tell him, "I think we better each go our own ways. You drink too much for me.

"Whatever you want, Babe."

Lynda, Barbara and I decide to take a vacation to Norway and visit Dad Jordan. Lynda points out, "Grandpa Jordan is the only grandparent we have." Grandpa and Randi say they'd enjoy seeing us. We take advantage of special airfares in July and fly to Oslo. Grandpa and Randi live in an A-Frame house with many gardens at Slependen. We can walk to the train station for the commute into the city to see the parks and museums. We spend a few days with Aunt Molle and visit with cousins at their summer home at Drobak. We take a week-long tour where we travel by train to Trondheim, by steamer to Bergen, and then by train again, through the mountains, back to Oslo. Visiting Norway is a great adventure for us. The down side is all the news from the U.S. seems to be about President Nixon getting impeached.

Back home, in August, Brad comes by and says he is now working as a machinist, his trade. He bought a house and joined Alcoholics Anonymous (AA). I am cautious but pleased.

I take a sabbatical at the University of Idaho to go back to school for a semester. I find renters for the house and an apartment in Moscow for me and the two girls. Brad cooks a farewell dinner for my daughters and me. I don't find the other men I meet are as much fun as Brad. I read *Games Alcoholics Play* and other similar books for I want to learn about alcoholics.

At the end of my sabbatical, I am offered a temporary position at the state extension office in Moscow. I sell the Mtn. Home house and find a nice rental home ten miles away in Pullman. The summer of 1974, we move to Lewiston and I begin a position as home economist on the Nez Perce Indian Reservation.

At Lewiston, I write Brad. He immediately answers with one of his humorous letters. After another four letters, he writes, "How about mucking me out of Nevada. Let's get married. I'll find a job where you are."

Suddenly, I have to decide. Yes, I tell myself, I love him. But can we make a go of marriage?

"All right," I say. "I'll come and get you, but I'll take a rain-check on the marriage until we both see how it works."

"Whatever you want, Babe."

I tell him, "The drinking is your problem. We aren't going to fight about it."

When we arrive home, he looks for work and applies for unemployment. Six weeks later, Brad finds a job and we get married. Francis Fleener, an Iowa State college friend, stands up with me for the home wedding. How different our lives have been. She is raising her family on a farm near Pullman.

Then Brad's job evaporates. A month later he announces he is moving out because he can't put up with my children. I am shocked. He goes on a drinking binge and is gone ten

Lynda and Marilyn visit Barbara in Idaho.

days. I fly to Boise to pick him up and drive him home.

Then Brad stops drinking completely—at least around me. He looks for work and signs up for unemployment again. He plants a big garden and each day when I return from work, he proudly shows me the shoots coming up or the ripe tomatoes. He has a green thumb. Often he is mowing the yard or trimming the bushes when I drive up. He takes pride in his meals and he introduces me to artichokes, egg plant, and avocados. I enjoy these surprises. He buys most of the groceries with his unemployment checks. I wonder if he is doing penance.

After graduating from college, Karen works for hospitals in Caldwell and Mtn. Home. In October of 1974, she quits her job and stops in Lewiston for a few days before she heads for Juneau in her little pickup. Eric and Sarah help her get settled and she starts a position as a medical technologist at the State Health Laboratory. Eric has started hand trolling in the summers and he and Sarah move to Sitka. Now two of Skip's children are back in Alaska.

Brad and I spend the evenings playing games. Our favorite is Scrabble because we are so evenly matched. When we play cards with friends, Brad announces that he is only drinking coffee. Camping on weekends and holidays offers a change of pace. After I attend a workshop in a nearby town, he arrives to take me home. He looks jaunty in a new straw hat. It matches him exactly. Being a history buff, he insists that we stop at every roadside historical marker. I am very happy. Seven months later Brad finds an excellent machinist job that uses all of his skills. Even though he works nights, I feel happy about our life.

Barbara is the best stu-

Marilyn marries Bill Bradbury in a small home wedding in 1974.

dent of my four children. In the middle of her senior year at Lewiston High School in 1975, I suggest that she see if she has enough credits to graduate. The crowded high school is encouraging good students to finish early. She attends Lewis-Clark State College the spring semester. Then she walks up for her high school graduation with Jack Leachman, whom she starts dating steadily.

One night Brad brings home a bottle of wine and says, "Let's have some of this instead of coffee." I don't know what to say.

"Don't look like the world came to an end. A little wine won't hurt us, Babe."

I am spinning down an endless pit. His moods go from one extreme to the other. I consider carefully each comment I make. One time he'll agree with me, and the next he'll fly into a rage. He finds more and more fault. Barbara has left for college at the University of Idaho. I am on edge. As Brad won't stop until the bottle is empty, I drink half so we'll finish it sooner. Soon my work suffers.

When his friends, Bob and Laura Cockran, come over for cards the next time, he slips out for a bottle of wine. On Saturdays when I am at the beauty parlor, he'll take three hours to buy groceries. I wonder if he is stopping at the bar. Whenever I suggest we go out on weekends, he says, "All you want to do is go, go, go."

Like a parent refusing a child something she really wants, Brad vetoes my idea of going away for our first anniversary. A month later, I come home on a Friday night to find no Brad and no dinner. By 9:00, I am so worried I drive from bar to bar searching for his truck. Finally I find him sitting in a bar with another woman whom he tells me he took to lunch earlier in the day. When he runs down my daughter in a loud voice, I walk out.

I think of packing all his things and setting them on the doorstep. Another part of me feels I might yet save our marriage. I cry and cry that night. Brad comes home the next afternoon but he's decided he's moving out. I make a big mistake by not insisting that he leave immediately. I don't want to be petty. For ten days, he only sleeps here and picks a fight whenever our paths cross.

After church on Sunday, I ask our new minister to stop by the house. When he arrives that afternoon, Brad walks in very drunk. The minister knows it is useless to talk to a drunk and he departs. He leaves two cards: one for AA and one for Al-Anon.

Brad unleashes his fury on me immediately. I shiver at his insults until I'm shaking uncontrollably. I cover my face with my hands and lay my forehead on the table, and sob. Lynda hears my sobs and comes into the kitchen and says, "Stop it, Brad. You're hurting my mother, and I love her." She runs to me and puts her arms around my shoulders.

He walks out and slams the door. Crying, I stand up and put my arms around Lynda. We must stick together. The next day Brad is gone for good.

Barbara spends the summer with us in Lewiston. She is still dating Jack. She gets a job waiting tables at a nice restaurant and also takes summer school courses. With her high grades, she receives several scholarships. She hopes to graduate from the University of Idaho in 1978. One of the reasons she is in a hurry is because her Social Security survivor's benefits will run out when she reaches 22.

I keep busy in my position as home economist on the Nez Perce Reservation. I get a divorce from Brad. I find inspiration in Katherine Mansfield's book, *Each Day a New Beginning.*

> *When we begin to take our failures non-seriously, it means we are ceasing to be afraid of them. It is of immense importance to learn to laugh at ourselves. When we no longer fear failure, we are free to attempt greater feats. We dare to learn more, and life is fuller for it— not just our own lives, but the lives that we touch. Laughter over our mistakes eases the risk of trying again. Laughter keeps us young, and the light hearted find more pleasure in each day.*[9]

I am concerned when I hear at a workshop that there is a movement to replace the white workers on reservations with Indians or do away with our programs. Then in September, Bob Black, my supervisor from the University of Idaho, tells me, "I've got bad news for you, Marilyn. The Bureau of Indian Affairs superintendent has informed the university that they are not going to fund your program for another year."

"Will I lose my job?"

"You are an associate professor and have tenure. We have two openings. One is about 65 miles from here in Nez Perce and the other is in the southeast corner of the state."

I want to look them over and see what housing is available. As Lynda has just started high school, I'd rather not move her again. We have moved four times in the past four years. My world is crumbling. I never seriously considered that my position is in jeopardy.

I visit both towns and am shown the available housing. The southeast town is ninety percent Mormon. I recall our minister in Mtn. Home saying, "When the Mormons make up over 50% of the population, they play a different game. All social life revolves around the church. If you don't belong then you and your children have no social life."

In this town I inquire about housing. The real estate agent shows me a waiting list of 21 names. "There's nothing here," he says.

As I am near the Utah border, I decide to see if the Utah Extension Service has any openings for a foods and nutrition major. They have none. I look at the other county. It, too, has little housing. I'm worried. I am going backwards not forward. I know the university has a rule that they won't move you for two years. I can't see Lynda and me spending two years in either town.

I consider all of my options. I inquire about other positions at the University of Idaho, such as their audio-visual department. I find one position at $4,000 less than my present salary. I ask about openings at any of the local companies. Again nothing.

I must make a decision, for my position will terminate on September 30. My supervisor wants to know if I'll take either job because they need to advertise these vacancies. While driving the 16 miles to work Monday morning, suddenly I decide to talk to Superintendent Vincent Little with the Bureau of Indian Affairs (BIA). Maybe they have another position I can fill. I make an appointment to see him at 8:30 a.m. I'm optimistic for I've always had a cordial relationship with him.

"Mr. Little," I say, "I would certainly like to keep working on the reservation. Might you have another position for me? What the university is offering me is totally unsatisfactory."

"I asked about you when this came up. They said not to worry because they had another position for you. I've watched you work with our young people in the summer day camp. You've done a good job here. This is a budget problem with us. Let me see what I can do."

This is the turning point. BIA had always paid a large portion of my salary to the university. Between the BIA and the university, they decide to fund my position for another year. I say thank you to BIA and the Nez Perce tribal leaders, who elected to keep me. With no money for my secretary, Sharon Kemp, I sadly let her go. At least, I'm still here for another year, but no one knows how much longer.

I had taken the federal civil service exam when I received my master's degree. I keep my name on its registry as a writer-editor. In November, I receive a long letter from the Civil Service Commission. They ask if I wish to be considered for a position. Down in the bottom right-hand corner is typed: Location of position: US Forest Service, Petersburg, Alaska.

I can't believe it. To return to Petersburg will be the answer to my dreams. Happily, I fill out the application and anxiously wait.

My first grandchild is born to Eric and Sarah in Sitka. They name their son Kris, after Skip's father.

After Christmas, I call the Juneau office of the Forest Service, "I'm Marilyn Jordan. I applied for your opening for a Writer-Editor at Petersburg. I'm wondering about the status of the position."

"We have offered it to a veteran, but if he doesn't take it, your name is next. Are you still interested?"

"I certainly am."

Three weeks later I am offered the position in Petersburg and I accept it.

I am walking on air for my dreams are coming true. For the first time in all my moves, I have the luxury of professional movers packing my possessions. We don't know when our furniture will arrive in Alaska, but we will live temporarily in a Forest Service trailer. The Forest Service makes ferry reservations for Lynda and me to leave Seattle on March 22.

I put my house on the market and have a yard sale. As Barbara is attending the University of Idaho, she won't be going with us. Lynda takes her Sheltie, Dandy, and I take my Mother's gloxinia that I have grown since she died in 1970.

I write a farewell letter to the people I have worked with on the reservation:

Dear Nez Perce Friends:

I have enjoyed the two and a half years that I've spent with you and feel sad that I'll be leaving you.

These are some of the things I'll remember: how proud I was of the Te-Toh-Ken 4-H Club riding in the parades and Grand Entry. The Indian costumes and red vests that many parents, my secretary, Sharon Kemp, and I worked on added a great deal to their appearance in the parades. How well behaved the children always were.

Jonathan Yearout family took a Japanese Exchange girl into their home for three weeks, and how she won all of our hearts and fit into life on the Reservation so well. Indian fry bread was one of the most popular items at the Nez Perce County 4-H Carnival. 500 4-H youth from all over Idaho learned more of the Indian culture when our Indian youth and adults danced at the Gem State 4-H Club Congress.

It took lots of nerve for our children to take part in the 4-H County horse show and fair, but our Te-Toh-Ken Club was always there.

I felt good when our Nez Perce women had a booth and sang Nez Perce songs at the District Homemakers Meeting. You were a receptive audience at my workshops and programs at both Lapwai and Kamiah. The Head Start children watched Rip Rocket fly through the air to teach them about nutrition.

I enjoyed taking part in your many activities. You always made me feel welcome. I dug roots with Elsie and Helen, gave thanks at the Root Feast, learned more about your people at the Recognition Dinners and General Council Meetings, caught a glimpse of your culture at the War Dances and Talmaks, and learned about the Coeur d' Alenes when we had exchanges. I loved being part of the BIA basketball team when we played the Tribe.

You are a fun-loving people and, as Rick Ellenwood says, a compassionate people. Many of you went the second mile with me. I will be forever grateful and humble.

You have a great deal to be proud of—yourselves and your accomplishments. I'm sure you will find new horizons and new opportunities for your people.

The best of everything to all of you.
Marilyn E. Jordan

I stand on the deck of the ferry coming into Alaskan waters. Having bid farewell to my life in Idaho, I recall my trip with Skip 31 years ago. I hope that Alaska will be as good to me now as she was the first time. What a great feeling!!

The Nez Perce 4-H club in a Lewiston parade.

CHAPTER TWENTY-SEVEN
Return To Alaska

LYNDA, DANDY AND I ARRIVE IN PETERSBURG on March 25, 1977. The snow line is almost down to the shore on the mountain across the Narrows. The town no longer has the boardwalks, but the store fronts have rosemaling to show the Norwegian heritage. The post office and bank are new. An airport has been built up on the muskeg to handle the jets and the harbor has a new float. Still, most of the town is familiar. I remember when Louie Lahmeyer finished building the new Hammer and Wikan store before we left over ten years ago.

While the movers are putting my furniture in storage, a woman comes out of another doorway in the building and invites me to come in for a cup of coffee. She introduces herself as Harriet Thompson.

Carefully reading the many posters hanging on its walls, I discover I'm in the Alcoholism Center. I remark, "Two years ago I married an alcoholic. When I refused to play his games, he moved out."

"Do you realize that 75% of those who marry one alcoholic marry a second one?" Harriet asks.

"Oh, no! I'd never want that much unhappiness again."

"Why don't you come to our Al-Anon group?"

"Will I be eligible? Doesn't the spouse have to go to AA?"

"It doesn't matter whether you're still married or he is seeking help," Harriet says as she pours me another cup of coffee. "Al-Anon is for the 50 million Americans whose lives are touched by alcoholism of a family member or a friend. I've seen families of alcoholics needing help as much or even more than the alcoholic."

Another six weeks passes before I hesitantly creep into an Al-Anon meeting. In dismay I see that I can't sit in a dark corner because everyone sits around one big table. My resolve to say nothing vanishes in the friendly atmosphere. Toward the end of the meeting, I mention my worry of finding a house to buy.

One girl turns around and looks at me, "I know a house that is just being listed tonight."

I walk out of that meeting and call the number she gives me. Thanks to Al-Anon I'm the first one there, and I buy it. "See," I tell myself, "Already Al-Anon helps you solve your problems."

Listening to the Welcome more closely at the next meeting, I feel it talks directly to me when it says:

> We, too, were lonely and frustrated, but in Al-Anon, we dicover that no situation is really hopeless, and that it is possible for us to find contentment, and even happiness, whether the alcoholic is still drinking or not. So much depends on our own attitudes, and as we learn to place our problem in its true perspective, we find it loses its power to dominate our thoughts and ourlives.[10]

Marilyn finds Petersburg has many new buildings when she returns in 1977.

I'm lonesome. I immediately feel the warmness and caring of the group. As I listen to the discussion, I only wish that I had gone when I first met Brad.

One girl says, "I found that I was doing and saying the wrong things. I thought I could make the alcoholic stop drinking. One minute I was his persecutor, and the next his rescuer. I had to accept that alcoholism is a disease. You don't punish a diabetic. I never realized that the alcoholic already felt guilty."

Surprisingly, I was right to maintain an emotional detachment from Brad's drinking. I did provide a crutch by allowing him to stay at my house. Another points out, "If you refuse to play the alcoholic's game, he has only two choices: to change himself or the find someone else who will play his games." Brad didn't want to change himself. I don't know whether his new wife allowed him to play his games.

I find that we go to Al-Anon for ourselves. If the alcoholic stops drinking, that is merely a bonus. I did Brad a disservice by not seeking help and by letting him intimidate me into doing nothing. Brad couldn't see that Al-Anon would help me change my attitude toward his drinking and "get off his back." Two and a half years after our divorce, Brad died of a heart attack. I wonder if his heavy drinking made him more susceptible to it. I will never know if he kept everyone around him from seeking help.

A new acquaintance from another town shows up unannounced. Al-Anon gives me courage to tell him that my home is no place to sleep off a drunk. I take him downtown and tell him not to come back. At midnight he rings my doorbell. I tell him I'll call the police if he doesn't leave. I also learn never to make threats that I don't intend to carry out. I call the police, and they take him downtown.

This is a happy ending, which my Al-Anon group tells me that I helped make because I refused to be his crutch. My friend decides to straighten out his life himself and immediately goes into an Alcoholic halfway house. Later, he attends school to become an alcoholic counselor.

I find one of the Al-Anon slogans is: "Let go and let God." When I did this, God lifted a great weight from my shoulders. Hazelton's Food for Thought said: "By getting in touch with our Higher Power, we cultivate a never-failing source of inner strength and direction."[11]

Reverend Dave Fulton asks the congregation to come to a short evening service. As I have nothing to do that October evening, I walk to church.

On the way home, I stop at the home of Lett and Ann Taylor, who were friends with Skip and me. While I'm there, her neighbor calls and asks if she'd like a salmon. She invites him over and then introduces me to Bill George, a widower. He's a Dutchman and shorter than my 5' 7".

We both feel that God planned for us to meet. I'm looking for a man who doesn't have a drinking problem, and he's looking for a woman who doesn't smoke. He's made a list of all the eligible women in town. After carefully considering each, he is ready to go South and look.

I tell him I can't figure out how to get my box springs upstairs in the house I just bought. He drives me home, and I show him the springs leaning against the wall. He ponders the problem and invites me to go trolling the next weekend on his boat the *Judith*. The box springs remain leaning against the wall.

I like getting on a boat again. Like old times, we wait expectantly for a bite. Suddenly, the starboard bow pole jerks. What excitement! I run out on deck and jump up and down. I think that minute Bill decides that I'm the girl for him. He had retired that spring as custodian at the school and now plans to troll full time.

Like Skip, he sets about to win me. He feels he should dangle some bait before me. His bait is getting a new troller built. He goes South at Thanksgiving to make arrangements with Chinook Marine in Port Townsend to finish a fiberglass hull that he bought. I find he is a good businessman and can offer me security.

Excitedly, he tells me, "The new boat will be done by April first, in time for fishing season." I recall Skip telling me many years ago that we must get to Alaska by April first.

When I was away from Alaska, I was like a fish out of water. I longed to return. Now I'm back and Bill George is tempting me to go back to the job I loved best, commercial salmon trolling. I agree and give up my Forest Service writing position.

Two weeks before our wedding, I warn Bill that company is coming. Six months after I first asked, I'm still waiting for him to get the box springs upstairs. Finally, he hangs a pulley on the overhang of the roof, and pulls it through an upstairs window.

My three daughters will be my bridesmaids. Eric's wife, Sarah, will play the flute. Bill chooses Jack Eddy for his best man and Eric and Gary Mahoney as ushers.

All my family will be in the wedding party. Barbara is still in college in Idaho and the only one of my children who has not moved back to Alaska. We talk Bill's 89 year-old mother into coming north with Barbara. It is the first and only time in her long life that Mother George flies. Karen's fiancé, Frank Glass, takes our wedding pictures. Two of the best pictures are 6'3" Eric walking 4'10" Mother George down the aisle, and Bill and me walking down the aisle after the service.

We are very happy. Bill and I fly on our honeymoon to Guam to visit his son and family. We enjoy island hopping across the Pacific with stops at Kwajalin, Marjoral and Truk. On our return trip, we visit three of the Hawaiian Islands.

We arrive in Port Townsend to find that the boat is far from done. We return to Petersburg for we don't want people to think that we've deserted 17-year-old Lynda. We pack a tent, cooking utensils and everything we'll need on the boat for our trip north.

For the second time in my life, I'm a bride aboard. I can hardly believe my good fortune. Skip was an excellent teacher and helped me love the fishing life. I admit fishing gets into my blood. An old fisherman said, "Once you fish, you aren't worth a damn for anything else."

Here I am again going fishing. Bill names our new boat *I Gotta*, because I'm always saying I gotta do this or that. As happened when Skip and I rebuilt *Nohusit*, *I Gotta* takes longer to complete than planned. We take a break from outfitting the boat and attend family graduations at the University of Idaho. Barbara graduates cum laude in Agricultural Economics and will start work in southern Idaho for the US Department of Agriculture. My brother-in-law, Gary Strine, receives his Ph.D. in Physics. Eric even takes a break from fishing to come from Alaska and be a part of this important occasion. I think again of what Skip is missing and how pleased he would be with his children's accomplishments.

On June 10, 1978, *I Gotta* is launched. We take her out the next day for a shakedown cruise. On a boat's first trip, you can't imagine how many items will light on the floor. Even though I've spent 20 seasons on a boat, I can't predict what will fall when the waves hit. With little ballast aboard, *I Gotta* bobs around like a cork in the wind. The stove falls over because the bolts don't hold. I laugh. That's what happened on *Salty's* first trip.

I find that life on a salmon troller has changed little through the years. A sense of humor is still the most necessary trait.

Eric escorts Mother George down the aisle of the Petersburg Lutheran Church during the wedding of Bill George and Marilyn.

Marilyn marries Bill George in March of 1978.

We see that it's still raining when we arrive in Ketchikan. I well remember that it rained 189 inches when Skip and I moved there in 1952. That year I pulled Eric, age two, and Karen, age one, around in a wagon. I draped a heavy plastic over them to make a tent.

Downtown Ketchikan has changed much since I lived there. They filled areas, widened streets, and replaced many old buildings burned by Ketchikan's firebug of the fifties. The Ketchikan Cold Storage is gone, and tugs bring in the freight in vans. No longer can longshoremen strikes bring Alaska's economy to a standstill as happened in the 1940s and 50s.

The house built at the turn of the century that we rented is torn down for the tunnel. How I remember the first night we lived in it. I dreamed that I was in Chicago and the El was going by. All the plank streets have been replaced.

Fishermen are always hurrying to get their gear in the water and Bill is no exception. Before we leave Ketchikan, the electric throttle stops. We have Alaska Airlines gold streak a new one from Seattle. Every day lost means money out of our pockets.

Along Ship Island, so named because it looks like a ship from a distance, our new fathometer shows herring or needlefish that salmon eat. I recall that Skip and I only used a pike pole and a chart to show us the depth. Two boats

Marilyn and Bill George are proud of their new fiberglass troller, I Gotta.

are fishing there, a good sign. We decide that I will fish the starboard side and Bill the port side.

We have no more than put our last lure out than the bell for my heavy lead line rings. I forgot the thrill of seeing a salmon jerk the pole. I push the gurdy into gear and start in the stainless steel line.

When I come to the leader that is stretched out behind the boat, I call to Bill, "Bring the gun, it's a big one." The salmon jumps out of the water behind us. Bill pulls the leader alongside the boat and shoots the shining fish.

That day we land 50 cohoes, 25 humpies and six kings. After eight days of good fishing, we troll toward Ketchikan with our catch. I study the Alaska Fish & Game regulation book and find no closures for this area.

At Point Caamano, one of the few places with a Spanish name, we find a number of sport fishermen with their lines in the water. Suddenly a women comes out on deck waving a white towel and calls, "This area is closed to you."

We immediately pull in our gear and head for Ketchikan. I laugh, "That's what happened to Skip and me. Here is the closure in the front of the book. Let's be the first to unload tomorrow."

I stand on the dock to check our weights. A man comes up, "Did you know you were in a closed area? Some there wanted to report you."

"We had no idea. Thanks for not reporting us. We really need the money from these fish."

We make two good fishing trips in that area.

The Fourth of July is enjoyable at Meyers Chuck with an old-fashioned Alaskan potluck with fresh crab, smoked salmon, barbecued chicken, salads of home-

Otto Kruse makes rolls in I Gotta's oven.

grown vegetables, and blueberry pie. Petersburg Fisheries, which has a salmon-buying station there, furnishes the beverages. I love the camaraderie with the old fishermen like Whiskey Bill, Blackie Lindsay, and the little children. Bob Meyers bought fish in this picturesque cove in the early years and it is named after him.

Alaska's Fourth of July resembles Christmas in other places. The fishermen have their first money since the end of the previous season. Everyone sees hopeful signs that this will be a big year.

After visiting with Lynda in Petersburg, we unload all the tools, tent and other items we took south last April. In July, Bill and I head for Chatham Straits where Skip and I fished.

A call on the Citizen Band (CB) radio says, "Where's the Tebenkof fleet?"

Someone replies, "I think the five of us are it."

I can't believe that such a change has taken place. In the 1950s, 50 to 100 trollers kept three fish buyers busy. To make their expenses, the power trollers must now fish outside waters and leave this area to the hand-trollers.

In February of 1979, Karen and Frank Glass are married at the Chapel by the Lake in Juneau. Eric takes on what would be his father's honor and gives his sister away. Both Barbara and Lynda come for the wedding. Barbara and Jack Leachman are married that fall on Karen's birthday, October seventh, in Lewiston, Idaho. Eric walks Barbara down the aisle. We're happy to welcome two new sons-in-law to our family.

In the summer of 1979, Bill and I encourage the Kruses to come to Alaska and again go trolling with us. Seven of them had gone out on *Nohusit* in 1965. Their son, Eric, was a baby and Ani wasn't born when they came the first time. We wonder if six of us can get along for five days on a 37-foot boat, which is much smaller than 45-foot *Nohusit*. We encourage them to bring their two-man tent in case they are too crowded in our two bunks in the bow section .

We run *I Gotta* into Ketchikan to meet Otto, Verna, and their two teenagers, Anilise and Eric. They arrive by ferry from Prince Rupert. Ketchikan is situated on Revillagigedo Island which was named in 1892 by the Spanish explorer Caamano for Don Horcasitas, Count of Revilla Gigedo. Originally Vancouver Island was named Vancouver-Revillagigedo, but the later name was eventually dropped. Revilla Gigedo was Viceroy of Mexico from 1788 to 1794.

The Kruse family has come across Canada from Iowa to Prince Rupert by train. We walk the short distance from the ferry terminal to Bar Harbor. Proudly, we help them aboard and find places to stow away the few bags they bring.

To give our friends a better perspective of the area, we climb the steep hill in this older part of town. We pass frame homes with well-kept yards and many flowers. On top of the hill is the modern high school and community college. From this vantage point, the many floats and boats at Bar Harbor stand out. The little ferry heads across Tongass Narrows to Gravina Island. Just then the Alaska Airlines 727 jet lands on the Gravina runway. The airline maintenance workers cut all the trees on the north end of the island for the long north-south landing strip. We watch "the big bird" turn and come back to the terminal building. Many kinds of boats are running up and down the channel. We point out the trollers, gillnetters, seiners and tug boats.

Coming down the hill, we shop in as modern stores as any in Iowa for groceries and drug items. The prices surprise our friends for they are only a nickel a can higher than at home. On the bus trip downtown, the wide streets, the number of modern buildings and the ability to build the homes straight up the mountainside impress our guests.

Ani excitedly points out the "*Love Boat* that's on TV," actually the *Island Princess*. Teenagers on the bus start a conversation with Eric. Their friendliness surprises him.

While Verna and I prepare dinner on *I Gotta*, Bill gives Ani and Eric lines to fish off the dock. Suddenly, Eric calls, "I've got something."

Bill runs over with the gaff hook. Excitedly, Eric reels in the fish. Leaning over to gaff it, Bill says, "It's a dogfish, a kind of shark." He hits the gaff on the dock in his effort to get it. "Doggone, I broke the gaff."

When the sun sets at 10:30 p.m. that July night, our friends see how long our days are. The long poles of the boats silhouette against the brilliant red and gold sunset.

Everyone is soon ready for bed. Otto and Verna sleep in the bottom bunk with Eric and Ani in the top. Their heads are in opposite directions with their feet meeting in the middle of the extra long bunks. Bill and I sleep in a double bed in the pilothouse.

The sun's high in the sky at 6 a.m. when we untie the lines and head *I Gotta* out Tongass Narrows. We dodge many logs and other debris. We run by Alaska's first pulp mill and the abandoned Guard Island light station.

They've built many homes along the Narrows. When we come to Ship Island, we slow the engine for fishing. When we're running, our two 40-foot trolling poles stand upright in the cross-tree on the mast. Bill stands by the mast amidships to let them down. They are at 45-degree angles to the water. We climb into the trolling pit to put out our gear. Our friends sit on the hatch for a better view.

Handling the starboard lines, I put over the 40-pound lead. Then I hook a rubber snubber with a lure on the end of the monofilament leader at each three fathom marker until I have 15 fathoms of line out. I no more than put the second line out when the bell rings on the heavy line.

"Is it a salmon?" everyone asks in unison.

"It sure jerks like one."

I shove the hydraulic gurdy into gear to wind in the stainless steel line. As each hook comes in, I coil it on the stern. On the bottom lure, the snubber is stretched taut. Carefully, I hook the leader onto the wire hung between the troller pit and the side of the boat. I pull the 16-foot leader in until I see a large fin out the water.

"It's a big one," I call excitedly to Bill.

I hook the snubber onto my soaker line, which gives the salmon more running line if it sounds. Suddenly, it jumps out of water with a big splash and the line runs out through my fingers. I keep just enough tension on the line so the fish can't turn and throw the hook. The purple sheen of the salmon is so beautiful. Slowly, I work it close enough for Bill to shoot it with his 22 pistol. Everyone claps when he pulls it aboard.

We wait anxiously for Bill to clean it to find its weight. Hooking the scales in its gills, Bill reads, "Seventeen pounds. It will make mild-cure, which brings the highest price. We should get around $38 for it."

In the next three hours we catch three smaller kings, a coho, and eight humpies. Bill throws the fish onto the ice in our fish hold. When we anchor that night, he'll climb into the hold and carefully put ice around them and in their bellies.

When the wind comes up, we run into Meyers Chuck. Fishing off the dock, Ani meets a woman who shows her the sea life in the tide pools. The rest of us visit old friends, Nondas and Ted Haux. We admire the gardens, buy a few items at the store, and watch a retired logger split wood.

The next morning we head for Onslow Island, an hour's run north.

"Here come the porpoises," Bill calls.

A school of Dall Porpoises, distinguished by their white bellies, is heading for the boat. We help Ani and Eric onto the bow to watch them crisscrossing in front of the boat. Seagulls squawk over some feed. Along Eagle Island, a very large bald eagle leaves its perch at the top of a tree and swoops down on a frightened seagull that drops its fish. The eagle glides down and grabs it with its long talons. Flapping its large wings, the eagle heads back to its perch.

"See," Bill says, "the eagle is a perfect politician. It takes just enough from the other birds so they won't starve but keep working for him." Bill entertains all of us with his stories and jokes.

Various kinds of ducks are diving on the feed, and a flock of snipe flies in unison overhead and suddenly changes direction. We spot a humpback whale breach and blow in Clarence Straits. Time speeds by because something different is always happening.

I steer too near a reef and hook one of our leads on bottom. In order to dislodge the lead, I give the boat full-throttle. *I Gotta* jumps ahead like a bucking horse and pours black smoke out of the exhaust. Finally the lead pulls loose before it breaks the line, but the jerk pulls out the bolt holding one side of the spring onto the pole. We continue to fish with it, but that evening Bill lets down the pole to fix it.

Coming in from the trolling pit, Bill says, "The great, gray sinker-eater almost got our lead that time."

Our friends see that trolling is more than dragging your lures through deep water. Fishing is ever changing. Where and how you catch fish yesterday may not work today. My years of experience help but are no recipe for success. Only one axiom we are sure of: you never catch fish with your gear on deck.

We point out the very poor stand of timber on the south end of Etolin Island. We anchor that night at a float on Brownson Island. Here, three abandoned houses sit on the beach, a reminder of by-gone times when a troll fleet winter fished that area. Ani finds more shells on our hike along the beach to an old Indian grave that I'd first seen in 1947. We finally find it, but now you can only see the buried outline of the logs around it. Our friends, Shirley and Chuck Piedra, who live in a float house, are not at home.

At Navy Creek by Burnett Inlet, we show the Kruses the Forest Service's fish ladder. Bill solves our problem of how to get six people ashore in a two-man skiff. He fastens a fish line from a pole on deck to the skiff. Two row ashore. Then those on deck reel the line back for two more to go ashore. The last two take the pole with them. Sadly, we find few fish up the creek. When we return to the boat the procedure is reversed with those on shore reeling the boat back.

Otto says, "I was afraid the line would break and the skiff would get away. I figured how I'd swim out to it."

Bill says, "I have a heavy line. I don't worry."

Otto and Eric go out in the skiff sport fishing. The waves on the beach frighten them and they soon return. It isn't calm like inside Tebenkof where they were on their first trip on *Nohusit*.

We visit the men building new holding tanks at the non-profit aquaculture facilities in Burnett Inlet. At the abandoned cannery that housed the Aleuts during WWII, we crawl around the old machinery and fallen-down buildings. I recall our fishing here on Skip's and my first trip in 1946.

"There's a black bear," Bill calls, pointing to one running into the brush. We had seen many kinds of animals but still hope to see a deer and a wolf.

Knowing what ravenous appetites we have on the boat, I bought lots of groceries. Still we run out of bread. Otto offers to make some. Tasting his bread and rolls, I point out, "You have the same knack for bread baking that your father had." (He'd been our town's baker.) This pleases Otto.

The next day we head for Petersburg. Little did our friends realize that they are enjoying a rare treat with the sun shining, the wind remaining light and variable, and calm water. We point out the logged areas and pass a tug as we run from marker to marker in Wrangell Narrows.

Upon leaving, each of them write what they think of their vacation aboard *I Gotta*.

Eric writes:
   Alaska
   Indescribable beauty
   Never to be forgotten
   Makes one proud to know
   Alaska's part of America.
   Unique beauty
   Uncontaminated by man
   With litter and pollution.

Vast wilderness with many
Plants, sea and land animals
Preserves this indescribable beauty.

Ani writes:

I Gotta seemed like an awfully small boat when we first
boarded her, and you know what a sardine might feel like
sleeping in cramped quarters with Eric, Mom and Dad.
The first day I got a little seasick and spent most of the
day in the bunk—the fresh air really felt wonderful when I
awoke. I got to steer the boat and was sure I would run
into one of those large islands.

My favorite things were: the beautiful background of
mountains, looking for and at the sea life in the tide pools
at Meyers Chuck, "Indian Grave Island" where as soon as I
stepped into the trees, it was like stepping into another
world with beautiful greens I had never seen—touching
the ground was like touching velvet. I'll never forget this
wonderful vacation.

Otto & Verna write:

Our whole family feels very fortunate in having friends in
Alaska with whom we could go fishing on their
commercial boat. Learning about the boat, types of fish,
methods of fishing, cleaning, preserving, selling and
processing were all very interesting. The evening trips
to Meyers Chuck with its "frontier" type of living, and old
Indian grave Marilyn had discovered, "up creek" to look
for salmon and picking blueberries for delicious pancakes
the next morning, some of the history connected with
abandoned homes, old canneries and the logging
industry all combined to make the time pass all too
quickly.

Most enjoyable of all was being together again with old
friends and new friends on a small fishing boat—six of

us—eating, sleeping, visiting, working, playing and learning together with a minimum of problems. Oh, that all of us could be put on a small boat—we soon would learn to work together to make our world the kind of place God meant it to be.

Thanks so much again, Marilyn and Bill, for making such a wonderful adventure possible for us.

The Kruses fly to Sitka on July 17 and see my new grandson, Karl, who is born that day to Eric and Sarah.

My daughter Barbara and her husband, Jack, come to Alaska on their honeymoon in 1980. They troll with us on *I Gotta* around Onslow Island. We put them on a small float plane at Meyers Chuck, and they visit Eric's family in Sitka and Karen's in Juneau. Barbara does not seem destined to return to Alaska. She was only eight when her father died and she doesn't have the connection to this life that my older children do.

Over the years we have many visitors: my brother Lynn, my brother Dick, his wife Charlotte, and son Jim. Joe and Joan Bova go out with us when we fish Chatham Straits. Joe, too, had been a grade and high school classmate of mine. Then my college roommate, Ruth, and her husband, Elmer Elliott, fly to Gedney Harbor, fish, and run through the fog with us to Petersburg. My friend from the Extension Service, Jean Annest, fishes Ernest Sound with us. Like Skip, I enjoy showing our family and friends the life of a troller. I want to share the wonders of Alaska with others.

CHAPTER TWENTY-EIGHT
Second Chance

ON THE MORNING OF THE FOURTH OF JULY 1980, Bill and I fish from *I Gotta*, along a reef at Onslow Island. I'm pulling in the gear on my starboard side. "Doggone it," I think, "I didn't put a long leader on that plug when I moved it from the top spread to the next to the bottom."

"Throw me a long leader," I call to Bill.

Reluctantly, he climbs from his seat, turns out from the reef, and pulls a leader out of the drawer. With a look that says, "That woman is never satisfied," he throws the leader at me with great disdain. I hook the plug on the leader and put the line out with the remaining leaders down. I climb out of the troller pit and walk into the pilot house.

"Isn't that line jiggling that I just put out?"

"I don't see anything," he growls. Making a success of this trolling life isn't easy. We're together 24 hours a day, and many marriages can't take this much "togetherness."

I gaze at the line a minute and say, "I'm going to pull it."

When I put the hydraulic gurdy into gear, I notice it drags

Marilyn can barely raise a king salmon she has caught.

back farther than usual. It may be a big halibut and I groan because they've closed its season. We'll have to shake it. Finally, I come to the leader I'd just put out. Our homemade snubber stretches out to the size of a pencil. Carefully, I pull back on the leader stretched around the stern of the boat. My heart pounds. Whatever it is, it is big.

I carefully hook the snubber into my soaker line and slowly pull in the leader. The fish's big fin breaks water about 30 feet behind the boat. A salmon!

Then the salmon jumps out of water, and the leader zings through my fingers. I'm careful to keep enough tension on the leader so the salmon can't turn and break loose. Bill climbs into the troller pit beside me as I pull in the leader again. This time he grabs the leader when I work the fish alongside. He aims and shoots the fish. Now he easily digs the gaff into its head and pulls it aboard. What a beautiful fish!

"This is our biggest fish of the year," I exclaim. I kiss my husband. We're both happy. The perfect way to celebrate the Fourth. It dresses out at 46 pounds. The thrill of landing a king salmon is as great today as it was when I landed my first one in 1946.

We work to make a success of this life. To us this is the perfect way to spend our retirement. First we make fishing a game. We kid each other, make jokes and like my mother said, "Do not take thyself too damn seriously." We work at keeping friction to a minimum. Bill gives me the lines on one side. This leads to our competing against each other. Why will my lines catch most of the fish one day, and Bill's the next? The one who isn't catching anything will play

Marilyn paints coho spoons.

"musical chairs" with his gear. This competition causes us to fish better and working my gear keeps me from becoming bored. Each season I do more of the fishing. Bill fillets the herring, and this year I cut it up and put it on my hootchies. Next year, I may learn to tie my leaders. I never clean or ice the fish although I know some women do.

I tell my daughter, Lynda, who lives at home during the summer while she attends college, "We don't know where we're going yet. We'll probably untie the boat and go whichever way the tide is running."

I still feel as much exhilaration when we pull back the throttle and head for the fishing grounds as I did in 1946. Can it be 34 years ago when I first started fishing Southeast Alaska with Skip? It's you against the elements in your efforts to find the salmon. It would be great if you could run to a place, throw over your gear, and have the fish start jumping aboard.

Even though Bill is a pessimist, I suspect he is just trying to bait me when he declares, "I know this is going to be a disaster." He knows I'm sure we're going to find many fish this time. I work harder to prove my optimism is right. Without high hopes, why are we going out?

On one trip we throw in our gear the first morning, and after three hours, we have not one bite. Then I list all the places in each direction where we could look for fish. We hear on the radio that someone tried each of these places and left. Another hour passes and still nothing. What are we going to do?

I finally say, "There's an old adage, 'When you don't know where to go, stay where you are.' Oh, hell, let's stay here."

By nightfall, we have eight big kings, and in four days, we have a good trip. The first quality you need in this business is patience. I'm always sure the kings are there. We aren't catching them because we don't have the right lure. It's the wrong stage of the tide, or they're only biting at dawn or dusk. Perseverance is the second quality needed.

Bill says, "I'm going to take a nap. If you want to fish, you can fish your side only." With only two lines out, I troll back and forth. Nothing!

He arises and says, "Are you satisfied there's nothing here?"

"All right, you win. I'll pull in my gear."

When I bring it in, I find a 20 pound king on the bottom spread of the heavy line. I will never know whether it got on as I pulled in my gear, or I dragged it for awhile. All of my gear is now on deck.

The fish sparks Bill's enthusiasm. He is as excited as I am when we catch

Marilyn is proud of the many king salmon she catches.

fish. We run to another hole and put in all of our gear. By nightfall we land ten big kings. Bill says, "The number of fish in *I Gotta's* hold is what matters, not who catches them."

My weakness is birds. If I see the big divers, I'm sure the fish are there or soon will be. One time a troller is running through an area in our direction when a school of herring suddenly surfaces. Gulls swoop down on them, and three whales swim through the herring with their mouths open. The troller stops dead in the water.

We imagine his saying, "My God, look!" A couple of minutes later two people run out to the troller pit and throw in their gear. They make one pass through the area and continue on their way. Happily, we are alone again. That troller needs my perseverance and belief in birds.

I feel we're playing the old shell game of figuring out under which group of birds are the salmon. The salmon are never under all of them. I must admit that no birds were around when we had our best fishing this year.

Bill says, "You can't sell birds."

"What else shows where the fish are?"

The best sign is to find a group of boats going back and forth with everyone working their gear. In 1980, my son Eric has a 20-foot hand troller, which he named *Hootchie*. We spot him as part of such a group this summer. We both leave the buying station in the evening and head for an anchorage.

"Look at all those birds working on the herring, Bill."

"I don't care how many birds there are. I'm tired and we're heading for harbor. We're supposed to be retired, you know."

Eric calls us on the CB. "This looks good, Mom, I'm going to cruise through it." In a few minutes, he says, "I'm throwing in my gear."

It is dark when he comes along side. "The finning cohoes caused me to throw in my gear. Look, I got ten in that hour!"

The next morning he heads out in the dark. He has a favorite shallow spot along the shore. We fish along a reef by ourselves.

"Look, Bill, more and more boats are going over where Eric is. We only have a dozen cohoes. Maybe the fish are over there."

We call Eric on the CB but he doesn't answer. We troll over to where Eric is winding in his lines as fast as he can with his hand gurdy. Salmon are flopping every place. Someone is in the trolling pit in each of the dozen hand trollers and half-dozen power trollers.

"I must have at least 40 cohoes and half dozen kings," he calls when he comes out into deep water to let another boat take its turn. We power trollers can't get into that shallow water. Hundreds of divers are working and great flocks of seagulls are diving into the water. How exciting! Eric doubles us on cohoes and has three times more kings. He is still talking about the day he beat us.

Each day afloat is different. I always find something new to see or photograph. I enjoy these times and I want to share that joy with others. I think of Don Blanding, the Poet Laureate of the Hawaiian Island in the 1950s, who wrote about his search for God:

> *My friend , with casual grace and cool aplomb,*
> *Tossed me a verbal super-atom bomb...*
> *Joy is an inside job, he said. The phrase*
> *circled within my mind. To my amaze*
> *I realized that it said something older,*
> *Beauty is in the Eyes of the Beholder.*[12]

Our search for fish frustrates us, but with our retirement income we don't need to catch fish to make a living. Skip and I needed it, sometimes desperately. I recall a page from a Workman Page-A-Day calendar which said:"I give myself permission to enjoy my journey through life. I envision the world as a great place to live in. This vision comes true every day."[13]

I feel the more we need to find the fish, the more elusive they are. Often we're right ahead or right behind them. Our remedy: relax. We're trying too hard. Luck always plays a part, but experience helps us know where to look. In time we see patterns in the way the fish act. It adds to the fun to test out our theories about the habits of fish. We hope our record keeping will help with this.

No two years are alike. Where we found fish in '78 and '79, we find none in 1980. What lures fished well those years, don't fish this year. Why? All I can say is that it keeps the stores selling more lures.

We fishermen like being our own bosses. The Parable of the Ten Virgins awaiting the bridegroom is applicable to fishing. Five were prepared and five unprepared. A friend comes to where we are catching fish, but he must mark a line and make up gear before he starts fishing. When he is ready the next day, the fish are gone. Many times in order to get our gear in the water, we make do with what we have. Bill makes up more gear while I steer.

Bill says, "The kings are like gold. They're where you find them, and often you must dig them out of the rocks." He asks me, "What are you doing out here in deep water?" Other times he accuses me, "You're risking our leads just to see how close you can get to bottom."

Some get their thrills from a slot machine. I admit I get my thrills from steering along a reef and not having to speed up once because I get too close to bottom.

I tell Bill when we lose a lead, "I learned from Ed Wellesley the first year, that it's the cost of doing business. You can't get uptight about it. Just throw over some more gear."

In the fog, Bill peers into the radar. He suddenly sees the depth sounder showing eight fathoms when we have out 20 fathoms of gear.

"Take the wheel," he commands as he dashes for the troller pit.

"Which way do I turn?"

"To the port."

I speed up the engine. In horror I see six fathoms... four fathoms... two fathoms. I'm running up on the reef! I put my weight on the wheel to turn it as sharp as possible to the port. Crash, bang! One lead goes. Another big jerk—the other lead goes. Then the depth starts dropping—10... 12... 15... 20 fathoms. We are in deep water. *I Gotta* didn't sit on the reef. I'm shaking.

I walk to the pilot house door to watch Bill pull in the gear. Only the two heavy leads are gone. We're lucky that the light leads, the lines and leaders are intact.

We fish protected waters, which Bill calls the infirmary of the Old Trollers Home. I love Bill's sense of humor. He always has a snappy come back.

Occasionally, the wind blows, but I can count on one hand the number of times we put out the stabilizers this summer. When it gets rough, we head for one of the nearby protected harbors and hike on the beach. We don't need to roll around in "outside" waters.

No other place offers the peace and tranquillity of the Alaskan fishing grounds. We're often miles from any human habitation, and the only boat in the area. Each day the lighting is different. I will always remember the rising sun throwing a red spotlight on a tree-covered mountainside, the rainbow forming a perfect bow above scattered islands, and the moon rising over a secluded harbor.

Each year more of the old timers are gone. I know we hadn't seen Oskar Oglend on the *Teddy* this season, but he might be fishing other places. I feel bad when I read in the *Alaska Magazine* that he died on June 11 at the age of 82.

Bill and I are looking forward to pitting our wits against the salmon next year. No other life has the pitch of excitement, challenges and beautiful scenery that trolling has. Will we still be trolling when we are 82 as Oskar was?

Like the gong for a prize fighter's first round, the moment arrives in April for our first trip of the 1981 salmon trolling season. For the last two months Bill and I worked on our gear to prepare our *I Gotta* for our fourth season. After warming up her engine, Bill unties her from our stall in Petersburg harbor and pushes us out with his foot. Then I put her in reverse backing her out into the channel.

We head south on a most beautiful day. The snow on the towering mainland peaks stands out against the crystal clear blue sky. The red markers in Wrangell Narrows contrast against the evergreens along the water's edge. We seldom find fish the first place we try. That day we try three bays and only catch three fiddlers, salmon too small to sell.

"Let's stop in and see D. Anderson on the south end of Etolin," I suggest. "He's always happy to see us, and we can give him one of our fiddlers."

"That's a good idea, but I don't want to stay all night in there. I don't like picking our way through all those rocks at low water. I want to get our gear in early tomorrow."

After tying to D.'s float, we hike overland to his float house that he's pulled up on the beach. He happily greets us and accepts our salmon. I'm surprised at how much he's aged since last season. He lives here alone year around. He proudly shows the wolf skins from his trapping that winter. We only stay an hour.

As the suns sets, we run to our "God's pocket" on Onslow Island, which Vancouver named for George Onslow, who became the Earl of Onslow. Suddenly, our tranquility is broken by the howl of a wolf. Then a second one howls which is followed by two more. My hair stands on end.

Early the next morning we put out our lures along Onslow Island. Suddenly, logs and kelp surround us. The highest tide of the year floats this moving mass of debris off the beaches. I can see no place to turn *I Gotta* to get away from it. Bill runs back to the troller pit and pulls a line closer to the boat to keep from hitting a log. I pride myself on my ability to dodge logs, but in all my years of fishing I never saw anything like this. By the time we troll into relatively clear water, I see nothing is going right. To add to our frustration, no fish are biting.

"Let's pull in our gear and visit Chuck and Shirley Piedra at Brownson Island. This isn't our day," I say.

"Sounds like a winner. I'll call them on the VHF and see if they're home."

Even though no one answers, we continue to their float-house. We spot the *Mercedes'* poles when we round the point. Chuck is working on the boat. They are a young couple in their late twenties or early thirties.

After tying *I Gotta* to the float, Bill says, "You've done a lot of work around here this winter, Chuck."

"Yep, I put three new logs under the float. It was ready to sink."

"The boat looks good, too."

"Always something to do on these old wooden boats."

At a certain stage of the tide, the end of the float goes dry. To get to the Piedra's float house, we crawl down on the beach. Elizabeth, their nine-year-old, comes to visit us. I love her little smile.

"I see you've lost some teeth. How are you doing on your lessons?"

"I'm not quite done yet, but I'll be done by the time we go fishing. Mom will be down in a little while. She's taking a bath."

When Shirley comes down, I say, "I'm cooking a pot roast in the oven. Why don't we eat together so we can have a longer visit."

Shirley thinks it is a good idea. I remember the time we made ice cream in their hand-freezer using ice from our hold. We don't have time that day since we plan to troll up into Ernest Sound that afternoon.

"We're going into Wrangell tomorrow," Chuck says. "Let's keep in touch on the VHF."

Ernest Sound stretches northeastward from Lemesurier Point to the high snow-capped peaks on the mainland. All sizes of islands and clusters of rocks dot the area. Seldom do ocean swells come in this far. No longer is Ernest Sound a winter fishing area, and only a few Wrangell boats fish it in the spring and summer.

We troll for four hours and catch not one salable fish. Even though I work my lines from time to time, I'm bored with no action. "Bill, do you think we're too early for the fish?"

"They aren't here. Where are we going to spend the night? It gets dark around eight now and I don't want to be groping around in the dark anchoring."

"There's Anita Bay."

"We can't get there by dark."

"There's Old Town and Olive Cove. I've not anchored in either for years."

"Anything closer?"

"Mel Gadd has a house near Thom's Place, but I heard on the VHF that they are going to town today."

"I like the small float by the Black Can in Zimovia Straits. Remember when we were in there last year and the fellow who owns the house told us we could use the float anytime."

Turning into the cove upon passing the Black Can, we find a small cruiser tied to the float. "Is it Curly Rathbone and his wife?" I ask. "We met them in here last year."

"No, it's the *Lady Blue*."

Even though we can see two fellows and a girl aboard, no one comes out to help us tie-up. Coming alongside the dock, I steer while Bill puts our lines around the piling instead of tying to the float. It's easier to do this. We ate supper on our way, so we crawl into our double bed in the pilothouse. Surprising how tired you get when you are out in this invigorating air.

About 5 a.m. I suddenly sense that Bill is up. I think he decided on an early start and won't need my help untying the boat like he does when we anchor. Peacefully, I roll over.

Then I hear him call, "Put her in gear."

I jump out of bed. Where is he? He isn't on the bow or the float. I run to the pilothouse door. Not on deck. Then I peer over the side. He is standing on the beach pushing *I Gotta* with a pike pole. He has on only his shorts and shoes. I run back to the wheel to push the starter. Which way do I turn to swing the stern to the port? He always does the docking or tells me what to do. With the extra high tide, the boat's lines went over the top of the pilings, and *I Gotta* floated in on the beach in front of the cabin. She is still floating. Every second counts.

Needing help to keep her from setting down, I honk our horn to raise the *Lady Blue*'s crew. Figuring they can pull us free with their skiff, the two fellows try to start their outboard on their skiff. Unfortunately, the outboard won't start. Cautiously, I put *I Gotta* in forward gear. Yes, she goes into gear.

"Speed her up," Bill yells.

Nothing happens.

"Try reverse."

She is moving. I look out of the pilothouse door. We are heading for the beach 100 feet behind us. I turn the wheel. Nothing happens. I feel Bill again pushing the boat out. I point her out of the cove. I give her full throttle in reverse gear. The fellows give up and go to the *Lady Blue*.

"Put her alongside the float," Bill yells to me.

To do this, I take her out of gear and slow her down. Then I put her in forward gear and turn the wheel hard port. She only goes straight ahead. Maybe I should turn it starboard, I think. I swing the wheel hard that way. Still I'm going ahead. We are heading at Bill and the beach. I take her out of gear. This is a mistake. I should have put her in reverse.

"I can't do anything," I call in panic. "She isn't responding."

In dismay I see we are crosswise in the same place we were when I awakened. We got *I Gotta* out once, can we do it again before she sits down on the bottom? Bill scales the six feet up the stern of *I Gotta*. This is a feat as there is no place to hang onto, and Bill is only 5'4" tall. His adrenaline must help him. He runs up on the bow and cinches a line around a piling.

"Put her in reverse, and speed her up," he orders. At last she is moving.

He calls, "Get the *Lady Blue* started and push us alongside the float."

In a matter of minutes, the *Lady Blue* pushes us alongside the float, and Bill ties us up. I turn off our motor and collapse onto the couch.

Why can't we steer *I Gotta* ? Bill climbs into the engine room and finds the shaft is turning when the engine is running. Could we have lost the rudder or propeller or both? Bill makes arrangements with the crew on the *Lady Blue* to tow us into Wrangell. We'll be able to put *I Gotta* on the grid to find out what is wrong. We are lucky she has no serious damage.

After the men fashion a bridle from *Lady Blue*'s stern to our bow, we start. We run *I Gotta*'s engine, thus making the towing easier. We know the hardest part of the trip is getting through Zimovia Straits. On the 90-degree turns, *I Gotta* could yaw and hit a buoy or a shallow area. Arriving at the narrowest part, the fellows slow down the *Lady Blue* and shorten the tow line.

Bill says, "We could have lost our rudder on the beach in there. I'll call Chuck and ask him to look for it when he gets there. They should be there around low tide. Did you feel any bumps?"

No, I didn't feel anything. We tell the Piedras of our mishap. Chuck says they'll be at the Black Can in a couple of hours as they already left Brownson. On the 20-mile trip into Wrangell, we have smooth running as the water is calm.

When Bill is on the bow adjusting the tow line upon our arrival in Wrangell harbor, I call Chuck. Chuck's voice comes back. "We have your rudder. I repeat, we have your rudder."

"Thank you, Chuck," I call back. "We'll go on the grid at high water. What size bolts are on it? We'll have to buy them before the stores close."

Chuck measures them and calls back the size. Chuck and Shirley arrive at high water, and he tows us to the grid with his skiff at 5 p.m.—12 hours after our mishap.

Later Chuck relates, "It was just low tide when we got there. We rowed into the beach. I told Shirley that it wasn't there. Suddenly, the sunlight caught something bright. It was the rudder's collar. Its green color blended into the seaweed. I almost missed it because I was looking for a metal rudder not a fiberglass one."

When the tide drops, we find that the shipyard put in galvanized bolts instead of stainless. In a matter of time, electrolysis would have caused them to drop off. If we lost the rudder in Wrangell Narrows or Snow Pass, the tide might have swept us onto a rock or beach when we were unable to steer. This time we were never in danger. Only *I Gotta* was in danger. If Chuck hadn't found the rudder, we would be forced to order another. This could easily have taken a week. All it cost us are six stainless bolts. Truly, it is a lucky accident.

A 55-mile gale blows the next three days. We are happy to be safely tied to the Wrangell dock and not standing anchor watch in some bay. We visit our old friends Stan and Eva Miller, Annie and Harvey Armstrong and Irene Ingle.

"I admire how your fast thinking saved *I Gotta*," I tell Bill. "The good Lord has his arm around us. He also sends good friends like the Piedras and the crew on the *Lady Blue* to help us when we really need them."

CHAPTER TWENTY-NINE
End Of An Era

LIKE RIP VAN WINKLE WHEN HE RETURNED, I find few familiar faces either on the fishing grounds or in the towns. Many of the Tebenkof fishermen have either died or retired. Sadly, I learn that Dave Harrison on the *Norma*, Irish Bennett, David Stuteen from Kake, and Little Joe Cash on the *Flicka* have died. In 1978 Barbara and Orwan Simpson bought fish on *NEFCO XI* for the last year. They began buying fish in '59. Orwan worked in town for Petersburg Fisheries until he retires in 1984 and they moved to Greenbank, Washington.

In 1946 I wrote that I had difficulty seeing where humans had disturbed the wilderness. Now, people have logged great areas to supply two pulp mills and many small sawmills. Both pulp mills will close in the 1990s. Our worries of the second growth being too thin and scattered proved groundless.

Rip Van Winkle returned to find his house gone to decay.[14] I return to Petersburg to find that Skip's and my house, having fallen into decay, was burned by the city. They tore down our house in Ketchikan, and the cabin we built on our homesite in Wrangell was also burned after Madge Gillen died.

Rip returned to find a busy, bustling, disputatious tone about [the town] instead of the accustomed phlegm and drowsy tranquility.[15] I also find that the Alaska I knew before statehood had a tranquility that no longer exists. We watch TV instead of visiting, and we rush and drive ourselves instead of enjoying each day to the fullest.

I know I was like "a fish out of water" the 11 years I was gone from Alaska. Perhaps I can erase those years from my memory as if I had been asleep like Rip van Winkle. Rip spent his later years telling whoever would listen about life before he went to sleep. Like Rip, I feel the need to get the message out about what Alaska was like before.

Bill and I fly to Fairbanks for Lynda's college graduation in broadcast journalism in May of 1985. Now all four of Skip's and my children have graduated from college. This is a time to be proud. Lynda has a job as

Bill lands a fish.

videographer at a Fairbanks television station. We also visit Jean Annest, my old friend from Idaho. She is now a Camp Fire Director in Fairbanks. I enjoy keeping in touch with good friends and sharing my Alaskan experiences.

I have the most fun when Bill and I are working together aboard *I Gotta*. No two days are alike. Nothing has the excitement that fishing does. But little do I realize when we agree to take an Alaska Department of Fish and Game (ADF&G) observer aboard *I Gotta* that it might be an end of an era for us.

ADF&G had hired eight observers to go out for eight to 12 days on salmon trollers to check on the hooking mortality of kings during a coho-only fishery. On August 27, Tom Huffman flies on Alaska Island Air from Petersburg to become part of our crew. We meet Tom for the first time and hope he'll enjoy his time on *I Gotta*. The two bunks in the bow section will be like his personal stateroom. With our fishing inside waters, it will be

Marilyn works the gear on I Gotta.

different from the previous two boats he'd been on out in the ocean.

Bill points out, "When we're on a single-species fishery, we fish shallow in deep water, use no bait and go like hell."

With Tom aboard, we run back to our fishing grounds in Tebenkof Bay to put in our gear. Tom shows us his logs and how he records the king's injuries, whether they are minor or serious, or if the king is dead. We carefully release each king. For the cohoes we keep, he takes scale samples, measures length and weight, and checks on the sex. For both species, he records our distance from shore, gear depth we are fishing, depth the fish is hooked and gear on which it is hooked.

Tom learns first-hand the problems of the troller. We have a good catch of cohoes and some kings the day before the 39-hour August seine opening. Eight trollers join us inside of Troller Islands. Then ADF&G opens Tebenkof to seining for the first time this year.

"Look," I point. "That seiner is going to set right in the middle of our drag. I can remember when we caught 100 cohoes in here at Gap Point this time of year."

The other trollers soon take off when it becomes evident that the seiners will catch the majority of the cohoes. The day before, we caught 40 cohoes; today we get five. Soon we, too, give up.

After unloading our fish on *NEFCO XI* to Eddie Haugen, we buy fresh fruit, vegetables and meat. We take on some additional ice and head up the Straits. We arrive at Pybus Bay as the sun sets. When we see five Kake hand trollers still fishing, we decide that they must be getting fish.

The next morning we are first out. We look for a jumper and head for it. "Where's Bergmann's closure marker?" I ask. "I don't want to take a chance of getting pinched." (A friend had gotten fined for fishing over the line here.)

Bill points out both ends of the line. Why is it, I wonder, that the best fishing is always over the line? Tom is busy recording our catch and taking scale samples. The next morning we start out early. When Tom arises, I say, "We've already got 22, and it's only 9 a.m. This should be a good day."

Then we spot a pod of killer whales coming into the bay. Two hours later we see them heading down the straits. They scare the salmon which either hide under rocks or take off. We end up with only 30 for the day.

The next day we fish all morning and are skunked for cohoes. Tom duly records the two kings we hook. Again, where to go is the question. We throw in our lures at Cape Fanshaw with great expectations. We catch only kings.

Surprisingly they are not on the bottom lures. Our strategy of fishing shallow in deep water isn't working. We end with only six cohoes for the day.

We run into Petersburg and Tom calls his bosses. He tells us of another observer program in which we retain the kings. He will take the gonads of the kings, and the State will sell the kings. This is to determine the fish's age and when they will spawn.

Early the next morning we head south and throw in our gear at the south mouth of Wrangell Narrows. Bill is steering among the rocks when suddenly my light line hangs up. He speeds up, but to no avail as the tide runs too hard. With a mighty jerk, the line breaks at the tag.

"Look," I point. "The bag is still floating back there. Maybe we can pick it up." We both work feverishly to pull in the other three lines by the time we turn *I Gotta* around. We run back to our float bag.

"Put the boat alongside the bag," Bill commands. "Be careful and don't get the line in the wheel. That heavy steel line will stop the boat dead in the water."

Slowly I maneuver *I Gotta* toward the float. I must head the bow right for it. If it is in the right spot, it will disappear from sight when it passes the bow. Bill stands in the troller pit ready with our longest gaff to pull the line in to grab as it floats by. I take the boat out of gear to ensure that we won't get the line in the wheel.

"I've got it," Bill calls. I watch him pull it over the side.

"Now bring me the green box with the crimping tool and the sleeves."

Obediently I hand them to him. He splices the two lines together. Slowly I put *I Gotta* in gear and he puts the gurdy into gear to wind in the line. We see that the lead is still hooked on bottom.

"Take her out of gear." He jerks and jerks, then pulls on the line. With a big lurch, it comes free. He puts the gurdy in gear and starts winding in the line. Then he instructs me to put the boat in gear. When the lead finally comes out of water, we haven't lost even one spread.

"How lucky can you be?" Bill comments. "Tom, now you can see what it is like out here when everything goes wrong. We only got six cohoes for three hours. We might as well go someplace else. How about Snow Pass?"

We find only one boat there, and he picks up his gear and leaves soon after we arrive. Another friend, Bus Goldsberry on the *LaDonna Rae* makes one pass and takes off for town. It doesn't look good. Other years six to ten boats fished here, and everyone caught fish. Another friend comes by and

344 Following the Alaskan Dream

says he has a hot tip and is heading down the Straits. We end with 17 big cohoes and nine kings for Tom. Quite a few of them are sub-legal and one is marked, which makes Tom happy.

The next morning we catch only five cohoes and eight kings. When the wind comes up we run into Exchange Cove to wait for a more favorable tide later in the day. On spotting an outhouse and a picnic table, we wonder if the Forest Service expects tourists here. Two campers, one with an inflatable boat on top, come over the hill and park beside the table.

We put over our skiff and row ashore. We visit with the four men who have driven around Prince of Wales Island. They came from Craig that day and report many salmon in the creeks along the way. They are from Montana. They launch their boat to catch a salmon and we return to I Gotta. We put in our gear. In two hours of fishing, we don't get a strike. Our dilemma is where to go now.

"Maybe the cohoes returned to Pybus," I say. "The tide is right to go back through the Narrows. The past years have been good here. Probably that seine opening in Area Six last week took all the cohoes around here."

The next morning we leave Petersburg by 5 a.m. We try many places on our way to Pybus but only catch five cohoes. Even though we spot many jumpers, we only land three cohoes and two kings inside the bay. We troll down the beach to Chapin Bay and catch two more cohoes.

Chapin is one of my favorite bays. As an isthmus on the left side almost covers the opening, you cannot see the bay. Suddenly you are in a secluded anchorage with towering mountains on all sides. We show Tom the hole in the top of one mountain. Each year the second-growth trees are higher. It was logged in the early 1960s.

The wind is blowing at least 30 miles per hour and making four- to five-foot seas the next morning. We throw over the stabilizers and run at half speed. We hear one of the Kake hand trollers call another hand troller. "Where are they opening the seining?"

"Right where you've got your pick, buddy. Right there in Port Camden."

"That's what I was afraid of. There goes our fishing here."

We learn that they'd gone there after we left them at Pybus and had three good days of fishing. We decide it is no use for us to go there now. We catch eight kings with adipose clipped fins while Tom is with us from September 4 to 11. ADF&G tells us where they came from. Bill is so discouraged about the whole trolling business that he comes to town and puts a For Sale sign on *I Gotta*.

I ask myself, "Is this an end of an era?" I started trolling with Skip in 1946. We fished until his death in 1965. I married Bill in 1978. I have thoroughly enjoyed commercial fishing these 28 seasons. It will truly be retirement when and if we sell *I Gotta*. I must admit I'll be very happy if we don't sell her. I keep feeling that the boat is a luxury that we can afford. If the Legislature votes to let us sport fish off a commercial boat, Bill is more inclined to keep it.

I doubt if Tom Huffman thought that he might be part of "The End of an Era" when he flew out and joined us.

CHAPTER THIRTY
She Loves Salmon Trolling

I DREAM THAT BILL AND I will salmon troll into our 80s like Jackie O'Donnell and Oskar Oglend. Perhaps I'll be like George Bernard Shaw, who wrote:

> I want to be thoroughly used up when I die, for the harder I work the more I live. I rejoice in life for its own sake. Life is no 'brief candle' for me. It is a sort of splendid torch which I have got hold of for the moment, and I want to make it burn as brightly as possible before handing it on to future generations.[16]

At the end of the 1986 season when I am 65, Bill talks me into selling our troller, *I Gotta*. Now that he is 71, he claims that his legs can't take a rolling boat anymore. A boat is different from a house. It becomes a part of you. With great sadness I reluctantly agree to give up commercial trolling. I persuade Bill to sell *I Gotta* to my son, Eric. I am afraid that Eric's old boat will sink with him, Sarah and my grandsons. At least we keep our troller in the family. With a heavy heart, I cry when I watch Eric run *I Gotta* out of Petersburg Harbor on his way to Sitka.

Two years later, Eric calls on his radiophone, "The Fish and Game just announced a three day king salmon opening. How would you like to fish with me and your grandson, Kris?

"I'd love to," I reply.

Hurriedly, I pack my clothes and fly to Sitka. When Eric and Kris meet me at the airport, I'm surprised how much 14-year-old Kris has grown. Of all the grandchildren, he looks the most like his grandfather. Skip was only 6' tall while Eric is 6'3". Kris will probably be as big as Eric.

I admit that Eric surpasses his dad and Bill as a fisherman. Maybe it's because he's been on a fishing boat every year since we took him out on *Salty* at six months.

After scouting various places, Eric decides where to start. I'm so excited that I sleep lightly. Eric and I pull anchor and start trolling at 3 a.m. I make breakfast and we wait. By 9 a.m. we only land seven kings. Eric declares that we must do better than this. We run 3 1/2 hours and put our lures in the water. Not one king takes our lures in a half hour. On a hunch, Eric returns at 5:30 p.m. to where we started. I steer while Kris and Eric put out the gear. Having learned to steer with the wheel, I over steer because the automatic pilot responds slower.

"Look at your line, Kris! It's jerking with fish already," Eric says excitedly.

I admire how adeptly Eric and Kris work the lines. In four hours, the three of us pull 51 kings. We consider this our lucky place for we found fish here in the past.

With great expectations, Eric and I put in the gear at 3 a.m. Immediately the lines jerk.

"They're still here," Eric says as he gleefully hits me on the back. By 4 a.m., the back deck is covered with salmon.

"Get Kris up," Eric commands.

I shake him, "Kris, we need you."

Kris jumps out of the bunk. While he pulls on his pants and shirt, he strides to the pilothouse door.

"This is IT," his dad exclaims. "I haven't time to clean fish. You must land fish as well as clean."

The salmon literally jump into the boat when Eric fishes.

I keep my eyes on the depth sounder in this difficult place to fish.

"This is great, Grandma," Kris says as he pulls on his boots.

"It's what we dream about," I answer.

For breakfast, I take some fruit and toast out to them. In this shallow water, we are surprised at how many kings we land from a line. We've never experienced such fishing. By 8 a.m., we have 50 kings.

Kris comments, "The

Marilyn lands a chum salmon.

silver of the kings is everywhere. We can't see the deck or most of the hatch, just huge king salmon."

Once I turn the wheel too sharply. Eric yells, "Mom. You're running over the float."

I look out of the window. The float is going in the opposite direction past me. I know I'm in trouble. If the heavy line tangles with the light line, we'll lose valuable time untangling it. Luckily at the last minute, the float turns around and comes toward us.

Eric climbs into the hold and makes beds of ice for the kings. Then Kris ices them. I see that Eric is training his boys well.

Our old friend from Wrangell, Bob Rooney, who now has the *Dorothy*, arrives. I wish I could figure a way to tip him off that the kings are here.

"It's like old times for the Jordans and Rooneys to fish together," I say on the radiophone. I'm leery about saying much since our experience in '55.

"Look," Kris calls, "A triple header!" (three fish on one line.) I hear the excitement in his voice. A triple header of kings doesn't happen often. He grins at me.

When you're landing that many big kings, every muscle in your body aches, but you forget it in the excitement.

Knowing how much I enjoy working the gear, Eric suggests, "Mom, why don't you go out and work the lines while I eat and rest?" I'm happy for Eric to steer when three more trollers arrive. We can no longer fish along the reef in both directions.

Gleefully, Kris and I land fish. "Who's going to catch the 100th king for the day?" I ask.

We both wait. We have a couple of strikes but the fish are gone. That

When the Georges sell I Gotta, Bill buys a sport fishing boat and fishes for personal use. Bill proudly displays what he caught on his sport pole.

100th king eludes us. At last, Kris puts his gurdy in gear. I watch as he carefully pulls in the leader. When he works it close enough to gaff, the salmon suddenly jumps out of water and throws the hook.

"I've got one on my heavy line. Maybe I'll get it." I say. When I come to the bottom leader, I see a big silver flash in the water.

"It's really big, Kris. Will you land it?"

"I lost the last one," he replies.

"That happens. Try again."

Eric comes to the pilot-house door, "Do you want me to land it?"

"I'll do it, Dad," Kris says confidently. This time he digs the gaff into it and pulls the big fish over the side.

"It'll easily make 40 pounds," I say, patting him on the back. "We both caught it, Kris. We can always remember our 100th king."

We fish until dark. That day we end with 106 kings, which is the most the Jordans ever caught in one day. The salmon disappear by the next noon. We end with 272 kings for the three-day opening. Working with my grandson forms a special bond between us that we'll always remember.

Another year I fish Cross Sound and Icy Straits with Eric's younger son, Karl. Eric tells us, "We gaff cohoes on this boat. We don't sling them aboard."

Marilyn loves Grandson's Kris's smile when we hit the mother lode.

When Karl and I are in the troller pit, he winks at me to tell me that Eric isn't watching. I sling the coho aboard. We have fun conspiring against him. Sometimes the fish come off the hook and Eric accuses me, "You lost that fish because you didn't gaff it."

"From the first year, I've had trouble with moving targets. If they aren't hooked well, I gaff them." I know the reason grandchildren and grandparents get along so well is that they have a common enemy.

Another year, Eric puts slush tanks into *I Gotta.* When in Elfin Cove, I return to the boat and see the hatch cover lying at an angle over one tank. Thinking it is safe, I step on it. Like a diving board, it dumps me into the icy water of that tank.

"Help," I yell. I stick out both arms and hold the sides of the tank to keep myself from going under. Only my feet dangle in the water. Luckily, the tank is full of water or I might have broken my ankles. Eric runs out of the pilothouse and tries to pull me out, but he's at the wrong angle.

I say, "Just help me get my knee on the edge and I can pull myself out." He insists I take a warm shower. I assure him that I'm not hurt.

Eric says, "Remember on *Nohusit,* the collapsible bath tub made in the frame of a folding cot. You heated water in a copper boiler and all of us took baths. Now the buying scows have showers."

I ask my children what they remember about growing up on a salmon troller. Barbara recalls all the good things. "Dad had such a positive attitude which made a difference. Something was always happening aboard. Living

Grandson Karl gaffs a king salmon.

on the boat was like taking an extended car camping trip across the country each summer. We had this huge vacation where we visited different places and met interesting people. Having both you and Dad around during the winters was special. We had a fantastic childhood. Even if money was short, we made up for it with the experiences. We did a lot of traveling but weren't too nomadic for we always had roots in Southeast. No two days were ever the same on the boat. Whenever we went out on deck, we put on life preservers, just like we put on a jacket."

Karen was also positive, "What an idyllic life for us! We found so much to see and do. I have such positive memories about life on the boat."

Eric was older when we fished. He says, "How close our family was, created a very positive experience." He adds a word of caution, "There was pain associated with it. Dad felt guilty that he wasn't fishing every minute. He was nervous about the safety aspects of having all of us aboard. Those were the days before survival suits, Emergency Position Indicator Radio Beacons, and life rafts."

"I know," I say. "Your dad confided to me that he was worried he might not save all of you if something happened." I'm more philosophical. After *Nohusit* blew up, I figure as long as we keep our heads and don't panic, we can face whatever happens.

I'm glad Skip's and my children look happily on their salmon trolling days as a good family experience. Surely this molds their lives.

I hope someday my grandsons tell their children, "You should have seen your great grandmother landing salmon. She really loved salmon trolling."

Don Blanding, Poet Laureate of the Hawaiian Islands in the 1950s noted: "Your joy must be woven, by you for you."[17]

My joy is hunting the elusive salmon and planning activities with my husband, children and grandchildren. As I look back on my many years, I know Blanding is right, "Joy is an Inside Job."

EPILOGUE

I hope this book has shown my love for life. Although life has not always been easy, I feel Alaska has been good to me. In Petersburg, Mary & Norman Armin wrote this for my birthday:

April 13th, Petersburg will come alive to celebrate Marilyn George's birthday...Number 75!

She's been around this old town awhile to compare
And knows who's done what to whom, why, when and where.
Marilyn is a poet of literary mind.
She's a friend...true blue, faithful and kind.
She's a reporter...though factual and rare she be.
She's a fisherman, whether it be calm or rough seas.
Marilyn is a Mother and one of the best;
She always kept her children warm, fed and dressed.
She's a Grandmother. Her rocking chair is rocking
While old father time is patiently "tick-tocking."

Marilyn is a wife...makes a nice cozy home
And she never stays away too long when she does roam.
Her thoughts are of Bill wherever she goes
And she will return home, this he knows.

Marilyn shares the love of her community in her writing
Tailored to catch each personality to be enlightening.
She is a member of several organizations
And she's not shy to ask you to join in these relations.

Marilyn is a lady of knowledge;
Worked up to Associate Professor in an Idaho College.
Whether it be by brain or brawn, she is a hard worker
And has no tolerance for a person who is a shirker.

M stands for majestic
A stands for artistic
R stands for researcher
I stands for idealist
L stands for learned
Y stands for yielding
N stand for novelist

It takes many words to describe her
And she brings out different feelings from one to another
But to be so spiritual, generous and kind
Makes us all of the same mind.

THANK YOU, MARILYN. YOU'RE A GOOD TEACHER.

As Alaska has fulfilled my many dreams, I want to end with Alaska's Flag Song, which Penny Ripple sang at my 75th birthday. Marie Drake wrote it in 1935, before Alaska became a state.

Eight stars of gold on a field of blue —
Alaska's flag. May it mean to you
The blue of the sea, the evening sky,
The mountain lakes, and the flow'rs nearby;
The gold of the early sourdough's dreams,
The precious gold of the hills and streams;
The brilliant stars in the northern sky,
The "Bear"—the "Dipper"—and shining high,
The great North Star with its steady light
Over land and sea a beacon bright,
Alaska's flag—to Alaskans dear,
The simple flag of a last frontier.[18]

Map
Map of Southeast Alaska by Laura Lucas Design

Preface
Essay titled "Attitude" by Charles Swindoll. Often quoted.

[1] Ralph Waldo Emerson, *Nature; Addresses and Lectures*, (1849) (Literary Classics of US, Library of America, Viking Press, 1983,) Ch. VIII Prospects, p. 47.

[2] Henry David Thoreau, *Walden*, (Boston, Ticknor & Fields, 1854, Longriver Press, 1976,) Ch. 2, p. 77.

[3] Unknown.

[4] Unknown.

[5] Emerson, p. 47.

[6] Thoreau, p. 77.

[7] Unknown.

[8] Joseph Fort Newton, "Life's Unfinished Symphony," *A Treasury of Inspiration*, (Thomas V. Crowell, 1951,) Reprinted in Wisdom, June 1956, p. 15.

[9] Katherine Mansfield, *Each Day a New Beginning*, (Center City, MN, Hazelden, 1984,) February 3.

[10] Al-Anon Family Groups, *Suggested Opening*, p.149, published by Al-Anon Family Group Headquarters, New York, N.Y., 1957.

[11] *Food for Thought*, July 31, Hazelden, Center City, MN, 1980.

[12] Don Blanding, *Joy Is An Inside Job*, (New York, Dodd, Mead, & Co., 1953,) p. 26.

[13] C. Donald Walters, *Page-A-Day Calendar*, "Secrets of Life," (New York, Workman Publishing Co. 1995).

[14] Washington Irving, *A History of New York From the Beginning of the World to the End of the Dutch Dynasty*, (NY, NY, The Library of America, Literary Classics of the US, Inc. 1983,) p. 778.

[15] Ibid. p. 770.

[16] Archibald Henderson, *George Bernard Shaw, His Life and Works, A Critical Biography*, (Stewart & Kidd, 1911) p. 504.

[17] Blanding, p. 83.

[18] Marie Drake, Alaska Flag Song, (Alaska Territorial Department of Education School Bulletin, Oct. 1935.) Cover.

ACKNOWLEDGMENTS

PARTS OF THIS BOOK WERE ADAPTED FROM articles that first appeared in various magazines and newspapers:

Preface: *Senior Voice*, December 1994, "Campfires to Home Fires, Strengthening Family Ties;" *Senior Voice*, August '94, "Return to Iowa;" *Senior Voice*, April '95, "Writing - A Novel Way to Elderhostel;" *Alaska Women Speak*, Summer '95, "Trolling and Traveling with Grandsons;" *Senior Voice*, November '96, "Planning a Family Reunion: How the Frink Family Did It;" *Senior Voice*, September '96, "Our Gal Marilyn Survives Hell's Canyon;" *Senior Voice*, March '96, "Alaskan Flies South For Writers' Workshop;" *Alaska Women Speak*, Spring '97 "Joy is an Inside Job;" *Senior Voice*, March '97, "The Days Spent Afloat Are The Best, By Far;" *Senior Voice*, April '98, "Alaskans Study 'Writing Yourself.'"

Chapters 2-9 are based on six articles in *Alaska Sportsman*. September 1947 to February 1948, titled "Trolling Poles."

Chapter 10, *Southeastern Log*, December '87, "My First Alaska Christmas."

Chapters 12-14 are based on articles in *Household*. March 1955, titled "We Go Fishing Everyday." and articles in the *Ketchikan Daily News*, March 1953.

Chapters 14-15 are based on articles in *Singer Light*, Spring 1955, called "Troller Wives" and articles in the *Ketchikan Daily News*, March 1954.

Chapter 21, *Alaska Women Speak*, Fall '98, "An Answer to a Prayer."

Chapter 22, *Alaska Women Speak*, Spring '98, "Children Aboard."

Chapter 23, is based on articles in the *Petersburg Press*, *The Alaska Fisherman*; and two issues of *The Pilot: a Guide to Scenic Southeast*, 1964 and 1965, called "Petersburg-The Hub of a Sportsman's Paradise," "Hidden Among the Islands," "Adventure on a Riverboat," "Redpath Special News Bulletin: Adventure Among the Islands;" and *Iowa State University Alumnus*, December, 1965.

Chapter 26, *Alaska Women Speak Summer*, '98, "Women in Transition - Change Doesn't Scare Me;" *Mtn. Home News* and *Glenns Ferry Gazette*, various articles, "News Notes from Marilyn Jordan, Elmore County Home Extension Agent;" *Alaska* magazine, July '78, "Salmon Surprise of '77."

Chapter 28, *Alaska Fishermen's Journal*, November '80, "How to Enjoy Your Retirement;" *New Alaskan*, November '80 "Like a Fish out of Water;" *New Alaskan*, June-July '81, "Guests Aboard;" *New Alaskan*, May '82, "Lucky Accident."

Chapter 29, *Senior Voice*, December '94, "Campfires to Home Fires, Strengthening Family Ties;" *Senior Voice*, August '94, "Return to Iowa;" *Senior Voice*, April '95, "Writing - A Novel Way to Elderhostel;" *Alaska Women Speak*, Summer '95, "Trolling and Traveling with Grandsons."

Chapter 29, *New Alaskan*, May '86, "An Observer on the *I Gotta*" and "The Fishing Was So Poor That It May Be The End Of An Era!"

Chapter 30, *Pacific Fishing*, April '96, "Around the Bar."

Additional articles related to this book are: *Pacific Fishing*, November '84, "Living on the Least Common Denominator;" *Alaskan Southeaster*, May '96, "Let Me Go Back to Where the Cement Grows," and *Alaska Women Speak*, Spring '96; *Alaska Fishermen's Journal*, August 1996, "My Alaska - Looking Back on 50 Years;" *Senior Voice* December, '97, "Christmas Has Always Been For Sharing."

PEOPLE

I have listed when a person is first listed in the book. If they are found in later chapters, these chapters are not listed. I have listed separately those in preface and epilogue. Where one of a couple is listed and spouse listed later, two chapters are given. Where children are often listed in different places than parents, this is noted. With all the years that have passed, I can not remember all the names of people in the book. I am sure we have errors and I apologize for this. Some, who I could not remember, I gave fictitious names.

In Preface: Amber Dahlin, Professor Roy Paul Nelson, Chris Weiss, Joy Jenkins, Emery Tobin, Ethel Dassow, Robert Crossley, Lew Williams, Jr., Bob Pickrell, John van Amerongen, Dave Fremming, MaryLee Hayes, Judy Sarber, Leslie Croxton, Bill Moulton, Mike Stainbrook, Betty Winship, Marjorie Colpitts, Elaine Colvin, C. Terry Cline, Lee Ribich, Drake Hokanson, Jane Evanson, Jocelyn Bartkevicius, John Thorndike, Ken Waldman, Jackie O'Donnell, R.N. DeArmond, Angus Cameron, and Laura Lucas.

For additional copies:

Marilyn George
PO Box 1031
Petersburg, AK 99833
margeorg@alaska.net
www.alaska.net/~margeorg/
Phone & FAX 907-772-4515

add $7 for postage & handling